THE VIKING COLLECTION
Studies in Northern Civilization

General Editors

Margaret Clunies Ross
Matthew Driscoll
Mats Malm

Volume 20

Már Jónsson

ARNAS MAGNÆUS PHILOLOGUS
(1663–1730)

UNIVERSITY PRESS OF SOUTHERN DENMARK
2012

© The Viking Collection and Már Jónsson
Layout: Sverrir Sveinsson
Printing and binding: Special-Trykkeriet Viborg a-s

ISBN 978-87-7674-646-9
ISSN 0108-8408

Contents

Abbreviations	7
1. Introduction	9
Aims	9
Sources	14
Disposition	19
2. Background	25
Septentrional studies	25
Revival	30
Destruction	36
Competition	40
3. Beginnings	47
The task	47
The assistant	53
First vellums	61
Philological fury	67
4. Erudition	81
Antiquitates	81
Íslendingabók	89
Survival	97

5. Success 105
Leipzig 105
Collection 115
Positions 123

6. Iceland 133
Politics 133
Acquisitions 142
Apographa 153
Disgrace 161

7. Copenhagen 169
Back home 169
Manuscripts 179
Work 188
Writings 199

8. Last months 203
Conflagration 203
Death 210

List of figures 217

References 219

Index of manuscripts 249

Index of names 257

Abbreviations

AM: Manuscripts in Stofnun Árna Magnússonar í íslenskum fræðum in Reykjavík and Den Arnamagnæanske Samling in Copenhagen.

AMKat.: Kålund, Kristian, ed. 1388–94. *Katalog over den Arnamagnæanske håndskriftsamling.* 2 vols. Copenhagen: Gyldendal.

Aug: Manuscripts in the Herzog August Bibliothek in Wolfenbüttel.

Barth.: Manuscripts in Thomas Bartholin's collection in the Royal Library in Copenhagen.

BE: Jón Ólafsson. 1836. 'Biographiske Efterretninger om Arne Magnussen'. Editor E.C. Werlauff. *Nordisk Tidsskrift for Oldkyndighed* 3: 1–166.

BL: Manuscripts in the British Library in London.

BT: Kålund, Kristian, ed. 1916a. Árni Magnússon, *Brevveksling med Torfæus (Þormóður Torfason).* Copenhagen: Gyldendal.

DG: Manuscripts in the University Library in Uppsala.

Don. var.: Manuscripts in the Royal Library in Copenhagen.

Emb: Kålund, Kristian, ed. 1916b. Árni Magnússon, *Embedsskrivelser og andre offenlige aktstykker.* Copenhagen: Gyldendal.

GKS: Manuscripts in the Royal Library in Copenhagen.

ÍB: Manuscripts in the National Library in Reykjavík.

ÍÆ: Páll Eggert Ólason 1948–52. *Íslenzkar æviskrár frá landnámstímum til ársloka 1940.* 5 vols. Reykjavík: Hið íslenska bókmenntafélag.

JS: Manuscripts in the National Library in Reykjavík.

Lbs: Manuscripts in the National Library in Reykjavík.

LS: Finnur Jónsson 1930b. *Árni Magnússons levned og skrifter.* 2 vols. Copenhagen: Gyldendal.

NB: Manuscripts in the National Library in Oslo.

NKS: Manuscripts in the Royal Library in Copenhagen.

Abbreviations

NRA: Manuscripts in the State Archives in Oslo.

Papp.: Manuscripts in the Royal Library in Stockholm.

PB: Kålund, Kristian, ed. 1920. *Arne Magnussons private brevveksling.* Copenhagen: Gyldendal.

Perg.: Manuscripts in the Royal Library in Stockholm.

RA: Documents in the State Archives in Copenhagen.

Registre: *Ordbog over det norrøne prosasprog. Registre.* Copenhagen: Den Arnamagnæanske Kommission, 1989.

Sigilla: Magnús Már Lárusson and Jónas Kristjánsson, ed. 1965–7. *Sigilla Islandica.* 2 vols. Icelandic Manuscripts, Series in octavo 1–2. Reykjavík: The Manuscript Institute of Iceland.

Thott: Manuscripts in the Royal Library in Copenhagen.

UB: Manuscripts in the National Library in Oslo.

Weiss: Manuscripts in the Herzog August Bibliothek in Wolfenbüttel.

1
Introduction

> And never throughout eternity will there
> be any Iceland except for the Iceland that
> Arnas Arnæus has bought with his life.
>
> Og aldrei um eilífð verður til neitt Ísland
> utan það Ísland sem Arnas Arnæus
> hefur keypt fyrir sitt líf.
>
> Halldór Laxness, *Iceland's bell* 1941–3
> (2003: 122; 1993: 140)

In this book I will describe the endeavours of a man who, at the age of only thirty, exclaimed that he desired to possess every remnant of medieval parchment to be had in Iceland, and then spent the rest of his life pursuing that goal. This was Árni Magnússon – 'Arne Magnussen' as he wrote his name in Danish or Latinised as 'Arnas Magnæus'. He was born at Kvennabrekka in the West of Iceland in 1663 and died in Copenhagen in 1730. His collection of Icelandic medieval manuscripts is the biggest in the world; had it not been for his single-minded pursuit of them, most of these pieces would surely now be lost.

Aims

In around 1150 the so-called First Grammarian noted that since Icelanders now wrote so much they needed an alphabet suited to the sounds of their language. In his treatise, he mentions Ari fróði's Book of Icelanders (*Íslendingabók*) and some recently written laws, but also genealogies and interpretations of sacred writings (Hreinn Benediktsson 1972: 208). Already then, less than three centuries after the first inhabitants settled in Iceland, literature was thriving. As it happens, the oldest manuscript preserved is a single leaf with an intriguing 'tabula computistica' (AM 732 a VII 4to) covering the years 1121–39, and it is similar to the one used by Ari fróði. The oldest extant fragment of a devotional text (AM 237 a fol.) was written in the mid-twelfth century (Ólafía Einarsdóttir 1964: 95–9; Hreinn Benediktsson 1965: 13–14). Some registers of church property (*máldagar*) had been written by the time the First Grammatical Treatise was composed; the oldest one extant, its first lines written in the 1180s, is from Reykholt in Borgarfjörður (Guðvarður Már Gunnlaugsson 2000: 17). During the next two centuries or so, Icelandic literature and historiography flourished, becoming, in the words of Margaret Clunies Ross, 'one of the most copious and original literatures produced by any European society in the Middle Ages' (Clunies Ross 1998: 8). There is no need here to provide more than a simple list of genres: Eddic and skaldic poetry, hagiography, Bible translations and other devotional works, sagas of Icelanders and contemporary sagas of bishops and chieftains, sagas of Norwegian and Danish kings, romances (*lygisögur*), chivalric sagas (*riddarasögur*) and sagas of ancient times (*fornaldarsögur*).

Students and scholars in their hundreds now pore over these texts, extracting their meaning and investigating their relations to one another, most of the time oblivious to the circumstances that led to their being preserved at all for posterity. This should not be so. Detailed knowledge of the preservation of medieval texts is necessary for their understanding and interpretation, for a variety of reasons which should become clear from this book on Árni Magnússon, by far the most tenacious and successful collector of Icelandic medieval manuscripts. How is it, for example, that some texts are preserved only in seventeenth-century transcriptions? In some cases this is because a number of vellums were destroyed in the Great Fire of Copenhagen in 1728 but had been copied some decades earlier. A more important reason is that after such copies were made on paper, the less readable vellum exemplars were thrown away or the leaves used as covers for printed books or paper manuscripts. Another question could then be: why are there so many fragmentary texts? That is simply because Árni, from early on, was acutely aware that every single scrap of vellum had potential value for its text. Awareness of issues such as these provides an interesting and fruitful perspective on Icelandic medieval texts, and of course the history of manuscript preservation as such has a momentum of its own as part of the history of erudition in Europe, where scholars like Árni actively searched for remnants of their countries' medieval literature and historiography.

Table 1. Icelandic manuscripts and charters

Period	Manuscripts		Charters	
	Vellum	Paper	Vellum	Paper
1101–1200	13	0	1	0
1201–1300	102	0	6	0
1301–1400	319	0	128	0
1401–1500	231	0	515	1
1501–1600	211	55	1370	189
Total	876	55	2020	190

Manuscripts: Based on all available catalogues and *Registre*. Liturgical and other Latin fragments and manuscripts in the Arnamagnæan and other Icelandic collections (min. 212 items) are left out, since their provenance has not been determined in a systematic way, although some were certainly written in Iceland. Charters: For the period until 1570, see Arna Björk Stefánsdóttir 2008: 23; she worked with *Islandske originaldiplomer* and *Diplomatarium Islandicum*. For the period 1571–1600, counting was done in the relevant collections and the numbers are provisional.

There are fewer than a thousand extant vellum manuscripts, many of them fragments, written in Iceland in the vernacular, as well as about two thousand charters written on parchment (see Table 1). Little is known about the turnover of manuscripts in medieval times but it is indeed striking that among preserved manuscripts there are very few cases where we have a vellum and its direct copy, even among the numerous manuscripts of *Jónsbók*, the lawbook of 1281 (Már Jónsson 2001: 381–2). None of the exemplars used in the compilation of *Flateyjarbók* (GKS 1005 fol.) survive, although it is certain that the two scribes used a number of manuscripts in their work (Rowe 2005: 16). This probably means that hundreds or even thousands of manuscripts had perished even before the end of the fifteenth century. Árni Magnússon himself touched on this issue in a short rumination on receiving a liturgical manuscript from Ormur Daðason in 1726, as he found pasted to the cover an early thirteenth-century bifolium containing text from *Veraldar saga* (AM 655 VII–VIII 4to) which appeared to be much older than the Lutheran Reformation. He concluded that this showed that people had cared as little for old Icelandic books then as was still the case: 'Siest so hier af, ad þeir elldri menn hafa um þvilikar gamlar Iislendskar bækur vered älika hirdulauser og vær' (cf. Jakob Benediktsson 1944: xxvi, xxxiii).

The destruction of vellums in the seventeenth century was no less severe. The printing of books at the bishopric of Hólar in the North of Iceland, which started around 1530, created a demand for sturdy protective covers, satisfied partly by the re-use of old vellum leaves. Paradoxically, the renewed interest in medieval texts, due to the interplay of foreign fascination with early Icelandic culture and a parallel local awakening, reinforced these destructive tendencies. Some of the medieval manuscripts that now surfaced were sent to Copenhagen but more often a readable copy was made for an Icelandic readership and the exemplar destined for re-use. Thus, when Helgi Grímsson produced a copy of *Óláfs saga Tryggvasonar* (Papp. 22 fol.) at Hítardalur, shortly before 1650, he had before him a partly mutilated vellum, of which only six leaves are now preserved (AM 325 VIII 2 c, e–h 4to), gathered by Árni Magnússon and his friends in five places between 1703 and 1721 (Ólafur Halldórsson 1958–2000, III: clv–clviii, ccxiii–ccxvii). Some vellums were simply kept in unknown private libraries and never copied. An example of this is a fourteenth-century collection of sagas (AM 564 a 4to) which Árni acquired in parts in 1716 and later (Hast 1960: 89–91). In a sense it can be argued that Árni came too late, since much had already been lost, but had it not been for his systematic effort we would now have even fewer Icelandic medieval manuscripts than we do.

Árni's collection of manuscripts and documents, now in the joint custody of the two institutes in Copenhagen and Reykjavík that bear his name, contains 656 out of the 876 vellums in Table 1; that is, three out of every four. More importantly, it contains an even higher proportion of fragments (see Table 2). In Árni's collection there are 118 single leaves and 174 bifolia, with 161 more fragments from three to twelve leaves in length. This adds up to 426 fragments or 75% of his vellums and 81% of all extant fragments. There are 149 codices of more than 40 leaves in his collection or 59% of all such manuscripts. Some of these complete or almost complete vellums, and even items that we would call fragments, were actually pieced together by Árni himself out of leaves acquired in different places, so the proportion of fragments in the table should in fact be higher. A good example is the *Sturlunga saga* manuscript *Reykjarfjarðarbók* (AM 122 b fol.) with its 30 preserved leaves, out of perhaps 180 originally, which Árni obtained in at least ten lots over a period of thirty years (Már Jónsson 2009a). It should be noted that out of 55 surviving sixteenth-century paper manuscripts written in Iceland, 37 are in Árni's collection; again, three out of every four. Of the 64 vellums produced in Iceland in the seventeenth century, however, 'only' 30 are in Árni's collection. As for the charters, of those written before 1600 the great majority is in his collection. In addition he had 6000 transcriptions (*apographa*) made, hundreds of them from charters that are now lost (see pp. 153–60).

Table 2. Icelandic vellums 1101–1600 according to number of leaves

Leaves	Manuscripts	Árni's collection	%	Other collections	%
1–2	367	292	80	75	20
3–12	161	134	83	27	17
13–40	94	81	86	13	14
41 +	254	149	59	105	41
Total	876	656	75	220	25

Five AM-fragments that entered the collection after Árni's death are excluded from the column on his collection. Two manuscripts are included which he had on loan but are now in the National Archives (Þjóðskjalasafn Íslands) in Reykjavík.

Although the emphasis here will be on Árni's Icelandic vellums it needs to be remembered that he did not only collect manuscripts and documents from his native country. He acquired around 2000 Norwegian charters and had 3000 transcriptions made, in addition to 1700 Danish charters and 1400 transcriptions. He also acquired 49 Norwegian vellum manuscripts and fragments, out of the 157 items extant. The Arnamagnæan collection also includes several Danish and a few Swedish legal codices and prayer books, along with a number of manuscripts written in Latin, German, Dutch, Spanish and Italian. Mention will be made of these items where relevant.

Sources

I have examined all the available sources on Árni Magnússon's life and work, not only his hundreds of letters and thousands of notes on manuscripts but also the transcriptions he made himself or had others make for him, as well as his working papers, many of them only drafts and not always easy to date. From a historian's point of view it is fortunate that Árni finished few of the scholarly projects he undertook, as he then retained his working drafts and notes, presumably hoping to return to them at some point. Thus, although no evidence remains of his preparations for an edition of a Danish chronicle, published in Leipzig in 1695 (see p. 113), the papers concerning his unfinished edition of *Íslendingabók* survive (AM 364 4to, AM 254 8vo). Árni never kept a diary as some contemporary scholars did, such as the French scholar Bernard de Montfaucon, who in Florence on 4 March 1699 was allowed 'to transcribe what I thought fit out of the Library of St. Laurence; so that I spent almost all the following Days in that Library' (Montfaucon 1725: 253; cf. Ultee 1981: 31–2). Árni's copious notes on manuscripts and documents, not all of them available in print, can be seen as a substitute for a diary, however, as they certainly were kept in order to preserve information for posterity. Lamentably, Árni did not start writing such notes until after 1700 and, strangely enough, often made no annotations at all on manuscripts that one would have thought deserved it. In some cases later scholars have managed to throw light on important or not so important issues relating to Árni's research; these studies will be extensively cited here, both in Icelandic and other languages, so that

Sources

inquisitive readers with an interest in Old Norse texts and Early Modern scholarship will have the chance to pursue these and related matters.

Árni rarely recorded the dates of his transcriptions and other working papers, which means that often they can only be dated on the basis of his quite distinct and always recognisable handwriting, which did undergo changes over time. Even competent scholars have gone astray, though: Ludvig Holm-Olsen, for example, dated a transcription on the basis of its use in a book published in 1689 and Desmond Slay ventured to date another transcription to the period before 1697 on the basis of orthography (Holm-Olsen 1952: 59–61; Slay 1960a: 114–15); Árni's handwriting shows that he wrote both manuscripts in the years 1685–6. The first scholar to identify certain features in Árni's handwriting was Stefán Karlsson, based on a transcription dated by Árni himself to 1686 (Stefán Karlsson 1970b: 288–90). Such studies, a necessity if one is to understand Árni's development, require the comparison of all relevant sources, starting with dates that he provides in his notes and transcriptions, but also his dated letters as well as 'external' information as to where he lived, with whom he worked, what vellum manuscripts he used and whether the transcriptions were at some point sent to someone else. In most cases his handwriting can be pinned down to a certain period, for instance the winter of 1684–5 or the important year 1686. The evidence for the years 1687–93 is harder to assess, since his handwriting had stabilised at that point. After that it changed slowly, although there is a clear difference, for instance, between the years 1696, 1710 and 1724.

All in all Árni left notes, recorded on small slips of paper, with at least 1400 out of his almost 2400 manuscripts, some of them extensive and detailed but many more far too short for a historian's taste. They are a major source for this book. Often he revised his notes, adding information or correcting himself, for instance if he had become the happy owner of a manuscript that he had previously borrowed or he knew something more about scribes and former owners. Before 1700 Árni sometimes indicated the year of acquisition on the front page of a manuscript, such as AM 412 4to acquired in 1689 and AM 408 h 2 4to in 1697. His oldest dated slips were written in the years 1701 and 1703 (e.g. AM 128 8vo, AM 129 8vo). They are irregular in size but soon enough Árni started to use standardised paper in octavo and quarto, and had his scribes do that too when they wrote notes for him. This may have begun in the winter of 1707–8 when he decided to make an inventory of his vellums (see p. 152). Most of these notes, though, were written after Árni got his manuscripts back to Copenhagen in 1721 and started organising his collection, recording what he thought would be useful for later scholars (see p. 184).

Compared to preserved collections of private letters to and from renowned contemporary scholars in Europe, the number of extant letters to and from Árni is small. We may note, for comparison, that more than twenty thousand letters are preserved to and from the librarian Antonio Magliabechi in Florence, while the philosopher and historian Gottfried Wilhelm Leibniz in Hanover left drafts and copies of ten thousand letters and kept almost as many letters which he had received (Dibon 1976; Doni Garfagnini 1988; Utermoehlen 1976). Around 2500 letters from close to six hundred learned men to the scholar Johann Albert Fabricius in Hamburg are preserved (Erik Petersen 1998: 9, 784). Even if Árni's correspondence while royal commissioner in Iceland with fellow officials, friends and foes, is included, the published volumes of his letters contain just over 1200 items to or from 243 men and 17 women. Fewer than 200 of these letters are from the years before 1700. Árni's correspondence was edited by Kristian Kålund and published in 1916–20, though partly in excerpts (see *BT*; *PB*; *Emb*). A few important letters and numerous extracts from the year 1729 were added by Jón K. Margeirsson in 1975 and some stray letters or drafts discovered among Árni's papers have been published by Jón Helgason (1975a).[1]

A number of letters from foreign scholars to Árni in the years 1693–1701 are preserved (*PB*: 71–2, 82–4, 149–52, 203–9, 266–9, 358–9, 363, 384–400). The oldest extant letter from Iceland was written by Bishop Þórður Þorláksson on 20 August 1689, but Árni's answer is lost (*PB*: 548–50). Four letters from the farmer Skúli Ólafsson from 1696–9 are extant (*PB*: 346–8), but otherwise letters from Iceland before 1702 are only preserved in bits and pieces, as Árni frequently copied or cut out statements relating to manuscripts in order to put them with his notes,

---

[1] In the margins of the Arnamagnæan Institute's copy of *PB* Jón indicates four more letters; see pp. 8, 313, 510, 653.

for instance on the two extant vellums of *Sturlunga saga* (*PB*: 245, 343, 532).

The 160 letters between Árni and the scholar Þormóður Torfason, perhaps better known as Torfæus, are a special case. The first one, written by Þormóður on 12 November 1688, is preserved in his copybook (*BT*: 1–4). Árni's first letters to Þormóður are lost and the oldest one now extant was written on 4 April 1689. Árni received that letter and many others together with Þormóður's manuscripts at his death in 1719, but had himself started to keep the letters from Þormóður in 1703 (*BT*: 374). At that time he also began to keep letters from other Icelanders. The oldest extant one was written in December 1702 by Árni's uncle, the Reverend Páll Ketilsson (*PB*: 274). Árni's decision to keep all correspondence can be linked to his writing of notes on manuscripts in order to record what he knew about their acquisition. It also marks a turning point in the preservation of letters that he himself wrote. Just over 300 dispatched letters are extant, including originals of some 110, more than half of them to Þormóður. Some found their way to the Arnamagnæan collection after Árni's death, such as his letters to Frederik Rostgaard through Jakob Langebek in the late eighteenth century (*PB*: 394–400; Weber 1775). Others are there because Árni seems to have actively sought to acquire his own letters from the people to whom he had sent them. Two of his letters to Magnús Jónsson at Vigur from 1691 and 1695 are thus preserved, as well as eighteen letters to his close friend Bishop Björn Þorleifsson (*PB*: 241–5, 550–610). Árni may have obtained these letters from the heirs of those to whom they had been written, just as he acquired his own letters to Þormóður. While in Iceland, from 1702 onwards, Árni also started keeping drafts of letters that he wrote, or had his assistants keep copies or make excerpts. Thus, while many letters written by and to Árni are lost, the rate of preservation is much higher than is the norm for Icelanders in these decades.

There exist several valuable descriptions of Árni by his contemporaries. In seventeenth- and eighteenth-century Europe it was common that devoted friends or disciples wrote about learned men shortly after their death. Even if they had led quiet lives they were thought to be interesting on account of their studies or ideas. Other scholars relished reading these tales, or that was at least the argument put forward by Pierre Bayle when he announced in March 1684 that his new journal *Nouvelles de la république des lettres* would contain such scholarly obituaries (5v–6r). In this vein, Thierry Ruinart wrote about Jean Mabillon in 1709, two years after he had passed away (Ruinart 1933: 10). Johann Georg von Eckhardt wrote about Leibniz in 1717, only a few months after his death (Eberhard and von Eckhart 1982: 125), and Hermann Samuel Reimarus wrote immediately about his father-in-law Fabricius, who died on 30 April 1736 (Erik Petersen 1998: 21). In this respect Árni was served by two men who knew him well. In the summer of 1730, seven months after Árni's death, his older brother Jón Magnússon wrote a short biography in Icelandic (AM 1037 4to) for Hans Gram and Thomas Bartholin the youngest, Árni's friends and colleagues who managed his estate (*PB*: 302; *LS* I, 2: 3). Although the brothers were not in fact raised together we can be fairly certain that Jón is a reliable witness regarding Árni's youth. Jón Ólafsson of Grunnavík, Árni's assistant and scribe from 1726 onwards, wrote a biography of Árni in Danish in 1738 (AM 1027 4to). His source for Árni's early years was Jón Magnússon's text, whereas for the later years he used some letters and more importantly relied on conversations with Árni (Jón Helgason 1925: 200–3; Jón Ólafsson 2005: 17). At times Jón recounts what Árni told him, for instance on the circumstances in which he got employment in 1684 and 1697 (see pp. 56, 114). Later, Jón wrote another biography, this time in Icelandic, which he finished on 7 January 1759, exactly 29 years after Árni's death. As before Jón relied on his memory of their conversations, but now excused himself by saying that he had only known Árni during his final years. He had also spoken to truthful men and used some letters and other documents. He remembered having read Jón Magnússon's biography, to which he no longer had access, as was also the case with his own earlier biography in Danish (*LS* I, 2: 9–10; Þorkell Jóhannesson 1950: 3; cf. Jón Helgason 1925: 297–300). The Icelandic biography is thus somewhat less reliable than the Danish one, but contains some interesting details which can be used with care.

Disposition

Árni Magnússon's persistence and remarkable results are the subject of this book, which is intended as an essay in understanding how a series of coincidences, combined with one individual's astonishing determination, brought together a great collection of manuscripts and documents, items which until that time were dispersed far and wide, threatened with destruction. The reader seeking fuller details of personal and political matters relating to Árni should consult my biography in Icelandic (Már Jónsson 1998). The diachronic framework employed there will also be used in the present volume and its emphasis will be on Árni's development as collector and scholar. The approach is thus quite traditional and is (indeed) inspired by E.C. Werlauff's argument of 1836:

> When one considers a collection of manuscripts such as the Arnamagnæan, the most spectacular and the best of its kind, it will always be interesting to know its origins, learn about its growth, and investigate the fortunate and not so fortunate circumstances through which it reached its present state.
>
> Ved en Samling af haandskrevne Monumenter, som den Arne-Magnæanske, den eneste og fortrinligste i sit Slags, bliver det altid interessant, at kiende dens første Oprindelse, bemærke dens successive Forøgelse, og undersøge de heldige eller uheldige Omstændigheder, gjennem hvilke den naaede sit nærværende Standpunkt (*BE*: 83).

When Árni began serious antiquarian and historical research in 1684, hundreds of erudite books were published each year in Oxford, Leiden, Amsterdam, Leipzig and Paris. Huge libraries were being established and learned journals had taken over as the most important medium of scholarly discussion and dissemination (Israel 2001: 119–55). The two principal problems of ambitious scholarship were, for one thing, how to locate, acquire and establish the required texts; and secondly, how to use them with discernment by sifting fact from fiction. Both tasks were fraught with difficulties. Nobody knew exactly what was available in collections and libraries spread all over Europe, nor was there agreement on the quality and reliability of manuscripts and documents (Erik Petersen 1998: 244). Árni emerged from an Icelandic tradition of learning that was neither strict in its methods nor critical in its attitude towards texts. As a young man, working for Thomas Bartholin the younger from 1684 to 1690, he identified strongly with European scholarship as it had developed since the early sixteenth century and, in doing so, applied new insights to Icelandic manuscripts and texts (see chapters 2–3). As early as 1690, after being fascinated with manuscripts for at least six years, Árni expressed his wish to live by scholarship alone: 'vid antiqvitet ad lifa' (*BT*: 34). Through his diligence he managed to do exactly that.

Árni's determination to collect manuscripts was strenghtened by his failure to produce editions of Icelandic texts, as he gradually realised that he did not have the talent to be a productive scholar in the sense of pouring out learned books, which was the goal of most contemporary scholars who sought recognition (cf. Grafton 1985; Gasnault 2008). His contribution would therefore be to collect and transcribe manuscripts and documents, or in other words to provide materials for others to work on (see chapter 4). In 1697 he became secretary to the Danish Royal Archives and four years later professor at Copenhagen University. He had reached his goal of being able to live off scholarly work and could also boast of the best collection of Icelandic texts ever put together (see chapter 5). His scholarly endeavours were interrupted when, in May 1702, King Frederik IV required him to report on the harsh socio-economic conditions in Iceland and suggest ways to promote economic recovery. The task took longer than planned and the Royal Commission, composed of Árni and his friend Páll Vídalín, came into conflict with other officials. While in Iceland Árni used the opportunity to collect manuscripts, and he and his assistants spent the winters at Skálholt copying documents (see chapter 6). Árni left Iceland for Copenhagen in the autumn of 1712. After that he rarely meddled in politics and concentrated on his ever-growing collection, but also renewed his own scholarly activity, although he yet again abandoned all ideas of editing Icelandic texts (see chapter 7). The Great Fire of Copenhagen in October 1728 nearly annihilated his efforts but he did not give up, writing some months before he died to the son of the recently deceased Páll Vídalín that as long as he lived he would want all the old documents that could be found (Jón K. Margeirsson 1975: 136). Árni died shortly afterwards, on 7 January 1730, at the age of 66. Although his efforts were not met with unanimous praise at the time, his reputation slowly but steadily grew and has now reached quasi-heroic proportions (see chapter 8).

Some readers of the present work may find that reference is made to an overwhelmingly large number of manuscripts. The reason is simple. Manuscripts were what mattered most to Árni Magnússon for almost half a century. A nascent fascination became an infatuation of almost obsessive proportions. In order to explain the nature, extent and contours of this engagement the manuscript shelfmarks have to be cited and sufficient detail provided so that the curious reader can go further, should he or she so desire. If no reference is given, the information provided is taken from the manuscript itself or Kristian Kålund's superb catalogue of Árni's collection (*AMKat.*). Other readers may feel that too many details of Árni's personal life and circumstances are provided. Again, the reason is simple. If this extraordinary collection of manuscripts is to be explained the life of the collector has to be investigated. Manuscripts and documents did not just arrive at his door. He had intentions and wishes, he wrote letters and talked to people; in short, he made a sustained effort which gave results which have left traces. There is no lack of evidence, as already explained, but it is fragmentary in the sense that Árni's statements or activities most commonly concern one manuscript or one document at a time. These scattered bits of information have to be compared with each other and put into context, so that one can gauge their relevance and thereby reach a satisfying and plausible level of generalisation. The basic approach here is empirical and I do hope that I have succeeded in choosing the right bits and pieces of information, which together provide a coherent and convincing image of this enchanting man.

It is not possible fully to explain exactly where Árni's urge to collect manuscripts and documents came from. One way would perhaps be to talk of 'destiny', in the sense that most of these objects would otherwise have been destroyed and that Árni was therefore 'produced' by historical circumstances – someone had to do this! His motives were neither political nor religious, as was common among contemporary scholars and collectors (Chiffoleau 2008: 183, 226, 230; Gasnault 2008: 130–1). Árni collected manuscripts and documents for 'purely' scholarly reasons, if that word can be used, although it could also be tempting to see a clue to the reason for his personal desire for these objects in Jón Ólafsson's biography of 1738. If we are to believe Jón, Árni was above medium height, thick-set, massive and masculine, with dark hair. His face was perfectly shaped and his demeanour was that of a level-headed, serious-minded and thoughtful individual. He was nonetheless a man of great passions, but controlled them with exceptional strength of mind. Something was wrong, though, and Jón claims that over Árni's blue eyes and eyebrows there was a shadow which hinted at hidden things in his heart: 'Dog var ligesom han havde nogen Skygge... over Øinene og Øiebrynene, det er det slags noget, at en mærker paa forborgne Ting i Hiertet' (*BE*: 42; cf. Finnur Jónsson 1930a: 195). What could these secrets have been? It is indeed the case that Árni became extremely angry when criticised and often exhibited great impatience in his requests for information, but what more can be said? It is certain that Árni was a person driven by great emotions. Was it because he grew up with his grandparents and spent most of his life away from his family? Does it relate to the fact that he married late in life to a much older woman and had no children? Such questions have no answers and I will not pursue them any further. Árni did what he did because he did what he did.

The devastating fire of 1728 could have wiped out everything Árni had done, which would have caused irremediable damage to Icelandic culture and identity. In 1929, Halldór Hermannsson wrote on Árni's loss of manuscripts: 'One shudders at the thought that the whole might have perished' (67). That is true indeed, but one also shudders at the thought of what would have happened had Árni not appeared on the scene to collect these manuscripts. Most of them would surely have vanished. He was certainly aware of this himself and explained to King Frederik IV on 12 November 1720 that he had tried to save manuscripts as well as documents from destruction, since Icelanders did not care for such things (see p. 183). This book is a modest contribution to the study of his efforts, so that they are not consigned to oblivion, and in the hope that there are indeed some now who care greatly for such things. Writing it has taken too long. In 1995–8 I received a grant from the Carlsberg Foundation in order to do research on Árni. The result was my biography of him, published in Reykjavík in 1998. The original plan was to produce a Danish version but that never happened and recurrent pangs of conscience resulted in my decision, in the autumn of 2007, to write this short volume in English. It is partly based on the biography but in 2008–9 I did more research in the Arnamagnæan collections in Reykjavík and Copenhagen, mostly on Árni's later years. My thanks go to the Carlsberg Foundation for its generous original support, to the University of Iceland for a research leave in 2008 and to the Icelandic *Alþingi* for the use of the Jón Sigurðsson apartment in Copenhagen in October that same year. I decided to face my implied audience directly and write the book in English myself, instead of leaving too many things to a translator. Diligent friends, Andrew Wawn, Patricia Pires Boulhosa and Gísli Baldur Róbertsson, have read the whole thing, suggesting some changes and correcting the language, as well as style and tenor; the same goes for the editors of this series, Margaret Clunies Ross, Mats Malm and Matthew James Driscoll.

2
Background

> We denie not but that some woorthy actes of our forefathers be reserued in the songs and poemes of our contreymen, as also in prose.
>
> Qvin veterum gesta aliqvot cantibus et poëmatibus nostratium, ut et soluta oratione, apud nos conserventur, non negamus.
>
> Arngrímur Jónsson, *Brevis Commentarius* 1593
> (Hakluyt 1598: 584; Jakob Benediktsson 1950–7, I: 72)

This chapter traces the origins of medieval Scandinavian studies and their development in Norway, Denmark, Sweden and Iceland until the appointment of Thomas Bartholin the younger as royal antiquarian to King Christian V of Denmark-Norway in 1684. These scholarly strivings will be looked at in the context of the concomitant destruction of vellum manuscripts in Iceland as well as Norway.

Septentrional studies

In 1424 the Florentine scholar Poggio Bracciolini expressed his hope that the monastery at Sorø in Denmark would have some valuable manuscripts of classical texts. He had in Rome met with a learned man of the 'Gothic nation' who talked about two large volumes containing the Roman history of Livy (Ellen Jørgensen 1915; Ellen Jørgensen 1931: 38–9). Poggio did not have the means himself to travel or to send someone else to inquire further into this matter, but in 1451 he played a part in sending Enoch di Ascoli to Germany and Denmark, as the envoy of Pope Nicholas V, to look for the Livy volumes. They were not found, but Enoch returned four years later with a manuscript containing the first-century Pseudo-Virgilian poems 'Elegiae in Maecenatem', which he had indeed acquired in Denmark (Sabbadini 1905–14, II: 115, 118, 140; Walser 1914: 227–8). The frenetic search for manuscripts of classical texts, initiated in Italy and France in the late thirteenth century, had thus reached the North, where quite a few manuscripts containing works from Graeco-Roman Antiquity came to light (Reynolds and Wilson 1991: 130–9). In 1416, to take only one further example, Poggio had visited the monastery of St. Gallen in Switzerland and identified works by Quintilian, Asconius and Valerius Flaccus. On 16 December he wrote to his friend Guarino Veronensis asserting that the manuscripts had not been kept in an orderly library but 'thrown into the lowest apartment or dungeon of a tower' unfit for criminals (Shepherd 1802: 108–9; Harth 1984–7, II: 155; Fubini 1964–9, III, vol. I: 28–9; IV: 719; Heer 1938: 184–5). Works in Latin were among the first texts printed after the invention of movable type in around 1450. In Italy, two out of three books published in 1469–72 were texts of this kind or related subjects such as Latin grammars. Approximately thirty thousand books were printed in Europe before the year 1500, a quarter of them in Italy, where at least a thousand editions of Latin authors were published, two hundred of them works by Cicero, whose collected writings first appeared in print in Milan in 1498–9 (Scholderer 1949: 26–33, 40–2; Reynolds and Wilson 1991: 155–6; British Library, Incunabula Short Title Catalogue, at www.bl.uk/catalogues/istc).

Scholars in Northern Europe, influenced by Italian humanists and publishers, now started inquiring into the history of their native lands. Bede's *Ecclesiastical History of the English People* (*Historia ecclesiastica gentis Anglorum*) was printed as early as 1475–80 in Strasbourg (Frantzen 1990: 152). Interesting texts were rediscovered, such as the plays and poetry of the tenth-century nun Hrotsvitha of Gandersheim, edited and published by Konrad Celtis in Nürnberg in 1501. The enterprising printer Jodocus Badius (Josse Bade) published a number of medieval Latin texts in Paris, such as Geoffrey of Monmouth's *History of the Kings of Britain* (*Historia regum Britanniæ*) in 1508. *The History of the Franks* (*Historia Francorum*) by Gregory of Tours appeared in 1512, followed in the next two years by the writings of other medieval historians, such as Siegebert of Gembloux, Aimonius of Fleury and Liutprand of Cremona (Ellen Jørgensen 1931: 34; Wattenbach-Levison 1952–63: 5–6).

In the spring of 1514 Badius issued the early thirteenth-century *History of the Danes* (*Gesta Danorum*) by Saxo Grammaticus, a sprawling mixture of legend and history which traces the origins of the Danish kingdom from before the foundation of Rome and goes right up to the author's own times. Saxo describes in detail the amazing feats of Denmark's first kings, as well as the more sober events of later centuries. The editor was a Danish student of theology, Christiern Pedersen, who had come to Paris in 1508. Inspired by the flurry of editions of medieval texts he asked influential friends in Denmark for help with obtaining texts that could be published. When no such assistance was forthcoming he travelled to Copenhagen himself, returning in 1512 with a manuscript of *Gesta Danorum* acquired from the archbishop of Lund (Boserup 1981: 11; Ellen Jørgensen 1931: 62–3, 70). The book may have been intended to show that Denmark was 'a cultural nation on a par with the rest of Europe' and it was ready just in time for the marriage of King Christian II of Denmark to Elisabeth, sister of Archduke Charles, Holy Roman Emperor *in spe*, in June 1514 (Friis-Jensen 1989: 149–50, 152).

The barrenness of the Icelandic soil, Saxo claimed in his introduction, offered to the inhabitants no means of self-indulgence and so instead they devoted their time to investigating the history of their own and other nations; their results he had used in his work (Saxo 1979–80, I: 5). This inspired Christiern Pedersen and later scholars to think that historical treasures might be available in Iceland or at least texts written in Old Norse. Back in Denmark from Paris, Pedersen decided to publish a Danish translation of Saxo with a commentary of his own. He hired a Norwegian man of law who was able to read the old sagas of Norwegian kings, which contained descriptions of the same events as could be read in Saxo. This unknown individual produced some extracts from manuscripts, probably in Bergen during the 1530s (Jon Gunnar Jørgensen 2007: 21–4). While the Icelandic language had remained largely unchanged, Danish and Norwegian had undergone changes, particularly under the influence of German, to the extent that by the end of the fourteenth century the medieval languages had become incomprehensible. In Norway, though, knowledge of law required a good understanding of Old Norwegian, as the national law of 1274 was still in use. Around 1550,

Background

the lawman Laurents Hanssøn produced a translation of parts of the early thirteenth-century saga of Norwegian kings, *Heimskringla*. He also knew *Orkneyinga saga*, *Jómsvíkinga saga*, *Óláfs saga Tryggvasonar*, *Konungs skuggsjá* and *Eyrbyggja saga*, but complained that very few codices were available, few Norwegians could read the texts and hardly anyone understood them: 'Ere nu all faa bøgher i Norige... faa ere och de som dem lese kunne, æn ferre ere de som forstaa dem' (Storm 1899: 3–4). In spite of the language barrier, however, a thriving milieu for medieval studies had by then developed among scholars and officials in Bergen (Jon Gunnar Jørgensen 1996: 214–18, 229; Sigurður Pétursson 2007: 147).

In the 1530s, the exiled Swedish bishop Johannes Magnus, who resided in Rome, wrote a response to Saxo, whose depiction of the Swedes in *Gesta Danorum* had been less than flattering. *The History of the Kings of the Goths and Swedes* (*Historia de Omnibus Gothorum Sueonumque Regibus*), published in Rome in 1554 (ten years after Johannes Magnus died), presents a list of 143 Swedish kings from King Magog, son of Japhet, up to Gustav Vasa who had been crowned in 1523. As Saxo had done before him Johannes Magnus invented many of these kings, but his efforts nonetheless gave the Swedes an even more remarkable royal genealogy than the Danes. According to him, the Swedes alone descended from the ancient Goths, who went on to conquer most of Europe, whereas the Danes had originally been chased out of Sweden and settled on uninhabited islands to the south and west (Johannesson 1991: 5, 29, 73, 127–8; Akhøj Nielsen 2004: 164–6). A second edition printed in Basel in 1558 attracted the attention of Danish scholars. Hans Münster, professor of theology at Copenhagen University, wrote from London on 16 October 1559 to a friend that the book was selling well. It was full of slander and calumnies about Denmark and such nonsense, he argued, should be refuted elegantly by learned men skilled in Danish history: 'homines antiquitatis rerum Danicarum peritos' (Ellen Jørgensen 1931: 87–8, 222).

In 1552, King Christian III had assigned to Hans Svaning the task of composing a history of Denmark based on Saxo and later sources. Svaning was also asked to write a rebuttal of Johannes Magnus, which he did anonymously in a pamphlet published in 1561, where he claimed that it was the Danes and not the Swedes who were descended from the Goths, whose origins could be traced to the region of Scania (Skåne), at that time part of Denmark. Svaning went on to write more than a thousand pages on Danish history from the earliest times, providing the names of all kings from Dan to Christian I, but that book was never published. The two countries were at war from 1563 to 1570; the Treaty of Stettin, which ended the war, stipulated, among other things, that no inhabitant of either country was allowed to publish anything offensive to the other's kings or authorities (Skovgaard-Petersen 1993: 114–16; Ellen Jørgensen 1931: 88–90; Ilsøe 1973: 48–51; Akhøj Nielsen 2004: 166–8).

In 1575 a Danish translation of Saxo's *Gesta Danorum*, based on Pedersen's edition, was published in Copenhagen by Anders Sørensen Vedel in an effort to make it more widely available among the general reading public and thus preserve the glory of the forefathers: 'vore Forfædris gode rycte oc prijs' (Vedel 1967: Ci–v). Vedel promoted the reading of these old stories not only for entertainment but, more importantly, in order to understand how God protected those who behaved well and punished those who did not, and how rulers should govern their states with justice and piety (Vedel 1967: Aij-r). Saxo had these qualities, just like classical authors, but a translation was needed because not many people could read Latin; even learned men complained that Saxo's language was difficult to understand (Vedel 1967: Biv-v). In 1578, Vedel replaced Svaning, his father-in-law, as royal historiographer. A year later he published the first edition of Adam of Bremen's late eleventh-century *History of the Church of Hamburg* (*Gesta Hammaburgensis ecclesiae pontificum*). He used a now lost vellum manuscript of the monastery of Sorø but made aleatory changes to the text. It appears that aided by an unidentified Icelander he made some effort to read Icelandic manuscripts, as he copied a few sentences and made a list of interesting words and common abbreviations (Akhøj Nielsen 2004: 172–6, 218–19, 615–30; Skovgaard-Petersen 2002a: 104–10).

Background

Revival

Medieval Latin texts concerning the history of the northernmost regions of Europe had thus begun to appear in print and scholars started using them, but Icelandic sources were as yet absent. In the autumn of 1592 the Reverend Arngrímur Jónsson came to Copenhagen on behalf of his uncle, Bishop Guðbrandur Þorláksson of Hólar. At Guðbrandur's instigation Arngrímur had written a booklet refuting calumnies made by foreign authors about Iceland, *Brevis Commentarius de Islandia*. It was printed in Copenhagen in 1593. Arngrímur cites a number of Icelandic medieval texts, such as *Landnámabók*, *Njáls saga*, *Hungrvaka*, *Jóns saga helga* and *Konungs skuggsjá*, thereby confirming Saxo's claim that there were abundant sources on medieval Scandinavian history to be had in Iceland. In Copenhagen Arngrímur met with the royal chancellor, Arild Huitfeldt, who in 1590 had published a Latin translation of the medieval laws of Scania and was now at work on an extensive history of Denmark in Danish, later published in ten volumes (1595–1604). Danish scholars asked Arngrímur to translate relevant Icelandic texts into Latin so that they could use them in their work, among them *Jómsvíkinga saga* from a manuscript in Huitfeldt's possession. Arngrímur also produced an abridged version of the since lost *Skjöldunga saga* (Jakob Benediktsson 1950–7, IV: 12, 40–1, 107–40, 149–50; Akhøj Nielsen 2004: 247–8). Huitfeldt continued his editorial work in 1594 by publishing a Danish translation of the thirteenth-century Norwegian court law (*Hirðskrá*) and financing the publication of a translation, or rather a paraphrase, of *Heimskringla* made by the Norwegian Matthis Størssøn half a century earlier (Storm 1873: 204, 212, 266–71; Rørdam 1896: 138–41; Ekrem 1994: 402–4). The editor was Jens Mortensen, who explained in his preface that since the saga revealed that Norwegians had performed remarkable deeds he had decided to publish it in Danish so that anyone could read it (Mortensen 1594: 4r).

Niels Krag replaced Vedel as royal historiographer in 1595. A year later King Christian IV decreed that Icelanders should provide Arngrímur Jónsson with whatever material he wished to consult. In a letter to Arngrímur in 1597 Krag mentioned that he and other scholars had manuscripts written in Icelandic which confirmed Saxo's claim of the reliability of Icelandic authors. Arngrímur now sent two compilations written in Latin, one on Danish history (*Rerum Danicarum fragmenta*) and the other on Norwegian history (*Supplementum historiæ Norvagicæ*). He used a number of hitherto unknown sources and borrowed many manuscripts (Jakob Benediktsson 1950–7, IV: 12–14, 182, 190, 224–5; Ellen Jørgensen 1931: 92–104; Adolf D. Jørgensen 1884: 26–30). Arngrímur was confident that Icelandic sources were more trustworthy than foreign ones. He had numerous objections to Saxo, who was considered infallible by his Danish patrons, finding it peculiar that Saxo praised Icelandic sources while so often disagreeing with them. Nowhere in his printed works does Arngrímur criticise Saxo, however, and in private letters he indicated that his criticism was meant for Krag alone (Jakob Benediktsson 1950–7, IV: 59–60). Perhaps because of these critical views, Huitfeldt hardly used the *Supplementum* and it was only in 1644 that Arngrímur's ideas on Saxo were mentioned by Stephan Stephanius in a new edition of *Gesta Danorum* (Jakob Benediktsson 1950–7, IV: 71–2, 182–3; Ellen Jørgensen 1931: 129–31).

Little by little manuscripts arrived from Iceland and Norway to fill the public and private collections in Copenhagen. In published and unpublished works Vedel mentions three manuscripts of sagas of Norwegian kings. When Krag died in 1602 only two of these were found, one of them now extant, *Eirspennill* (AM 47 fol.), which contains a note indicating that Vedel owned it in 1570 (Akhøj Nielsen 2004: 23–25, 227–36, 249–55, 266–8; Birket Smith 1882: 106–11, 121). That manuscript, written in Iceland in the early fourteenth century, seems to have come to Denmark from Norway. In 1588 Huitfeldt had acquired a manuscript of *Knýtlinga saga* from Iceland which after his death came to the University Library. In 1619 that library acquired the entire collection of the Norwegian doctor Henrik Høyer, who possessed several manuscripts of kings' sagas, such as *Kringla, Fagurskinna A, Fagurskinna B, Gullinskinna* and *Jöfraskinna*; all of them destroyed in the Great Fire of 1728 (Birket-Smith 1882: 24–6, 127–35; Kålund 1900: xx–xxi).

Among the men who were infected by this new interest in septentrional studies was Ole Worm, professor of medicine at the University of

Copenhagen. In a letter to his friend Bertel Knudsen in 1626 he explained that he did not know what storm had driven him out on the 'deep ocean of antiquities' where no harbour could be seen (Schepelern 1965–8, I: 114; cf. Valdimar Tr. Hafstein 2003). Four years earlier Worm had persuaded King Christian IV to request that all bishops in Denmark and Norway should search for documents and runestones and send them to Copenhagen (Werlauff 1832: 286–90; Ellen Jørgensen 1931: 121). In 1623, after reading Arngrímur Jónsson's book on Icelandic history (*Crymogæa*) of 1609, Worm contacted Þorlákur Skúlason, a former student of his and now schoolmaster of the cathedral school at Hólar in Northern Iceland, asking whether it was true that the Icelandic language had not changed much since ancient times (Jakob Benediktsson 1948: xv–xvii; Jakob Benediktsson 1950–7, IV: 72). This was the beginning of a fruitful scholarly relationship between Worm and several Icelandic scholars. In 1626 Þorlákur could inform Worm that Arngrímur Jónsson had just sent a manuscript called *Skálda* to Chancellor Christian Friis of Kragerup. On Þorlákur's request Arngrímur explained to Worm that Friis had asked him to gather historical sources and added that he considered it unlikely that more could be found in Iceland. Nonetheless, he provided Worm with a few manuscripts which he had borrowed from people with the promise to return them in due course (Jakob Benediktsson 1948: 1–2; Jakob Benediktsson 1950–7, IV: 78n; Schepelern 1965–8, I: 108–9).

Þorlákur Skúlason became bishop of Hólar in 1627 and after that strove to establish a library of medieval texts containing mostly sagas of bishops; he borrowed old vellum manuscripts as well as more contemporary transcriptions to have them copied. He never considered publishing any of these texts, though, and at the printing press which had been established at Hólar almost a hundred years earlier he printed only books for Lutheran edification. Bishop Þorlákur sent both manuscripts and erudite ruminations of his own to Worm and was his most important contact in Iceland (Springborg 1977: 61–6; Stefán Karlsson 2000: 383–403). He was not alone, though, and in the autumn of 1632 the Reverend Magnús Ólafsson at Laufás wrote to Worm that laymen who had manuscripts would not lend them, but lay on them like serpents on gold, to no use for anyone: 'ut angvis auro incubant, nullo cum fructu' (Jakob Benediktsson

1948: 225; Schepelern 1965–8, I: 273). He may have been thinking about men like the Magistrate Magnús Björnsson at Munkaþverá in Eyjafjörður, who possessed many distinguished manuscripts, such as *Möðruvallabók* (AM 132 fol.), another compilation of *Íslendingasögur* and some younger sagas (AM 152 fol.), *Óláfs saga Tryggvasonar* and *Óláfs saga helga* (AM 61 fol.), *Karlamagnús saga* and other sagas (AM 180 a–b fol.) and *Stjórn*, *Rómverja sögur*, *Alexanders saga* and *Gyðinga saga* (AM 226 fol.), besides two manuscripts of *heilagramannasögur* (AM 232 fol., AM 233 a fol.) (Sigurjón Páll Ísaksson 1994: 142–5).

There were discrepant opinions among Icelandic scholars about the existence and availability of manuscripts in Iceland. Some, like Arngrímur Jónsson, asserted that nothing more was to be found in the country, and others, like Magnús Ólafsson, claimed that there were manuscripts around but the owners would not let go of them. It turned out that Arngrímur was wrong. In 1635 Bishop Þorlákur informed Ole Worm that he had heard of an old manuscript which might contain something of use, written by Haukr the magistrate. This most probably referred to the vellum known as *Hauksbók* and Þorlákur may have known the part containing *Landnámabók* (AM 371 4to), earlier used by Arngrímur in his writings. Worm eagerly waited for the manuscript and repeated his request in the spring of 1638. Þorlákur replied on 9 September that Arngrímur had translated some of the text and would send it to Copenhagen (Jakob Benediktsson 1948: 290–300; Jón Helgason 1960a: xxvi–xxvii). A year later Þorlákur sent a recent transcription of *Knýtlinga saga* (AM 1005 4to) and Worm asked the Icelandic student Einar Magnússon to translate parts of it (Petersens and Olson 1919–25: xxii–xxv). Worm thus gradually managed to collect quite a large number of Icelandic vellum manuscripts, most of which later ended up in Árni Magnússon's collection (AM 68 fol., AM 227 fol., AM 242 fol., AM 310 4to, AM 580 4to, AM 20 a 8vo), as well as most of Worm's paper manuscripts (AM 102 4to, AM 414 4to, AM 490 4to, AM 762 4to, AM 1005 4to, AM 160 I 8vo).

In 1633 Worm published a new translation of *Heimskringla* made by the Norwegian priest Peder Claussøn in 1599–1600. Worm had been encouraged by a bookseller who claimed that the edition of 1594 was out of stock and there was great demand for the text. In his introduction Worm claimed to have published the best available translation and informed the reader that he had compared it to several manuscripts written in both Icelandic and Danish. He had also provided information on the kings of Norway until the unification with Denmark at the end of the fourteenth century (Worm 1633: preface; Werlauff 1832: 352–4). By now, Icelandic sources had been established as fundamental to the study of the earliest history of the kingdom of Denmark and Norway. This was not recognised by everyone, however; the Dutch scholars Johannes Pontanus and Johannes Meursius, for example, royal historiographers to King Christian IV, published books, respectively in 1631 and 1638, on the history of Denmark until 1448, using only the work of other scholars and completely disregarding unpublished Danish and Icelandic sources (Skovgaard-Petersen 2002a: 154–202, 240–6; Ellen Jørgensen 1931: 155–9; cf. Jakob Benediktsson 1950–7, IV: 419).

The learned Brynjólfur Sveinsson became bishop of Skálholt in 1639 and wanted to further the scholarly use of the medieval texts of his country by publishing them in the vernacular with a Latin translation and commentary. In 1647 he asked King Frederik III for permission to establish a printing press in Skálholt for this purpose. Ole Worm supported the idea but Bishop Þorlákur Skúlason protested that he would be forced to close down his press since the diocese of Skálholt was much bigger than the diocese of Hólar. He offered to print the medieval texts at Hólar, but Brynjólfur would not accept this. In the end no permission was granted and Worm suggested to the king that Brynjólfur should spend some time in Copenhagen working on these editions. Brynjólfur turned down the offer in the autumn of 1650 with the excuse that he was busy building a cathedral (Halldór Hermannsson 1922: vi–vii; Jakob Benediktsson 1948: 105–14, 321–7, 407; Schepelern 1965–8, III: 316, 333–4, 344, 374, 378–9).

King Frederik III had ambitious plans for the Royal Library in Copenhagen and in the spring of 1656 he asked Bishop Brynjólfur to obtain some Icelandic manuscripts for him. The royal request was announced at the yearly assembly at the *Alþingi* and Brynjólfur promised to pay well for the manuscripts or return them after they had been transcribed. No manuscripts were offered, but from his own collection the bishop sent *Flateyjarbók* (GKS 1005 fol.), *Grágás* (GKS 1157 fol.)

and *Völsunga saga* and *Ragnars saga loðbrókar* (NKS 1824 b 4to), along with some paper manuscripts. He took the occasion to encourage the royal librarian Wilhelm Lange to publish editions of Icelandic texts with Latin translations in order that European scholars would get to know them, and only Icelanders, he argued, could undertake that kind of work. To keep manuscripts locked away in foreign libraries, he contended, where nobody would ever understand them, did not amount to preserving antiquities but to eradicating them: 'id vere antiqvitates non conservare sed extingvere est' (Jón Helgason 1942: 72; Kålund 1900: xxxvii–xxxviii; Halldór Hermannsson 1929: 46–8). Although the bishop did not get a direct answer, the subsequent hiring of the recently defrocked Reverend Þórarinn Eiríksson can be seen as a compromise. Þórarinn was preparing a Latin translation of *Hálfdanar saga* for print when he drowned in Copenhagen in 1659 (Kålund 1900: xxxix; Halldór Hermannsson 1922: 40).

Another Icelander, Þormóður Torfason (Torfæus), was then hired as royal translator and in 1662 was sent to Iceland to gather more manuscripts. Bishop Gísli Þorláksson of Hólar, son of Bishop Þorlákur Skúlason, was also to provide him with two copies of every book printed there. Bishop Brynjólfur Sveinsson again handed over several remarkable manuscripts: The Codex Regius of the Poetic Edda (GKS 2365 4to), the Codex Regius of *Snorra Edda* (GKS 2367 4to), *Jónsbók* (GKS 3270 4to), *Morkinskinna* (GKS 1009 fol.), *Njáls saga* (GKS 2870 4to), a collection of *Íslendingasögur* (now lost), *Rímfræði* (GKS 1812 4to), *Konungsannáll* (GKS 2087 4to) and a collection of romances (GKS 2845 4to). Þormóður himself acquired a few more manuscripts for the king: *Hrokkinskinna* (GKS 1010 fol.), *Tómas saga* and *Óláfs saga helga* (GKS 1008 fol.) and *Njáls saga* (GKS 2868 or 2869 4to) (Kålund 1900: xli). Three years after returning to Copenhagen Þormóður was given a lucrative administrative position (*Cammererer*) in Stavanger in Norway and settled at the farm Stangeland, where he lived for the rest of his life. He kept in touch with the learned men of Copenhagen and was appointed royal antiquarian in 1667 in order to write a book on medieval government and produce a 'corpus historicum' from the Icelandic texts he had already translated into Danish (Halldór Hermannsson 1954: 68–74; Ólafur Halldórsson 1992: 11–14; Jón Eiríksson 2009: 28–75).

Background

Destruction

Not all owners of manuscripts were as careful as Magnús Björnsson and Brynjólfur Sveinsson, who kept their collections in good condition. The renewed interest in Icelandic texts paradoxically had a downside in the sense that many vellum manuscripts were destroyed after being copied for people who could not easily read the medieval handwriting. In a seventeenth-century note written on an empty page of a manuscript of *Jónsbók* from the early fourteenth century, a reader expresses gratitude for the loan of the manuscript but complains that the book is hardly legible: 'lýtt lesande' (AM 169 4to: 25v). Such vellum manuscripts were in danger of being taken apart so that their leaves could be used as flyleaves and covers for the printed books which poured out of the Hólar press. Vellum leaves and strips were also used as covers and for support in the binding of manuscripts (Gjerløw 1980, I: 3–4, 53). Whole vellums could also perish out of pure neglect, and not only in Iceland. In the sixteenth century it was common practice for scholars in Europe to throw away manuscripts which had been used in the preparation of printed editions. The manuscript of Saxo's *Gesta Danorum*, for example, disappeared after the book was published in 1514. The same fate presumably befell a fifth-century manuscript of Pliny's letters, borrowed by the Venetian printer Aldus Manutius from the Monastery of St. Victor in Paris, and several manuscripts used by the scholars Beatus Rhenanus and Gelenius (Reynolds and Wilson 1991: 139–40; Schoeck 1982: 16).

In England a great many medieval manuscripts were dispersed after the dissolution of the monasteries in the 1530s. Many were destroyed and the leaves reused for the bindings of books; others ended up in private libraries of collectors who appreciated them, such as the Archbishops Matthew Parker in the 1560s and James Ussher a few decades later (C.E. Wright 1949–53: 208–20; O'Sullivan 1956: 35). In Iceland the Reformation of 1540–51 meant that liturgical and hagiographical manuscripts came to be regarded as obsolete and thus disposable. Two leaves from a manuscript of *Margrétar saga* (AM 428 b 12mo), to take just one example, were discovered by Árni Magnússon in 1725 when he took a close look at the binding of the copybook of Bishop Ólafur Hjaltason at

Hólar. An almost systematic destruction of vellum manuscripts written in the vernacular commenced at the end of the sixteenth century, although when exactly it began and how it developed is not easy to ascertain, since most of the evidence has disappeared. There are cases, however, where transcriptions are preserved of vellums which must have been destroyed soon after they were copied, as they have never resurfaced. In 1595 Páll Jónsson at Þernuvík made a copy of *Snorra Edda* from a vellum which according to Anthony Faulkes was written in the mid-thirteenth century (1985: 21); the exemplar has not been preserved. A few years later Gunnlaugur Ormsson produced a summary of *Guðmundar saga* (AM 111 8vo) from a manuscript which has similarly disappeared (Stefán Karlsson 1983: cxxxii–cxxxv). Many of the hundreds of fragments that Árni Magnússon later collected appear to have been part of complete codices in the early seventeenth century which then vanished. A manuscript of *Egils saga* (AM 162 A δ fol.) may have been intact in the first years of that century, when Magnús Gunnlaugsson wrote his name in a margin, or at least larger than the quire of eight leaves now extant (Speed Kjeldsen 2005: 71–2). In 1710 Árni himself removed three vellum leaves of *Knýtlinga saga* (AM 20 b II fol.) from the cover of a paper manuscript and concluded that they might have been placed there a hundred years earlier.

In spite of the rising interest in antiquarian studies the destruction continued unabated. In 1632 the Reverend Magnús Ólafsson had a complete manuscript of *Orkneyinga saga* of which only two leaves now remain (Widding 1963: 97). Even some of the manuscripts that Bishop Þorlákur Skúlason at Hólar had transcribed are lost. According to Jón Helgason, a paper manuscript of *Egils saga* which belonged to Þorlákur in 1641 (AM 458 4to) provides 'a glimpse of a vellum codex that can scarcely have been younger than the thirteenth century' (Jón Helgason 2005: 27). The bishop had two copies made of *Þorláks saga* (AM 380 4to, AM 379 4to), both from a manuscript of which only four leaves are now extant (AM 383 IV 4to). A vellum manuscript of *biskupasögur* (AM 219 fol.) was at Hólar when Jón Pálsson copied *Guðmundar saga* (AM 398 4to). Árni Magnússon later noted the provenance of eleven of the seventeen preserved leaves and had acquired all of them from Skagafjörður and Eyjafjörður. Three of them had belonged to the Reverend Ólafur Hallsson, the resident priest at Hólar in 1635–9. Peter Foote fittingly asks: 'Might it be that as soon as the copy of the saga in AM 398 4to had been made, that part of the vellum became fair game for pillagers?' (2003: 181*). Something similar may have happened to a badly preserved vellum containing a grammatical treatise (AM 757 a 4to), where Grímur Magnússon wrote his name as owner in 1646. According to the Reverend Torfi Jónsson at Gaulverjabær, in a letter to Þormóður Torfason on 8 August 1684, a vellum containing Ari fróði's *Íslendingabók* had been found among papers in the cathedral at Skálholt (AM 285 b fol. IV: 21v–22r). Scholars agree, based on the orthography of two copies made by the Reverend Jón Erlendsson in around 1650, that the manuscript may have been written as early as the late twelfth century (Jón Jóhannesson 1956: ix, xix; Björn Sigfússon 1944: 20–33; Finnur Jónsson 1887: xi). The manuscript then vanished and, as he never asked anyone about it, Árni must have been told early on that it was irretrievable. Bishop Brynjólfur, for one, was aware of the destruction going on and in his aforementioned letter to the royal librarian Lange in 1656 he explained that manuscripts which were hard to read, and perhaps already damaged, were threatened with re-use as book covers and binding material (Jón Helgason 1942: 70). Brynjólfur may even have used vellum leaves to bind items in his own library, as a manuscript containing verdicts, written by Jón Erlendsson, turned out to be bound in four leaves from a vellum containing *Saulus saga ok Nikanors* (AM 162 C fol.).

Manuscripts were also re-used in Norway and Denmark. A fragment of a vellum manuscript of *Gesta Danorum* has recently been found in the bindings of accounts revised in the Royal Exchequer (*Rentekammer*) in Copenhagen in the years 1623–42 (Riis 2006: 11–12). From 1846 onwards, numerous vellum fragments were found in the bindings of Norwegian account books from the first half of the seventeenth century. A fragment of the Norwegian national law of 1274 (NRA 2) was thus used as a cover for accounts from Sunnmøre before 1633. Three fragments from one manuscript contain passages of *Jóns saga helga*, *Nikulás saga* and *Páls saga postula* (NRA 57, 69, 80), two of them with the marginal notes 'Nordfjord 1623' and 'Nordfjord 1628'. It has not been possible to ascertain who used these manuscript as book covers; either local officials all over the district or royal secretaries located in Bergen, or both (Foote 2003: 54*–55*; Eken 1963: xiii–xv, xviii–xx; Johnsen 1908: 93, 96). In Iceland the destruction of vellums appears to have reached its climax in the decades 1660–80, while Árni Magnússon was growing up. Only a few (but telling) examples will be provided here. After Magistrate Magnús Björnsson died on 6 December 1662 his manuscript of *Karlamagnús saga* (AM 180 a–b fol.) was disassembled. Árni later spent years putting it together again, as he described in a note:

> This book was in many parts in the north, and I have acquired it from various persons. Some part of it from Skúli Ólafsson, another from Magnús Jónsson at Leirá, who had acquired what he had in various places. A few bits and damaged leaves have come to me in Iceland after 1702, each piece from a different place.

> Þesse bok var komin i marga parta nordur i lande, og hefi eg hana feinged af ymsum. Nockurn part þar af hiá Skula Olafssyne, nockurn part fra Magnuse Jonssyne á Leira, en Magnus hafde sitt feinged i ymsum stödum. Nockra smageira og mutilerud blöd hefi eg feinged a Islande epter 1702, sitt ur hverium stad (*AMKat*. I: 147).

The manuscript *Reykjarfjarðarbók* (AM 122 b fol.) of *Sturlunga saga* had been complete when Björn Jónsson at Skarðsá used it in 1635. The owner may have been Sheriff Jón Magnússon the elder at Hagi on Barðaströnd. He died in 1641 and his son Gísli Jónsson at Reykjarfjörður in Arnarfjörður became the owner of the stately volume. Years later, Magnús Jónsson at Vigur told Árni Magnússon in a letter that in his youth, probably in 1662, he borrowed from Gísli a manuscript of *Sturlunga saga* which, for most people, was not easy to read: 'ei öllum læsileg'. In 1676 or 1677 Árni Guðmundsson borrowed the manuscript from Gísli but did not take good care of it. After he got it back a year later Gísli removed some leaves and gave them to various people. In

1710 Torfi Hallsson confirmed to Árni Magnússon that by 1674–8 the manuscript had been taken out of its binding. Gísli had then started removing leaves in order to make sheeths for knives and covers for books. Accordingly, *Reykjarfjarðarbók* must have been in a dismal state by the time Gísli and his wife Guðný Jónsdóttir died in October 1679 (Már Jónsson 2009a: 88; Gísli Baldur Róbertsson 2005: 189–90; *PB*: 169–70, 245). Similarly, in around 1676, a leaf of a theological text (AM 655 I 4to) was used as a cover for a paper manuscript which belonged to Þorsteinn Þórðarson at Skarð on Skarðsströnd. Soon after that, Steindór Ormsson made a copy (AM 630 4to) of a vellum manuscript of *postulasögur* which then was taken apart and re-used to make shoes with. Only fourteen leaves (AM 652 4to) survive (Jón Ma. Ásgeirsson and Þórður Ingi Guðjónsson 2007: 169–72). The interest shown by some learned Icelanders and Danes from the 1630s and onwards may thus have helped to save a number of medieval manuscripts but it also had a deleterious effect on their preservation in the sense that some of them were discarded as soon as their texts had been reproduced on paper in writing that was easier to read.

Competition

In Sweden, Johannes Bureus had been appointed royal antiquarian as early as 1628; he was to search for 'old monuments' and have them printed for the honour and fame of his country. Bureus had already translated some Icelandic texts, albeit not very well (Gödel 1897: 216–25). His main interest lay in the study of runes, perhaps because there were no saga manuscripts in Sweden at the time – a situation which was about to change. In 1652 the Swedish Chancellor Magnus de la Gardie bought the manuscripts of the Danish scholar Stephanus Stephanius from his widow and gave them to Uppsala University Library in 1669. This collection included Icelandic vellum manuscripts such as *Óláfs saga helga* (DG 8), *Óláfs saga Tryggvasonar* (DG 4–7), *Snorra Edda* (DG 11), *Grettis saga* (DG 10), *Jónsbók* (DG 9) and *Heimskringla* (now lost). The *Snorra Edda* manuscript had come to Stephanius from Bishop Brynjólfur in 1639 and those of *Jónsbók* and *Grettis saga* a year or two afterwards

(Gödel 1892: 2–16; Gödel 1897: 73, 91–4; Kålund 1900: xxi–xxii; Ellen Jørgensen 1917: 20–3). In 1658, when the Swedish army conquered Seeland, the huge library of the Danish magistrate Jørgen Seefeldt was taken to Sweden by Korfitz Ulfeldt, King Frederik III's brother-in-law. Seefeldt's manuscripts were placed in the Royal Library in Stockholm in 1661; it seems that he had two copies of *Jónsbók* (both lost) and a collection of *biskupasögur* (Perg. 5 fol.) which had been sent to him as a gift by Bishop Brynjólfur in 1656 (Gödel 1897: 104–13; Kålund 1900: xxii–xxiv; Halldór Hermannsson 1929: 52–3; Chesnutt 2005a: 210).

Also in 1658, a Swedish warship captured a Danish merchant ship on its way from Iceland to Copenhagen and took it to Gothenburg. One of the passengers on board was the young Jón Jónsson from Rúgstaðir in Eyjafjörður, who had taken with him a few manuscripts to read containing several sagas in which ancient Swedish kings figure prominently: *Heiðreks saga*, *Bósa saga ok Herrauðs*, *Gautreks saga* and *Hrólfs saga Gautrekssonar*. Jón was sent to Uppsala where the historian Olof Verelius, later professor of antiquities, needed help with the medieval language. Jón never returned to Iceland, working instead as a scribe and translator for the Swedish Institute of Antiquities from its foundation in 1667. With his help Verelius published *Gautreks saga ok Hrólfs* in 1664, a fragment of *Óláfs saga Tryggvasonar* in 1665, *Herrauðs ok Bósa saga* in 1666 and *Hervarar saga* in 1672 (Gödel 1897: 81–3, 113–21, 246–55; Schück 1932–44, I: 200–41; Wallette 1999: 10–11; Jón Helgason 1958: 87–8; Halldór Hermannsson 1929: 53–4). In the preface to his first edition, signed on 16 October 1664, Verelius asserted that Gautrekr and Hrólfr had lived more than a thousand years earlier, and although those were heathen times and their domains not extensive they were great kings (Verelius 1664: preface, 2v). The language had changed for the worse, Verelius argued, and it was now impossible to understand what was spoken eight centuries ago. The saga was therefore published both in the purported Gothic language (*götska*), as in the manuscript, meant for those who wished to learn that language, and in a Swedish translation for those who only wanted to understand the story. In his preface to *Herrauðs ok Bósa saga* Verelius argued that past events and deeds had been neglected, old customs abandoned and the language of the forefathers destroyed

(Verelius 1664: 3r; Verelius 1666: preface). The text was once again given in *götska* along with a Swedish translation, followed by a detailed Latin commentary, a format also adopted in *Hervarar saga* in 1672. Latin translations of medieval Icelandic texts first appeared in Denmark in 1665, when Peder Resen, professor of law and mayor of Copenhagen, published *Snorra Edda*, *Hávamál* and *Völuspá* based on work done by Icelandic students and scholars in Copenhagen in previous years. Resen wrote two prefaces to his edition of *Snorra Edda*, putting less emphasis on patriotic pride or national glory than Vedel, Worm and Verelius had done before, although his excessive erudition, loaded with references to Latin, Greek and Hebrew texts as well as Egyptian hieroglyphs, clearly indicated that he thought that Nordic literature was no less important. Resen provided not only a Danish translation of these texts but also one into Latin for the scholarly world. In 1666 Jan Dolmer published the late thirteenth-century Norwegian court law (*Hirðskrá*) in Old Norwegian with a Danish translation. He subsequently translated the text into Latin and, in a further effort to promote Nordic medieval texts among foreign scholars, Resen published it in three languages in 1673 (Faulkes 1977, II: 11; Ellen Jørgensen 1931: 133–5; Dolmer 1673).

On 7 June 1681 the Icelander Hannes Þorleifsson was appointed to the position as royal antiquarian. He was 26 years old and had studied for six years at Copenhagen University, establishing his scholarly credentials with a now lost collection of Icelandic proverbs. His letter of appointment probably reflects his own aspirations and shows great ambition. He was to publish medieval texts, particularly from Iceland, with Danish and Latin translations and commentary. He was also to obtain old manuscripts for the Royal Library, report on Icelandic antiquities and search for natural objects for the Royal Museum. Moreover, he was expected to write a political and natural history of Iceland. Hannes went to Iceland in the spring of 1682 and had his letter of appointment read at the *Alþingi* (*Lovsamling* I: 381–3; *BE*: 90–1; *Alþingisbækur* VII, 587; Már Jónsson 1998: 33–4, 353). Late in the autumn he departed from Iceland on board a merchant ship that left Skagaströnd and was lost soon after its departure. In the subsequent months flotsam appeared on the north-eastern shores of Iceland which was thought to come from that ship (*Annálar* I: 393;

Alþingisbækur VII: 622–4). Before leaving, Hannes had visited his friend Jón Torfason in Gaulverjabær; it was Jón who told Þormóður Torfason about the tragic event in a letter dated 30 July 1683. In another letter, that same day, Jón's father, the Reverend Torfi Jónsson, described Hannes to Þormóður as a well-mannered and learned young man· 'juvenis optimus et eruditissimus' (AM 285 b fol. IV: 7v, 9r).

One of the tasks with which Hannes had been charged was to collect manuscripts. It is not known how many he acquired in Iceland or what they contained. Magnús Jónsson at Vigur some years later thought that Hannes had taken *Reykjarfjarðarbók* (AM 122 b fol.) with him (*PB*: 245), but that proved to be wrong. On 2 May 1697 Árni Magnússon asked the Reverend Björn Þorleifsson to inquire into the manuscripts which Hannes might have taken with him. An Icelandic student in Copenhagen had claimed that Hannes had acquired from the sheriff in Skagafjarðarsýsla, Þorsteinn Þorleifsson, several vellum manuscripts, such as *Njáls saga*, *Kirjalax saga* and *Karlamagnús saga*. Þorsteinn was Björn's father-in-law and Árni wanted to know which sagas Hannes had acquired from him and how many manuscripts. A year later Árni insisted on the matter and received some information. However, he lost his note containing the answers and in the spring of 1700 repeated his questions, adding that he wished to know which of the manuscripts were on paper and which on parchment (*PB*: 557, 559, 572). An answer is not preserved. In 1702 Guðmundur Þorleifsson, brother of Hannes, told Árni that he had taken with him a copy of the tenth-century law of Úlfljótur (*Úlfljótslög*). The incredulous Árni did not believe this and noted that Guðmundur must have made it up (AM 364 4to: 140r).

Another manuscript hunter, the boisterous Icelander Jón Eggertsson, had intended to travel on the same ship as Hannes but did not reach Skagaströnd in time. When in Copenhagen in the autumn of 1680 in order to settle a legal dispute, Jón had come into contact with Swedish scholars and been hired to transcribe manuscripts. In March 1682 Jón presented a copy of *Kringla* to the Swedish scholar Johan Gabriel Sparwenfeld, who was in Copenhagen at the time (Bjarni Einarsson 1955: xi–xiv; Jon Gunnar Jörgensen 2007: 118–22; Gödel 1897: 191; Jacobowsky 1932: 46–7). Sparwenfeld had become interested in Icelandic texts when he was prisoner of war in Norway during the winter of 1677–8 and acquired *Bergsbók* (Perg. 1 fol.), which contained texts of *Óláfs saga helga* and *Óláfs saga Tryggvasonar*. Eager to increase the manuscript collection of the Swedish Institute of Antiquities, its director Johan Hadorph now hired Jón Eggertsson to travel to Iceland to collect manuscripts, which he did in the summer of 1682 with good results.

VELLUM MANUSCRIPTS ACQUIRED BY JÓN EGGERTSSON

The Icelandic Homily book (Perg. 15 4to)
Heiðarvíga saga (Perg. 18 4to)
Óláfs saga helga (Perg. 4 4to)
Maríu saga (Perg. 1 8vo)
Romances (Perg. 7 fol.)
Þórðar saga hreðu (Perg. 8 4to)
Nikulás saga (Perg. 16 4to)
Alexanders saga (Perg. 24 4to)

Jón may have misled people by saying that he worked for the Danish king. In 1684, at the *Alþingi*, Þorsteinn Þórðarson was quoted as having given Jón a collection of sagas for the king, but it was not clear which king he had meant. Jón's travel expenses amounted to 179 rigsdaler; out of which 155 were paid for about fifty manuscripts, many of them on vellum. In his report to the Institute of Antiquities, Jón explained that the sum was high because the Danish royal antiquarian had published a decree prohibiting the sale of manuscripts to countries other than Denmark (Klemming 1880–2: 33–41; Gödel 1897: 192–4; Bjarni Einarsson 1955: xvi–xix; Jucknies 2009: 46–52; Kålund 1900: xxvi–xxviii; Halldór Hermannsson 1929: 56–7). There is no other source for this claim, however, and no such prohibition is mentioned in Hannes Þorleifsson's letter of appointment. Jón Eggertsson left Iceland in the summer of 1683 on a Dutch ship bound for Amsterdam. Four young Icelanders went with him, two of whom brought the manuscripts to Stockholm while Jón stayed behind in Copenhagen in order to pursue his disputes with Icelandic and Danish officials, keeping with him some paper manuscripts (Gödel 1897: 196–

9; Kålund 1900: xxxii–xxxiv). That same autumn, a young Icelander, Árni Magnússon, arrived in Copenhagen and enrolled at the university. He would in due course follow up the feats of previous collectors of manuscripts with even better results, as he not only looked for complete codices, like Bishop Brynjólfur and Jón Eggertsson had done, but also tracked down every single remnant of vellum which had survived the horrendous destruction of manuscripts which had taken place in the preceding decades.

3
Beginnings

> I have an Icelander with me whose name is Árni Magnússon; in the spring he will travel to Iceland for me and get whatever old books he can track down.
>
> Jeg hafver en Ißlender hos mig, som heeder Arnas Magnussen, hand skal til foraaret reÿße op for mig til Ißland, og indsancke hvis gamle böger hand kand offverkomme.
>
> Thomas Bartholin 24 January 1685
> (AM 285 b fol. I: 2r; Aðalgeir
> Kristjánsson 1975: 380)

This chapter treats Árni Magnússon's apprenticeship with Thomas Bartholin and his first tentative but nevertheless impressive steps as a scholar, as he strove to position himself in the world of learning by defining the subjects that he wished to study and the methods he would apply.

The task

Hannes Þorleifsson's successor as royal antiquarian was Thomas Bartholin the younger, born on 29 March 1659. He was the son of Thomas Bartholin the elder, professor of medicine, who was so influential at Copenhagen University that his four sons were all made professors at an early age. Their sister Margrethe, a poet, was married in 1671 to Christian Müller, first resident governor (*amtmaður*) of Iceland in 1688 (Ehrencron-Müller I: 264, 269, 272, 290–1). Young Thomas, from here on referred to simply as Bartholin, entered the university at the age of fourteen (Birket Smith 1890–1912, II: 38). He displayed an early interest in books; one of his surviving notebooks contains numerous titles on theology, the most recent of which had been published in 1674 (Don. var. 153 4to: 47, 56). In 1676 Bartholin published a booklet on the early medieval Lombards who conquered parts of Italy, a popular subject among learned men at the time. In a journal edited by his father he published articles on diving in ancient times, glaciers in Iceland and the history of the Order of the Dannebrog (Bartholin 1676; *Acta Medica* 4 (1676): 57–63, 66–74, 107–15). That same year he edited, under the title *De libris legendis*, seven of his father's lectures from 1672 on how to read books. In these lectures Bartholin the elder had recommended the consultation of a list of typical errors in textual criticism compiled by Caspar Scoppe in his *De arte critica* of 1597. Bartholin the elder also quoted the contemporary scholar Johann Friedrich Gronovius, who opined that the older a manuscript was the more reliable it was likely to be, unless it had been corrected too much or added to (Skovgaard-Petersen 2007: 137).

A few weeks before finishing his studies, in the summer of 1677, Bartholin received a letter of expectation to become professor of history and the constitution of Denmark when a position became vacant (Birket Smith 1890–1912, II: 70; Rørdam 1893–7: 221–2; Slottved 1978: 18–19, 211). Rasmus Vinding had at that point taught history at the university for almost two decades; he was 62 years old and would live for another seven (Ilsøe and Hørby 1980: 313–19). In order to strengthen his academic position Bartholin published a book on the ninth-century legendary hero Holger the Dane. Latin poems by various learned Danes and a poem in Icelandic by Hannes Þorleifsson 'amicus' adorn the preface, dated 4 August 1677. Bartholin mostly discusses claims and opinions put forth by other scholars and cites a plethora of sources from France and Spain, in addition to Danish ones, thus demonstrating his substantial learning (Bartholin 1677). Bartholin now went on to further study in Leiden, Oxford, London and Paris. In 1678, while in Leiden, he contributed to his father's journal with a note on earthworms (*Acta Medica* 5 (1677–9): 24). In England he read widely about the country's history during the period of Danish rule, as can be seen from preserved lists of books which he read or bought (Barth. F III: 2–3, 10–11).

Bartholin returned to Copenhagen when his father died in 1680, but left again for Leipzig two years later. In the autumn of 1683 he returned to become professor at the University of Copenhagen and that winter he probably taught what the catalogue of lectures calls 'Origins of History and Society' (Ehrencron-Müller I: 290; Ilsøe and Hørby 1980: 320–1; Tamm 1991: 281). Bartholin was appointed royal antiquarian on 23

The task

February 1684 and became secretary to the Royal Archives six months later, a new office to which no-one had previously been appointed. The archive was kept in the cellar of Rosenborg castle on the outskirts of the city; a register of documents had just been made and 24 bookshelves installed (Adolf D. Jørgensen 1884: 47–9, 263). In a single year Bartholin thus became omnipresent as Denmark's official scholar; only the royally-funded task of writing history was in the hands of other men. In 1682, Þormóður Torfason had been appointed to write a history of Norway and Willum Worm, professor of medicine and director of the Royal Library, had been at work on a history of Denmark since 1679 (Ehrencron-Müller IX: 200). By 1684, King Christian V had become even more ambitious than his grandfather, King Christian IV, who had 'only' had two historiographers working for him (Skovgaard-Petersen 2002a: 27–8).

As a rule, historiographers traced events in chronological order, using annals, narratives and charters as sources, whereas antiquarians studied customs and mores, working with coins and inscriptions; they even performed archaeological excavations (Momigliano 1990: 54–8, 71–5; Piggott 1956: 93–114; Schnapp 1993: 122–81; Schnapp 1997: 121–77; Levine 1987: 73–103). According to his letter of appointment as royal antiquarian, Bartholin's task was a combination of these two roles. Unlike his predecessor, Hannes Þorleifsson, Bartholin was not responsible for writing about natural history; instead, he was to produce editions of Danish and Icelandic medieval texts in their original language, complete with translations and commentary: 'med tilbørlig Udtolkning og Forklaring'. He was already working on a book about the ancient culture and customs of the Danes (*BE*: 54–5).

The notes Bartholin took in preparation for writing this book are extant in four impressive folio volumes in the Royal Library in Copenhagen, numbered from ten to thirteen in the collection of his papers (these numbers will be used here). Bartholin presumably began using the tenth volume just after his appointment as royal antiquarian in February 1684, although he may have started earlier, secure in the knowledge that he would be appointed. He divided the pages into two columns and wrote compactly, leaving no margins. He put a caption on top of each page, starting, perhaps not surprisingly, with Danish history ('Historia

49

Danorum') and some lines from Saxo Grammaticus. His next caption concerned medieval historians ('Historici'), with a first quotation from *The History of the Goths* by Jordanes (called 'Jornandes'). The third and fourth captions cover gods and sacrifice (Barth. X: 1–6). The volume has more than a hundred captions, each of them followed by passages from medieval texts on at least two pages. If the allotted space was not sufficient Bartholin continued on the next empty page without providing cross-references. Passages on burial practices ('Funera'), for example, are to be found in four different places in the volume (Barth. X: 121–2, 201–2, 249–50, 342–3).

In the eleventh volume there are from two to thirty quotations under each caption and Bartholin now wrote across the whole page, making the texts easier to read. He started with readily available scholarly books and editions of Latin medieval texts, such as those by William of Malmesbury, Adam of Bremen and Ordericus Vitalis. He then examined editions of Icelandic medieval texts, starting with *Gautreks saga ok Hrólfs*, published in 1664 with a Swedish translation (see p. 41). Sometimes he presented these texts with a short introduction in Latin, but more often he just gave the Icelandic text with a Latin translation. It is not likely that he began learning Icelandic until he had secured the position as antiquarian, and at first he probably used the Swedish translation as the basis for his Latin versions of the chosen passages, but with experience he came to understand the language well enough to be able to spot relevant sentences without looking at the translation. His transcriptions from the editions produced in Sweden are very accurate, as can be seen in these sentences from *Hervarar saga* (Barth. X: 77; Verelius 1672: 96):

Bartholin	*Verelius*
Þad bar til eitt sinn ad Godmundr Kongur liek ad tafli, ok var à han tafli miog leikid. Þa spurdi Kongur ef nockur madur væri sà þar, er honum kunni rad til tafls ad leggia? Þà stod upp Hervardr, oc gieck til taflsins: oc hafdi han litla hrid radid taflïnu, adr Kongi gieck betur.	Þad bar til eitt sinn ad Godmundr Kongur liek ad tafli, ok var à han tafli miog leikid. Þa spurdi Kongur ef nockur madur væri sà þar, er honum kunni rad til tafls ad leggia? Þà stod upp Hervardr, oc gieck til taflsins: oc hafdi han litla hrid radid taflïnu, adr Kongi gieck betur.

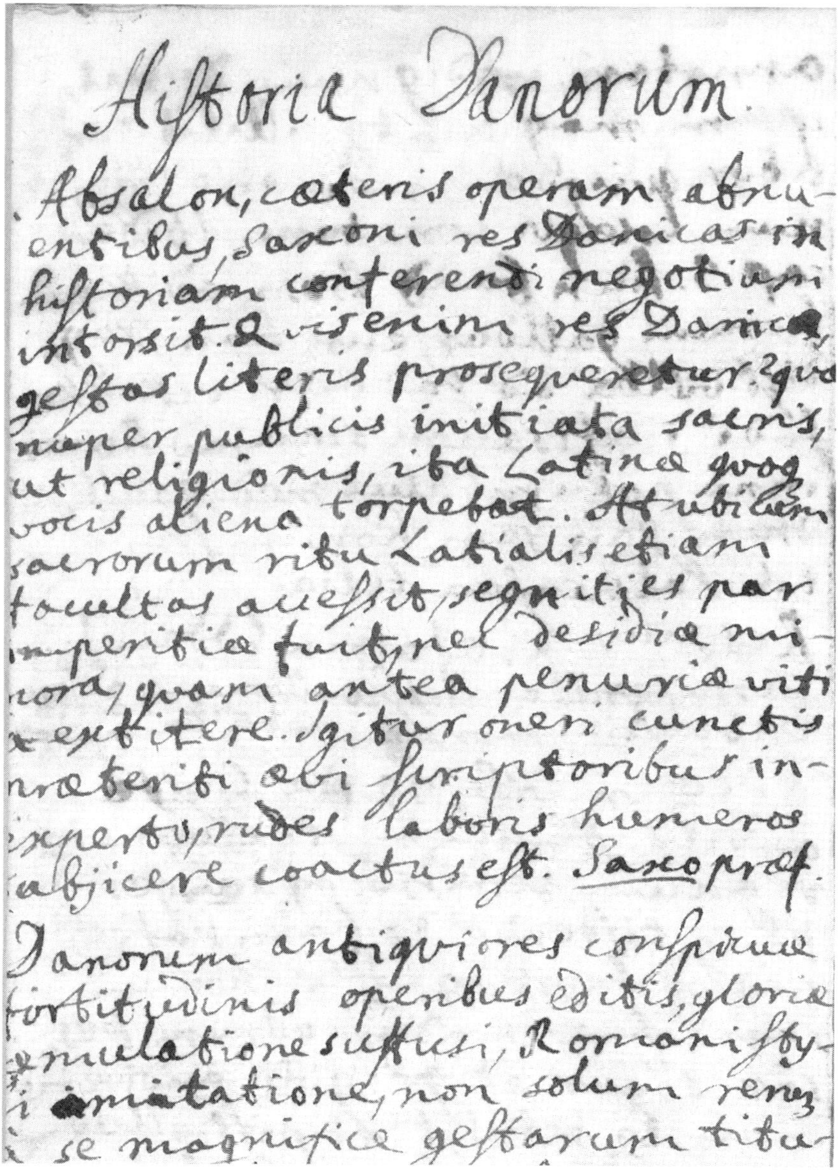
Historia Danorum.

Absalon, cæteris operam abnuentibus, Saxoni res Danicas in historiam conferendi negotium intorsit. Quis enim res Danicas gestas literis prosequeretur? quae nuper publicis initiata sacris, ut religionis, ita Latinae quoq. vocis aliena torpebat. At ubi cum sacrorum ritu Latialis etiam facultas accessit, segnities par imperitiae fuit, nec desidia minora, quam antea penuria vitia extitere. Igitur onere cunctis nostratibus abi scriptoribus inexpertis, rudes laboris humeros subjicere coactus est. Saxo praef.

Danorum antiquiores conspicuae fortitudinis operibus editis, gloriae æmulatione suffusi, Romani styli imitatione, non solum rerum se magnifice gestarum titu-

Figure 1. This is how Thomas Bartholin, then 25 years old, began his painstaking preparations for a book on the fearlessness of his remote ancestors as they faced death (Barth. X: 1).

Bartholin next worked with Peder Resen's editions of *Snorra Edda* and the eddic poems published in Copenhagen in 1665. He also took a number of sentences from Ole Worm's edition of the dictionary *Specimen Lexici Runici*, published in Copenhagen in 1650, which contains material from a number of Icelandic sagas, including *Grettis saga*, *Orkneyinga saga* and *Egils saga* (Faulkes 1964: 54, 137; cf. Magnús Ólafsson 2010). Judging from the saga titles Bartholin still had some problems with the language, since he confused the grammatical cases, for instance writing 'Finnbogu Ramms saga' and 'Draumu Jons saga' instead of 'Finnboga Ramma saga' and 'Drauma Jons saga'. Despite such slips he may well have understood the texts and was probably the first Danish scholar to learn more than the rudiments of Icelandic.

The first Icelandic manuscripts used by Bartholin were provided by Jón Eggertsson, who was jailed in Copenhagen in April 1684 for debts to the king and mismanagement of royal property in Iceland. A further reason may well have been that Jón had sent the manuscripts acquired in Iceland in 1682 to Sweden; at least that is what Johann Hadorph, head of the Swedish Institute of Antiquities, stated in a memorandum to the Swedish government: 'för misstanckar att hijt försåldt Manuscripta' (Gödel 1897: 203–4; Bjarni Einarsson 1955: xxxiii). During his imprisonment Jón was clearly in contact with Bartholin. Jón had with him two recently copied manuscripts containing texts, somewhat garbled, of a number of sagas. It seems that Bartholin copied dozens of sentences from *Víglundar saga* and *Jökuls þáttr Búasonar* in one of these manuscripts (Papp. 16 4to) and from *Norna-Gests þáttr*, *Finnboga saga ramma* and *Drauma-Jóns saga* in the other (Papp. 15 4to), accompanied, as usual, by Latin translations. Jón may have given advice on the choice of these sagas, perhaps in response to Bartholin's inquiries, and it cannot be excluded that he copied the five sagas, converting the abbreviated script of these manuscripts into a more readable version (Már Jónsson 1998: 36–7). An unidentified Icelander had done exactly that for Swedish scholars, according to Hadorph in a letter to Magnus de la Gardie on 1 December 1682, with the aim of making the texts more readable: 'att dhe läsas kunna' (Gödel 1897: 178).

Bartholin subsequently worked on *Bárðar saga Snæfellsáss*, using an unidentified manuscript, and was helped by an unknown Icelander who copied out lengthy passages (Barth. XI: 19–21, 31–2). It is unlikely that the copyist was Frans Ibsson, hired by Bartholin as an assistant in the spring of 1684. Frans was a Dane who had lived for ten years in Iceland as Bishop Þórður Þorláksson's foster-son at Skálholt, before being sent to Copenhagen to study at the university (ÍÆ II: 17–18). His later handwriting, as seen in the manuscripts AM 372 4to and AM 408 g 4to, does not resemble the hand in the passages from *Bárðar saga*. His hand has not been found in the Bartholinian volumes at all and it is not known what his duties for Bartholin were. After finishing his studies in the spring of 1684, Frans decided to return to Iceland. Asked by Bartholin to recommend someone to replace him he suggested Árni Magnússon, his roommate in the university dormitory (*Regensen*). Árni was twenty years old and had registered at the university on 25 September 1683 as 'Arnas Magnæus'. Three other Icelanders had arrived that autumn to take their place among that year's intake, which in all comprised 161 students (Bjarni Jónsson 1949: 41–5; Birket Smith 1890–1912, II: 127; Tamm 1991: 314). Frans was then in his second year and Þórður Þorkelsson Vídalín in his third; it was he who had helped Jón Eggertsson to copy *Kringla* in 1682 (Jon Gunnar Jörgensen 2007: 196–7).

The assistant

Árni Magnússon's parents were the Reverend Magnús Jónsson and Guðrún Ketilsdóttir at Kvennabrekka in Dalasýsla in the western part of Iceland. Magnús had studied for two years at the University of Copenhagen before assuming responsibility for the parish from his father, the Reverend Jón Ormsson, in 1657. Guðrún was the daughter of the Reverend Ketill Jörundsson at nearby Hvammur in Hvammsfjörður. Their first child, Gísli, died in infancy and Jón, their second, was born in 1662 (the exact date is unknown). Their third son, Árni, was born on 13 November 1663. Two years later Magnús had a child out of wedlock, as a result of which he was dismissed from the parish. According to his brother Jón, Árni was already living with his grandparents at Hvammur when this happened (*LS* I, 2: 3). For a few years Magnús and Guðrún lived in the vicinity but around 1676 they moved away with Jón and two younger boys, Magnús (born in 1669) and Þórður (born a year later). By 1682 they had settled at Sauðafell and Magnús became sheriff of Dalasýsla.

Ketill Jörundsson, Árni's maternal grandfather and his first teacher of Icelandic and Latin, was born in 1603 and had spent a year or two at Copenhagen University. He had been a teacher and rector at the cathedral school at Skálholt before moving to Hvammur in 1638. His wife was Guðlaug Erasmusdóttir, daughter of the Reverend Erasmus Pálsson. Ketill died in 1670 and his son Páll replaced him as vicar and as Árni's teacher. Guðlaug died six years later and Árni remained at Hvammur with the Reverend Páll, his wife Elín Björnsdóttir and their three sons, Páll, Ketill and Böðvar, born in the years 1669–71 (Már Jónsson 1998: 19–22; Finnur Jónsson 1930a: 5–8). Páll Ketilsson had studied at Copenhagen University in 1663–5 and may have copied manuscripts for his father. Later he acquired important vellums for his nephew but was never a scholar in his own right (Seelow 1979; Kålund 1909: 28; Jón Þorkelsson 1879–89: 740–1; AM 534 4to: note). In a letter from Páll to Árni dated 8 May 1710 there is a curious remark which could indicate that there had been some kind of animosity between the two, due to Árni's stay with Páll as a child. As he finishes the letter Páll expresses his gratitude for Árni's assistance in later years and then asks forgiveness for the treatment he received in childhood: 'og firergjeffníngar bón, um vidhöndlan mína í barnæsku ydar" (JS 98 fol.: 8 May 1710; partially printed in *PB*: 275–6).[1] This seems more than pure formality and my suspicion is that Páll felt that he may have treated his own sons better than he treated his somwehat older and much more talented nephew. There is no indication, however, that Árni was not on good terms with Páll, and while in Iceland he often stayed with him and his family (see pp. 137, 162)

Árni's interest in manuscripts seems to have emerged in his youth, as the few notes he ever wrote about those years concern such matters. His grandfather Ketill had been greatly interested in medieval texts and as early as around 1636 he made a copy of *Langfeðgatal*, probably for Bishop Gísli Oddsson (Stefán Karlsson 1977: 679–81). About twenty manuscripts in Ketill's distinct hand have survived, most of them in

---

[1] I thank Gísli Baldur Róbertsson for bringing this letter to my attention.

his grandson's collection, but they are hard to date. It seems unlikely, though, that he copied many of them before 1638, as has been suggested in respect of his two copies of *Egils saga* (Chesnutt 2005b: 257). Most of his transcriptions were probably made after he came to Hvammur. It is certain that in 1663 he worked on *Laxdæla saga* and *Vatnsdæla saga*; four years later he was busy with *Sturlunga saga* (Már Jónsson 1998: 24, 351). When Árni was around forty he reminisced that the *konungasögur* manuscript *Hulda* (AM 66 fol.) had been at Hvammur in his youth ('ungdæmi'). That would have been after 1671, if his notes on the manuscript are correct (*AMKat*. I: 44–5; Kålund 1909: 22; Louis-Jensen 1968: 15–18). He also remembered that *Kálfalækjarbók* (AM 133 fol.), a vellum containing *Njáls saga*, had been at Hvammur in his childhood ('barndæmi') (*PB*: 522; Jón Þorkelsson 1879–89: 672). He later recalled that in his youth ('ungdæmi') a manuscript of *Óláfs saga helga* had been on loan from Skarð on Skarðsströnd (AM 53 fol.: note; Johnsen and Jón Helgason 1941: 978). On yet another occasion he wrote that a recent transcription of *Jómsvíkinga saga* was a copy of a paper manuscript that he, in his young years ('á mínum ungu dögum'), had seen on Hrappsey, an island close to Hvammur (AM 288 4to: note).

Ketill certainly used *Kálfalækjarbók* to write variants in his own copy of *Njáls saga* (AM 470 4to). The manuscript may have been kept at Hvammur for some years after his death, as it is not likely that a seven-year-old Árni would have had much interest in a medieval manuscript, unless it was used to teach him to read. Árni could have seen the other vellums during the time he lived in Iceland until the summer of 1683, when he left for Copenhagen; during the winter he was at school in Skálholt but spent the summers in Hvammur. There is no indication that he worked on manuscripts during his three years at school, which began in the autumn of 1680, whereas his friend Jón Halldórsson (who finished school in 1685) borrowed two vellum manuscripts at Skálholt containing annals and made his own conflated version (AM 411 4to) (*LS* II: 163–4; *AMKat*. I: 616–17; Storm 1888: lxvii). His brother Jón claimed later that Árni made a good impression at Skálholt and was considered by his fellow students to be among the best (*LS* I, 2: 4).

Beginnings

According to Jón Ólafsson, in his Danish biography of 1738, Bartholin was impressed with Árni too, as he was more knowledgeable than Frans Ibsson and could explain things better; accordingly he got the job as assistant (*BE*: 15). It is likely that Jón's story was based on Árni's recollections more than forty years later. A longer account, found in Jón's Icelandic biography of 1759, narrates the event as a premonition of Árni's destiny. Jón identifies the encounter as the origin of Árni's good fortune. After Bartholin first contacted him, Árni fell ill and lay in bed for some weeks. At Bartholin's insistence he went to meet him and accepted the offer to replace Frans Ibsson. This may have taken place in July or August 1684. Bartholin showed Árni a manuscript containing *Njáls saga* and according to Jón he did a good job of reading and translating the text, explaining every single word (*LS* I, 2: 13; Finnur Jónsson 1930a: 10). There is no reason to doubt that Bartholin tested Árni in some way and liked what he heard and saw. Their collaboration over the following six years was a success and they worked well together.

Most Icelandic students at Copenhagen University returned to Iceland to become clergymen of some distinction. This had been the case with Árni's father, his uncle and both grandfathers. Had Árni left for Iceland after graduation he would still have been able to pursue his scholarly interests, but would certainly have achieved less significant results had he not become the assistant to the royal antiquarian. Árni was lucky, to say the least, but he was also the right man at the right time and in the right place. Hannes Þorleifsson drowned in 1682 and his successor, Thomas Bartholin, needed an Icelandic assistant, as Frans Ibsson, who happened to know Árni well, wished to return to Iceland. Later, around 1720, Árni claimed credit for most of the Icelandic texts that Bartholin and Þormóður Torfason introduced to readers in their books (AM 1 e ß II fol.: 53r); as regards Bartholin, it is certain that Árni prepared most of the Icelandic texts that appeared in *Antiquitates* in 1689 (see p. 82).

When Árni joined him as his assistant Bartholin was gathering passages from an unidentified manuscript of *Óláfs saga Tryggvasonar*. At first the two young men worked together. Bartholin wrote a short introduction, Árni copied the Icelandic text and Bartholin did the translation (Barth. X: 15, 21, 67, 276). It was not long before Árni also took

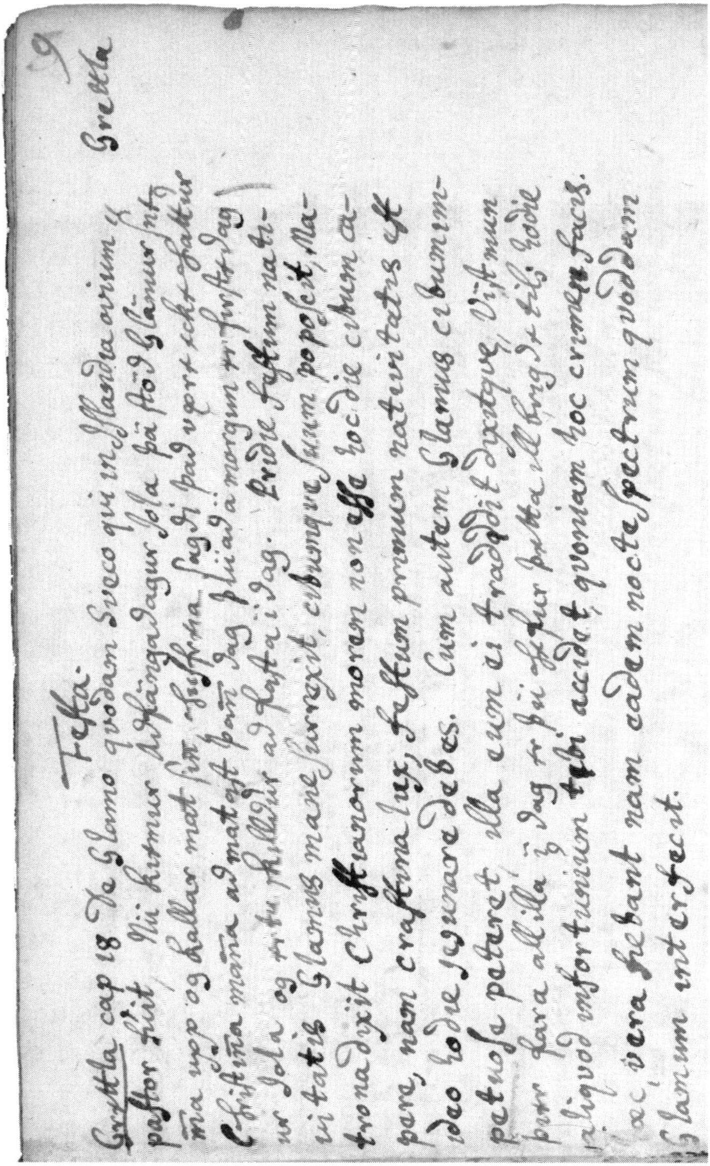

Figure 2. This image shows Árni's work procedure. He first wrote a short introduction ('De Glamo ... pastor fuit'), then copied the relevant text ('Nú kiemur ... ad fasta í dag') and produced a translation ('Pridie festum... hodie jejunare debes'). There follows another citation with the same structure: 'Cum autem...' etc. (Barth. XII: 9).

over the translations. Together they wrote around seventy passages from *Vatnsdœla saga* and more than a hundred from *Egils saga*. From chapter 27 of *Egils saga* Árni took over the writing while Bartholin resumed his search for printed books. After *Egils saga*, Árni tackled *Grettis saga* alone. He wrote passages from its first chapters between Bartholin's citations in the eleventh volume, but soon enough got a volume for himself; the twelfth according to the modern shelfmark. Bartholin completed the eleventh volume and started on the thirteenth, which he never finished.

Árni's work on the twelfth volume was done in the winter of 1684–5, with a few passages written in 1688 or perhaps later (Barth. XII: 461–5). In addition to *Vatnsdœla saga*, *Egils saga* and *Grettis saga* Árni perused 36 other sagas and two short sixteenth-century texts. Like Bartholin, he wrote compactly and within narrow margins. The captions are similar but, unlike Bartholin, Árni provided cross-references when he had to continue the text on another page. He thus began a long citation about sorcery from *Þorsteins þáttr bœjarmagns* on page 20, but as he ran out of space he continued forty pages later, since he had already used the intervening pages for other material (Barth. XII: 20, 61–2). After *Grettis saga* Árni worked on *Þorsteins þáttr*. He perused each saga individually and the final product always had the same characteristics: a title for the saga, chapter numbers, a short introduction, the Icelandic passage and a Latin translation. The length of passages varies from just a few lines to a whole page, as when he quotes from *Landnámabók* on Bede, and even several pages as when copying text from *Eiríks saga rauða* (Barth. XII: 133, 291–7).

It can be estimated that by 1684 around fifty medieval Icelandic manuscripts and many more younger manuscripts on paper had been sent abroad. The collections in Stockholm and Uppsala were unavailable to Bartholin and Árni. Manuscripts which belonged to the Royal Library and the University Library in Copenhagen were also inaccessible, as Þormóður Torfason had taken most of the important ones with him to Norway. This meant that the two scholars had to rely on private collections kept in Copenhagen. The bulk of the manuscripts which they used, in addition to those lent by Jón Eggertsson (see p. 52), belonged to Peder Resen, who had at least 54 Icelandic and Norwegian manuscripts, ten of which were medieval vellums. Some of them had been sent from Iceland. In 1663 Þórður Þorláksson, later bishop, gave Resen a vellum of *Óláfs saga Tryggvasonar* and the Reverend Torfi Jónsson may have sent *Konungs skuggsjá* in 1678. Resen also had medieval annals and a manuscript of *Óláfs saga helga* (both lost), besides the still extant *Guðmundar saga góða* (AM 399 4to), but it is not known how or when he acquired them (Kålund 1900: xv–xvii; Stefán Karlsson 1970a: 274–6; Jón Helgason 1985: 38–9).

One of Resen's paper manuscripts had been written by the Reverend Þorsteinn Björnsson at Útskálar around 1650. Torfi Jónsson mentions it in a letter to Þormóður on 8 August 1684 and it probably came to Copenhagen that autumn (AM 285 b fol. IV: 20v). Árni Magnússon later made a table of its contents and when the list is compared with the order in which he used its sagas in his twelfth volume, striking similarities appear (see next page). From *Droplaugarsona saga* onwards the sequence is the same, although Árni skipped *Njáls saga* after *Brodd-Helga saga*. *Víglundar saga*, *Jökuls þáttr* and *Finnboga saga* were in Resen's manuscript but Bartholin had already read them in the manuscript borrowed from Jón Eggertsson (Már Jónsson 1998: 38–9).

Árni made use of other recent transcriptions from Iceland, such as *Knýtlinga saga* (AM 1005 4to) which Ole Worm had obtained from Bishop Þorlákur Skúlason in 1639 (Jakob Benediktsson 1948: 502; Petersens and Olson 1919–25: xxii–xxv). An unidentified Icelander copied that transcription and Árni corrected a few errors (for example, on the first page King Sveinn is wrongly taken as King Sverrir, a mistake Árni put right). He also prepared a Latin translation (AM 20 h fol.). With another unknown Icelander, Árni copied *Hrólfs saga kraka* (AM 922 4to) from a paper transcription and translated it into Latin (Slay 1960a: 114–15). He also made a copy of *Konungs skuggsjá* (AM 243 n fol.), again with an unknown scribe, from a vellum (now lost) which belonged to Resen. Árni commented at one point that a leaf was missing in his original and corrected the other scribe's errors; they both used their own spelling (Holm-Olsen 1952: 57–8).

Apart from *Konungs skuggsjá* the only vellum used by Árni in his work for Bartholin was a single leaf, since lost, containing text from

The order of sagas in Árni's twelfth volume

Texts in Peder Resen's manuscript are in italics. In that manuscript, *Landnámabók* came first and was followed by *Þorsteins þáttr uxafóts*; otherwise the order of texts is identical.

1. Óláfs saga Tryggvasonar
2. Vatnsdæla saga
3. Egils saga
4. Grettis saga
5. Þorsteins þáttr bæjarmagns
6. Orms þáttr Stórólfssonar
7. Óláfs saga helga
8. Þorsteins þáttr uxafóts
9. Göngu-Hrólfs saga
10. *Landnámabók*
11. *Droplaugarsona saga*
12. *Brodd-Helga saga*
13. *Ölkofra þáttr*
14. *Búa saga* (*Kjalnesinga saga*)
15. *Harðar saga ok Hólmverja*
16. *Krókarefs saga*
17. *Gísla saga hin skemmri*
18. *Eiríks saga rauða*
19. *Þórðar saga hreðu*
20. *Þorleifs þáttr jarlaskálds*
21. *Sneglu-Halla þáttr*
22. *Stúfs þáttr Kattarsonar*
23. *Hallfreðar saga vandræðaskálds*
24. *Af forfeðrum Grettis*
25. *Bandamanna saga*
26. *Ljósvetninga saga*
27. *Jóns saga biskups*
28. *Ögmundar saga biskups*
29. *Fríheitabréf Eggerts Eggertssonar*
30. Laxdæla saga
31. Þormóðar saga Kolbrúnarskálds
32. Ketils saga hængs
33. Gríms saga loðinkinna
34. Örvar-Odds saga
35. Njáls saga
36. Sturlaugs saga starfsama
37. Hálfdanar saga Eysteinssonar
38. Herrauðs saga ok Bósa
39. Gunnars þáttr Keldugnúpsfífls
40. Hákonar þáttr norræna
41. Kormáks saga
42. Víga-Glúms saga

Kristni saga. In the margin of his volume, alongside sentences from *Jóns saga biskups* and *Landnámabók*, Árni added variants and words from what he calls a fragment of a vellum manuscript: 'Fragmentum qvoddam in membrana manuscriptum' (Barth. XII: 135, cf. 131, 286, 349, 352, 358; Ólafur Halldórsson 1990: 465–6; Foote 2003: 189*–191*). *Jóns saga biskups* was one of the last texts that Árni worked with, probably in the spring of 1685. Strangely enough, other Resenian vellums were not used, nor any of the codices that had belonged to Ole Worm and were now in the library of his son Willum, such as the *Codex Wormianus* (AM 242 fol.), containing *Snorra Edda* and the grammatical treatises, and a fourteenth-century collection of romances (AM 580 4to).

First vellums

Bartholin's research into medieval Icelandic texts was a part of a scholarly project financed by King Christian V (see p. 49). Bartholin knew Willum Worm, as did Þormóður Torfason, but the two did not know each other. In 1684 Þormóður sent some sections from his history of Norway to Worm. Bartholin got to read them and took the opportunity to make contact with the author. He wrote to Þormóður on 24 January 1685 and cited his chief interest as preparing an edition of *Jómsvíkinga saga*, a dramatic and fanciful narrative about medieval Danish kings; it would be provided with a translation and commentary. He wanted Þormóður's help. A Latin translation of the whole saga made by Arngrímur Jónsson in 1592–3 was accessible in the University Library, but the manuscript Bartholin had, with the text in Icelandic, lacked the first part: 'den første part fattis mig original texten'. He knew that Þormóður had many old manuscripts, one of them containing *Jómsvíkinga saga*, and asked for a transcription of the first chapters. He also informed Þormóður that he had an Icelandic assistant, Árni Magnússon, who would go to Iceland in the spring in search of manuscripts. Bartholin also asked, somewhat naïvely, whether Þormóður could not provide him with a list of the most important and rare manuscripts that he had seen or knew of, so that they could be traced in Iceland: 'thi saa kunde ieg derefter lade dem i Ißland opspørge' (AM 285 b fol. I: 1r–2r; Aðalgeir Kristjánsson 1975: 380).

Bartholin's inquiry illustrates the problems facing late seventeenth-century scholars. They sought out manuscripts because they recognised them as the key element in their research, despite the difficulty caused by their physical dispersal and the variable state of their preservation. *Jómsvíkinga saga* was not complete. The text of Bartholin's transcription can be identified as being derived from a manuscript from the mid-sixteenth century (AM 510 4to), where the first seven chapters are missing. Bartholin knew that the saga was not complete because he had seen Arngrímur Jónsson's translation (Ólafur Halldórsson 1969: 11; Jakob Benediktsson 1950–7, IV: 171–2). Until he had the whole text, he thought, he could not publish the saga. It is interesting that he did not want a copy of the part of the text he already had and it probably did not worry him whether other manuscripts had a different or even a better text. He used whatever material he had at hand and only searched for those sections that he did not have, not for other versions of the same work.

Among the vellum manuscripts Þormóður had with him at Stangeland was *Flateyjarbók* (GKS 1005 fol.), where most of *Jómsvíkinga saga* is to be found incorporated into *Óláfs saga Tryggvasonar*. It would not have been difficult to comply with Bartholin's request, but for some reason Þormóður never did (Ólafur Halldórsson 1969: 9). As for Icelandic manuscripts in general, Þormóður was hardly the right man to ask. He had brought some manuscripts from Iceland for the king in 1662 (see p. 35) but had only vague ideas as to what else might be available or where it could be found. He thus repeatedly asked the Reverend Torfi Jónsson for information. On 24 April 1683, for instance, Þormóður indicated that he did not need romances such as *Sigurgarðs saga*, *Sigurðar saga þögla* or *Mágus saga*, but rather a variety of other works, such as *Haraldar saga hilditannar*, *Sturlunga saga*, *Íslendinga saga*, *Vémundar saga*, *Vilmundar saga*, *Þóris saga háleggs*, *Ögmundar saga akraspillis*, *Helga saga Droplaugarsonar* and *Gunnars saga þiðrandabana*. A year later Þormóður still wanted *Haraldar saga* and added *Amlóða saga* and *Hrómundar saga Gripssonar*, which he had heard of but not read. He was also looking for *Andra saga* (AM 285 b fol. IV: 4v, 13v). Torfi had not even heard of some of these sagas and sent ten copies of Þormóður's list out to friends, but without expecting much by way of return. He explained on 6 August 1685 that some men knew as little as himself whereas others pretended to know nothing but lay on their manuscripts like serpents on gold: 'Sumer þikjast ey vita neitt aff þeim ad seigia og liggia þoo sem ormar a gulle' (AM 285 b fol. IV: 24r). Torfi's efforts proved not to be in vain, however, as he was able to send copies of the sagas of Egill einhendi, Hálfdan Eysteinsson, Sörli sterki, Gunnlaugur ormstunga, Vallna-Ljótur, Illugi gríðarfóstri and Glúmur, with a promise of more to come, perhaps even *Laxdæla saga* (AM 285 b fol. IV: 24v).

As for Bartholin and Árni, the ground covered in their work during the winter of 1684–5 reveals that they knew a significant part of the medieval Icelandic corpus, but mostly from recent transcriptions. As noted, they had access to Resen's library but made only limited use of his vellums. Manuscripts which belonged to the king and the university were with Þormóður at Stangeland and little was known about what could be had in Iceland. Jón Eggertsson must have bragged about his impressive acquisitions for the Swedish Institute of Antiquities, for the competitive Bartholin reacted by asking King Christian V on 4 April 1685 to ensure that Icelanders would only be allowed to sell manuscripts to Denmark. He pointed out that one of his responsibilities was to publish Icelandic medieval texts, for which purpose he had hired Icelandic students who knew the old language well. One of them was being sent to Iceland in the spring to collect more manuscripts. The Swedes, he claimed, had acquired some remarkable manuscripts and published a number of texts, resulting in a considerable loss of prestige for the Danes. Bartholin suggested that Christopher Heidemann, the newly-appointed royal administrator (*landfógeti*), should publish a prohibition stating that Icelanders were forbidden to sell saga manuscripts and other documents to foreigners. Heidemann should also try to acquire as many manuscripts as possible and send them to Denmark. That same day the king signed an almost identically-phrased letter to Heidemann, who had it read at the *Alþingi* in July (Aðalgeir Kristjánsson 1975: 377–8; *Alþingisbækur* VIII: 63–4; *Lovsamling* I: 437–8).

Árni Magnússon studied at Copenhagen University for two years. His subject was theology, as was the case with most students at the university. On 11 October 1684 he participated in a public exercise with his schoolmate Hans Steenbuch, who went on to become professor of theology. Steenbuch discussed the words of Christ on the Mount of Olives: 'Keep awake, then, for you do not know when the master of the house will come. Evening or midnight, cock-crow or early dawn' (Mark. 13.35). He cited classical texts on the crowing of cocks and explained what had been written about the verse by earlier scholars. Árni's response is not included in the printed version of the dissertation but he may have been impressed to learn that the King James' Bible, first published in Oxford in 1611, had been based on more than one hundred manuscripts (Steenbuch 1684: 5). In the spring of 1685 Árni qualified as 'attestatus' in theology and, in order to have done so, would have shown a secure knowledge of both the Bible and of the learning of the Church. He was ready to leave for Iceland in his mission to find as many 'old books' as he could find (Már Jónsson 1998: 26, 48). At a later date, his brother Jón wrote that Árni had also planned to take leave of friends and family, expecting that this would be his last visit to Iceland. He knew that his father was dead. Magnús Jónsson had travelled to Copenhagen with his son and spent the winter of 1683–4 negotiating prices of goods with merchants on behalf of the *Alþingi*. On his way back he became sick and barely reached his home in Sauðafell before dying (*LS* I, 2: 5; *Annálar* II: 266; III: 340). Árni was in Iceland when the inheritance was divided on 4 August 1685 and each of the four brothers received no more than eight hundreds in landed property. They got somewhat more when their mother died five years later, so that the total inheritance from their parents for each of them amounted to an average farm (Már Jónsson 1998: 48, 95–6). Árni planned to sail to Denmark from Rif on Snæfellsnes in the autumn but the ship sank in the harbour in very bad weather. He could not secure passage on another ship but managed to send a letter to Bartholin. He spent the winter in Hvammur and gave instruction in Latin to his younger cousins (*LS* I, 2: 5; *BE*: 16).

On 26 September 1685 Bartholin wrote to Þormóður expressing his eagerness to see what Árni would bring back with him (AM 285 b fol. I: 3r–v; Aðalgeir Kristjánsson 1975: 381–2). In another letter four months later Bartholin explained that Árni had not been able to leave Iceland but his luggage had been salvaged. He also mentioned that Bishop Þórður Þorláksson had sent him on loan a vellum of *Sverris saga* (AM 81 a fol.) which Árni, when he arrived, could transcribe for Þormóður if he did not have a copy of the saga already. Another Icelander, Björn Magnússon, had given Bartholin a vellum, the now famous *Möðruvallabók* (AM 132 fol.), but the new owner was not impressed as it only contained sagas of Icelanders: 'ickun particulares Islandicæ historiæ'. *Kormáks saga* was interesting, though, as it was replete with antiquities: 'heel fuld af Antiqviteter'. Bartholin added that he had a manuscript of *Hrólfs saga kraka* (probably AM 922 4to written by Árni) which contained a different version of the saga from that which Þormóður had used in his earlier work on Danish kings. Bartholin's version of *Knýtlinga saga*, on the other hand, was corrupt: 'heel ucorrect skrefven' (probably AM 20 h fol.). He also had other Icelandic sagas such as *Landnámabók*, *Vatnsdæla saga* and *Egils saga* (AM 285 b fol. I: 4r–v).

In the spring of 1686 Þormóður sent his secretary, Árni Hákonarson, to Copenhagen with a manuscript of *Ragnars saga loðbrókar* for Bartholin, who wanted to have a copy made (AM 285 b fol. I: 8r). Bartholin still looked forward to seeing what Árni would bring back from Iceland, but his hopes were dashed when it came to light that it was nothing of particular interest, except for two copies of the Poetic Edda, a defective *Grágás* and *Áns saga bogsveigis* (AM 285 b fol. I: 13r). These items could not live up to the expectations that a year and a half of absence had raised. Torfi Jónsson had in fact met Árni at Þingvellir in the summer of 1686 and found him entertaining; in a letter to Þormóður on 5 August he mentioned two sagas in Árni's possession, at least *Andra saga* and perhaps also *Víga-Skúta saga* (AM 285 b fol. IV: 28v; cf. *LS* I, 1: 10n; Aðalgeir Kristjánsson 1975: 380). That was nothing remarkable either and Bartholin was justly disappointed, although it is difficult to decide what could reasonably have been expected of Árni at that point in his life, when he was so young and without money or influence. He did not have the means to travel around the country or hire assistants, as Jón Eggertsson had done in 1682 (see p. 44). Heidemann had sent the scholarly-inclined sheriff of Árnessýsla, Einar Eyjólfsson, around with a list of nearly a hundred sagas, without results. Árni, however, spent most of his time in Dalasýsla, though he did go to the Alþingi both summers while in Iceland (Már Jónsson 1998: 49). In 1685 he had a discussion there with the local priest, the Reverend Árni Þorvarðsson, who informed him that he had lent an old fragment of *Elucidarius* to Magistrate Lauritz Gottrup, who had not returned it (*LS* II: 183).

Besides working for Bartholin Árni had a private agenda which turned out to be more rewarding. His family had local influence and from people in Dalasýsla he acquired for himself no fewer than three fourteenth-century law manuscripts, in which Bartholin would not have been interested: *Ljárskógabók* (AM 344 fol.), *Staðarfellsbók* (AM 346 fol.) and *Belgsdalsbók* (AM 347 fol.). They all contain *Jónsbók* and *Kristinréttr Árna biskups*, as well as royal and ecclesiastical decrees. *Belgsdalsbók* also contains the *Kristinna laga þáttr* of *Grágás* (*AMKat*. I: 279–83). Árni acquired *Ljárskógabók* from Ingibjörg Jónsdóttir at Ljárskógar in 1686, apparently in exchange for a paper manuscript containing an Icelandic translation of a Danish version of *Trójumanna saga* (*LS* II: 174–6; *PB*: 538–9). *Staðarfellsbók* came from Björn Jónsson at Staðarfell and *Belgsdalsbók* from the Reverend Jón Loftsson at Belgsdalur. Árni apparently started working on these manuscripts right away. In *Staðarfellsbók*, the Icelandic tithe law of 1096–7 ends abruptly; *Belgsdalsbók* contains more of the text, which Árni now added to *Staðarfellsbók* (AM 346 fol.: 24r; AM 347 fol.: 79v). He also corrected some passages in the *Jónsbók* text in *Staðarfellsbók*, enhanced chapter headings and added text which had disappeared because of damage to the manuscript.

In *Ljárskógabók* Árni made several conjectures at points where text was missing or hard to decipher, especially at the end (AM 344 fol.: 75v–78v). The vellum's last leaf is badly cut. Árni copied the text that could still be read, which he erroneously thought came from Bishop Jón Sigurðarson's Statutes of 1345, whereas it actually belongs to Archbishop Páll's Statutes of 1342. He then wrote what can be called his first codicological report, concluding quite correctly that the last nine lines could not be read and that one of the two columns was completely torn off, whereas the remaining column gets thinner, its width spanning three fingers at the top but only a thumb at the bottom (Már Jónsson 1998: 56–7).

While in Iceland Árni also acquired a number of recent transcriptions. Among these were at least six manuscripts produced by his grandfather Ketill: *Kjalnesinga saga* (AM 504 4to), *Flóamanna saga* (AM 516 4to), *Bandamanna saga* (AM 554 a β 4to), *Hænsa-Þóris saga* (AM 554 a δ 4to), *Gísla saga Súrssonar* (AM 481 4to) and *Harðar saga* (AM 499 4to). A seventh manuscript, Ketill's copy of *Egils saga* (AM 453 4to), may also have become part cf Árni's library at this time (Louis-Jensen 1994: 518n; Chesnutt 2005b: 250n). A transcription of eddic poems made by Ketill, in the possession of Árni's paternal uncle Vigfús Jónsson, was copied by the Reverend Páll Ketilsson, Árni's maternal uncle. in the winter of 1685–6. Árni took it with him to Copenhagen and gave it to Peder Resen (AM 254 8vo: 359r). In Iceland Árni also received a manuscript of *Svarfdæla saga* from Árni Álfsson which came to be copied in Copenhagen by Jón Eggertsson a year or two later (AM 484 4to; Jónas Kristjánsson 1966: xxvii–xxix). Þorsteinn Þórðarson at Skarð gave Árni a transcription of *Eyrbyggja saga* (AM 447 4to), written by Þorsteinn himself in his youth with corrections made by his father, the Reverend Þórður Jónsson at Hítardalur. That transcription turned out to be covered by two vellum leaves from a manuscript of *Heimskringla*. A third leaf from the same codex had been used to cover a booklet belonging to Árni's father: 'kver er att hafde fadir minn' (AM 39 fol.: notes). Árni wrote these notes later and it cannot be known whether he noticed the three leaves already in 1685–6. A single leaf from a thirteenth-century collection of homilies (AM 686 c 4to) was certainly in his hands in 1686, when he made a copy of it (AM 686 d 4to).

Philological fury

In the last years of the fifteenth century the scholar Angelo Poliziano, who worked under the patronage of Lorenzo di Medici in Florence, undertook groundbreaking studies of classical manuscripts. He came to be known for his book *Miscellanea*, printed in 1488, containing a hundred short chapters on classical texts, where he discussed names, coins, inscriptions, the orthography of manuscripts, variant readings and conjectures. He claimed that it was useless, as scholars tended to do, to have too much faith in a text as it appeared in the majority of available manuscripts. Instead he saw the need to assess each manuscript's age and other qualities. Manuscripts which derived from the same extant exemplar were useless as witnesses of the original text. Old manuscripts were of greater interest than young ones, but if younger manuscripts derived from old and good copies, which were lost, they could be used as independent witnesses. Poliziano believed in getting as close to the original text as possible and criticised other scholars for putting more work into conjectures than into looking for better manuscripts. He thus formulated two important principles in textual criticism: the valuelessness of copies derived from known manuscripts (*eliminatio codicum descriptorum*) and the possible utility of younger manuscripts (*recentiores non deteriores*) (Timpanaro 1990: 5–7; Grafton 1983, I: 27–31; Grafton 1991: 57–62; Reynolds and Wilson 1991: 143–6).

Not all scholars heeded such advice. The first edition of the New Testament in Greek, produced by Erasmus of Rotterdam in Basel in 1516, was based on at least five manuscripts, all of them unknown except for a twelfth-century vellum which would now be regarded as without value. According to L.D. Reynolds and N.G. Wilson, Erasmus was 'aware of the likely value of really old manuscripts' although in most of his editions 'he relied on rather late books of no great merit, despite the evident possibility of discovering better and older texts by inquiry from his many correspondents.' He even supplemented the Greek text with his own translations from the Latin Vulgate, thereby revealing 'a lack of a set of logical principles for the evaluation of manuscripts'. In his editions of Seneca from 1515 and 1529, Erasmus had access to a ninth-century vellum, but, being 'inhibited by the critical methods of his day', he only 'drew on it spasmodically to emend what he had before him' (Reynolds and Wilson 1991: 160–3; cf. Timpanaro 1990: 17–18).

Learned Icelanders in the seventeenth century also knew that older vellum manuscripts were more important for scholarship than newly-made paper transcriptions, and were aware that copies should be made with care. In a letter to Þormóður Torfason in the summer of 1663, Bishop Brynjólfur Sveinsson wrote that although the king had received a more beautiful copy of the Poetic Edda, none could be as valuable as the one Þormóður had taken with him, because it had the authority of age and was correctly written: 'riett stafad og skrifad'. The beautiful manuscript to which Brynjólfur referred was a recent transcription of the Codex Regius, which in his opinion needed to be preserved (Jón Helgason 1942: 163). Þormóður himself preferred vellums and in letters to the Reverend Torfi Jónsson in 1684 frequently cited sentences found in all available vellums or in some of them (AM 285 b fol. IV: 10r, 13r, 14r). Often though, Þormóður's desire for old vellums was constrained by circumstances and he had no choice but to rely on paper copies.

When Árni started working for Bartholin his standards were not very exacting. He took whatever manuscripts were available and used his own orthography in his transcriptions. This is not surprising, since that is what even the best Icelandic scribes had always done. There were, of course, no official rules of orthography at the time so that each scribe developed his own, although within generally acknowledged constraints. Ketill Jörundsson, for instance, copied *Egils saga* (AM 453 4to) from a sixteenth-century manuscript of which three leaves remain (AM 162 A α fol.). He followed the text closely but used his own personal system of abbreviations and orthography (Chesnutt 2005b: 246, 257). Hákon Ormsson, to take another example, copied parts of *Grágás* (AM 339 fol.) and did not omit a word but used his own spelling, as did the industrious Reverend Jón Erlendsson when he copied *Kristinréttr Árna biskups* (AM 355 b fol.); altogether he wrote more than a hundred manuscripts (Guðrún Ása Grímsdóttir 2007). An example of Jón's method is a copy of *Bevers saga* (AM 179 fol.) from a vellum which ended up in Stockholm (Perg. 6 4to). According to Christopher Sanders, Jón did a good job but did not produce 'a mirror-image of the exemplar'. The orthography and abbreviations were 'sometimes faithful... but by no means consistently so', and he emended errors and 'passages that are difficult to decipher' (2001: xciv). This way of proceeding was followed even by a professional scribe such as Jón Vigfússon, who worked in Sweden. In 1690 he copied *Trójumanna saga* (Papp. 58 fol.) from the now-lost fourteenth-century saga collection *Ormsbók*. On his method, Jonna Louis-Jensen concluded: 'He makes no attempt to reproduce his exemplar letter for letter but uses his own orthography and inflexions. He frequently substitutes one word for another, changes the word order and tries to emend passages which he did not understand' (1963: xxi). This is what Árni was familiar with and practised himself when he started out as a scholar. Soon enough he developed his own, more exacting method.

Árni's enthusiasm after acquiring his first vellums may have prompted him to adopt higher standards. He began copying manuscripts as exactly as possible and even to imitate the letter-forms and abbreviations used by the medieval scribes. This practice can be seen in his transcriptions made in 1685–6, which have been described by Stefán Karlsson as extremely meticulous and 'almost diplomatic' (1970b: 290–1). While in Iceland, Árni copied the legal text *Járnsíða* of 1271–3 from *Staðarhólsbók* (AM 334 fol.), the owner of which, Bjarni Pétursson, the sheriff of Dalasýsla, lived at Staðarhóll close to Hvammur (*ÍÆ* I: 188). A copy of *Grágás* from *Staðarhólsbók*, by Árni's brother Jón, may also have been made at this time (AM 122 4to). Árni made first one copy of *Járnsíða* (AM 119 4to) and then immediately made another (AM 1021 4to). The scribe of *Staðarhólsbók* had used the letter 'ð', but Árni writes 'd' everywhere in accordance with the current practice in Iceland at the time. On rereading AM 119 4to, however, he added strokes to the letter 'd' on the first six pages, thus changing them to 'ð'. He imitated the majority of the abbreviations and superscript signs (*bönd*) but occasionally expanded them. He sometimes wrote a majuscule when *Staðarhólsbók* uses a minuscule at the beginning of a sentence. His punctuation was also inconsistent, as he neither followed *Staðarhólsbók* nor his own practice. Although his method lacked consistency, these transcriptions are much more exact than those he had produced up until that time.

On further scrutiny these transcriptions turn out to be a little less perfect. There is a lacuna in *Staðarhólsbók* between leaves 104 and 105, and Árni wrote in the margin of folio 104v that something was lacking: 'hier vantar'. In AM 119 4to he left twelve empty pages, probably hoping at some point to be able to fill the lacuna, but in AM 1021 4to only indicated the lacuna with a single empty line (AM 119 4to: 68–79; AM 1021 4to: 21r). In places where some text is missing in *Staðarhólsbók*, or Árni thought that something was not right, he consulted *Jónsbók* to emend

Járnsíða. On the last leaf of *Staðarhólsbók*, four lines have been cut out along with parts of a further eight lines (AM 334 fol.: 108r). In AM 119 4to Árni worked as Erasmus had done two centuries earlier, silently filling the lacuna with the corresponding text in *Jónsbók* but adopting the orthography of *Staðarhólsbók* (Már Jónsson 1998a: 58–9). AM 1021 4to was made for Sigurður Björnsson, the scribe of the *Alþingi* and later magistrate, perhaps in exchange for the loan of the Norwegian national law of 1274 and the older church law of Eiðsivaþing (AM 68 4to), which Árni copied (AM 67 4to and AM 77 d 4to) for his own use (Stefán Karlsson 1970b: 289n). He also made a copy of *Bjarkeyjarréttur* (AM 123 a 4to), but used a recent paper copy borrowed from the farm Vatnshorn in Dalasýsla (Hagland and Sandnes 1997: xxiii–xxiv).

Árni was only 22 years old when he experimented with making diplomatic transcriptions of medieval texts. He may have found inspiration in Bartholin's enormous library, which held at least 2500 books. Bartholin owned numerous printed editions of medieval texts and many important books of scholarship, such as the collected works of Angelo Poliziano (Paris 1519) and a 1620 edition of Lorenzo Valla's critique of the Donation of Constantine. He also had books by Joseph Scaliger, Isaac Casaubon, Jean Mabillon and other living or recently deceased scholarly luminaries, and subscribed to erudite journals published in Amsterdam and Leipzig (*Catalogus Librorum*: 9, 13–14, 21, 42–3, 49, 55, 54, 102–3). Exactitude was the order of the day among scholars such as the French Étienne Baluze, who in the last decade of the seventeenth century published a series of editions of texts concerning ecclesiastical history. In his prefaces and letters he repeatedly scolded scholars who were careless in their transcriptions and was extremely conscientious himself, although not perfect (Gasnault 2008: 138–9). The English scholar Thomas Hearne similarly informed a friend that Humfrey Wanley 'was so exact a man, that his copies are next to originals' (C.E. Wright 1960: 129).

Árni may also have been inspired by discussions with Icelandic scholars such as Einar Eyjólfsson and Bishop Þórður Þorláksson, who in 1685–6 were at work on editions of *Landnámabók* and *Íslendingabók*, published at Skálholt in 1688. They sought to come as close as possible to the style and spelling used 'by our forefathers' (*Sagan Landnama*, preface, explanations). Special fonts were even carved for the press in preparation for the edition of *Íslendingabók* so that the old orthography could be reproduced (*Schedæ Ara Prests froda*: preface, 17). That edition was probably based on a meticulous transcription made by Jón Erlendsson in around 1650 (AM 113 a fol.). Jón had in fact made two transcriptions of *Íslendingabók* for Bishop Brynjólfur Sveinsson, of which the other (AM 113 b fol.) was even better. Both come close to being diplomatic. The orthography of the original manuscript (now lost) emerges clearly from the transcription, although Jón's own orthography shows here and there, and occasionally he omitted a word. Such exact transcriptions were exceptional at the time but not unknown, as witnessed by the *Snorra Edda* manuscript *Codex Trajectinus* from around 1595, where, according to Anthony Faulkes, the scribe 'preserved surprisingly many features of the orthography of his exemplar' (1985: 19). In 1685–6 Árni made a virtue of this kind of exactitude, surpassing his contemporaries in his zeal for the systematic production of accurate transcriptions.

Back in Copenhagen in the autumn of 1686, Árni's first project was to copy a now-lost manuscript written in the last years of the fourteenth century (*Vatnshyrna*). Its owner, Árni Hákonarson from Vatnshorn, had just sold it to Peder Resen (Louis-Jensen 1994: 516; Jón Helgason 1985: 48–9). Four decades later, Árni Magnússon made a list of its contents: *Flóamanna saga, Laxdæla saga, Hænsa-Þóris saga, Vatnsdæla saga, Eyrbyggja saga, Kjalnesinga saga, Króka-Refs saga, Stjörnu-Odda draumr, Bergbúa þáttr* and two other dream tales (Stefán Karlsson 1970a: 271; AM 226 a 8vo: 58r–59v). In the autumn of 1686 he borrowed the manuscript from Resen and seems to have started out by making copies of the dream tales. The four short texts were at first together in one volume, but at some point later in life Árni divided it in two. To the right of the title in his copy of *Stjörnu-Odda draumr* he writes that the text is copied from a very old vellum: 'Skrifadr epter miög gamallri Membrana' (AM 555 h 4to: 1r). At the beginning of the other tales Árni claims to have used the same vellum (AM 564 c 4to). Árni's transcription of *Vatnshyrna* is diplomatic, apart from some inconsistencies in the use of 'ok and 'oc' for the Tironian nota 'et' (Stefán Karlsson 1970b: 290–6). Just as his grandfather had done in his copies, Árni numbered the

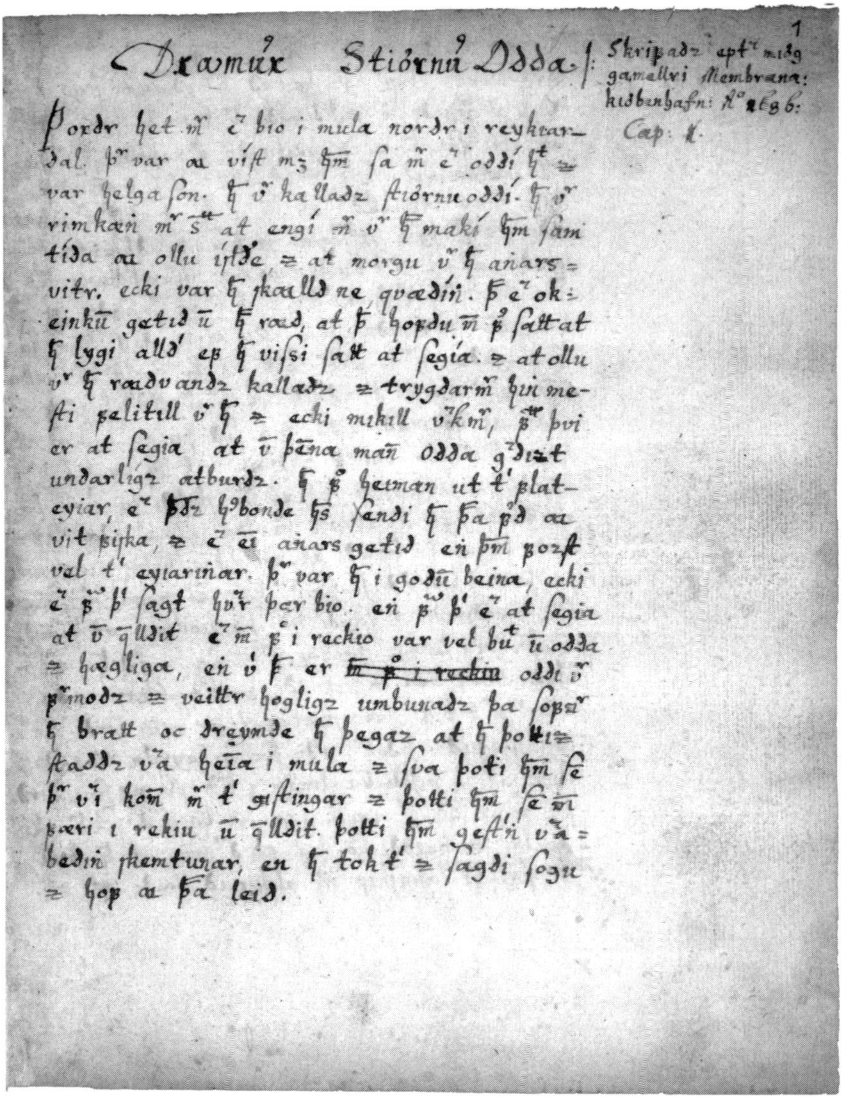

Figure 3. The first page of Árni's first copy from Vatnshyrna, where he proudly added a note of his own (AM 555 h 4to: 1r).

chapters in the margins, but provided no pagination. He wrote the poetry in continuous lines, as was customary at the time, but put a 'v.' in the margins for every two lines. He emended the text in a few places, putting whatever he added within brackets. A few corrections, mostly in the verses, indicate that he may have checked his transcription, or at least some of it.

On 19 November 1686 Ásgeir Jónsson registered as a student at Copenhagen University (Bjarni Jónsson 1949: 47–8). He was six years older than Árni and had some limited experience in transcribing manuscripts. Árni may actually have known Ásgeir from Iceland, as he had worked for Þorsteinn Þórðarson at Skarð, close to Hvammur (Már Jónsson 2009b: 291–2). Árni now engaged him to work on a transcription of the whole of *Vatnshyrna*. With the exception of *Króka-Refs saga*, all the sagas in *Vatnshyrna* are extant in Ásgeir's hand: *Laxdæla saga* (ÍB 225 4to), *Eyrbyggja saga* (AM 448 4to), *Hænsa-Þóris saga* (AM 501 4to), *Kjalnesinga saga* (AM 503 4to), *Flóamanna saga* (AM 517 4to) and *Vatnsdæla saga* (AM 559 4to). Árni's contribution was limited to writing twelve pages of *Eyrbyggja saga* and most of its verses. Ásgeir's transcriptions of *Vatnshyrna* are not as exact as Árni's dream tales. Ásgeir expanded most abbreviations or used his own as he saw fit, and at times his personal orthography appears. Árni accepted this and only made a few corrections, for instance in *Laxdæla saga* (Kålund 1889–91: xvii; Már Jónsson 1998: 61). Furthermore, it seems that Ásgeir did not copy all the sagas directly from *Vatnshyrna* but to some extent used transcriptions made by Ketill Jörundsson which were in Árni's possession following his trip to Iceland (see p. 67). Árni may actually first have compared Ketill's manuscripts with *Vatnshyrna*, putting variants in the margins and between the lines: the whole of *Flóamanna saga* (AM 516 4to), ten pages of *Hænsa-Þóris saga* (AM 554 a δ 4to) and as much of *Kjalnesinga saga* (AM 504 4to). Árni then had Ásgeir transcribe Ketill's copies and not *Vatnshyrna* itself. Strangely enough, Árni's additions to his grandfather's copies appear with few if any changes in Ásgeir's transcriptions (AM 517 4to, AM 501 4to, AM 503 4to), along with numerous words that Ketill had put within parentheses and can hardly have been in *Vatnshyrna* (Már Jónsson 1997a: 119-27; Már Jónsson 1998: 61). This hypothesis has been disputed by Stefán Karlsson, who claims that only *Vatnshyrna* was used in this project, and further investigation is required (Ólafur Halldórsson 1999: 247–8; Stefán Karlsson 2000: 358; Guðvarður Már Gunnlaugsson 2001: 113). In the autumn of 1686 five Icelandic students arrived in Copenhagen, in addition to the six already there. A further two arrived in 1687 (Bjarni Jónsson 1949: 44–50). Most of these young men became Árni's lifelong friends, such as Páll Vídalín (who would later become a magistrate), Björn Þorleifsson, Steinn Jónsson and Jón Vídalín (all later bishops), Arngrímur Vídalín (later a schoolmaster), Hákon Hannesson (later a sheriff), Gísli Einarsson, Geir Markússon, Þorlákur Grímsson, Jón Halldórsson, Eyjólfur Björnsson, Guðmundur Guðmundsson and Jón Gíslason (later clergymen). During the winter of 1586–7 Helgi Ólafsson was in Copenhagen and copied texts on behalf of the Swedish Institute of Antiquities (Gödel 1897: 188; Gödel 1897–1900: 145–8). Jón Eggertsson remained in jail until the spring of 1687 but all the same collaborated with Helgi and continued making copies after he was set free. Jón produced two bulky volumes, at least one of which arrived in Stockholm on 5 October 1687. He was still in touch with Bartholin and particularly with Árni, from whom he borrowed some transcriptions. Jón falsely wrote in his own copy that *Stjörnu-Odda draumr*, which he had without doubt copied from Árni's transcription, was copied from 'a very old vellum' in Copenhagen in 1687, and the other dream tales from the same manuscript (Papp. 67 fol.: 1r, 11v, 13v, 14r). He also claimed to have copied *Flóamanna saga*, *Bandamanna saga* and *Hávarðar saga Ísfirðings* from an old vellum (Papp. 60 fol.: 60, 165, 245, 595), but most certainly copied at least the last item from a manuscript written by Ketill Jörundsson (AM 502 4to). Jón also made a copy of *Svarfdæla saga* for Árni (AM 484 4to) and another for the Swedes (Papp. 67 fol.: 15r–55r, Jónas Kristjánsson 1966: xxvii–xxviii; Jucknies 2009: 58–9, 67–81). During a visit to Jón in prison Árni wrote six lines at the bottom of a page in the middle of *Böðvars þáttr bjarka* (Papp. 60 fol.: 59).

Late in 1686, it seems, Bartholin finished collecting materials for his book on the fearlessness of the ancient Danes, published in 1689 (see p. 82). His next project was an ecclesiastical history of Denmark, in which he aimed to provide the same kind of detailed chronological survey that scholars had produced for other countries; such as the Lutheran *Magdeburger Zenturien* of 1559–74 or the *Annales* of the Italian scholar Baronius published in 1601–8 (Neveu 1966: 154, 166–7; Heussi 1904: 8–9, 24). For this project, Bartholin had a royal letter dated 1687 which ordered the bishops in Denmark, Norway and Iceland to provide documents and information (*Lovsamling* I: 465–6). As he had done before, Bartholin used large folio volumes but now wanted entire texts of sagas and annals, Danish and Norwegian law, and documents of all kinds (Barth. B–K). He had reached a similar conclusion to the French scholar Dom Lobineau, who in a history of Languedoc (published in 1708) argued that copies of entire texts were to be preferred to extracts and summaries, since the latter could not be trusted and few people could actually do them well (Auger 2003: 108). Bartholin now copied some of this material himself, but the bulk of it was done by Árni and his Icelandic friends. The originals were to be found in the University Library and the Royal Archives in Copenhagen, but also in the private libraries of officials or wealthy men such as Magistrate Holger Parsberg, Count Otto Rantzau, Professor Johan Bircherod and Etatsråd Jens Rosencrantz. Helgi Ólafsson worked with Árni and Bartholin on a volume produced in 1686–7. Another volume was the collaborative work of six Icelanders: Steinn Jónsson, Geir Markússon, Þorlákur Grímsson, Árni Hákonarson, Guðmundur Guðmundsson and Gísli Einarsson. In the final nine volumes Árni Magnússon wrote at least two thousand pages and the other scribes combined twice as much.[1] Ólafur Halldórsson has analysed one of these transcriptions and concluded that Árni copied *Danakonungatal* 'letter by letter from the original, though not without a good deal of mistakes' (2006: 122). Most of the texts concerned Danish history and reveal Bartholin's 'real' interests, as he totally disregarded all things Icelandic. In another series of eight volumes, Bartholin allocated two pages to each year, writing short notes on the relevant events and referring to his other volumes for the appropriate texts (Barth. XIV–XXI).

---

[1] In AM 1045 4to, Árni mentions the scribes but provides no information on what they wrote. On these men, see *ÍÆ* and Bjarni Jónsson 1949. Árni's contribution is listed in Finnur Jónsson 1930a: 16n.

Árni also made copies for Bartholin in separate smaller volumes, such as the church law of Scania (AM 907 4to) and medieval Danish annals (AM 300 4to, AM 844 4to). He gathered information on the history of the church in Denmark, Norway and Iceland from Icelandic works such as annals, *Landnámabók, Hungrvaka* and *Guðmundar saga*, as well as from Arngrímur Jónsson's *Crymogæa* of 1609 (AM 429 b 3 4to). He also translated Icelandic and Norwegian texts into Latin, mostly charters and official documents, but also *Jóns saga helga* (AM 222 fol.) and church law (AM 352 fol., AM 355 a fol.) (Foote 2003: 123*; Westergård-Nielsen 1971: 54–5). For the legal material, Árni used three fourteenth-century vellums of *Jónsbók* which Bartholin had received on loan from Bishop Þórður Þorláksson in 1687 (AM 351 fol., AM 354 fol., AM 175 a, c 4to). For himself, Árni copied a sentence from the Icelandic church law of 1275 as it appeared in the vellum AM 351 fol. in the margin of his recently acquired *Staðarfellsbók* (AM 346 fol.: 9v; Westergård-Nielsen 1971: 83r; *Norges gamle love* IV: 536). Bishop Þórður had also sent to Bartholin a vellum of hagiographic sagas (AM 234 fol.), in which Árni underlined rare words with red chalk, such as 'olmleikr' (excitation), 'remían' (shouting) and 'vandrækiligan' (disregarded) (AM 234 fol.: notes, 1v, 2v; Jón Helgason 1975b: 407–8; Foote 2003: 12*n). Árni at this time also had access to a vellum containing *Jóns saga postula* (AM 649 a 4to) and produced an apparently random list of more than a hundred words, each followed by an Icelandic synonym or a Danish or Latin translation (AM 649 b 4to: 1r–2v).

Árni produced even more transcriptions on his own account or had his friends make them. He obviously wanted to gather as many Icelandic texts as possible in careful copies based on old manuscripts. Bartholin only desired information on Danish history, whereas Árni wished to know more about Icelandic history and literature. His work on *Vatnshyrna* was part of that project, but it seems that he realised that the newly-developed diplomatic method was too time-consuming, and also that it was not a realistic requirement for copyists other than himself. He may have changed his mind when he toiled alongside Ásgeir on *Eyrbyggja saga* (AM 448 4to). Árni transcribed the first twelve pages and Ásgeir the rest of the prose, while Árni copied all the poetry, dividing the poems into separate lines for easier reading. Ásgeir kept writing in a mixture of his own style and that of the exemplar, whereas Árni now expanded all abbreviations but otherwise maintained the orthography of the original. This is how he worked for the rest of his life, although he did not completely give up the diplomatic method and would make an exception if he found a text particularly interesting (see pp. 79, 157, 195).

Árni's next project, begun in the winter of 1687–8, was *Möðruvallabók* (AM 132 fol.), which had been in Bartholin's library since 1685 (see p. 65). Árni may have thought that he already had good enough texts of *Njáls saga, Laxdæla saga, Finnboga saga* and *Bandamanna saga*, since he did not make copies of these sagas from *Möðruvallabók*. Ásgeir copied *Ölkofra þáttr* (AM 1008 VI 4to) and *Droplaugarsona saga* (JS 435 II 4to) but together they copied *Kormáks saga* (AM 505 4to), *Víga-Glúms saga* (AM 508 4to) and *Fóstbrœðra saga* (AM 566 b 4to). Eyjólfur Björnsson now worked for Árni too, copying *Egils saga* (AM 460 4to) and *Hallfreðar saga* (AM 497 4to). Eyjólfur was three years younger than Árni and studied at the university in 1687–9 (*ÍÆ* I: 451–2). In what Árni transcribed he followed the orthography of *Möðruvallabók* carefully but expanded all abbreviations. He wrote personal names with an initial capital letter, something which is seldom done in *Möðruvallabók*, but did not use capital letters at the beginning of sentences if the manuscript used lower case. Following the practice of the manuscript he used 'ð', but added some modern punctuation. Eyjólfur worked in the same way, whereas Ásgeir was attentive to the spelling of *Möðruvallabók* as before, but either expanded the abbreviations in his own way or copied them as they appeared in the manuscript (McKinnell 1970: 315–16; Loth 1960: 208–10; Stefán Karlsson 1970b: 298). Árni did not systematically compare his assistants' copies to the original and only made some minor changes in Eyjólfur's copies of *Egils saga* and *Hallfreðar saga* (Már Jónsson 1998: 67).

Other projects involved Norwegian law and *konungasögur*, available on vellum in private libraries in Copenhagen. Árni's main purpose seems to have been to acquire as many texts as he could find, for reading and research. The quality of the transcriptions is the same as in the transcriptions from *Möðruvallabók*. Árni borrowed from Willum

Worm a manuscript containing *Óláfs saga helga* (AM 68 fol.) and *Óláfs saga Tryggvasonar* (AM 310 4to). Ásgeir copied both of them (AM 77 a fol., AM 311 4to) and Eyjólfur made another copy of *Óláfs saga Tryggvasonar* (AM 312 4to). From *Fríssbók* (AM 45 fol.), the property of Jens Rosencrantz, Ásgeir and Eyjólfur copied *Hákonar saga Hákonarsonar* (AM 89 fol.). From *Eirspennill* (AM 47 fol.), which also belonged to Rosencrantz, Eyjólfur copied *Heimskringla* (AM 40 fol.), *Sverris saga*, *Hákonar saga Sverrissonar* (AM 87 fol.) and *Hákonar saga Hákonarsonar* (AM 88 fol.), whereas Jón Vídalín made another copy of *Hákonar saga Sverrissonar* (AM 328 4to). Eyjólfur made two copies (AM 302 4to, AM 51 fol.) of the so-called *Fagurskinna B*, held by the Copenhagen University Library, and Ásgeir made a further copy (NB Oslo 371 fol.) (Loth 1960c; Seelow 1997; Már Jónsson 2009b: 287). In the autumn of 1686 Árni had bought *Hulda* (AM 66 fol.) and *Stephanus saga* (AM 661 4to) from Árni Hákonarson. Ásgeir now transcribed *Hulda* (NB Oslo 372 fol.), preserving the abbreviations as they were in the manuscript, as Árni later reminisced (Louis-Jensen 1968: 18). Eyjólfur copied *Ólafs saga helga* (AM 78 a fol.) from a vellum that belonged to Resen and is now lost. Ásgeir and Eyjólfur together transcribed *Guðmundar saga* (AM 401 4to) from another vellum (AM 399 4to) in Resen's library (Stefán Karlsson 1983: xcviii–cv). They also copied *Hrómundar saga Gripssonar* (AM 587 b 4to). Árni himself copied *Knýtlinga saga* (AM 13 fol.) from a vellum in the University Library and made another copy with most of the text (AM 20 d fol.), which he sent to Þormóður in the spring of 1690 (Már Jónsson 1998: 70–1).

In 1688 Árni made an elaborate copy of the older *Gulaþingslög* (AM 308 fol.) from a thirteenth-century vellum that belonged to Count Otto Rantzau (Eithun, Rindal and Ulseth 1994: 17–20). The rubrics are in red, as in the exemplar, but Árni did not reproduce the green initials. He copied the text in great detail and made a list of things that he had emended or regarded as errors in the vellum, putting additions in brackets and using noughts – 0000 – in order to indicate damaged letters. He added comments when something was missing (AM 308 fol.: 88). He later made a copy (AM Steph. 1 a) of his copy and gave it away to an unknown recipient after Ásgeir had copied it (AM 66 4to). Árni also made a partial copy of the older *Frostaþingslög* (AM 312 fol.) from a manuscript that belonged to Resen; Ásgeir transcribed the whole text (AM 310 fol.) and then made another copy (AM 311 fol.) for Þormóður (Már Jónsson 2009b: 287).

By 1689, after four years of intense activity, Árni Magnússon had a sizeable collection of good transcriptions and some vellums of his own. He had no plans for producing editions of *Íslendingasögur* or *konungasögur*. The market for such books in Iceland was diminutive and there was limited interest among scholars in Europe. In Sweden, sagas had been printed in order to celebrate the country's glorious past. The Institute of Antiquities had the means to publish such books without the necessity of selling too many of them. In Denmark such a luxury was unthinkable. All editions in Copenhagen so far had been financed by individuals like Ole Worm and Peder Resen, but there were no such patrons around when Árni appeared on the scene. His goal was to put together a good private collection and the best way to acquire old texts of some quality was to make copies of vellums held in public and private libraries. Jón Eggertsson and Helgi Ólafsson made copies with the intention of selling them, and being absolutely faithful to the text of their exemplars was not their main preoccupation. Árni mostly worked for himself and after his initial engagement with Bartholin in 1684–5 he became more demanding, testing more than one way of making good copies. At first he was fascinated by diplomatic transcriptions but soon turned to what would nowadays be called semi-normalised transcriptions, where abbreviations are expanded but the orthography otherwise preserved. Árni may have changed his mind as he found out, as early as 1686, that strictly diplomatic copies are extremely time-consuming. He also realised that his friends and fellow students were not capable of working that way, and may thus have decided that it was not necessary to produce diplomatic copies. Less detailed ones, meticulously done of course, were good enough.

4
Erudition

It is certain that I know no-one better than Árni Magnússon and no-one like him, and although you may think it unlikely, I find him better than Sæmundur fróði and Snorri Sturluson in many things, even most.

Það er vist jeg öngvan veit betri enn Arna Magnusson og öngvan hans lika, og þo þer þyche oliklegt betra enn Sæmund froda, Snorra Sturluson i mörgu ja velflestu.

> Þormóður Torfason to Bishop Þórður Þorláksson
> in the spring of 1691 (AM 283 fol.: 150v)

This chapter shows how Árni Magnússon managed to established himself as a scholar and a collector, even while he was still the assistant of Thomas Bartholin the younger, who in 1689 published a book based on their work on medieval Icelandic texts. Árni strove for independence by working on *Íslendingabók*, without finishing an edition, but had far more success in his search for manuscripts.

Antiquitates

On 30 September 1686 Thomas Bartholin wrote to Þormóður Torfason at Stangeland and asked to borrow the Codex Regius of *Grágás* (GKS 1157 fol.). Þormóður was reticent to send the vellum during the winter and promised to do so in the spring. On 24 June 1687 Bartholin asked for the Codex Regius of the Poetic Edda (GKS 2365 4to), promising to keep it for no longer than a month. He also suggested that Þormóður should come to Copenhagen so that they could discuss scholarly matters on a daily basis. Þormóður liked the idea and in a letter to the royal historiographer Willum Worm on 14 February 1688 he explained that he wished to travel to the city and stay for some time, meet with Bartholin, buy books and hire a scribe. A few weeks later Þormóður sent salmon and oysters to the wife of an important official in Copenhagen but had decided not to go there himself. He then changed his mind again and arrived in Copenhagen in early August (Már Jónsson 1998: 73–4, 360). Despite a 27-year difference in their ages, Þormóður and Árni immediately became very good friends. On 23 October Þormóður left Copenhagen again in the company of Ásgeir Jónsson, whom he had hired as scribe and assistant. On 12 November, a few days after he arrived at Stangeland, Þormóður thanked Árni for their interesting conversations, asked him to look for the deerskin underpants which he had probably left behind in the guesthouse and expressed his hope that their friendship would continue (*BT*: 1–3). Þormóður's liking for Árni appears even more clearly in a letter of 23 February 1689, where he asks Árni not to convey his greetings to Bartholin, so that Bartholin would not know that he had written to Árni first (*BT*: 5).

During the winter of 1688–9 Árni read proofs and supervised the printing of Bartholin's book on the fearlessness of the ancient Danes in the face of death, *Antiquitatum Danicarum de causis contemptæ a Danis adhuc gentilibus mortis libri tres*. Professor Ole Borch signed the permit for publication on 5 September 1688. In a letter to Þormóður on 4 April 1689 Árni predicted that the book would come out before the end of June (*BT*: 8). So it did, printed at the University Press by Johan Philip Bockenhoffer. The book was dedicated to Matthias Moth, who had recently become the first secretary of the Danish Chancery (*Danske kancelli*). In his preface, Bartholin argues that old manuscripts need to be saved from oblivion and brought into the light; he also thanks the learned Arnas Magnæus for his translations of ancient Icelandic poetry. A Latin poem by Professor Holgeir Jacobsen is followed by Árni's elaborate skaldic poem in Icelandic, in 22 eight-line stanzas, where he praises Bartholin for his interest in antiquarian studies and his diligence in learning the old language (Bartholin 1689: b3r–b4v). Árni later wrote a learned commentary on his own poem for friends; it is preserved in a copy (BL Add. 11.1184) written in the late eighteenth century (Már Jónsson 2006; cf. Már Jónsson 1998: 82; *PB*: 555). The tenth stanza will suffice to illustrate the nature of the poem, with Árni's text to the left and the numbering he provided in his commentary to the right:

Antiquitates

Nu ræþr fornra fræþa	Nu [1] ræþr [2] fornra [3] fræþa [4]
fiolauþigr, hve dauþir	fiólauþigr [5] hve [7] dauþir [9]
laungo lista drengir	laungo [8] lista [10] drengir [11]
lifat hofþo skrifa,	lifat [13] hofþo [12] skrifa [6],
kennir hann oss hve kunno	kennir [14] hann [15] oss [16] hve [17] kunno [24]
kindir Belltis strindar	kindir [20] Belltis [18] strindar [19]
gondlar veþri vandar	gondlar [22] veþri [23] vandar [21]
va galldrs tolom hallda.	Va-galldrs [26] tólom [27] hallda [25].

In his commentary Árni shows the correct order of his poetic words by putting numbers after each of them. He then explains the more difficult expressions, for example that 'Belltis strind' is Denmark, as it is on both sides of the Sound between Seeland and Fyn, and so 'Belltis strindar kindir' signifies all Danes. 'Va' is killing, just as in *Völuspá*, and 'Galldr' a poem, as the poet Sighvatr has it, which means that 'va galldr' becomes the sound of weapons: 'vopna hliomur' – in other words a battle. Árni finally provides the meaning of the stanza as a whole, which is that Bartholin, highly learned in ancient studies, shows how the old Danes lived and recounts how brave they were in battles, in which they were greatly experienced (*LS* II: 307; BL Add. 11.1184: 72r).

Antiquitates is a book in three parts of just over 700 pages in length and filled with quotations from medieval Icelandic texts. The first chapters are based on *Jómsvíkinga saga*. Instead of preparing an edition of the saga, as he had planned (see p. 61), Bartholin quoted the saga extensively and provided some comments in order to support his main argument, which was that the ancient Danes had not been afraid of dying even though they were not Christians. This argument is repeated throughout the book as Bartholin discusses themes of medieval culture, such as fame and honour, blood brotherhood (*fóstbræðralag*), berserks, battles and weaponry, life after death, immortality, ghosts and monsters, sacrifice, burial mounds, runestones, pagan gods, destiny, predictions, witchcraft, curses, defamy, plunder, killings and revenge. A few pages are devoted to a discussion of the value of medieval poetry and sagas as sources, with a succinct history of Icelandic literature and historiography. Bartholin's opinion was that poetry, kings' sagas and *Landnámabók* could be trust-

Erudition

ed for historical information, unlike the *fornaldarsögur* that Swedish scholars mistakenly valued so greatly (Bartholin 1689: 183–203; cf. Finnur Jónsson 1930a: 14–16).[1] On the use of skaldic and eddic poetry, Bartholin approvingly cited the English scholar Robert Sheringham, who in his 1670 book on the oldest history of England, *De Anglorum gentis origine disceptatio*, had claimed that such texts could be used as sources for religious ideas and social mores in pagan times. Bartholin emphasised that a scholar had to be very careful in distinguishing fact from fable. He therefore rejected the scathing attacks by the French scholar Pierre-Daniel Huet on the truthfulness of eddic poetry and other Northern texts in his *Traité de l'origine des romans* from 1670, cited in *Antiquitates* in a Latin translation of 1682 (Bartholin 1689: 193–4, 199; Huet 1942: 213–14; Sheringham 1670: 264–5; cf. Fell 1996: 28–9; Sveinbjörn Rafnsson 1987: 301–2, 311–12). Bartholin would also have agreed with Þormóður Torfason, who on 30 April 1689 wrote to Árni Magnússon that although *Alexanders saga*, *Hrólfs saga kraka*, *Þiðreks saga* and *Sigurðar saga þögla* could not be used as evidence for historical events, they were necessary for the understanding of the language: 'omissanlegar thil þess gamla mals skilnings' (*BT*: 11–12).

The Icelandic material in *Antiquitates* came from Bartholin's four volumes of textual passages made in 1684–5 (see pp. 49–53, 56–58), with some additions from Árni's more recent transcriptions, such as *Stjörnu-Odda draumr* in *Vatnshyrna* (Bartholin 1689: 261–2). *Grágás* is cited from a copy of *Staðarhólsbók*, perhaps AM 122 4to (Bartholin 1689: 37–8). When Þormóður had visited Copenhagen in August 1688 he had brought with him *Flateyjarbók* and the Codex Regius of the Poetic Edda (Már Jónsson 1998: 35, 360). Árni perused both manuscripts for Bartholin and passages from them appear in *Antiquitates* (Bartholin 1689: 78, 178). At the end of that book there is an alphabetical list of almost 70 medieval Icelandic texts, starting with 'Æfi Noregs konunga' and ending with 'Þormodar saga Kolbrunarskalldz' (Bartholin 1689: 'Index manuscriptorum'; Baumgarten 1984: 128–34).

Most of the Icelandic texts that appeared in *Antiquitates* had never

---

[1] Baumgarten 1984: 3–88 provides a resumé of *Antiquitates*, of which a Danish excerpt was made c. 1770, see NKS 637 4to.

been printed before. The spelling is somewhat more simplified than in Árni's transcriptions from *Möðruvallabók* (see p. 78), presumably because of the printer's demands. There are no diacritics over long vowels and the letter 'ð' is not reproduced. The character 'þ' is badly rendered at the beginning of the book but is better done later on. All Icelandic texts are translated into Latin, the poems paraphrased and some of them explained in detail. Bartholin compares Icelandic texts to Greek and Roman classical texts, as well as medieval Latin writings, and frequently refers to recent scholarly works, such as Jean Mabillon's *De re diplomatica* from 1681 and his *Museum Italicum* from 1687 (Bartholin 1689: 128, 215, 483, 579–80, 662; cf. Malm 1996: 61–7; Kirby 1997: 60–7). *Antiquitates* is replete with citations and is in many places little more than a list of examples with short comments in between. These passages and paraphrases from sagas and poems would later inspire scholars and poets, but not until after the mid-eighteenth century when the book came to be praised by scholars all over Europe (Baumgarten 1984: 91–2). In fact the book was hardly referred to in the first decades after its publication. The English scholar William Temple may indeed have known it, or at least the title, when he wrote his essay *Of Heroick Virtue*, published in 1690, as he mentions 'a fearlessness of Death' among 'those Northern People' (Baumgarten 1984: 89–90; Seaton 1935: 265), whereas his countryman George Hickes does not mention it in his voluminous survey of 1705: *Compendium Linguarum vett. septentrionalium thesaurus grammaticocriticus et archæologicus* (Fell 1996: 34–53). In 1714 the book appeared as 'Thomæ BARTHOLINI Antiquitatis Danicæ, in 4. Hafniæ 1689' among other books on Nordic history in Johann Burckhardt Mencke's catalogue of historical works in print, *Catalogue des principaux historiens* (Mencke 1714: 415). The inevitable conclusion to be drawn is that in its first decades of existence *Antiquitates* received almost no attention within the European Republic of Letters.

While Þormóður was in Copenhagen in the autumn of 1688 it was decided that Árni would travel to Stangeland and do research for Bartholin. On 23 February 1689 Þormóður wrote to Árni asking him to bring *Laxdæla saga* with him and whatever 'monumenta antiqvitatis' he had (*BT*: 4). On 4 April Árni suggested that Þormóður should prepare for his visit by having Ásgeir Jónsson copy parts of *Flateyjarbók*, such as *Hálfdanar saga svarta*, *Óláfs saga helga*, *Orkneyinga saga* and *Magnúss saga Hákonarsonar* (*BT*: 8). Árni repeated this request a month later, arguing that if those copies were made he could work for Þormóður with Ásgeir most of the time he stayed at Stangeland. Þormóður retorted that Ásgeir could not spare the time (*BT*: 15–16). On 1 July 1689 Bartholin sent a copy of *Antiquitates* to Þormóður with a call for collaboration to their mutual benefit. There should be no envy between them, Bartholin emphasised, since they both worked for the same king (AM 285 b fol. I: 31r). A few weeks later Árni left Copenhagen. He went first to Bergen and from there to Trondheim, where he made transcriptions of old charters in the cathedral and took notes from diverse documents. Finally, at Stangeland, he joined Ásgeir to copy texts from *Flateyjarbók*, using the same principle of word-for-word transcription as they had done in Copenhagen a year earlier (Már Jónsson 1998: 83–6; Már Jónsson 2009b: 288–9).

**COPIES MADE FROM *FLATEYJARBÓK*
AT STANGELAND IN 1689**

Árni:
Kristnisaga meistara Adams (AM 950 4to)
Sigurðar þáttr slefu (AM 329 1 4to)
From *Óláfs saga helga* (AM 1009 4to)
Sneglu-Halla þáttr (AM 349 4to)
Þorsteins þáttr tjaldstæðings (AM 349 4to)
Flateyjarannáll (AM 425 4to)

Ásgeir:
Óláfs saga helga, *Orkneyinga þáttr* and more (AM 69 fol.)
Grænlendingaþáttr (AM 1008 V 4to)
Helga þáttr ok Úlfs (AM 329 3 4to)
Játvarðar saga helga (AM 663 c 4to)
Hversu Noregr byggðist ok fannst (AM 1008 I 4to, AM 34 4 fol.)
Eiríks saga víðförla (lost)
Norna-Gests þáttr (AM 348 4to: 26–9)

Both of them:
Hemings þáttr (AM 326 b 4to)

They also transcribed texts from the vellum *Tómasskinna* (GKS 1008 fol.), which contained *Óláfs saga helga* and *Tómas saga erkibiskups* (Loth 1964: 25–6; Johnsen and Jón Helgason 1941: 1056–7). In a letter to Bartholin on 11 November, Þormóður explained that Árni had been allowed to see all the manuscripts at Stangeland and copy whatever he wanted. Þormóður had nothing to hide and did not envy Bartholin or for that matter anyone else: 'jeg aldrig haffuer enviderit nogen' (AM 282 fol.: 260v).

Árni also did some work on skaldic poetry for his own purposes (see image on next page). In 1687–8 he had compiled poems from two collections of kings' sagas (AM 66 fol., AM 61 fol.). In Stangeland he compared the texts in his compilation with the manuscripts of Norwegian kings' sagas kept there, writing variants in the margins or adding verses; although without ever indicating which manuscripts he used (AM 761 a–b 4to). Árni much later rearranged his compilation more or less alphabetically by author, but Kjartan Ottósson's reconstruction shows convincingly that when Árni left Stangeland the notebook had become a sizeable volume of 500 pages (Kjartan G. Ottósson 2006; cf. Finnur Jónsson 1930a: 134–5).

Árni left Stangeland in early December 1688 and brought with him Þormóður's manuscripts of two books on the history of the Orkney and the Faeroe Islands which were to be printed in Copenhagen (*BT*: 17–19; Ólafur Halldórsson 1992: 16–17). He travelled through Bergen, which he left on 15 January 1690. He spent some busy days in Christiania (now Oslo) before returning to Copenhagen, met with people and transcribed texts for Bartholin (*BT*: 30; Barth. C: 457–93; Barth. H: 575–96). Two days after Árni came back Bartholin sent him to Lund in Sweden, where he copied inscriptions in the cathedral and, with a local student, transcribed an old register of charters (Barth. K: 1–2, 5–24; AM 1045 4to: 34r; *BT*: 26, 30). After Easter he went to Ribe in Jutland and made copies of numerous charters and paraphrased others. He was back on 10 June (Barth. K: 330–528, 539–64; *BT*: 41). He had little interest in what he was doing and wrote to Þormóður that the documents he had seen were mostly Danish Episcopal statutes devoid of any relevance to political history. He had never in his life been so busy, he informed his friend. The

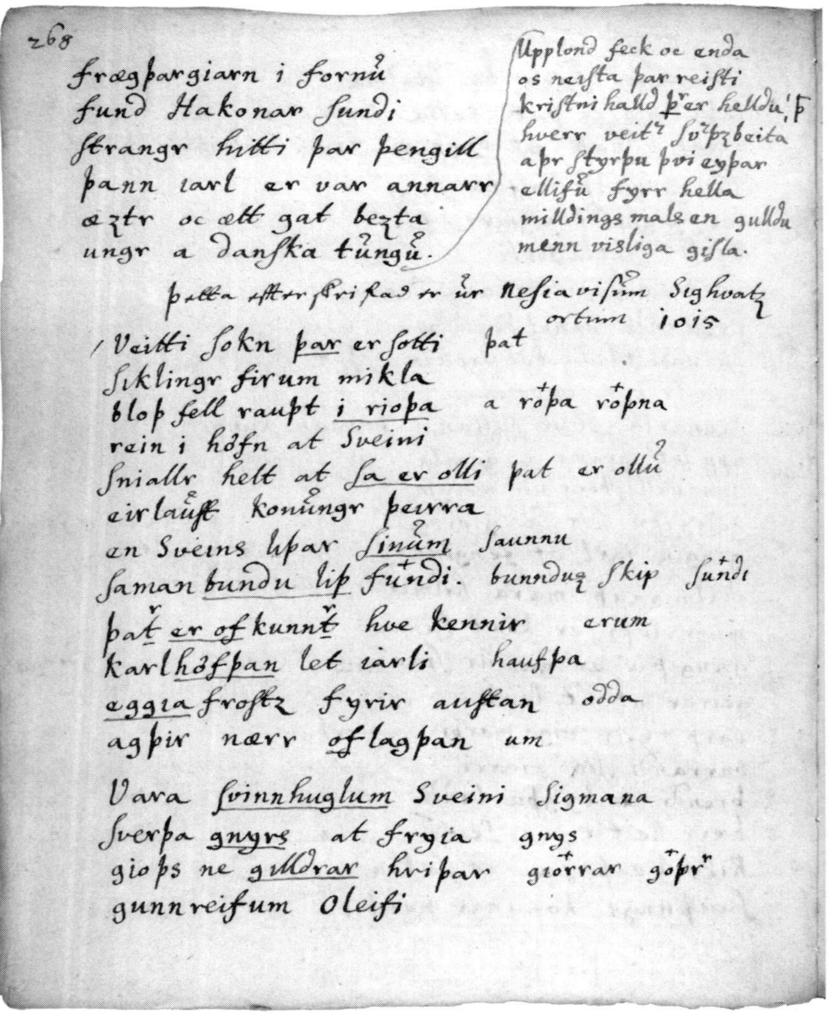

Figure 4. Árni transcribed these and many more verses by Sighvatr Þórðarson from the vellum manuscript AM 61 fol. He then added variants from one or more manuscripts kept at Stangeland (AM 761 b 4to: 291v).

main reason was that Bartholin wanted to finish the first volume of his ecclesiastical history, which would end with the tenth century (*BT*: 65).

Íslendingabók

When they first met in August 1688, Árni informed Þormóður that he intended to publish an edition of Ari fróði's *Íslendingabók*, which deals with the colonisation of Iceland in the late ninth century and its subsequent Christianisation. The text had just been published in Skálholt by Bishop Þórður Þorláksson alongside the much longer *Landnámabók*, and Árni had helped to distribute the books (*PB*: 548). He was already working on his own edition of *Íslendingabók*, a project which is mentioned in *Antiquitates* (Bartholin 1689: 198). He wanted to publish the text for a scholarly audience with a Latin translation and a detailed line-by-line commentary, in accordance with scholarly publishing practice at the time (Grafton 1983, I: 15–16; Murphy 1967: 52). *Íslendingabók* had been unknown until Bishop Brynjólfur Sveinsson found an old vellum at Skálholt and had the Reverend Jón Erlendsson make two copies of it, one of them somewhat better than the other (see pp. 38, 72). The vellum manuscript disappeared but many copies of Jón's transcriptions were made, most of them rather badly done. In around 1686, Árni got hold of one of these. Almost forty years later he claimed that as a young man he had transcribed the text as closely as he could at the time: 'so sem eg þá kunne' (AM 254 8vo: 11r). That may be true, but the text of his exemplar, unfortunately lost, appears not to have been particulary good.

The Skálholt edition of 1688 was based on one of the two transcriptions made by Jón Erlendsson (AM 113 a fol.), with some judicious corrections by Bishop Þórður and Einar Eyjólfsson. The editorial principles are explained in a short introduction but there is neither commentary nor translation. Árni must have realised that the text of this edition was better than the copy he had already made for himself (AM 365 4to). For some unknown reason he did not use the edition in his work but insisted that Þormóður should send him a manuscript of *Íslendingabók* (AM 113 g fol.) in his possession, even though Þormóður reported on 12

November 1688 that the manuscript contained exactly the same text as the one found in the printed edition, so that it would be unnecessary to send it (*BT*: 3). On 5 May 1689 Árni complained that he could not finish his book unless he saw the manuscript and that the delay had been extremely deleterious (*BT*: 14). Árni finally got the manuscript and on sending it back on 12 June he explained that his edition would not appear until some months later (*BT*: 42); something which did not happen. On the basis of Þormóður's manuscript he had added some variants to his own text but should have made more if he had wanted to do a thorough job of the comparison. His text was just as bad as before. In the autumn of 1691 he received from Iceland the two transcriptions made by Jón Erlendsson. AM 113 a fol. came from the Reverend Halldór Torfason at Gaulverjabær and AM 113 b fol. was given to Árni by Þórður Jónsson, who had spent the summer in Iceland (*ÍÆ* V: 103). Árni now corrected his working copy (AM 365 4to) in some places on the basis of AM 113 b fol., improving the text slightly, and also compared the two recently acquired manuscripts to each other (Már Jónsson 1998: 77–8).

Árni also translated *Íslendingabók* into Latin (AM 365 4to), most likely in 1687 or 1688 (*LS* II: 1–15), and produced a line-by-line commentary. Many of the comments are brief explanations of words and names. Some are longer and even constitute short essays, mostly on chronology, for instance concerning King Haraldr hárfagri, who according to *Íslendingabók* unified Norway in the mid-ninth century (AM 364 4to: 282r–290v; *LS* II: 29–33).[2] The most thorough part of the commentary (AM 1029 4to) concerns Sæmundur fróði, who was believed to be the author of the Poetic Edda, at the time consequently known as *Sæmundar Edda*. Árni traced the idea of Sæmundur's authorship to Bishop Brynjólfur Sveinsson and refuted it thoroughly by arguing that the poems were much older and had probably been composed by various authors in pagan times. There was no way of knowing, he claimed, who subsequently wrote the poems down from those who knew them by heart, as the sources kept such information hidden in deep silence: 'qvi qvisnam

---

[2] Finnur Jónsson's edition in *LS* II: 21–85 provides Árni's final version and does not take into account whether his text is written in 1688–90 or much later, nor does it show changes he made.

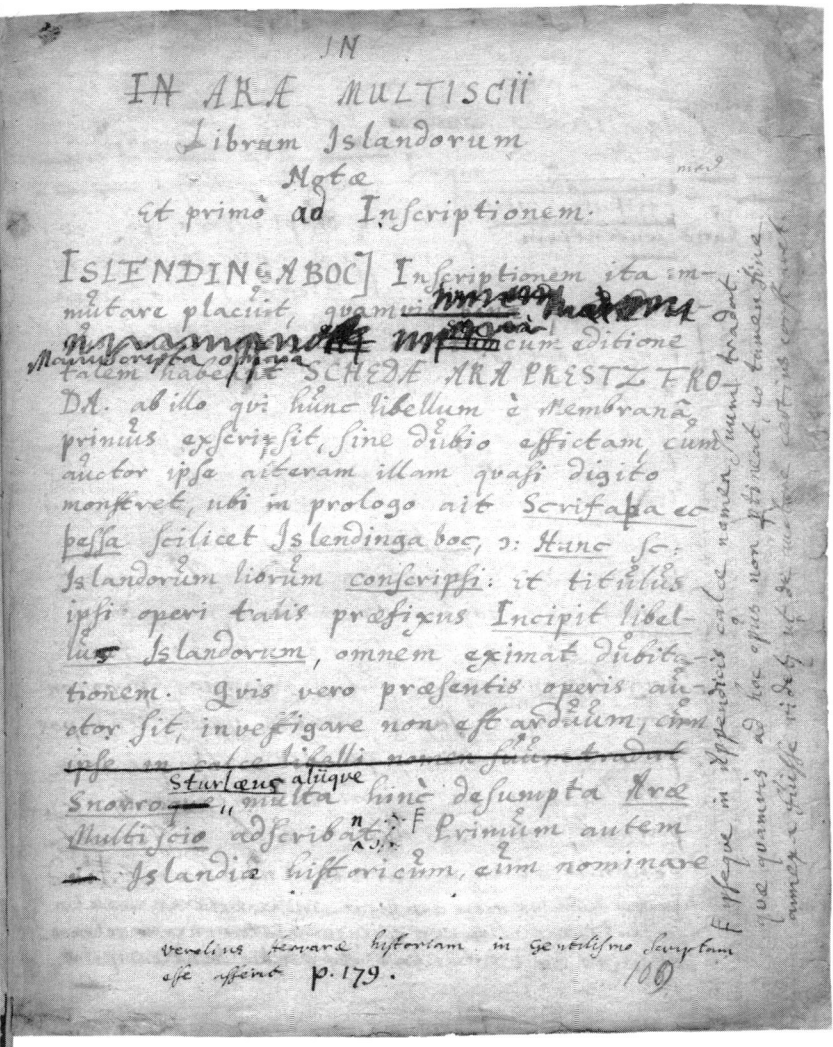

Figure 5. The first page of Árni's commentary on Íslendingabók, with some additions and corrections a few years later (AM 364 4to: 109r).

fuerit, antiqvitates alto silentio prætereunt' (*LS* II: 98–9; Árni Magnússon 2008: 154–5; cf. Gottskálk Jensson 2008; Finnur Jónsson 1930a: 124–6). In his commentary, Árni used the extensive knowledge of medieval texts he had acquired in the previous years, profusely citing other Icelandic works which mention the dramatic events recounted in *Íslendingabók*. Ari fróði's text is barely five thousand words in length but poses intricate questions on chronology, a subject which in 1690 became the matter of an almost feverish correspondence between Árni and Þormóður Torfason. It all began when Árni, on his way back from Stangeland, noticed that Þormóður, at the end of a manuscript of recent annals (AM 412 4to), had commented that King Haraldr hárfagri was born when King Gormr of Denmark had been in power for seven years. On 15 January 1690 Árni asked Þormóður where he had seen this information. Þormóður promptly replied that this was his hypothesis, as medieval annals indicated that Gormr became king in the year 840 and Haraldr was born in 848 (*BT*: 20, 23). Árni replied that there was so much confusion about Haraldr's origins and reign that it was not possible to be sure about anything (*BT*: 58–60). He preferred to use the year 930 as the point from which to work out Haraldr's biography and other issues in Norwegian and Icelandic history. Ari fróði, in *Íslendingabók*, stated that King Haraldr died at the age of eighty, one or two winters later, and Árni wondered whether he was then born in 851 or 852. Other medieval historians had accepted this uncertainty, Árni claimed, but either way changes would have to be made in the reigns of later kings. *Heimskringla* and other medieval sources followed the chronology in *Íslendingabók*, although not always consistently; sometimes, indeed, they seemed to have misunderstood it. Árni professed that foreign sources made matters even more confusing and concluded that he hardly knew how to proceed (*BT*: 72). Þormóður admitted that it would be impossible to reach a satisfying conclusion on a number of chronological details but insisted that only the oldest historians, such as Ari fróði, should be used as sources and not those authors who only followed in their footsteps. No author could be entirely trusted and all of them made conjectures which had to be assessed (*BT*: 53, 99–100). Therefore, Þormóður argued, a scholar like him had to work 'ex hypothesibus', but of course based on datable events (*BT*: 76). The scholar, or better still the community of scholars, should then decide which conjectures were correct. From a letter Þormóður wrote to Árni on 2 October 1690 it is clear that this group included the two of them, in addition to Bartholin (*BT*: 103).

Had it been published, Árni's edition of *Íslendingabók* would have added invaluably to European scholars' knowledge of Icelandic medieval history, first and foremost because of the Latin translation and detailed commentary, but also for its numerous citations of other texts, most of them available only in manuscripts. In a letter to Þormóður on 4 September 1690 Árni said that the book would be out at some point during that winter, and it was indeed accepted for publication in the spring of 1691 (*BT*: 67; AM 254 8vo: 16v). Árni, however, decided to abandon the project and his edition never appeared. Nowhere does he explain this sudden decision but may have reached some sort of a methodological deadlock, as he was unable to recover a satisfying text from the several manuscripts around him and had become hopelessly entangled in complex chronological issues. He may have thought that the edition would not be good enough, and, like Bartholin (see next page), feared the reaction of scholars abroad, perhaps mirroring his own critical attitude towards contemporary scholarship. If one is to believe Peder Deichmann, a Norwegian student of medicine who met him in 1691, Árni's judgment on Danish and Swedish erudition was extremely harsh. The runic inscriptions published by Ole Worm and other Danes were useless, Árni argued, because not a single one of them had correctly interpreted or translated the texts, although Swedish scholars had done a somewhat better job (UB Oslo. Ms. 4to 73: 109–13; *LS* I, 2: 154–6; *BT*: xxix–xxx).

The same attitude appears in a letter to the young and promising Frederik Rostgaard on 3 October 1691, in which Árni fiercely criticised German scholars who wished to dominate their Danish colleagues but had scant knowledge of old texts and took all their information from recent books. For that reason, he argued, the world was replete with false traditions written by tendentious authors whose errors were kept alive by younger scholars who took them for granted and did no research for themselves. The majority of the recent dissertations on Germany, Pommern, Poland, Denmark and Sweden should therefore be burnt. Árni clearly favoured scholars who published old sources instead of only writing on the results of their investigations. Not surprisingly, therefore, he lavished praise on French scholars who had brought to light all kinds of useful sources and always stated where they were to be found: 'med største candore altid sette hos hvor det eller det er fra' (*PB*: 389). This is probably what he intended to do with his scholarly edition of *Íslendingabók* and would have done had he finished it.

Árni adored such old texts and also took great care and pleasure in assessing their value. Along with Bartholin he can be said to belong to a group of moderately sceptical scholars and thinkers who wished to eradicate fables from historical discourse. Historical pyrrhonism (*pyrrhonismus historicus*), as it was called, had its roots in Greek scepticism, whose main thinker was the second-century philosopher Sextus Empiricus. Its main proponents in the late seventeenth century were Hermann Conring and Pierre Bayle. A valid conclusion could well be reached on historical matters, they asserted, but scholars should not claim to be sure of anything. There were many things that could be rejected, but fewer that could be stated with certitude, and nothing was beyond doubt (Scheele 1930: 21–67; Erasmus 1962: 71–6, 108–9; Völkel 1987: 99–185; Whelan 1989: 119–38). A historian would have to assess all available evidence and then decide which of the sources were more credible than others. This kind of work, Jean Mabillon wrote in an essay around 1677, would have to be based on a sincere love for the truth, the basic rule being that some things were indeed certain, others false and yet others doubtful. All arguments should be laid out and nothing kept back which could lead to credible results (Mabillon 1990: 108; cf. Grafton 1999: 258).

This critical attitude can be seen here and there in Bartholin's *Antiquitates* but even more clearly in his own assessment of the book. In a letter to Þormóður on 15 April 1690 Bartholin thanked him for praising the book but added that he himself was not happy with it, partly because he had not been critical enough. Although he had rejected *Þorsteins saga Víkingssonar* he now opined that he should have ignored all such 'fabulous' sagas. He feared that scholars abroad would despise him and regard the book as being built on a foundation of nonsense: 'nugalia fundamenta'. Bartholin added that he had been happy to hear from Árni that Þormóður, in his medieval history of Norway, intended to reject all fables: 'rehecere omnia fabulosa'; he finally advised him to throw out everything that even resembled fiction (AM 285 b fol. I: 33r). This was a far cry from Arngrímur Jónsson's uncritical attitude at the beginning of the century, which has been well described by Jakob Benediktsson: 'His credulous faith in his sources knows almost no bounds... Even the most extravagant exaggerations and fantastic tales are accepted by him in good faith' (1950–7, IV: 52). The prevailing attitude among earlier Danish scholars had been similar. In the preface to his translation of Saxo in 1575 Anders Sørensen Vedel thus emphasised that while not everything recounted in the text was altogether credible it could well be that things had indeed been different in pagan times; what was not considered as unbelievable in Rome or Constantinople might as well be true in Iceland. Vedel even argued that if Saxo were to be discarded the same fate should meet Herodotus, Plutarch and others (Vedel 1967: Biv–r). Ole Worm similarly claimed in 1633 that everything in *Heimskringla* was true and compared it with Greek and Roman works of history which had been proven to be truthful (Ole Worm 1633: preface).

The sagas published in Sweden were also presented as true stories about ancient times. In his preface to *Gautreks saga ok Hrólfs* in 1664, Olof Verelius argued that it narrated what had happened in the past: 'berättar hwad fordom skedt är' (Verelius 1664: preface). Two years later, in the preface to *Herrauðs ok Bósa saga*, he informed the reader that Herrauðr was mentioned by both Saxo and Johannes Magnus, but that Bósi was previously unknown. Verelius was not at all surprised by unbelievable happenings, such as people changing into animals or becoming invisible, as they happened in pagan times. Similar things were described in other Nordic texts but even more in the Old Testament and in works by Latin writers such as Virgil and Ovid, which meant that this saga also should be regarded as truthful (Verelius 1666: preface; cf. Malm 1996: 57–8). The greatest heights of credulity were soon afterwards reached by Olof Rudbeck, professor at Uppsala University, who in 1679–99 published the monumental *Atlantica*, where he connected the history of Sweden with the creation of the world, using whatever sources he could find to support his arguments, among others the recently published sagas (Eriksson 1984: 89–96, 99–101, 108–9).

Þormóður was far from being sceptically inclined and would gladly have accepted most of what Worm and Verelius had said. Bartholin was not the only one who tried to persuade him to change his scholarly ways; Árni did so too as he read through Þormóður's manuscript on the history of the Orkney Islands (see p. 87). In January 1690 Árni pointed out that the author of *Orkneyinga saga* had not been alive at the time of the events he described, thus implying that there was no reason to believe everything he said. Þormóður retorted that he had just stated his personal opinion: 'min opinio' (*BT*: 23). On 3 April Árni further suggested that Þormóður should remove some sentences about Angantýr and Herrauðr taken from *Friðþjófs saga* and *Örvar-Odds saga*, arguing that the story had been made up by Icelanders and would harm an otherwise good book (*BT*: 33; cf. Sveinbjörn Rafnsson 1987: 304). In his reply on 17 July, Þormóður explained that scholars could believe what they wanted but he sincerely considered these passages to be truthful (*BT*: 47). He could not see anything 'fabuleux' in *Friðþjófs saga*, as persons mentioned there also figured in *Gautreks saga* and even in Saxo, who also mentioned Örvar-Oddr and Angantýr; he would never declare that these men had not existed (*BT*: 49). He added that Árni ought to write a treatise on all these sagas, where he would distinguish between those which were authentic and those which should be rejected. It had to be explained, though, that there were fabulous elements even in the best sagas. This treatise could be put with the preface of his book (*BT*: 51). Four days later Þormóður wrote an equally defensive reply to Bartholin's letter of 15 April, claiming that foreign scholars were not always right. Nonetheless he had decided to cut out whatever appeared to be fictive: 'alt som siunis at haffue speciem fabulæ'. His book would for this reason become much shorter, he lamented, and a lot of his painstaking work would be wasted (AM 283 fol.: 69v).

On 4 September 1690 Árni insisted by expressing his disdain for *Hrólfs saga Gautrekssonar*, *Bósa saga*, *Þorsteins saga Víkingssonar*, *Sturlaugs saga starfsama* 'et similibus', such as *Egils saga einhenda*, *Friðþjófs saga*, *Sörla saga sterka* and *Örvar-Odds saga*, for the simple reason that neither the names nor the events ('res gestas') they contained appear in the writings of more trustworthy authors. These sagas were composed as late as the fourteenth century and yet their authors purported to know more than older authors like Ari fróði and Snorri Sturluson. This greatly reduced their credibility (*BT*: 66). Þormóður reacted on 10 October by complaining that if these sagas were made up in the fourteenth century and he was to disregard them completely, the first three parts of his planned book on the history of Norway would become very short. As before, he proposed to use whatever material he had found and now argued that the reader could decide what to believe. A lengthy treatise on the sources would have to be included and Saxo should not be spared criticism (*BT*: 94). Þormóður never really changed his mind on the Icelandic sagas and kept on defending their credibilty. Returning to the issue in a letter to Árni on 28 March 1691 he declared that he could not accept that *Hrólfs saga kraka* and *Ragnars saga loðbrókar* were fables and only admitted that they contained some hyperbole: 'utan það at þær seu ychtar'. He also found it unbelievable that Sigurðr Fáfnisbani and Brynhildr Buðladóttir had not existed (*BT*: 129).

Survival

In a letter to Þormóður on 3 April 1690, Árni explained that it was impossible for anyone to live off scholarship alone: 'vid antiqvitet ad lifa'. Árni had been offered the position of vice-magistrate in Iceland with 200 rigsdaler per year but feared that it would not be possible to live well without marriage to a woman of means; something, it seems, he did not desire. He was reluctant to look for a scholarly position in Sweden because he would not be allowed to return to Copenhagen on account of the political animosity between the two countries. He did not want to become a priest in Denmark and would rather be a judge or something similar but did not have contacts with men powerful enough to ensure him such a position. He was close to desperation ('sosem halfdesperat') and wished that he was eighty years old (*BT*: 34). Þormóður replied that he should become thirty before he wanted to be eighty and suggested a position as vice-bishop at Skálholt. He agreed that Árni should not move to Sweden and mentioned England as a more feasible option (*BT*: 40).

Árni asked on 12 June whether Þormóður knew of any positions in Norway and once again expressed his unwillingness to return to Iceland or move to Sweden (*BT*: 42). Such were his feelings at the age of 26, as he probably realised that he was stuck in a job with no future. The man who employed him, Thomas Bartholin, was only four years older and had gained all the positions to which a fledgling scholar could aspire. On 10 July, Þormóður speculated whether Willum Worm would soon become a member of the Supreme Court. Bartholin would then take over as royal historiographer for Denmark and Árni could replace him as royal antiquarian (*BT*: 44–5). As this was written, Þormóður did not know that Bartholin had become seriously ill with tuberculosis. He died on 5 November, a few days after his wife, Anne Tisdorph, gave birth to their first son (*BT*: 111n; Ehrencron-Müller I: 290–1). On 27 December Árni asked Þormóður to recommend him to Matthias Moth for the position as royal antiquarian, which Þormóður promptly did in unambiguous terms, claiming that Árni was the best scholar around and in possession of knowledge nobody else had (*BT*: 111–12; AM 283 fol.: 125v). On 22 April 1691 Árni told Þormóður that he did not dare to speak with Moth. Little by little, however, they became acquainted and by the autumn Árni was a regular guest at Moth's house for dinner (Már Jónsson 1998: 100; Finnur Jónsson 1930a: 19–20, 25).

In the spring of 1691, Árni was one of sixteen students to lodge in a new residence built in Store Kannikestræde with money donated by the recently-deceased Ole Borch, professor of chemistry (Olrik 1889: 7–15, 18–22, 47, 65; Julius Petersen 1898: 122–4, 135–7). In a letter to Frederik Rostgaard on 3 October Árni listed the names of the students and their fields of study, including himself: 'Arnas Magnæus, Philologus'. The students received a generous stipend of 58 rigsdaler per year; two students shared an apartment with two spacious rooms, a stove, two tables, two chairs and one bed. Every student had once a year to deliver a public lecture; originally it was Borch who chose the topics, such as what Eve might have said when the snake deceived her (*PB*: 387; Olrik 1889: 27–30). One of the three lectures given by Árni during his stay at the college followed this what-if formula, as he in 1691 discussed what Hannibal might have said when he lost his eye on the expedition over the Alps: 'Quid opportune potuerit dicere Hannibal, amisso in Alpibus oculo?' In 1692 and 1693, however, Árni talked on the christianisation of Norway: 'De initiis Christianæ religionis in Norvegia'. Copies of these lectures were kept in the college library but perished with the building in the Great Fire of 1728 (Már Jónsson 1998: 106–7, 362; Finnur Jónsson 1930a: 27).

After Bartholin's death Árni was hired by his family to finish the first volume of an ecclesiastical history of Denmark. He also arranged the sale of Bartholin's library, comprising some 2500 books, which took place on 15 June 1691. Árni himself acquired several manuscripts from the collection, such as *Óláfs saga Tryggvasonar* and *Óláfs saga helga* (AM 61 fol.), *Möðruvallabók* (AM 132 fol.), *Stjórn* (AM 228 fol.) and *Jónsbók* (AM 126 4to), which Hannes Þorleifsson had given to Bartholin in 1678 (Már Jónsson 1998: 102, 112). In the winter of 1691–2 Árni often declared himself to be busy, although he never mentioned the nature of his work (*BT*: 151; *PB*: 389). He was not at that time actually studying at the university and the stipend at Borchs Collegium was probably provided because of Bartholin's ecclesiastical history, which, however, he hardly touched. His writing only appears in the margins of one of the eight volumes in which Bartholin had ordered events chronologically (Barth. XVII: years 1038, 1085, 1099). Árni may have done some work in Moth's library but did not assist him in a project to produce a Danish dictionary. Shortly before Bartholin's death, Árni mentions in a letter to Þormóður the task of translating drafts for a new lawbook for Iceland which Icelandic officials had been asked to compose on the basis of King Christian V's Norwegian law (*Norske lov*) of 1687. Árni may have done some of this, although nothing in his hand has been preserved (Már Jónsson 1998: 95–6, 108; Gísli Baldur Róbertsson 2004: 47–8). His private projects are not well known either. In the summer of 1693 he hoped that some students would come from Iceland who were competent enough to transcribe some medieval law amendments for Þormóður (*BT*: 168). Only Jón Einarsson arrived that autumn, however (Bjarni Jónsson 1949: 53). He made no transcriptions for Árni, who apparently had no time any more for the copying of old texts. The only known transcriptions from the years 1691–4 were made by Jón Gíslason, who copied the church laws of Archbishop Jón rauðr and King Sverrir (AM 327 fol.) and the town law of Bergen (AM 76 a 4to).

It is certain, on the other hand, that Árni's collection of manuscripts kept growing. In a letter to Þormóður on 4 April 1689 he had emphasised the necessity of inquiring about such antiquities. Þormóður agreed and insisted that no bit of vellum should be lost: 'ætti því enginn leppur at tynast' (*BT*: 8–9, 12). In Bergen, on his way to Stangeland, Árni had acquired a manuscript of the Norwegian general law of 1274 (AM 78 4to) and a few weeks later he compared its text to a manuscript in Þormóður's possession (AM 65 4to). When passing through Bergen again Árni composed a poem about Schoolmaster Edvard Edvardsen, who gave him a manuscript of *Sverris saga* (AM 327 4to) (*LS* II: 309–10; Holm-Olsen 1981: 32–3). Árni also got hold of a manuscript containing *Örvar-Odds saga* and *Alexanders saga* (AM 344 a 4to, AM 519 a 4to), which Þormóður earlier had thought would be impossible to acquire from the heirs of the Reverend Geertz Miltzow (*BT*: 11, 14, 16, 20; Jón Helgason 1966: xiv–xv).

On Árni's instigation, Bishop Þórður Þorláksson at Skálholt had tried to locate the legendary *Hauksbók*, first mentioned in correspondence between various Icelanders and Ole Worm six decades earlier (see p. 33). On 20 August 1689 Þórður explained that those men who had knowledge about old manuscripts lay on that information as a serpent lies on gold ('ormur á gulli'), mostly because they were aware that few manuscripts remained in the country. Most of them had been taken to Copenhagen or elsewhere (*PB*: 549). Interestingly, Þórður used the same serpentine metaphor as the Reverend Torfi Jónsson four years earlier and the Reverend Magnús Ólafsson in 1632 (see pp. 32, 63). The great task for a collector of manuscripts, then, was to identify these 'serpents' and persuade them to let go of their 'gold'. Bishop Brynjólfur Sveinsson had indeed been quite successful in the years before 1662 and the results of Jón Eggertsson were encouraging. Nothing much had been found in the Danish campaign of 1685–6, however, although Árni did get a few vellums for himself (see pp. 64–7). Had Iceland now been emptied of manuscripts or were they hidden and only waiting to be found?

As it happened, many more manuscripts were discovered by Árni's tireless efforts in the following years. His dealings with friends and other informants in Iceland were fraught with frustration, though, because letters could only be sent with merchant ships that left Copenhagen in the spring and returned in the autumn. If someone did not reply or the answer was unsatisfactory, Árni would have to wait for a whole year. On 25 May 1691 he informed Magnús Jónsson at Vigur, an avid collector of manuscripts, that *Bjarnar saga Hítdælakappa* could not be completed. The same applied to other sagas which they had swapped earlier, Árni added, since they were copied from partly damaged manuscripts which were unique. With his letter Árni sent some shorter texts (*söguþættir*), one of which he had found in a fragment of *Víga-Skúta saga*. He had not yet received *Heiðarvíga saga* and *Víga-Styrs saga* from Sweden, nor a copy of *Virgils saga víðfræga* from a good friend. Magnús had complained that he provided more texts than he received and Árni now replied that it was difficult and expensive to get Icelanders in Copenhagen to transcribe texts. He would only be able to pay back with assistance on more mundane matters such as helping Magnús with an application to the king on testamentary dispositions (*PB*: 242–4; on Magnús, see Jón Helgason 1955: 7–14). That autumn, Árni received a vellum containing *Snorra Edda* (AM 748 II 4to) and some eddic poems (AM 748 I a–b 4to) from the Reverend Halldór Torfason at Gaulverjabær, son of the Reverend Torfi Jónsson. Árni also received the two copies of *Íslendingabók* made by Jón Erlendsson, mentioned earlier (p. 90). His field of interest expanded and he started to gather information on the younger Icelandic sagas, at first by producing and asking for summaries of individual texts, such as *Nítíða saga*, *Sigurðar saga þögla* and *Dámusta saga*. Such a collection in his hand is preserved, written in around 1690 (AM 576 c 4to), and from Einar Eyjólfsson, who died in 1695, he received another one, containing what he called 'extracta' (AM 576 a 4to); in his aforementioned letter to Magnús Jónsson at Vigur he called this sort of summary 'inntak' (*PB*: 244; *LS* II: 176–7; cf. Wäckerlin 2004).

In the autumn of 1692, two Icelandic clergymen came to Copenhagen hoping to fill the vacant position as bishop of Hólar. The Reverend Björn Þorleifsson at Oddi had been with Árni at school in Skálholt and had attended Copenhagen University in 1684–6. The more experienced

Reverend Einar Þorsteinsson at Múli got the position and Björn was made vice-bishop with a letter of expectation to succeed him (Bjarni Jónsson 1949: 45; ÍÆ I: 258, 395). Einar presented Árni with a now lost manuscript of *Kristinréttr Árna* of 1275, which the new owner promptly compared to a recent copy of his own (AM 182 a 4to). Einar also promised that on his return to Iceland he would send a copy of *Reykdæla saga* (Jón Helgason 1977: 51). Björn Þorleifsson had only shown Árni a volume containing several sagas, some of which were written by Jón Erlendsson, whereas he gave King Christian V a collection of sagas transcribed recently on parchment (GKS 1002–1003 fol.). When the king asked Árni to translate some of those sagas he replied that he had already translated the only one of interest, that is *Hrólfs saga kraka*. He argued that the other sagas were romances and pure fiction ('enten Romaner og pure Fabeler') but declared himself willing to translate them if the king so desired, adding that he had a number of more noteworthy Icelandic texts which he could translate (*BE*: 126–7; *PB*: 337; Slay 1960a: 23–24; Slay 1960b).

In the autumn of 1693 Árni first got news about *Reykjarfjarðarbók* (AM 122 b fol.) from Ari Þorkelsson, sheriff of Barðastrandarsýsla, who informed him that the Reverend Jón Ólafsson at Lambavatn had discovered some leaves of a vellum containing *Sturlunga saga*. Ari had seen one of them. Next spring, Árni asked Ari to acquire that leaf and gather more information about the other ones (*PB*: 532). At the same time he asked Björn Þorleifsson to specify which sagas, out of those he had with him in Copenhagen, had been transcribed by Jón Erlendsson. He also wanted a vellum of *Njáls saga* (AM 466 4to) which Björn had mentioned in conversations; that was the saga Árni now needed the most: 'su saga sem mig hellst vantar' (*PB*: 552). If Björn could not acquire the manuscript Árni wished to know who owned it, presumably intending to persuade the owner to sell it. Björn had also said that he knew about some old lawbooks and Árni wanted as many as he could get his hands on, the more the better. The next paragraph summarises his thoughts at the time and can be seen as a manifesto:

Survival

I have told my brother earlier how greatly I desire parchment books, even if it is only half a leaf or the smallest fragment, only if it is on parchment, and even though I already have a hundred copies of the same text; for which reason I often have dismantled books and removed their covers, if something of that kind was found.

[...] hefe eg og minum brodur til forna sagt hve superstitiosè eg pergaments bækur þráe, iafnvel þott þad ei være nema eitt half blad, eda ringasta rifrillde, þegar þad ickun være a pergament, og iafnvel þo eg 100 exemplaria af þvi sama hefde, hvar firir eg og offtlega hefi rúed qver og involucra af þeim tekið, þa nockud soddan hefur a vered (*PB*: 553).

The letter continues with a number of detailed requests. Árni urgently needed a vellum fragment containing *Klerkarímur*, *Ormarsrímur* and *Pontusrímur* which he had also asked for a year earlier. He promised to send it back next spring. He was grateful for what Björn had sent him the year before, but could not believe that a text of *Sturlaugs saga starfsama* had been copied correctly. He therefore sent it back and asked Björn to compare it with two other copies in his possession. Árni knew that Björn had two recent manuscripts of *Hrólfs saga kraka* and wanted one of them transcribed with wide margins and variants from the other one carefully written in the margins. Árni also wanted to know more about the poem *Einvaldsóður*, which he had seen in one of Björn's manuscripts. Finally, he inquired about the contents of a vellum that the Reverend Jón Sigmundsson at Þykkvabæjarklaustur had recently lent to Ólafur Einarsson, whose brother Ísleifur apparently collected sagas, and Árni wanted information on his manuscripts: 'mætti vita hveriar hann hefdi' (*PB*: 553–4). Such were the requests he would write in hundreds of letters and express in conversation over the years to come, as he relentlessly sought information on manuscripts and documents, which he then would want to own, or at least to copy.

5
Success

> I have so much to do, and almost all of it worthless, that I am sick of myself.
>
> Eg hefi so mikid ad giöra, og þó snart allt einskisvert, ad eg er leidur af mier sialfum.
>
> Árni Magnússon 2 October 1700 (*BT*: 310)

When Árni Magnússon's fellowship at Borchs Collegium expired in the spring of 1694 he had consolidated his scholarly standing. This chapter describes his two-and-a-half-year stay in Leipzig and his subsequent re-establishment in Copenhagen, where he first obtained the position of secretary to the Royal Archives and a few years later became professor at Copenhagen University. He kept collecting manuscripts and stated confidently in 1699 that he had the best collection of Icelandic texts ever assembled.

Leipzig

In May 1694 the Consistory of professors at Copenhagen University decided to send 'Arnas Magnæus Islandus' to the city of Stettin in Pommern in order to negotiate the donation of a collection of oriental manuscripts and printed books which the scholar Andreas Müller wished to give to the University Library on the promise that the collection would be kept intact (on the details of this trip, see Már Jónsson 1999). Müller claimed to have devised a key to the Chinese language but refused to publish the details, and the philosopher Gottfried Wilhelm Leibniz bemoaned in 1697 that either Müller 'esteemed his invention excessively or doubted that it should be brought to light while not sufficiently perfected' (Leibniz 1994: 56). Árni would not have had the means to travel or study in Europe on his own, as some of his fellow students and friends had done; his friend Frederik Rostgaard, for example, spent the years 1689–99 in Oxford, Giessen, Leiden, Paris, Milan, Rome, Naples and Leipzig, buying books and copying manuscripts in many outstanding libraries (*PB*: 386, 394–9; Weber 1775; Bruun 1870a: 18–77; Röhn 1994: 515–17). Established scholars also travelled to search for manuscripts and documents. Jean Mabillon travelled through Switzerland and southern Germany in 1683 and went to Italy two years later in the pursuit of sources relating to ecclesiastical history; Leibniz similarly went all over Italy in the years 1689–92 in search of information on the early history of the dukes of Braunschweig, his employers (Mabillon 2007: 82–98, 118–85; Bergkamp 1928: 52–71; Robinet 1988; Davillé 1909: 83–96; Antognazza 2009: 281–93).

Árni's journey to Germany was also seen by his patrons as an occasion for him to pursue research in connection with the Danish ecclesiastical history he had inherited from Thomas Bartholin. Matthias Moth was most certainly involved in the decision to allow Árni to travel, and also the renowned professor and scientist Ole Rømer, who was rector of the university at the time (Friedrichsen and Tortzen 2001: 57). Árni travelled via Rostock to Stettin and on 28 July complained to Þormóður Torfason that Stettin University was nothing to be proud of; if other German universities were no better, he added, there was no reason for Danes to study there at all (*BT*: 179). The negotiations with Andreas Müller came to nothing but Árni consulted some of his manuscripts and read in one of them that the Vatican Library had burnt down in 1527 and the City Library of Stettin half a century later. He saw a map of Europe made by Jesuit missionaries in China, in which Norway and Sweden were an island and Greenland only twice as big as Iceland. Denmark was so small that it could hardly be made out (AM 909 A 4to: 510r). Müller, on the other hand, saw Árni's edition of *Íslendingabók* and may have taken some notes, as Árni later reminisced (AM 254 8vo: 21r). As for the oriental manuscripts, Árni does not say a word about them in his letters or notes and may have been unaware of how keen scholars all over Europe would have been to know more about Müller's key to the Chinese language.

Leipzig

From Stettin Árni went to Berlin. In the library of the Elector of Brandenburg he was impressed with a printed catalogue of all books starting with the letter A. This was the first out of 24 planned volumes in alphabetical order and Árni doubted that such an undertaking could be accomplished by one man (AM 909 A 4to: 524r; cf. *LS* II: 202–3). Árni then headed for Leipzig. Out of 320 Danish, Norwegian and Icelandic students who went abroad in the last two decades of the seventeenth century, 62 studied in Leipzig, 72 in Leiden, 38 in Kiel and 34 in Oxford (Helk 1991, I: 84–5; cf. Erik Petersen 1998: 129). Árni's Danish friend Niels Foss was already in Leipzig and three Norwegians that Árni knew were on their way (Helk 1991, II: 87, 113; Erler 1909, II: 50, 99, 111, 495). Árni enrolled for the autumn term 1694 as 'Dalas Arnas Magnenus Isla Island', as it says in the register, the first word undoubtedly referring to the district of Dalasýsla, his place of birth (Erler 1909, II: 71; Helk 1991, II: 188). For the next two years he spent most of his time in the University Library (Bibliotheca Paulina). The Swedish scholar Olof Celsius met him in the spring of 1696 and describes in his journal how they collected the keys from the librarian Christoph Pfautz in the morning and spent the whole day among the books and manuscripts. In their conversations Árni bragged that in Copenhagen he owned all Icelandic sagas: 'alla Isländske Sagor tillsammans'. He was highly critical of Swedish scholars who exaggerated the feats of Swedish medieval kings. He claimed to Celsius that Icelandic scholars who worked at the Swedish Institute of Antiquities were incompetent and did not transcribe their exemplars correctly; they used their own orthography based on the current pronunciation because they did not understand the abbreviations in the manuscripts (*LS* I, 2: 158–9). Similarly, Árni had some months earlier written to Þormóður from Stettin that two recently published Swedish books were so bad that one could touch the lies: 'ad madr kann ad þreifa a lígenni' (*BT*: 180).

The notes that Árni wrote while in Leipzig are easily recognisable because of the very thin paper he used (AM 909 A–E 4to, AM 231 a–f 8vo). Previously he had only worked with Icelandic, Norwegian and Danish manuscripts, but now came to see a greater variety. In order to find his way he used a catalogue published by Joachim Feller in 1686:

Success

Catalogus Codicum Mssctorum Bibliothecae Paulinae in Academia Lipsiensi. Out of nearly a thousand manuscripts listed there Árni seems to have taken a close look at around fifty. He had scant interest in biblical manuscripts or medieval theological works, of which there were many, preferring historical works and the lives of saints. Both categories relate to his obligatory work on Bartholin's church history. In Berlin he had consulted a manuscript with some information about a Danish bishop from the late fifteenth century (AM 909 B 4to: 576–82). In Leipzig he also found some texts concerning dioceses in the northern regions of Germany which he paraphrased or transcribed (AM 909 B 4to: 101–15, 583–609). Árni's interest in the lives of medieval saints was also relevant to his work on medieval Icelandic bishops' sagas and related to his admiration for the text editions being produced at the time in Antwerp and Paris. According to Celsius, Árni had plans to send a Latin translation of *Jóns saga helga* to the scholar Daniel Papebroch in Antwerp, but that probably never happened (*LS* I, 2: 159; Foote 2003: 123*).

The bulk of Árni's German notes consists of transcriptions of passages and lists of the content of manuscripts, but in rare moments his notes include an assessment of the material he was reading. After transcribing a passage from a manuscript containing saints' lives, to take an example, he observes that all the texts are short and of good quality: 'Omnes autem hæ vitæ breves sunt et exigui momenti' (AM 909 D 4to: 222v). Another such manuscript gets criticised for its lack of veracity, as it was replete with miracles and lies. The last part, though, was excellent (AM 909 E 4to: 70v). Árni was not a 'polyhistor' in the sense that he found all subjects within human experience fascinating (Grafton 1985: 33–4, 37–9; Erik Petersen 1998: 113–14). He concentrated on history and geography, ranging far and wide in those fields. He looked at travel books, atlases and general works on geography (AM 909 D 4to: 109–25, 416–19). He noted different ways of calculating the years from the creation of the world and made a list of books on the invention of writing (AM 909 A 4to: 320r, 324v). Books from the years 1480 to 1520 were one of his passions. He made extensive notes about the writings of the Italian humanist Flavio Biondo on the history of Rome and Italy, printed in Verona and Venice between 1481 and 1511, for example; even comparing those editions with

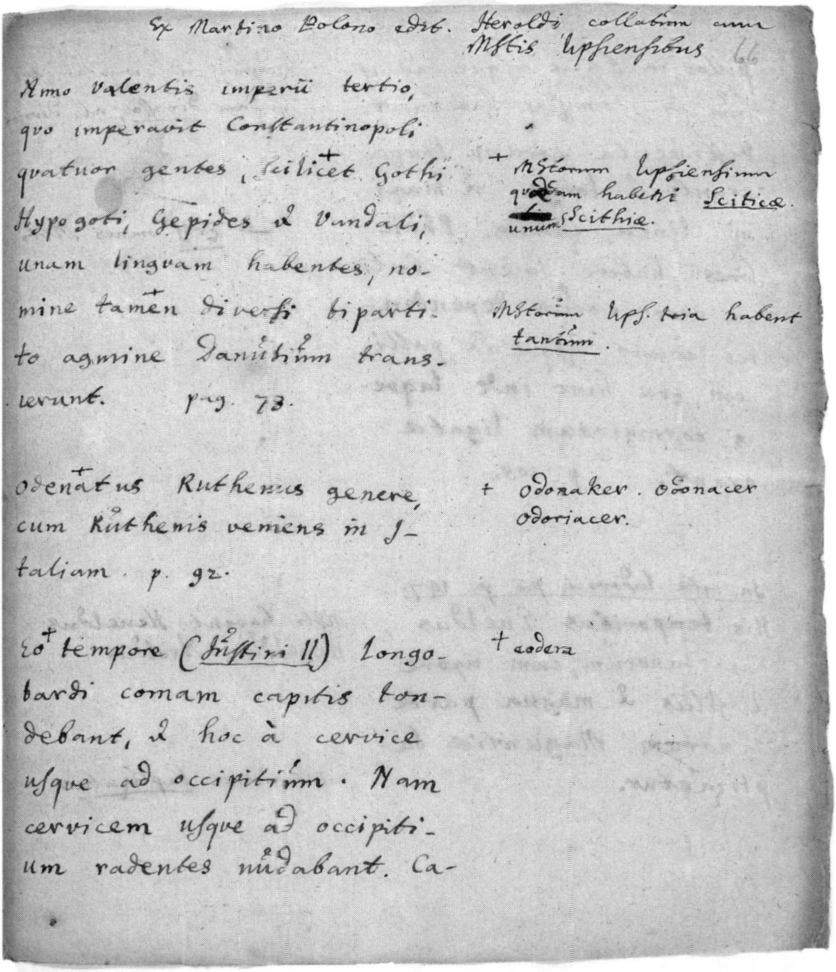
Ex Martino Polono edit. Heroldi collatum cum
MStis Upsensibus 66

Anno Valentis imperii tertio,
quo imperavit Constantinopoli,
quatuor gentes, scilicet Gothi,
Hypogoti, Gepides et Vandali,
unam linguam habentes, no-
mine tamen diversi biparti-
to agmine Danubium trans-
ierunt. pag. 73.

+ MStorum Upsiensium quaedam habent Scitice. unum Scithiae.

MStorum Ups. tria habent tantum.

Odenatus Ruthenus genere,
cum Ruthenis veniens in I-
taliam. p. 92.

+ Odoaker. Odonacer Odoriacer.

Eo tempore (Justini II) Longo-
bardi comam capitis ton-
debant, et hoc à cervice
usque ad occipitium. Nam
cervicem usque ad occipitium radentes nudabant. Ca-

+ eodem

Figure 6. One of Árni's extensive studies of books and manuscripts in Leipzig; see further on p. 110 (AM 909 E 4to: 66r).

Biondo's collected works published in 1531 (AM 909 A 4to: 59r–60r). After reading Jacopo Bracelli's description of Liguria, printed in Paris in 1520, which included some letters to Biondo, Árni emitted a rare burst of enthusiasm concerning that wonderful book, adding in parenthesis that he had read it: 'exiguum est opusculum (legi)' (AM 909 A 4to: 67r).

The first printed editions of medieval texts fascinated Árni, who noted that Konrad Peutinger observed that his 1515 edition of 'Jornandes de Rebus Gothorum' and 'Paulus Diaconus... de Gestis Langobardorum' was the first ever. Árni also noted that the same claim was made by Jodocus Badius in his edition of Gregory of Tours, printed in Paris in 1512 (AM 909 A 4to: 35r, 41r). From Konrad Celtis's edition of the plays of the illustrious nun Hrotsvitha, printed in Nürnberg in 1501, Árni copied the table of contents and the editor's statement that the manuscript was old and had been written by a woman (AM 909 A 4to: 34r). He also relished comparing printed editions with manuscripts that he had access to in the library. Thus, on six pages, he compared an edition of the thirteenth-century chronicle by Martinus Polonus with four manuscripts, using a printed edition as the main text and entering manuscript variants in a wide right-hand margin (AM 909 E 4to: 66r–68r). He also compared first printed editions with more recent editions, concluding at one point that Hermann Conring's edition of *Germania* by Tacitus from 1678 was better than the first edition of 1470. Árni compared the entire text of these two books line for line, but skipped obvious typographical errors: 'crassiora et manifesta typographica vitia omisi' (AM 909 D 4to: 170r). In general he was critical of recent editions in which the orthography had often been modernised and even the words changed, so that the text was corrupted and its meaning garbled (AM 909 E 4to: 94r).

Judging from Árni's letters to Þormóður in the years 1689–92 he was desperate to get a secure position in Copenhagen, something he expected Matthias Moth to provide (see p. 98). A few weeks after Árni left for Germany, Moth did exactly that, using his influence to obtain a letter of expectation for Árni to be made professor at Copenhagen University (*Emb*: 1). This meant that he would have to publish something in order to convince learned circles in Denmark that he deserved that coveted position. During his first months in Leipzig he went between publishers and printers asking for prices on behalf of Þormóður, who thought that it would be cheaper to print his book on the history of the Orkney Islands there rather than in Copenhagen. Árni concluded that this would be complicated and too costly; Holland might be a better choice (*BT*: 181–2). As for his own projects, Árni had brought with him a transcription of an early thirteenth-century fragment containing a narrative on Danish medieval kings (*Sögubrot af fornkonungum*). The fragment (AM 1 e β I fol.) had probably been given to him by Bishop Þórður Þorláksson of Skálholt in 1687 along with *Knýtlinga saga* (AM 20 b I fol.). In a letter to Þormóður on 2 March 1695 Árni asserted that his Icelandic-Latin edition of *Sögubrot* would be far more correct than current copies. The book would be ready in May and was to be dedicated to Moth, but nobody should know that until its publication (*BT*: 184).

The book was never published, which Árni, in a letter to Þormóður dated 29 June, blamed on the reluctance of printers who had problems with reproducing a text in Icelandic (*BT*: 189). Árni's meticulous transcription has been preserved (AM 1 d α fol.); in 1829 it was praised for its accuracy by Carl Christian Rafn who, after comparing it with the vellum, stated that not a single letter was out of place (Rafn 1829–30, I: xxiii; cf. Petersens and Olson 1919–25: ix). All abbreviations have been expanded but are indicated to a certain extent by dots under the added letters. Árni retained the letter 'ø' but not the 'r-rotunda' or 'ð', and for the small capital 'R' he used 'rr' (AM 1 e β I fol.: 1r; AM 1 d α fol.: 1r–v). He divided the pages with a drawn line and only wrote in the inner columns. After the transcription he wrote detailed notes on the errors and difficulties of the text, for instance that the spelling 'Sviþioð' occurs seven times in the fragment and the spelling 'Sviðioð' five times. He also speculated on the dubious truthfulness of the saga (AM 1 e β II fol.: 5r, 21r). The beginning of the text is missing in the vellum and Árni suggested what it may have contained (25r–v). A draft Latin translation of the text follows and Árni appears constantly to have changed his mind, crossing over entire paragraphs and making changes in almost every line (26r–30r). Árni's edition was thus far from ready, and this, rather than the reluctance of printers, was probably the reason why it was never finished or published (Már Jónsson 1998: 134–6, 367; Finnur Jónsson 1930a: 32–3).

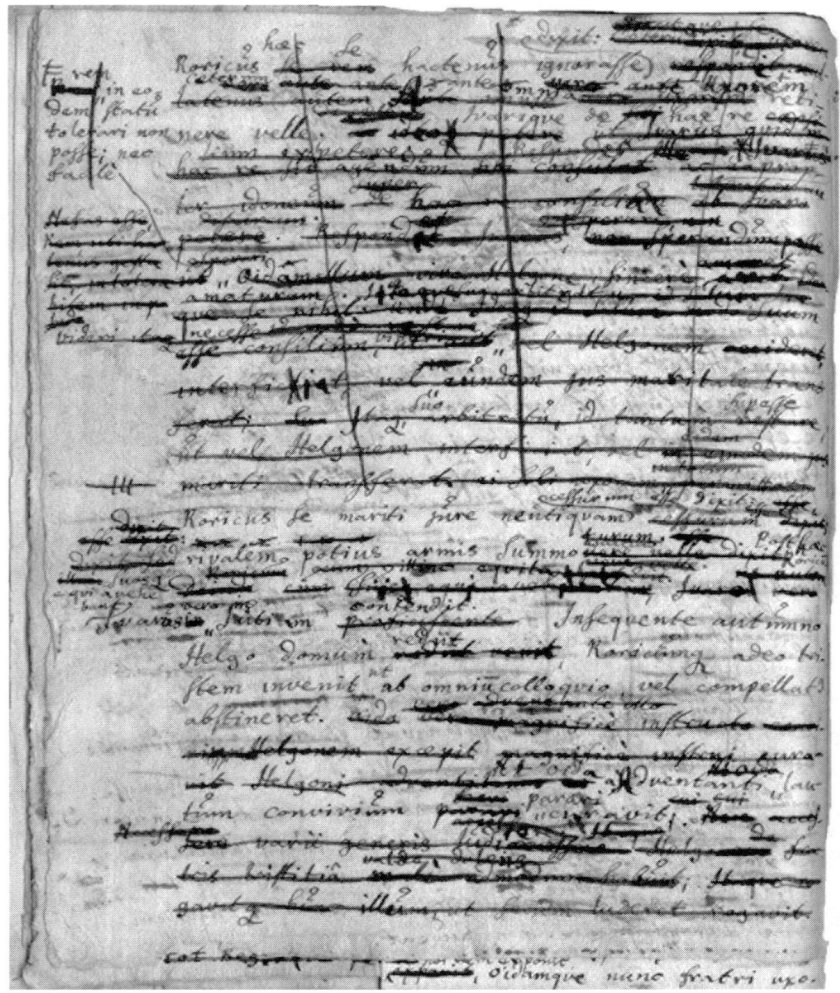

Figure 7. It seems unlikely that Árni would ever have managed to finish this draft of a translation of Sögubrot *(AM 1 e β II fol.: 28v).*

Leipzig

The only Icelandic texts published with Latin translations until then were the Poetic Edda and *Snorra Edda* in Copenhagen in 1665. Swedish editions had so far only contained Swedish translations (see p. 41). There was scant interest in Icelandic medieval literature in learned European circles and correspondingly little knowledge of it either. For example, neither Swedish nor Danish editions nor translations of Icelandic texts are mentioned in a general presentation on necessary learning for students at the University of Leipzig, published by Adam Rechenberg in 1691. Latin and Greek authors dominate and the only books on Danish history are Saxo's *Gesta Danorum* and the *Rerum Danicarum historia* by Johan Isaksen Pontanus, published in Amsterdam in 1631 (Rechenberg 1691: 155). The dominance of the classical languages among learned men may have influenced Árni's decision to edit a Latin text instead of an Icelandic one. He had also brought to Leipzig a transcription of a Danish medieval annal and when, on 29 June 1695, he informed Þormóður that *Sögubrot* would not appear in print he added that he would instead publish a 'Chronicon Sialandiæ' (*BT*: 189). This time Árni was both quick and efficient in his work. Before the end of the year the book was published with the title *Incerti Auctoris Chronica Danorum & præcipuè Sialandiæ*. The text was taken from an old vellum manuscript ('ex pervetusto codice membraneo') kept at the University Library in Copenhagen, which Thomas Bartholin had used in his book *Antiquitates* (Bartholin 1689: 131). In his edition, Árni added variants from a manuscript which he had come upon in Berlin on his way to Leipzig. The laudatory dedication to Moth is dated 12 August 1695 and in a short introduction addressed to the reader Árni laments Bartholin's early death. He mentions earlier Danish scholars who had referred to the chronicle and explains his own role as editor in terms of cleansing the innumerable errors committed by the scribe of the vellum, who had misunderstood some of the abbreviations and letter-forms that looked alike. There follows a list of his corrections and a few lines on the putative author of the annal, a Danish monk who died in 1283. Árni then asks the reader to be fair in his judgment of the work, but if praise was not forthcoming he promised to hide himself behind famous scholars, such as Goldast, Pistorius, Lindenbrog, Meibom, Twysden and Mabillon, who had published comparable texts

(Árni Magnússon 1695: preface; Sveinbjörn Rafnsson 1987: 307; Geertz 1917–22, II: 2–4, 12–13).

Árni left Leipzig in October or November 1696, travelling through Halle, Helmstedt and Wittenberg. His letters reveal that he would have wanted to go through Holland and England but could not afford it (Már Jónsson 1999: 230–1). In Lübeck he hoped to see a manuscript containing two historical works written at the end of the twelfth century, the *Historia Norwegica* by Theodoricus and the narrative of a Danish expedition to Palestine (*Profectio Danorum Hierosolymam*). The manuscript had been discovered in the City Library by Johann Kirchmann in the early 1620s and the text published by his grandson, Bernhard Caspar Kirchmann, in 1684. When Árni arrived in Lübeck the manuscript had disappeared (AM 909 C 4to: 114r; *PB*: 269; Skovgaard-Petersen 2002b: 108–11, 114–26).

As Árni returned to Copenhagen, some days before Christmas, Matthias Moth provided him with lodging and food (*PB*: 556; *BT*: 192). The positions which Thomas Bartholin had held in Copenhagen were all still vacant, even though more than six years had passed since he died. No royal antiquarian had been appointed and there was no professor of history at the university (Ilsøe and Hørby 1980: 325–6). An official in the Danish Chancery took care of the Royal Archives as Bartholin's secretarial position had not been filled. It may be presumed that Árni would have been interested in all of these jobs, and indeed, on 20 February 1697, Moth arranged a royal appointment for Árni to become the archival secretary (*Emb*: 5–6). In his Icelandic biography of 1759, Jón Ólafsson relates (allegedly following Árni himself) that at some point Moth asked Árni what he planned to do with himself. Árni saw no other option, owing to lack of money, than to go back to Iceland in the spring. Moth then suggested that he should rather try to provide for himself in Copenhagen. One evening, Jón Ólafsson continues, Árni was reading a book in his room in Moth's house. When summoned for dinner he claimed not to be hungry. Moth then left the house but not for long. He returned with a letter, put it on a dish and had it carried to Árni, asking whether he liked this dinner better: 'hvert honum liki þessi aftans kostur betur'. The letter revealed that the king had indeed appointed Árni as secretary to the Royal

Archives. He now stood up, went downstairs and thanked his patron kindly (*LS* I, 2: 15–16; cf. *BE*: 20–1). A week after the king signed this letter Árni happily informed Þormóður of the appointment and claimed that Reinhold Meier, head of the Royal Exchequer, had promised to take care of his salary. Árni wanted Þormóður to let Meyer know that he knew Árni well, as one hand washed another: 'manus manum lavat'. In his reply, Þormóður referred to Árni's earlier sulking comment that he wanted to be eighty and asked whether this was still so (*BT*: 193; see here on p. 97).

Collection

By the middle of the seventeenth century Icelandic manuscripts had become collectors' items in Europe, as learned men wanted to have samples of all kinds of writing in their libraries. In the autumn of 1645, Ole Worm sent a manuscript of *Jónsbók* to Gabriel Naudé, the librarian of Cardinal Mazarin in Paris (Werlauff 1832: 345n; Schepelern III: 136–7). The Dutch scholar Jacob Golius owned a manuscript of *Njáls saga* (AM 468 4to), brought to Holland by the Icelandic student Þorkell Arngrímsson in 1652. A vellum manuscript of *Jónsbók*, written in 1634, was apparently exported from Iceland on the false claim of being 350 years older and ended up in Dublin (Springborg 1969: 297–8, 306–9; Gísli Baldur Róbertsson 2010: 367). Three manuscripts had, at an unknown date, been acquired by the celebrated Ducal Library in Wolfenbüttel; a sixteenth-century vellum of *Jónsbók* (Weiss 103), a collection of *rímur* from around 1500 (Aug 42 7 4to), registered in the library as 'Mythologia Islandica', and not least a fourteenth-century manuscript containing *Eyrbyggja saga* and *Egils saga* (Aug 9 10 4to), registered as old Icelandic poems: 'Antiqui Poetae Islandici Poemata'. This suggests that mythology and ancient poetry may have been more saleable than other texts from Iceland (Ólafur Halldórsson 1968: xxxviii). In a note written in Leipzig Árni had likened the Wolfenbüttel library to the legendary library in Alexandria (AM 909 A 4to: 531r). He cannot at that point have known about the Icelandic manuscripts there and he did not go to Wolfenbüttel on his way back from Leipzig at the end of 1696, although it would not have been too much out of his way. Leibniz was head librarian in the

Ducal Library; he lived in Hanover but came regularly to Wolfenbüttel (von Heinemann 1894: 114–15; Müller and Krönert 1969: 142–4). He knew the representative of the Danish king there and actually had dinner with him on 23 August 1696 (Pertz 1847: 204). Leibniz would certainly have wanted to meet someone who had seen the oriental manuscripts of Andreas Müller and he had also become interested in Nordic matters. On 27 January 1697 he asked the Swedish scholar Johann Gabriel Sparwenfeld, who in 1684–94 had travelled widely in search for manuscripts relating to Northern antiquities, whether he knew anything about Icelandic bibles, asserting that eddic poems and Icelandic sagas were not at all remarkable because they were not that old: 'puisqve ces pieces ne sont pas fort anciennes' (Wieselgren 1883: 14; cf. Jacobowsky 1932: 50–72, 100–237, 257).

In the early months of 1697, as the dukes of Wolfenbüttel sent their librarian Lorenz Hertel to Stockholm in order to pay their respects to a new king, Leibniz decided to obtain Sparwenfeld's opinion on a manuscript apparently written in unrhymed verse in Icelandic or old Scandinavian: 'en Islandois ou en vieux Scandinavien'. The contents were otherwise unidentified. This was the manuscript containing *Egils saga* and *Eyrbyggja saga* (Aug 9 10 4to). Sparwenfeld must have heard about Árni and he persuaded Hertel to take the manuscript to Copenhagen. Leibniz agreed to that decision and expressed his hope that the manuscript would be of some use to 'Monsieur Arnas Magnæus' (Wieselgren 1883: 19, 28; cf. Ekenvall 1953: 26–30, 40; Palumbo 1993: 122).

In the spring Þormóður Torfason came to Copenhagen to oversee the publication of his book on the Orkney Islands. Ásgeir Jónsson came with him, hoping to secure a position as administrator or judge in Norway, or as scribe and scholar in Sweden. In 1692 the Institute of Antiquities had moved from Uppsala to Stockholm and a year later Johann Peringskiöld became its director. The two Icelanders who worked there had just died, Guðmundur Ólafsson in late 1695 and Guðmundur Guðmundsson in early 1697 (Schück 1932–44, IV: 13, 21–2). Þormóður and Ásgeir took with them some transcriptions for Árni, such as *Gísla saga* (AM 482 4to), *Fóstbræðra saga* (AM 566 a 4to), *Þorsteins þáttr Síðuhallssonar* (JS 435 III 4to) and *Hrafns saga Sveinbjarnarsonar* (AM 487 4to). Ásgeir had copied these texts from a manuscript which belonged to the king but later disappeared (Loth 1960a: xvii–xix, xxx–xxxi, liii–lvii, lxiv–lxv, lxviii–lxix). Árni may also have received transcriptions of texts for which he had asked Þormóður on 27 February 1697, where he also showed an increased attention to detail. Ásgeir was asked to transcribe the verses on Swedish kings in *Ynglingatal* from one of the two royal manuscripts of *Heimskringla* with great exactitude, so that abbreviations and letter-forms were shown: 'nempè observando omnes abbreviaturas, ductusqve literarum'. The text, Árni insisted, should be compared with the other vellum, letter for letter, so that he would get it absolutely right: 'ad eg það so ölldungis correct fá kunni'. He also needed the poem *Noregskonungatal* in *Flateyjarbók*, as the copy he had was inexact and could not be trusted (*BT*: 194). Even errors, he insisted five weeks later, should be reproduced if there were any: 'cum omnibus abbreviaturis et erratis, si qvædam in sint' (*BT*: 198).

Þormóður left for Stangeland again in late August but Ásgeir stayed on in Copenhagen. On 26 February 1698 Árni expected Ásgeir to leave for Sweden. That never happened and Ásgeir returned to Stangeland in April (*BT*: 202, 210, 216; Jon Gunnar Jørgensen 2007: 202). In the meantime he worked for Árni. His most important task was to make a copy of the two sagas in the Wolfenbüttel manuscript: *Eyrbyggja saga* (AM 450 a 4to) and *Egils saga* (AM 461 4to). Árni transcribed the first and last pages of the vellum as Ásgeir could not decipher them. Ásgeir copied the remaining text and filled the lacuna in *Eyrbyggja saga* from the copy of *Vatnshyrna* made in 1686–7 (see p. 74). He indicated a short lacuna in *Egils saga* with fourteen empty pages but filled a longer one with the text of *Möðruvallabók*. The longer lacuna in Aug 9 10 4to is close to the end of *Egils saga* where some leaves are missing in the middle of a quire. After considering the length of the missing text Árni concluded that the defective quire must have had twelve leaves, even though other quires in the manuscript had eight. The end of the saga was also missing and Árni decided that it would probably have been written on a single leaf appended to the manuscript, rather than at the beginning of a whole new quire (AM 461 4to: ad p. 602).

Another Icelander, Jón Torfason, helped Árni to compare Ásgeir's

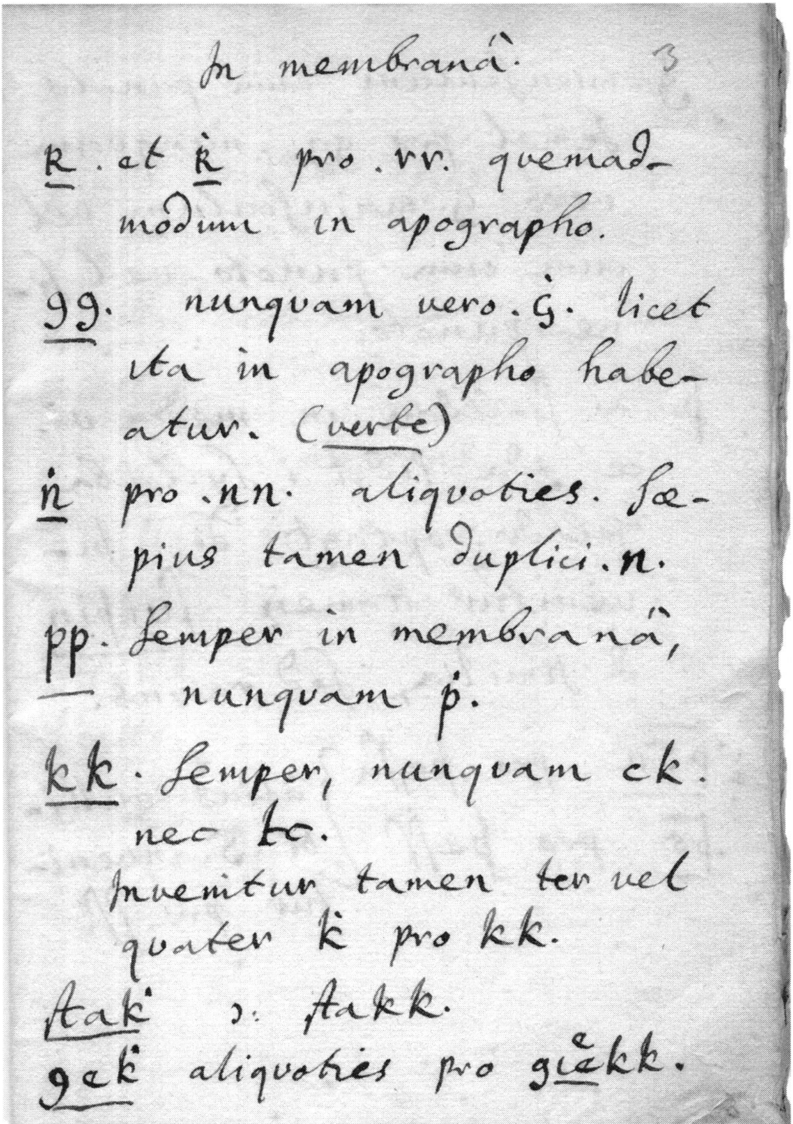

Success

> In membranâ. 3
>
> R̲. et k̲ pro. rr. quemad-
> modum in apographo.
>
> g̲g̲. nunquam vero. ǵ. licet
> ita in apographo habe-
> atur. (verbè)
>
> n̲ pro. nn. aliquoties. sæ-
> pius tamen duplici. n.
>
> p̲p̲. semper in membranâ,
> nunquam p.
>
> k̲k̲. semper, nunquam ck.
> nec tc.
> Invenitur tamen ter vel
> quater k̆ pro kk.
>
> ſtak̆ ɔ: ſtakk.
> gek̆ aliquoties pro gĕkk.

Figure 8. One of Árni's impressive notes on the orthography of the Wolfenbüttel vellum borrowed in 1697–1701 (AM 267 8vo: 3r).

transcriptions with the Wolfenbüttel manuscript. Jón had come to Copenhagen in 1691 but abandoned his studies for the army (*ÍÆ* III: 294). He was a capable scribe and for Árni he copied a late sixteenth-century manuscript containing poems, keeping each text separate: *Píslargrátur* (AM 715 d 4to), *Heimsádeila* (AM 716 n 4to), *Hugbót* (AM 716 o 4to) and *Hjónasinna* (AM 716 p 4to). Jón also copied sagas from paper manuscripts, such as *Króka-Refs saga* (AM 506 4to), *Víglundar saga* (AM 512 4to), *Þorsteins þáttr austfirska* (AM 562 k 4to), *Hungrvaka* (AM 376 4to) and *Örvar-Odds saga* with *Hálfdanar saga Eysteinssonar* (AM 344 b 4to). The checking of the Wolfenbüttel sagas was done in some hurry ('i nockrum flyter') but Árni was confident that the results could be trusted (AM 450 a 4to note). He made extensive notes on the manuscript itself, such as on individual letters, orthography and abbreviations, in Jón Helgason's words showing 'a perception of the characteristic features of Icelandic manuscripts that was exceptionally keen for that period'. Árni sent the manuscript back to Wolfenbüttel on 6 June 1701 with a short report in Latin on its contents (Jón Helgason 1956: xiv–xv, first pages of facsimile; Már Jónsson 1998: 159–62).

While in Copenhagen Ásgeir also transcribed some of Árni's vellums for him, such as *Gull-Þóris saga* (AM 495 4to) from a fifteenth-century manuscript (AM 561 4to), *Kristinna laga þáttr* of *Grágás* (AM 180 4to) from *Staðarfellsbók* (AM 346 fol.) and *Kristinréttr Árna* (AM 179 4to) from *Ljárskógabók* (AM 344 fol.), but also *Óláfs saga Tryggvasonar* (AM 58–60 fol.) from a vellum previously in Bartholin's library (AM 61 fol.) and *Sverris saga* (AM 79 fol.) from a vellum (AM 327 4to) acquired by Árni in Bergen in 1689. Two parts of *Hauksbók* (AM 371 4to, AM 544 4to) had come to Árni from Gaulverjabær in 1691 or 1692. Ásgeir now made two copies of *Skálda saga Haraldar hárfagra* (AM 67 a fol., AM 67 b fol.), one copy of *Hervarar saga ok Heiðreks* (AM 354 4to) and a partial copy of *Hemings þáttr* (AM 326 b 4to: 22–52). He transcribed the preface to *Óláfs saga helga* (AM 904 4to) from a manuscript given to Árni by the *Amtmaður* Christian Müller and made a copy (AM 41 fol.) of the entire kings' saga collection *Hulda* (AM 66 fol.) (Már Jónsson 2009b: 295–6). Most of these transcriptions remained in Árni's collection and it is not clear what he had in mind in having them produced. Perhaps he just wanted to have copies that were easier to read or he wished to have them at hand if he needed to lend them or give away in exhange of other manuscripts or personal favours. As before, Árni used every opportunity to make further inquiries on manuscripts. In the autumn of 1697 Jón Hákonarson sent Árni a paper transcription of *Hrafnkels saga* (AM 116 II 8vo) (Springborg 1969: 289–90). Ari Þorkelsson, sheriff of Barðastrandarsýsla, sent a vellum manuscript of *Stjórn* (AM 225 fol.). The Reverend Páll Ketilsson sent some leaves of the manuscript *Króksfjarðarbók* (AM 122 a fol.) of *Sturlunga saga* and most likely *Staðarhólsbók* (AM 334 fol.), containing *Grágás* and *Járnsíða*. The farmer Skúli Ólafsson in Skagafjörður sent a few vellum leaves containing *Vítus saga* and *Laurentius saga biskups* (AM 180 a–b fol.) and his father-in-law, the scholarly inclined Halldór Þorbergsson, provided a recent vellum containing magical incantations (AM 434 d 12mo). A year later Skúli sent four more vellum leaves, two of which he had not been able to read. In exchange for their effort Árni paid some of Halldór's debts and arranged for Skúli's two sons to attend the cathedral school at Hólar (*PB*: 346–8, 561, 570).

Þórður Jónsson came to Copenhagen in the autumn of 1697, hoping to be appointed bishop of Skálholt. Another candidate was the Reverend Jón Vídalín. Jón obtained the position but on Árni's initiative the two men reached an agreement. Þórður became rector of the school at Skálholt and his youngest sister Sigríður was to be Jón's wife (Jón Þorkelsson and Hannes Þorsteinsson 1903–10: 352). Þórður had brought with him some manuscripts for Árni. Bishop Jón was even more generous, and after settling in Skálholt in the autumn of 1699 he sent no fewer than fourteen vellum manuscripts which belonged to the cathedral. Árni had used some of them before but from now on could regard them as his own (Kålund 1909: 48–50, 61–2).

In the spring of 1698 Árni asked Magnús Jónsson at Vigur whether he knew what had become of the manuscript *Reykjarfjarðarbók* (AM 122 b fol.) containing *Sturlunga saga*, about which he had first heard five years earlier (see p. 102). Magnús had borrowed the manuscript three decades earlier but had not made a copy and erroneously thought that it had perished with Hannes Þorleifsson in 1682 (*PB*: 245). In the

> **VELLUMS PRESENTED TO ÁRNI
> BY THE TWO CANDIDATES FOR THE BISHOPRIC OF SKÁLHOLT**
>
> Þórður Jónsson:
> *Kálfalækjarbók* (AM 133 fol.)
> *Konungs skuggsjá* (AM 243 a fol.)
> *Konungs skuggsjá* (AM 243 d fol.)
> *Jónsbók* (AM 350 fol.)
> *Laurentius saga biskups* (AM 406 a I 4to)
>
> Jón Vídalín:
> *Karlamagnús saga* (lost)
> *Óláfs saga Tryggvasonar* (AM 62 fol.)
> *Sverris saga, Böglunga sögur* and *Hákonar saga Hákonarsonar*
>   (AM 81 a fol.)
> *Stjórn* (AM 227 fol.)
> *Heilagramannasögur* (AM 234 fol.)
> *Heilagramannasögur* (AM 235 fol.)
> *Jónsbók* and *Kristinréttr Árna* (AM 351 fol.)
> *Jónsbók* and *Kristinréttr Árna* (AM 354 fol.)
> *Jónsbók* and *Kristinréttr Árna* (AM 175 a, c 4to)
> *Lygisögur* and *ævintýri* (AM 335 4to)
> Annals (AM 420 a 4to)
> Annals (AM 420 b 4to)
> Annals (AM 420 c 4to)
> A theological compendium (AM 671 4to)

autumn of 1698 Páll Vídalín sent a manuscript of the Norwegian national law of 1274 (AM 69 4to) and Magnús Jónsson, brother of the Reverend Þórður Jónsson, brought with him from Iceland a vellum manuscript of *Barlaams saga ok Jósafats* (AM 232 fol.) (Kålund 1909: 7–8). A year later the Reverend Ísleifur Þorleifsson at Eyri in Skutulsfjörður sent fifteen liturgical fragments: 'pergaments skrædur eda bókaslitur'. In the spring of 1700 Árni returned nine of them and asked Ísleifur to look everywhere for more, as well as for documents older than 1580 (*PB*: 625–6). That autumn, Benedikt Magnússon provided some leaves of *Óláfs saga helga* which had been used as book covers (*BT*: 316). Next spring Árni spent two weeks writing many long letters to Iceland (*BT*: 344). He did the same a year later and the year after that. Only a few of these letters are preserved. On 20 May 1701, for instance, Árni asked his old friend the Reverend Hjalti Þorsteinsson at Vatnsfjörður whether he had any leaves from liturgical books that might contain something useful: 'eitthvad nytanlegt' (*PB*: 632). Hjalti may on that occasion have sent him a fifteenth-century compendium of theological texts (AM 624 4to). In the autumn of 1701 an unknown donor sent a vellum containing *Jómsvíkinga saga* and *Friðþjófs saga frækna*, as well as fragments of *Sverris saga* and *Hákonar saga Hákonarsonar* (*BT*: 355). Grímur Einarsson informed Árni of a very old manuscript on vellum ('skrædu afgamla, ä kalfskinn skrifada'), containing *Elucidarius* (probably AM 674 a 4to). The vellum had belonged to Grímur's father, Einar Eyjólfsson (see pp. 66, 71), but was now in the hands of Þórður Þorkelsson who did not want to give it back (*PB*: 119; Konráð Gíslason 1858: 83).

Icelandic manuscripts were also to be had in Copenhagen. In 1702, Árni bought at least thirty manuscripts at an auction of more than twenty thousand books and hundreds of manuscripts which had belonged to the Danish administrator Jens Rosencrantz, who died in 1695. Árni acquired two precious collections of kings' sagas, *Fríssbók* (AM 45 fol.) and *Eirspennill* (AM 47 fol.), but also *Konungs skuggsjá* (AM 243 b α fol.) and *Jónsbók* (AM 132 4to). He bought a recent transcription of *Íslendingasögur* (AM 128 fol.) and *Orkneyinga saga* in Danish (AM 103 fol.), as well as some Danish, Norwegian and Spanish manuscripts (Overgaard 1996: 262–73). With all these acquisitions Árni clearly had the most remarkable collection of Icelandic medieval manuscripts ever assembled under one roof. He was acutely aware of this himself and claimed in a letter to Johann Peringskiöld on 25 February 1699 that his collection of Icelandic vellums was the largest in Europe: 'Saasom ieg af dylige bøger haver saa stor collection in membranis som ieg neppe troor at nogen in Europa haver' (Gödel 1912: 270). This was certainly true and he had indeed more medieval Icelandic and Norwegian vellums than the Royal Library and the Copenhagen University Library together. The magnitude of his collection should not be exaggerated, however. Kristian Kålund and Jón Helgason have both asserted that most of the 193 vellums in a list that Árni made in 1707–8 were in his collection already when he left for Iceland in 1702 (Jón Helgason 1958: 92; Kålund 1909: vi). This is not correct, as a maximum of 52 vellums were in Árni's possession by 1702, fewer than one third of those in his collection. Many more were acquired in Iceland in subsequent years.

Positions

In a letter to Þormóður on 22 January 1698 Árni mentioned their earlier conversations ('gamla búdarhial') on marriage and thought that it would not be worth while to pursue such matters, but promised to let him know if something happened (*BT*: 208). He had not received any salary as secretary to the Royal Archives but frequently had dinner at Reinhold Meier's house and had given him transcriptions of kings' sagas produced by Ásgeir, just as Þormóður had done earlier. Meier was in a position to see to it that their wages were paid. On 10 July Árni appears to have been on the verge of giving up, despite spending as little money as possible. He complained to Þormóður that his positions as secretary to the archives and future professor meant that he could not earn money by giving private lessons in Latin to children. He also believed that nothing would be gained by leaving for Sweden or England. He regretted going to Leipzig, as he had spent all his money and received no pay since he came back (*BT*: 222–3).

A year later Árni explained to Bishop Björn Þorleifsson that he might get higher wages in England or Sweden but did not want to leave Copenhagen, mostly because his friends in Iceland relied on his help as an intermediary with the royal administration (*PB*: 564). It appears, though, that he made inquiries on scholarly employment in England, as the Danish priest in London, Iver Brinck, informed him on 5 August 1699 that the annual wages there could amount to 50 pounds. Brinck suggested that Árni should write to the scholar George Hickes, who was well connected (*PB*: 82–3). Hickes was greatly interested in septentrional studies and had in 1689 published a grammar of the Anglo-Saxon language (*Institutiones grammaticæ Anglo-Saxonicæ et Moeso-Gothicæ*), with Runólfur Jónsson's Icelandic grammar included (Hickes 1689: 97–132). Hickes was in contact with Swedish scholars and was at this time working on his *Thesaurus* (see p. 85), where a catalogue of all extant Anglo-Saxon manuscripts made by Humfrey Wanley was to appear (C.E. Wright 1960: 104–5; Ruth C. Wright 1939–40: 186; cf. Harris 1992). Hickes, indeed, wanted to correspond with Árni and in the summer of 1699, perhaps encouraged by Brinck, he wrote to ask about Icelandic manuscripts and books, claiming that Árni was the best scholar in the field. Árni did not reply and Hickes wrote again on 5 February 1700 (*PB*: 82–3, 204–9; Finnur Jónsson 1930a: 49–50; cf. Seaton 1935: 193–4). Árni never wrote back and it seems unlikely that he ever seriously considered leaving Copenhagen, either for Iceland or for other countries. In fact, he never really sought contact with foreign scholars and may even have been somewhat protective of his collection and his knowledge, wanting, for whatever reasons, to keep it for himself.

Árni's dealings with Swedish scholars were mostly competitive in nature, although he was willing to cooperate just as were other contemporary Danish scholars (Ilsøe 1988; Ellen Jørgensen 1931: 149–50). He continued to criticise Swedish scholars for their work. The first volume of *Heimskringla*, with Icelandic text and Swedish and Latin translations, was published by Peringskiöld in Stockholm in 1697. Árni saw a copy in the spring of 1698 and found it distasteful that the Swedes should be the first to bring out an edition of such an important text. In a letter to Þormóður on 10 July he insisted that manuscripts of kings' sagas should only be exchanged between Icelanders, as the Swedes had edited *Heimskringla* from transcriptions received from Copenhagen. They could have access to sagas of Icelanders, except for *Sturlunga saga*, as there were so many of them and it did not matter where they ended up: 'má alíka gillda hvar lenda' (*BT*: 216, 223–4). A few weeks later he wrote to Þormóður that there was not a single correct word in the Icelandic text in the edition of *Egils saga einhenda ok Ásmundar berserkjabana* published by Peter Salan five years earlier. The translation was even worse, he added, and the commentary a mess, its main purpose having been to disqualify Thomas Bartholin the younger as a scholar: 'Ecce nugas' (*BT*: 237).

Despite this hostility vis-à-vis the Swedes, Árni lent a manuscript of *Snorra Edda* to Peter Salan's brother Jonas when he came to Copenhagen in the summer of 1698, and was instead allowed to copy a transcription of that work which Jonas had made from a paper manuscript in Oxford. Árni correctly guessed that Salan's exemplar had been written by Jón Guðmundsson the learned in the mid-seventeenth century and that it derived from the Uppsala codex (DG 11) of *Snorra Edda* (AM 739 β 4to: 2r; AM 739 γ 4to: 1–14; Einar Gunnar Pétursson 1998, I: 40; Grape 1914: 238). In a letter to Þormóður later that year Árni regretted that he had given Reinhold Meier some transcriptions of kings' sagas and contemplated buying them back when Meier died, in order to prevent the Swedes from acquiring them for little money (*BT*: 275; cf. Schück 1932–44: IV: 135–41). When Meier died in 1701 Árni duly bought all his Icelandic manuscripts (Kålund 1909: 50–4).

On 4 February 1699 Árni informed Þormóður of what had just been published in Sweden and what was forthcoming (*BT*: 258). Only three weeks later, as he introduced himself in a letter to Peringskiöld, he pretended not to know what had been published in Sweden during the last decade and offered his assistance in preparing text editions. He pointed out that there were indeed errors in Swedish editions, such as that of *Egils saga einhenda*, which was so badly edited that even Icelanders had difficulties reading it. The Icelandic text of *Heimskringla* was inexact and some of the poems badly translated. He hoped that Peringskiöld would not be offended, as he wrote as a friend, and declared himself grateful for the effort put into these books. He also promised to send his own 1695 edition of a Danish chronicle, *Incerti Auctoris Chronica Danorum & præcipuè Sialandiæ*, as well as Þormóður's book on Danish medieval kings (*Series*) when it was published (Gödel 1912: 270–1).

Árni kept working for Matthias Moth, who apart from being the first secretary to the Danish Chancery was a judge in the Supreme Court. In early 1698 a case of witchcraft from the town of Tisted in Jutland was brought before the court and Árni read the proofs of a booklet on the case, most likely written by Moth himself, in which the belief in witchcraft was ridiculed. Árni helped Moth to move house in the early summer of 1698 and certainly wrote letters for him, although none have been preserved (Már Jónsson 1998: 152–3; Bæksted 1959–60, II: 308–9; Finnur Jónsson 1930a: 43–4). Árni's work on Bartholin's ecclesiastical history was still in progress. Between 31 July 1697 and 16 July 1698 he wrote to three bishops in Norway on behalf of Moth to ask for registers and documents. The bishop of Christiania (Oslo) sent some documents and the bishop of Bergen explained that he had none, as the cathedral archive had burnt down in 1620 (*PB*: 277–80, 364–5, 384–6). It came to light that Þormóður Torfason had borrowed all extant charters from the bishop of Stavanger and Árni immediately asked Þormóður to bring them when he next came to Copenhagen. By 29 October 1698 Árni had received 277 documents from Norway. In the spring of 1701 the bishop of Stavanger needed information on fishing rights which was contained in some of these documents, but instead of sending them back Árni asked for more, adding that he also wanted inscriptions and coins from before 1580. He received a further 47 charters (*BT*: 195, 198, 226, 231, 245, 263, 318, 344; *PB*: 487–91).

Árni also wrote to Icelandic bishops asking for documents. In the spring of 1697 he wanted Bishop Björn Þorleifsson to report on documents belonging to the churches that he inspected on his regular visitations through the diocese of Hólar. Árni explained that he needed dates and names rather than exact copies (*PB*: 557). Björn promised to do this and a year later Árni thanked him for what he had sent, adding that he had received documents from Norway and expected some from Skálholt. He now wanted to borrow every single letter written before 1580 that Bishop Björn could find at Hólar and promised to send them back undamaged the following year. A royal order procured by Moth accompanied the letter, in case of resistance (*PB*: 560, 562). On 29 October 1698 Árni informed Þormóður that he had received from Hólar a number of old documents of little worth as historical sources. He had also received all extant charters kept at Skálholt, which he thought were not worth much either (*BT*: 247). In the spring of 1699 he thanked Björn for what he had sent but still wanted more. He knew that in the days of Bishop Guðbrandur Þorláksson, who died in 1627, there had been more than 500 documents on parchment at Hólar. He had only received 153, one of which had the number 608 written on it. He returned all the documents that he had so far received from churches, so that nobody, he explained, would think that he intended to steal them. As usual he was convinced that much more was to be had: 'Eg þikest vita ad miklu fleiri muni þar t.l vera' (*PB*: 564–5). His insistence verges on rudeness, but at the end of this letter he apologises for all the wishes, presenting himself to his friend as 'a pretty girl' ('ein smuck pige') who would not do this to anyone else (*PB*: 566). On 10 May 1700 he wrote to Björn on charters again, stating that such 'popish rags' were incredibly valuable and he would accept whatever was found, although originals should not be sent due to the war between Denmark and Sweden (*PB*: 571).

As before, Árni was more than willing to help Þormóður Torfason with his books. As a young man Þormóður had composed a treatise on medieval Danish kings (*Series dynastarum et regum Daniæ*) which he had presented to King Frederik III in 1664. In the summer of 1692, while Þormóður was in Copenhagen, Árni had urged him to revise it for print (*BT*: 155–6, 162). Þormóður's book on the Orkney Islands (*Orcades*) came out in 1697, printed by Johan Lorentsen, who worked with Árni at the Royal Archives and was soon to become official printer and bookseller for the king and university (*BT*: 194, 207; Nyrop 1870, I: 217–19; Stolpe 1878–9, I: 252–4, 269). Árni disliked Lorentsen but asked him nonetheless, in the summer of 1698, whether he would be interested in publishing *Series*. Lorentsen refused, arguing that the book would not sell as it was written for the learned public. Árni and Þormóður subsequently opted for another bookseller (*BT*: 213, 232, 238, 249).

On 3 September 1698 Árni had read the whole book through with relish but claimed that a great deal of work remained to be done before it was ready to be printed. He disagreed with many things and sent a list of suggestions for changes (*BT*: 239). This meant a second discussion on chronology and fiction between the two of them, with similar arguments advanced on both sides as some years earlier (see pp. 92–3, 96–7). At the end of 1698 Þormóður was totally confused on the issue of Ragnar loðbrók and concluded that there might have been more than one man with that name. He insisted that he had not mixed fables with fact in his discussion of Saxo, but only tried to define the factual foundations of his narrative (*BT*: 251). A few weeks later he argued at length against Árni's critique of his genealogies (*BT*: 252–6) and on 11 February 1702 he went as far as to claim that he believed in giants: 'Nu trui jeg trollfolch se' (*BT*: 368).

Árni's contribution greatly influenced *Series*, especially the first part on sources where a clear distinction is made between texts that could be trusted, such as skaldic poetry and the works of Snorri Sturluson, and others that had little value (Sveinbjörn Rafnsson 1987: 303–4; Andersson 1964: 6–9; Finnur Jónsson 1930a: 44–7). Þormóður alone, however, was responsible for what was to outrage Danish scholars, namely a critique of Saxo's chronology and a list of kings based on Icelandic sources. Árni was aware of the book's explosive contents and on 2 October 1700 even expected that it would be banned. For that reason nobody got to read the sheets which had already been printed (*BT*: 311). Saxo's list of kings beginning with King Dan was generally accepted among scholars and officials, whereas Þormóður now insisted that Skjöldur had been the first king of Denmark, in keeping with the Icelandic sources. His ideas were highly controversial at first but came eventually to be accepted by most scholars. In 1729, for example, the historian and playwright Ludvig Holberg wrote in his description of Denmark and Norway, *Danmarks og Norges Beskrivelse,* that Þormóður's hypothesis was widely regarded to be the better one (Ellen Jørgensen 1931: 146–8; Carl S. Petersen 1920: 293–5).

The first part of *Series* was ready on 18 November 1699 and Árni had it bound for the finance minister Siegfried von Plessen (*BT*: 286). On 3 April 1700, in a letter to Þormóður, Árni thought that the whole book might be finished during the summer. Six months later he lamented that it would hardly be ready before Easter 1701 because he had an infinity of small tasks to attend to. He had so much to do, he asserted, and most of it pointless, that he was sick and tired of himself. He did not go into the details of what he was so busy doing but hinted at work in the archives (*BT*: 303–4, 310). Árni simultaneously complained to Þormóður that his own projects were being neglected as he had hardly touched any of his planned books since starting work on *Series*. Highly placed men had encouraged him to have something printed and thus recommend himself for advancement. So far he had not been able to do this and wanted Þormóður to tell these men that a reader of proofs should be rewarded as well as the author (*BT*: 312).

On 23 May 1701, as Þormóður prepared for yet another trip from Stangeland to Copenhagen, Árni asked him to bring two of the king's manuscripts containing medieval annals and a treatise on chronology. Þormóður should also bring some of his own manuscripts which Árni urgently needed to consult, such as *Gulaþingslög* on vellum, Icelandic annals, bishops' sagas and documents on the Orkney Islands, *Sturlunga saga* in the short version made by Björn Jónsson at Skarðsá, *Hálfsrekka saga* transcribed by the Reverend Páll Ketilsson and all manuscripts relating to law, as well as commentaries. Árni also wanted to see Icelandic, Norwegian and Danish lawbooks and amendments which he remembered seeing at Stangeland twelve years earlier, and last but not least each and every saga manuscript on paper that Þormóður had and did not care for, written by various Icelandic scribes. Árni argued that Þormóður had better copies of these sagas made by Ásgeir Jónsson, either from these paper manuscripts or from the much better vellums which Þormóður had on loan at Stangeland. In exchange Árni promised to send Þormóður printed books or whatever else he needed. He then repeated that he did not want the copies made by Ásgeir, but only the bad copies made by earlier scribes. If the trip was postponed, Árni wanted Þormóður to send these manucripts and he promised to return everything, if required (*BT*: 343). What can Árni have been thinking? He already had an excellent collection of vellums and good copies produced under his supervision, so the only answer to this question, as he does not explain the reason for his request, is that he considered that he could never be certain about the value of manuscripts and that even in apparently useless ones something of interest might be found. He had to see them all.

When King Christian V died on 26 August 1699 his son Frederik succeeded to the throne and appointed men whom he trusted to high positions. Two weeks later Matthias Moth had been stripped of all power. Reinhold Meier had lost his post and been given a lower one. With a new king, officials needed to have their letters of appointment confirmed. For Árni this meant that he needed royal confirmation for his positions at the archives and the university, although for the latter he only had a letter of expectation (*BT*: 247, 270–2; Bjerre Jensen 1987: 37–43). On 9 March 1700 his position at the Royal Archives was confirmed and his friend Frederik Rostgaard was appointed their director (*Emb*: 6; Bruun 1870a: 82; Adolf D. Jørgensen 1884: 58–9, 264–7). Soon after that, Árni got his wages at last. The first payment of 125 rigsdaler was paid out on 16 July; the same amount was paid three weeks later and the rest by the end of the year. His salary of 300 rigsdaler was just below that of top administrators such as the *Amtmaður* Christian Müller who received 400 rigsdaler (Már Jónsson 1998: 143). These payments went through despite the tense political situation which had developed after Swedish regiments had been sent to help build a fortress for the duke of Gottorp in the summer of 1699. In March 1700 King Frederik IV had sent soldiers to take over the duke's palaces. King Charles XII of Sweden, only eighteen years old, replied by having his navy fire on Copenhagen on 25 July. Ten days later Swedish soldiers went ashore between Humlebæk and Espergærde to the north of the city. King Fredrik gave in, the duke got to build his fortress and the Swedes left Seeland (Olsen 1970: 383–9).

As for the university, Árni was next in line for a position as professor with a letter of expectation from 14 July 1694. Christian Worm, son of Willum (see p. 49), had received such a letter a month later. In 1693–4 he had published in Copenhagen two impressive volumes on Jewish antiquities as they appeared in Roman texts: *De Corruptis Antiqvitatum Hebrærarum apud Tacitum et Martialem Vestigiis*. In 1693 he had borrowed the text and translation of *Íslendingabók* from Árni, who may have told him that his edition would not appear. Worm decided to do an edition himself, using Árni's text and translation but with his own commentary. First he asked Frederik Rostgaard for help. Rostgaard was in Oxford at the time and wrote to Árni on 8 May 1694 that an unnamed friend had contacted him about the printing of this work, and wanted to know about Árni's plans. Worm spent some time in Oxford during his travels around Europe in 1695–7 and the printing started, but was never finished (AM 254 8vo: 19r; Weber 1775: 119–20; *PB*: 394; Böðvar Kvaran 1971: 157–68). A copy, still extant, was sent to Árni by George Hickes in the late summer of 1699 (*PB*: 206; AM 369 4to). This incident did not prevent Árni and Christian Worm to be on friendly terms in the years to come (see p. 146).

Árni's only publication since arriving from Leipzig had appeared in 1701, being a short explanation of an inscription on King Óláfr helgi in the journal *Nova Literaria Maris Baltici et Septentrionis*, published in Lübeck (*LS* II: 114–15; cf. Ekenvall 1941: 189; Erik Petersen 1998: 315–16). A plan to prepare a catalogue of the manuscripts in the University Library, in which Árni would be responsible for the Icelandic ones, had come to nothing (RA. KU 12.03.14: 93r, 163r; Birket Smith 1882: 55). Despite this lack of productivity he considered himself entitled to a position when, on 22 May 1701, Professor Jørgen Seerup died. Seerup was a physician and had attended King Christian V in his last months; although he had never received a letter of expectation he was appointed professor of medicine (Ehrencron-Müller VII: 322; RA. KU 12.03.14: 211v). On 2 June Árni wrote to King Frederik IV referring to his letter of expectation from seven years earlier. He explained that he had for years worked on Danish history and antiquities and asked for the title of 'Professor Historiæ et Antiquitatum Danicarum' rather than the more general title of 'Professor Philosophiæ' as was customary for newcomers to the university. He promised to publish worthy books in the future. The king agreed to this on 22 October, the same day he confirmed the appointment of all the other professors (*Emb*: 8–10; RA. KU 12.03.14: 275v; Finnur Jónsson 1930a: 40–2). Árni could now be secure of decent earnings in two positions, both held earlier by his employer Thomas Bartholin. From now on he would be able to do whatever he desired.

6
Iceland

> I am here as in a prison and only expect
> to be released after two or three years.
>
> Eg er hier uppi eins og i fangelse, sie og
> ei, ad hiedan leysast kunni ennnu i 2, 3 ár.
>
> Árni Magnússon 26 September 1704 (*BT*: 390)

This chapter describes Árni Magnússon's dealings in the years 1702–12 as royal commissioner in his native Iceland, a country of just over fifty thousand mostly poor inhabitants living on six thousand farms. During the last few years of the seventeenth century winters had been bitter. Harvests and fisheries failed, cattle, horses and sheep died of cold and hunger. Famine was widespread and hundreds of poor people perished. The Danish royal administration decided that something needed to be done.

Politics

In the autumn of 1699 Árni lamented in a letter to Þormóður Torfason that only bad news came from Iceland. A year later nothing had changed (*BT*: 272, 313). Amidst the crisis, allegiance was sworn to King Frederik IV at the *Alþingi* in July 1700. In a letter addressed to him both bishops, both magistrates and numerous sheriffs and priests described the current difficulties, which they attributed to the wrath of God, who sought to punish Icelanders for their sins. They predicted that the whole country would be deserted within a few years and suggested that a representative be sent to Copenhagen to explain the situation. On 30 April 1701 the king agreed that Magistrate Lauritz Gottrup should come to meet him. Gottrup had come to Iceland as an assistant to Danish officials and was appointed

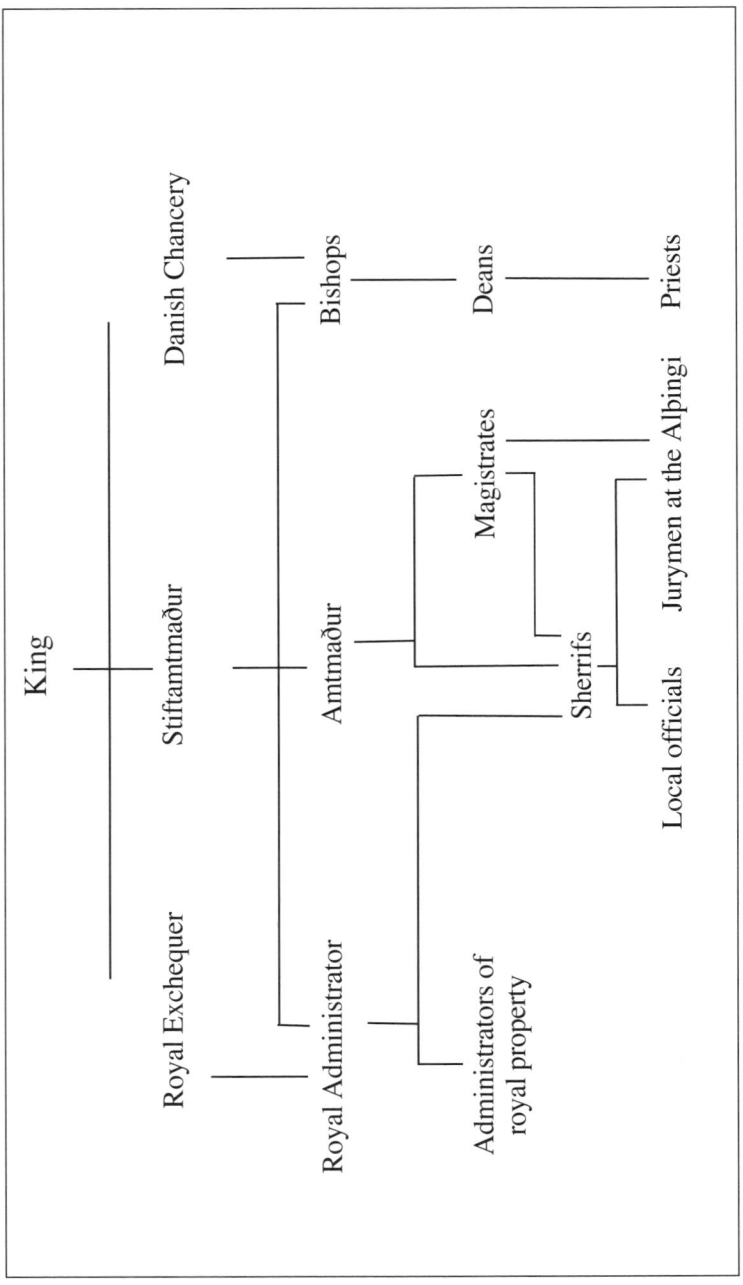

Figure 9. Royal administration in Iceland c. 1700 (see Már Jónsson 1998: 181).

magistrate (*lögmaður*) in 1695, the first Dane to occupy this position. He spent the winter of 1701–2 in Copenhagen and his expenses were covered by a special tax levied on landowners. Some officials, in particular the cousins Páll and Jón Vídalín, who were Árni's close friends, disapproved of his journey, arguing that it was too costly for a destitute country. They asked Árni to represent their views in Copenhagen, and later that winter the *Amtmaður* Müller asked for his advice. The extent of Árni's participation in the ensuing negotiations is unknown and in letters to Þormóður he merely noted that most of Gottrup's suggestions were unreasonable (*BT*: 350–1, 354). After protracted discussions within the administration King Frederik IV decided, on 15 April 1702, that a royal commission should go to Iceland and investigate conditions there. Ten days later Árni was appointed as head of that commission and the king accepted his proposal that Páll Vídalín would join him instead of the Norwegian Paul Beyer, who had worked intermittently in Iceland since 1688 (*Lovsamling* I: 580–1; Már Jónsson 1998: 186–9; Gunnar F. Guðmundsson 1990a: xxxiii–xxxiv).

Árni retained his positions at the Royal Archives and the university, and was granted four rigsdaler per week for himself and a servant for his journey to Iceland, with the addition of two rigsdaler per day to cover his expenses while there. Páll Vídalín would receive half as much. The stipend was to cover all costs, such as travel, paper and scribes. The king signed a letter of appointment on 22 May 1702. Five days later Professor Ole Rømer informed the assembly of professors at the university that the king had commanded Árni to go to Iceland, and that he would keep his income as professor (*Emb*: 10–11, 18–19; RA. KU 12.03.14: 296r–v). Jacob Rasch wrote to Þormóður Torfason that Árni spent the whole night of 29 May packing his books and luggage, and was still saying farewell to friends at half past four in the morning. In the end he had so much to do that he could hardly speak. According to Rasch, Árni expected to be in Iceland for a year and a half. The journey to Iceland was trouble-free and on 18 June Árni and the navigating officer found themselves enjoying the midnight sun just to the north of Langanes. Five days later the ship arrived at Hofsós (Már Jónsson 1998: 190–1; Finnur Jónsson 1930a: 59). Árni probably chose this specific ship and route so that he could visit

Bishop Björn Þorleifsson at Hólar, where he examined a sixteenth-century land register (AM 269 4to). Árni and Björn travelled to Þingvellir together, where they met Páll Vídalín, who until then was unaware of his new role as royal commissioner (*PB*: 578; *Annálar* I: 676). First and foremost, Árni and Páll were to investigate the terrible economic situation of the country. The first stage was to prepare a detailed land register (*jarðabók*), containing a description of all farms, and a census of people and cattle, information which would enable them to propose reforms. The royal letters regarding the commission were read in public at the *Alþingi* on 17 July 1702. Two days later Árni and Páll ordered all landowners to send a detailed inventory of their landed property within a year (*Alþingisbækur* IX: 203–4, 208–9; *Jarðabók* XIII: 3–11; *Emb*: 12–21; *Lovsamling* I: 584–92). They also asked Lauritz Gottrup to provide the accounts for his journey to Copenhagen, so that Icelandic landowners would not be subject to too much expense.

After the *Alþingi* Árni and Páll went to Bessastaðir, the official residence of the *Amtmaður* Christian Müller, to inquire about issues relating to royal administration in the country. In his first report to the Royal Exchequer on 31 July 1702, Árni emphasised the extreme poverty of most inhabitants as a result of the disastrous fishing season (*Emb*: 22–3). Páll then returned home to Víðidalstunga and Árni settled at Skálholt, where he would stay while in Iceland. Some weeks later he left with Bishop Jón Vídalín, who appears to have scheduled his visitation that year so that it coincided with Árni's travels. The two of them visited their friend the Reverend Jón Halldórsson at Hítardalur on 27 August and Árni met Páll Vídalín again at Hvammur in Hvammsfjörður, where Árni's younger brother, the Reverend Magnús Magnússon, now lived with his wife, Sigríður Jónsdóttir, who was Páll's sister (Már Jónsson 1998: 194–5).

From Hvammur the commissioners reported to Copenhagen on the dismal state of the judicial administration. They claimed that sheriffs were often so ignorant that they did not understand the law and either made their cases too complicated or prepared them so badly that they could not be resolved at the *Alþingi* but had to be sent back for further investigation. Even at the *Alþingi* the verdicts were poorly argued. There were no rules on how to appeal to the Upper Court (*yfirdómur*), over which the

Amtmaður presided. There was great uncertainty as to what was valid law, as innumerable amendments and decrees had been added to the legal code of 1281 (*Jónsbók*). Magistrates indiscriminately used King Christian IV's *Recess* of 1643, King Christian V's *Danske lov* of 1683 or the *Norske lov* of 1687, although none of these laws had been promulgated in Iceland, while drafts for a new Icelandic lawbook lay unfinished in Copenhagen. The magistrates Gottrup and Sigurður Björnsson were harshly criticised in this report, which concluded that several recent and not so recent examples of their faulty verdicts needed to be investigated. Árni and Páll argued that most Icelanders were worse off than ever before. Many farmers could not provide for their own needs and were deep in debt to merchants, who were partly to blame for the crisis, as were landowners and officials who did nothing to alleviate the abject poverty. A blatant lack of discipline was another reason for the troubles, with servants disobeying their masters and vagrants ready to steal rather than earn their living in an honest way (*Emb*: 40–9; Már Jónsson 1998: 195, 213–14).

The commissioners intended to travel all over the country and meet with the local people. Their first public meeting took place at Drangar at Skógarströnd in Snæfellsnessýsla on 27 September 1702 in the presence of Sheriff Jón Magnússon, who was Árni's brother and married to Kristín Vídalín, another of Páll's sisters. It took two days to produce a detailed description of thirty farms. The report shows the value of each farm, the names of its owners and the tenants, the annual rents and the number of cattle. Meadows, pastures and access to water are described, along with assets such as firewood, fisheries, boats and eider down, and also any damage due to rivers or mudslides. Important farmers in the community attested to the reliability of the report (*Jarðabók* V: 310–58; cf. Gunnar F. Guðmundsson 1990a: xliii–liii; Már Jónsson 1998: 194–9). Only two other communities were investigated that autumn, and while Páll took care of the land register Árni travelled to the small fishing villages on the edge of Snæfellsnes to look into complaints about merchants there. They met again at Staðarstaður, where the Reverend Páll Ketilsson, Árni's uncle, lived. On 21 October they wrote to all sheriffs, ordering them to produce a detailed census of all inhabitants. They also required tax reports from the last three years and information on the number of cattle on each farm in the country (*Emb*: 50–3).

Árni spent the winter of 1702–3 in Skálholt and undertook some scholarly work. He had brought with him the vellum charters from the bishopric of Hólar, which he had received in Copenhagen a few years earlier (see p. 126), but knew that there were more documents at the cathedral. Bishop Björn had sent him an old inventory of extant documents and Árni saw that some leaves were missing. On 11 March 1703 he asked the bishop to search for them and required a detailed list of all charters remaining at Hólar, while he would himself make a list of the charters he had on loan. Two months later Árni sent back documents that he had received earlier from the church of Goðdalir in Skagafjörður, explaining that he did not want the bishop to think that he intended to steal them (*PB*: 579, 581). Árni left Skálholt on 21 May and travelled to the west of Iceland again, where he met with Páll Vídalín. Most of June was spent in Barðastrandarsýsla compiling the land register (*Jarðabók* VI: 232–50, 292–337; *Annálar* I: 450, 679). On their return to Hvammur, letters from the king and the Royal Exchequer instructed them to be back in Copenhagen that autumn or pay for their passage themselves (*Lovsamling* I: 596–8; *Emb*: 53–4). At that point they had surveyed less than five percent of the country.

At the *Alþingi* in July 1703 sheriffs from all parts of the country handed over a remarkably thorough census of people and a fairly detailed tally of the cattle on every farm. After the assembly, Árni and Páll left for Bessastaðir and Viðey in heavy rain in order to inspect buildings owned by the king and then proceeded to compile a land register in Grindavík (*Jarðabók* III: 3–24; *Annálar* I: 454–5; AM 440 fol.: 46r–56r). On 28 August 1703 Árni wrote to Frederik Walter, an official at the royal court and an avid collector of books. The king, Árni asserted, would have to do something to improve the living conditions in Iceland and needed a detailed knowledge of the situation in order to act; that is why the land register had to be properly done. Admitting that the register would not be finished by the end of the year, Árni asked Walter to ensure that he would not lose his positions in Copenhagen, so that when his work in Iceland was finished he would, as before, be able to immerse himself in old books

Figure 10. Map of Iceland with some key localities

and documents: 'wie vorhin unter alten büchern und brieffschafter consummirt zu werden' (*PB*: 646; Finnur Jónsson 1930a: 102; on Walter, see Ehrencron-Müller VIII: 402). In a letter to King Frederik two days later Árni and Páll claimed that they would finish the land register in 1708, provided that they were free from other tasks. Due to the harsh climate and lack of fodder for horses they could only travel around the country from May to October. The roads were bad and many of them involved crossing dangerous rivers. It was difficult, they added, to describe in a few words just how arduous travelling really was. In July they had to spend more than a week at the *Alþingi* at Þingvellir, a delay that greatly disrupted their work (*Emb*: 60–2).

In February 1703 Árni had visited Magnús Sigurðsson, a wealthy farmer at Bræðratunga close to Skálholt, in order to inspect some documents and books. He spent two nights there and Magnús asked for assistance in a dispute concerning his wife, Þórdís Jónsdóttir, whose sister Sigríður was Bishop Jón Vídalín's wife.[1] Þórdís had first fled from her husband a year earlier after giving birth to their fourth child. After some time in Skálholt she returned to Bræðratunga and was there during Árni's visit. On 24 March 1703 Þórdís left Magnús again, pregnant with their fifth child. Magnús then started spreading a rumour that Þórdís was having an affair with Árni. Shortly afterwards Magnús came to Skálholt and again wanted Árni to negotiate on his behalf, apologising to Þórdís in the presence of the bishop. After returning to Bræðratunga Magnús wrote to Árni. He wanted his books back and complained that Árni had not supported his case. In an undated reply Árni denied that he had persuaded Þórdís not to return to Bræðratunga again and asserted that he would never influence any woman to leave her husband. In the early summer, Þórdís went to her mother at Leirá in Leirársveit where she gave birth to a daughter on 13 August.

In a letter to Árni on 8 April 1704 Magnús claimed that Þórdís and Árni had spent time alone together in Skálholt behind locked doors. Árni

---

[1] The following is based on a detailed account of the whole case in Már Jónsson 1998: 225–43. Most of the documents are only available in a Danish translation made by Árni as he prepared the case for the Supreme Court in Copenhagen; see AM 444 fol.: 1r–329v.

promptly replied that he would not allow anyone to circulate lies about him and a few days later he sued Magnús for libel. The local court assembled at the farm Vatnsleysa on 28 April where an angry Árni presented his accusations. All those present stated that nothing indecent was known to have happened between Árni and Þórdís. The verdict was that there was no truth in the rumours spread by Magnús. Accordingly, he was to pay a fine to the king and compensation to Árni. Magnús did not show up and continued with his insinuations. In a letter to Þórdís on 3 May he claimed that when Árni had spent the night at Bræðratunga he had coughed in the evening. She then left the bed, removed the key from the door and locked it, and then went to Árni's rocm. During the first days of July, with Magnús present at the *Alþingi*, his accusations were judged invalid. He was to pay a fine to the closest lepers' hospital, an appropriate compensation to Árni and all court costs (*Emb*: 87–95; *LS* I, 2: 166–80; *Alþingisbækur* IX: 254–6).

Between the trials at Vatnsleysa and the *Alþingi,* Árni travelled with Bishop Jón to Vestmannaeyjar where they arrived on 8 May 1704. Árni compiled a land register there and left on 10 June. In Skálholt, royal orders awaited him: the Royal Commission was to finish its work as soon as possible and send a report in the autumn on what had been done and what remained (*Lovsamling* I: 603–4). In late June Árni and Páll met at the *Alþingi* and after the assembly went to Bessastaðir for discussions with the *Amtmaður* Müller. For the next three months they worked on the land register in Rangárvallasýsla and Vestur-Skaftafellssýsla. Árni was annoyed with his native country after staying there for a year longer than he had intended. At Kirkjubæjarklaustur on the night of 25 September he bitterly complained to Þormóður Torfason that he felt as if in a prison and feared that he would have to stay for at least a further two or three years. He had no time for himself and was dissatisfied with his search for manuscripts, having found nothing remarkable except for a manuscript containing *Ólafs saga Tryggvasonar*, two leaves from *Hungrvaka* in Latin, a few legal codices and some old letters. Next to nothing of value was left in the country and what little remained was rotten and spoiled: 'það til baka hefur orded, er fued og fordiarfad' (*BT*: 390).

Iceland

Acquisitions

When Árni left for Iceland in 1702 he brought some manuscripts to read and study for the next year and a half, for instance a vellum of *Þiðreks saga* that perished in 1728. The manuscript was a gift from Þormóður Torfason (Kålund 1909: 45). On 3 May 1704, though, Árni wrote to Bishop Björn Þorleifsson that he could not provide his wife Þrúður Þorsteinsdóttir with anything to read, as the sagas he had with him were nothing special (*PB*: 583). If one is to believe his aforementioned letter to Þormóður later that year, Árni had not found many manuscripts either, but that claim is something of an exaggeration. A close look at Árni's notes, which he wrote quite systematically during his time in Iceland (see pp. 15–16), reveals that he started searching for manuscripts on his arrival and by the autumn of 1704 had acquired some quite interesting pieces. As before, Árni worked hard. He collected *Íslendingasögur, konungasögur, biskupasögur, heilagramannasögur, fornaldarsögur, lygisögur,* lawbooks, treatises on law, annals, genealogies and calendars, young and old. He even had *rímur* and other poetry written down from the recitations of old women and asked around for stories about renowned figures, not least Sæmundur fróði, although he himself did not believe any of them (Jón Helgason 1950: vi–vii; Jón Helgason 1963: 106, 110; Bjarni Einarsson 1955: xcvi–cxliv). He made inquiries about manuscripts wherever he went, although he may not have been quite as insistent as implied in the the depiction by Halldór Laxness in his novel *Iceland's Bell* (*Íslandsklukkan*) of 1941–3, where the character Arnas Arnæus searches feverishly in the dusty and rubbish-ridden bedstead of an old woman:

> After a long and thorough search through the old hay the noble visitor dragged out some wadded and hole-riddled parchment scraps that were so shrivelled, shrunken, and hardened by age that it was impossible to smooth them out... He blew on the parchment and scrutinised it, then took a silk handkerchief from his breast pocket and dusted it. "Membranum", he said finally (Halldór Laxness 2003: 23–4).

> Eftir lánga og nákvæma leit kom þar að hinn tigni gestur dró frammúr heyruddanum nokkur samanvöðluð skinnaræksn svo bögluð, skorpin og gamalhörðnuð að ógerlegt var að slétta úr þeim... Hann ýmist blés af skinninu eða rýndi í það, dró upp silkihandlínu úr brjóstvasa sínum og strauk með henni af því eða dustaði. Membrana, sagði hann að lokum (Halldór Laxness 1991: 31).

During his years in Iceland Árni obtained manuscripts from at least 170 individuals, mostly men, often receiving just one or two items from each. He received most of these manuscripts as gifts, rather than purchases. As a representative of the king he was a powerful man and people were eager to have him on their side. A few examples will serve to reveal Árni's methods and give some sense of the intensity of his search. For example, in 1702 Árni obtained a fourteenth-century vellum of *Þorláks saga helga* (AM 382 4:o) from the widow of Bishop Þórður Þorláksson, Guðrún Gísladóttir at Hlíðarendi (Kålund 1909: 32). Bishop Jón Vídalín gave him a fifteenth-century collection of *lygisögur* (AM 593 a–b 4to). Someone unknown provided a Latin church ritual from around 1200 (AM 98 I 8vo) and the farmer Jón Hákonarson gave Árni a recent transcript of *Snorra Edda* (AM 166 a 8vo). At the *Alþingi*, Snæbjörn Pálsson told Árni that he could keep a sixteenth-century vellum of *Konungs skuggsjá* (AM 243 e fol.) which his father, the sheriff Páll Torfason, had sent on loan to Copenhagen some years earlier.

In 1703 Árni acquired three leaves of *Óláfs saga Tryggvasonar* (AM 325 IX 1 a 4to) at Saurbær on Kjalarnes and at Þingvellir. At Saurbær, where Magistrate Sigurður Björnsson lived, Árni found yet another leaf of the same saga, which had been used as the cover for a printed book (AM 325 VIII 2 f 4to). While Árni was in Flatey in Breiðafjörður gathering information for the land register, Magnús Arason gave him a leaf from another codex of *Óláfs saga Tryggvasonar* (AM 54 fol.) and Guðrún Ögmundsdóttir came up with a leaf from *Trójumanna saga* (AM 598 II β 4to). In that same year, Bishop Jón Vídalín provided two more vellums of *Jónsbók*, one which had belonged to Ingibjörg Pálsdóttir (AM 343 fol.) and the other to the Reverend Árni Þorleifsson (AM 133 4to). Bishop

Iceland

Björn Þorleifsson presented Árni with eight leaves of a Latin *calendarium* (AM 249 d fol.). The Reverend Daði Steindórsson at Gufudalur, who was married to Árni's aunt, Jóhanna Jónsdóttir, gave him two leaves which dealt with church property and liturgy. The new owner commented, perhaps justifying the displacement of such material, that the leaves were of no use to the church (AM 266 4to). The wealthy Guðmundur Þorleifsson at Brokey, brother of the royal antiquarian Hannes Þorleifsson (see p. 42), furnished Árni with a collection of sagas and *rímur* transcribed by Árni's grandfather, Ketill Jörundsson (AM 554 h β 4to, AM 554 i 4to, AM 613 c 4to, AM 611 e 4to). To that manuscript was appended a copy of *Íslendingabók* prepared by the Reverend Páll Ketilsson in 1681 (AM 113 i fol.). Árni also received two recent copies of *Konungs skuggsjá* from the Reverend Þórður Jónsson (AM 243 d fol.) and Þorsteinn Ólafsson (AM 243 q fol.). The Reverend Skúli Þorláksson at Grenjaðarstaður provided a manuscript of kings' sagas (AM 304 4to) transcribed by Þorleifur Jónsson and Björn Jónsson at Skarðsá in the mid-seventeenth century (Jón Helgason 1970a: 4–7). At the *Alþingi*, Árni received a recent copy of *Laxdæla saga* (AM 554 d 4to) and Magnús Markússon gave him *Ívens saga Artúskappa* (AM 588 a 4to). An unnamed farmer came up with a recent transcript of *Snorra Edda* (AM 747 4to) which, though torn and mouldy, seemed to Árni well worth leafing through: 'Er þó verd ad hlaupast i gegnum' (*AMKat.* II: 173). Two former correspondents sent him items of interest. Halldór Þorbergsson had found vellum leaves containing royal amendments (*réttarbætur*) written in the early sixteenth century (AM 174 I A 4to) and Bjarni Bjarnason added seven leaves to a vellum of *Trójumanna saga* and *Bretasögur* (AM 573 4to) which he had sent to Copenhagen four years earlier (Kålund 1909: 46). The servant Jón Einarsson gave Árni a leaf from a thirteenth-century vellum of *Grágás* (AM 315 b fol.) and another leaf belonging to a late thirteenth-century *Jónsbók* (AM 134 4to); he was unable to remember where he had found them. Jón also possessed a leaf of *Heimskringla* (AM 325 VIII 1 4to); in February 1704 Árni obtained a second leaf from the same manuscript. His vellum acquisitions for the year 1704 appear within the frame.

> ## Vellums acquired by Árni Magnússon in 1704
>
> *Óláfs saga Tryggvasonar*, fourteenth century, 72 leaves
>   (AM 53 fol.)
> *Heimskringla*, fourteenth century, one leaf (AM 325 VIII 1 4to)
> *Egils saga*, thirteenth century, one leaf (AM 162 A θ fol.)
> *Gísla saga Súrssonar*, c. 1400, one leaf (AM 445 c I 4to)
> *Karlamagnús saga*, c. 1400, 73 leaves (AM 180 c fol.)
> *Barlaams saga ok Jósafats*, c. 1400, two leaves (AM 231 I fol.)
> *Heilagramannasögur*, fourteenth century, four leaves
>   (AM 233 a fol.)
> *Þorláks saga helga*, thirteenth century, two leaves (AM 383 I 4to)
> The Norwegian national law, fourteenth century, 66 leaves
>   (AM 68 4to)
> *Kristinna laga þáttr* and church statutes, c. 1400, two leaves
>   (AM 173 d B 1 4to, AM 173 d C 2 4to)
> Latin calendars, thirteenth to fifteenth century, 18 leaves
>   (AM 249 o fol., AM 249 q I–VIII fol.)

In the spring of 1705, hoping to make some progress on the land register, the commissioners split up. Árni worked in Mýrdalur while Páll took care of Kjós and Kjalarnes. Royal letters brought both good and bad news. The good news was that, on 15 May, King Frederik had accepted their arguments for the delay of the land register, although he insisted that they should complete it as soon as possible. The bad news was that he had been persuaded by Danish merchants, who had a monopoly on trade with Iceland, that instead of renting one or two harbours each they would be allowed to work together in a company. Árni and Páll strongly opposed this measure as detrimental to all Icelanders, since there would be no competition. They considered the matter important enough for Árni to depart from Keflavík for Copenhagen on 10 September. His arguments prevailed and on 25 January 1706 the king decided that current contracts for individual harbours would be extended for a year; after this period he would consult Árni's opinion: 'des Arnes Meinung' (*Lovsamling* I: 628; cf. *Emb*: 128–53; Már Jónsson 1998: 246–9).

In the spring of 1706 Árni realised that he would still have to spend some years in Iceland and decided to take most of his vellums with him. Among these manuscripts there were gifts he had just received from his colleague Christian Worm: *Óláfs saga helga* (AM 68 fol.), *Óláfs saga Tryggvasonar* (AM 310 4to) and *Elís saga, Bærings saga, Flóvents saga* and *Mágus saga* (AM 580 4to) (Ellen Jørgensen 1919). Árni's appetite for manuscripts had no limits, though, and he also tried to borrow vellums from the Royal Library. King Frederik had travelled to Norway in the summer of 1704 and visited Þormóður Torfason at Stangeland on 10 July. Þormóður, who had been asked to return the king's manuscripts six years previously, now handed them over to the royal librarian, who was in the king's retinue. The manuscripts were thus back in Copenhagen but Árni's request was turned down on 12 June 1706. He would only be allowed to use the manuscripts in Copenhagen (*BT*: x, 393; Kålund 1900: xlv).

He had more success with the University Library and on 8 June he was allowed to borrow five Icelandic manuscripts on the understanding that he would publish them in Iceland. *Consistorium* accepted this arrangement on the condition that in case of damage or loss, Árni would replace them with manuscripts from his own collection, which he had left in Copenhagen and were kept in the University Library. Three of the manuscripts he borrowed can be identified as *Knýtlinga saga* (now lost), *Guðmundar saga góða* (AM 399 4to) and *Guðmundar saga ok Nikulás saga* (lost) (*Emb*: 200; Kålund 1909: 64; Stefán Karlsson 1960: 187–8). Árni arrived in Þorlákshöfn on 8 July 1706 and was present at the *Alþingi*, confident of the support of the king. After the assembly Páll Vídalín compiled the land register in Ölfus and Selvogur while Árni attended to other matters. They met in Eyrarbakki before Páll returned to Víðidalstunga and Árni settled in Skálholt for the winter (AM 441 fol.: 138r; *Annálar* I: 702).

On 14 June 1705 the Reverend Jón Árnason at Staður in Steingrímsfjörður, later bishop at Skálholt, had written to Árni about a vellum that he believed to be very old: 'temmilega ad eg meina gamla'. He sent the first few lines and Árni asked him to buy the manuscript, irrespective of the cost: 'qvocunque prætio' (*AMKat.* II:41). This was *Veraldar saga* from around 1400 (AM 625 4to). That year, Magnús Arason sent three leaves of a sixteenth-century *Egils saga* (AM 162 A α fol) and, more spectacularly, a damaged bifolium from an illustrated *Physiologus* (AM 673 a I 4to), probably written c. 1200. Brynjólfur Þórðarson gave Árni a tiny vellum containing documents from the early sixteenth century (AM 191 4to) and parts of a slightly older vellum of *lygisögur* (AM 570 a–b 4to). Manuscripts of *Jónsbók* and the church law of 1275 were continually sent to him; the Reverend Jón Jónsson at Garpsdalur sent one such vellum and said that Árni could keep it if he wished (AM 128 4to). At the Alþingi Árni acquired another of his grandfather's manuscripts, a copy of *Eyrbyggja saga* (AM 442 4to); the manuscript also included *Laxdæla saga* which is now lost.

In 1706 Bishop Jón Vídalín found yet another vellum of *Jónsbók* (AM 151 4to) and Árni Hannesson discovered a leaf containing text from *Sverris saga* amongst a pile of rubbish at Ytri-Hólmur on Akranes. Árni Magnússon identified it as belonging to a vellum also containing *Magnúss saga lagabætis*, a leaf of which had been the cover of a book owned by the royal antiquarian Hannes Þorleifsson (AM 325 X 4to). Árni had long been acutely aware of the destruction of old manuscripts during the seventeenth century and judiciously attempted to identify the various fragments he was gathering. If his notes reveal the scale of the losses they also bring to light the extent to which the survival of these fragments and manuscripts depended on the efforts of Árni and his collaborators. A case in point was the rescue of a manuscript by Bishop Jón. Some years before Árni came to Iceland the *Amtmaður* Christian Müller was given a vellum containing *Péturs saga postula* (AM 658 III 4to) and texts on Christian virtues and church discipline (AM 684 4to), probably for use as covers for books. When Bishop Jón visited Bessastaðir on one occasion he saw Müller throw leaves of this manuscript out of the window in his living room. Jón had them retrieved but Müller insisted that they were useless: 'hann qvad ónytt vera' (*AMKat.* II: 72; cf. *LS* II: 186). Müller had also, at some point, been given a fourteenth-century manuscript of *Óláfs saga helga* (AM 325 V 4to) and when he gave it to Árni, perhaps as early as 1702, it lacked several leaves. Árni discovered two of those as the cover for a book belonging to Müller, who in 1704 gave Árni a few more. Two years later Árni received two leaves from Pétur Björnsson at Bustarfell in Vopnafjörður and suspected that they had originally come from Müller (*AMKat*. I: 555–6; Louis-Jensen 1979: 227–9). The complex network through which Árni acquired his manuscripts is illustrated by his acquisition of a fragmentary fourteenth-century collection of bishops' sagas (AM 219 fol.). In a note written c. 1725 he concluded that, even though the columns were not all equally long and wide, the 17 extant leaves had once belonged to a volume which had probably been torn apart somewhere in the North of Iceland. He had not recorded the provenance of all those leaves but remembered that three of them had been sent to Copenhagen before he went to Iceland: 'ante annum 1702'. In 1705 he had received two leaves from the Reverend Jón Torfason, who had obtained them in Eyjafjörður, and three leaves from Nikulás Einarsson. Another leaf was given to him in 1708 by the Reverend Þorlákur Grímsson who had acquired it in Eyjafjörður. At an unknown date Árni was presented with two leaves from Guðmundur Ólafsson, who had also received them in that region (*AMKat*. I: 178).

Before leaving for Iceland in 1702 Árni had received parts of *Hauksbók*, containing *Landnámabók* and *Kristni saga* (AM 371 4to), from the Reverend Ólafur Jónsson at Staður in Grunnavík. The leaves had belonged to his father, the Reverend Jón Torfason at Staður in Súgandafjörður, who had obtained them from a local farmer. When in Iceland, Árni received four more leaves, and on 17 April 1707 wrote to Ólafur with a number of questions that reveal his remarkable exactitude in the pursuit of manuscripts. What was the farmer's name and where did he live? How many leaves did Jón Torfason receive from the farmer and where had the farmer got them? How many years had passed since Jón acquired the fragment? Were the leaves loose or bound in quires? How thick was the manuscript? It was important to know the thickness, Árni argued, so that he could calculate how much of the manuscript had been lost. He also wanted to know what might have happened to missing leaves and whether there was any way of tracking them down. Árni explained that his questions were detailed because the fragment was among the most valuable of his many manuscripts. Even the smallest part was worth more than its weight in gold to him: 'mihi auro charior' (*PB*: 248–9). However, the Reverend Ólafur died that summer and when his father replied, on 28 December, he offered little additional information. The Reverend Jón only remembered that the farmer in question was Bjarni Indriðason at Skálavík and that the fragment only consisted of the fourteen leaves which Árni had received. Bjarni had acquired the fragment from his very old father who could barely read and could not recall where it came from. These were ignorant people, Jón explained, and it would be useless to pursue the matter any further (Jón Helgason 1960a: xxviii–xxix).

On 27 April 1707 Árni wrote two similar letters to the Westfjords on the subject of his vellums of *Sturlunga saga*. One of them went to Árni Guðmundsson at Bíldudalur, who in 1703 had provided Árni with some leaves of *Reykjarfjarðarbók* (AM 122 b fol.). Árni desired further details on its fate, or as he said in his letter:

> I would also like to request that if you, somewhere close to you or further away, get to know about the tiniest fragment from this book that you can acquire, that you do so, although you might think that it is worth little, and I will certainly remunerate your effort in any way that might please you. And you will hopefully understand how important it is to me to receive even a small leaf from this book, as I write to you in such detail.

> Þessu jafnframt vil eg ydur umbeded hafa, ef nockurstadar, nærre ydur, edur fiærre, vited til vera hid minsta ur optnefndre bók, sem i ydar vallde sie yfer ad komast þier þá vilied giöra so vel ad ná þvi sama, hversu litels vert sem synast kynne, og vil eg allt þetta ydar ómak gódu forskullda, ef nockud þar á mót ydur til vilia giört gæte. Og kunned þier vel skilia, hversu þægt mier mune hid minsta blad hier af, þar eg so itarlega hier um skrifa (*PB*: 170).

Árni's letter to the Reverend Páll Þórðarson was more complex as it concerned *Króksfjarðarbók* (AM 122 a fol.) of *Sturlunga saga* which the

Iceland

Reverend Páll Ketilsson had sent to Copenhagen (see p. 120), as well as a collection of sagas (AM 556 a–b 4to) and *Njáls saga* (AM 133 fol.). The three manuscripts had belonged to Þórður Steindórsson, Páll's father, who was still alive. The reply arrived in June and Árni's 23 questions had elicited little information. Þórður only remembered that Páll Ketilsson had acquired *Króksfjarðarbók* from him and that Finnur Jónsson at Kálfalækur had borrowed *Njáls saga*, but he could not remember where the saga collection had gone (*PB*: 520–1; Hast 1960: 15–16). All in all, the year 1707 yielded a good harvest of manuscripts for Árni, his dissatisfaction about spending too much time on other tasks notwithstanding; on 15 June 1707 he joked with Bishop Björn that the isolated island of Grímsey would have been a good place for him to pursue his studies, had the parish not been given to someone else (*PB*: 597). That same year, at Reykholt, Árni acquired yet another leaf containing *konungasögur* (AM 325 X 4to) and Guðrún Ögmundsdóttir sent a leaf from *Óláfs saga helga* (AM 325 XI 2 m 4to). The Reverend Jón Halldórsson at Hítardalur found one from a manuscript containing *Bjarnar saga Hítdælakappa* and *Kormáks saga* (AM 162 F fol.) and the Reverend Þorvaldur Stefánsson another from *Guðmundar saga góða* (AM 220 II fol.). Magistrate Sigurður Björnsson gave Árni a vellum of *Jónsbók* and *Kristinréttr Árna* (AM 155 a–b 4to) and his son, Sigurður Sigurðsson, gave him a fragment of *Stjórn* (AM 229 I fol.). Elín Þorláksdóttir provided a collection of sagas, transcribed by the Reverend Jón Pálsson at the bequest of her father, Bishop Þorlákur Skúlason (AM 496 4to, AM 329 2 4to). At the Alþingi Árni bought a vellum containing *Konungs skuggsjá* (AM 243 k fol.) and a theological treatise (AM 626 4to). He was also given a collection of early sixteenth-century *rímur* (AM 604 a–h 4to).

In the autumn of 1706 Árni asked Christian Reitzer to present his apologies to the French emissary in Copenhagen, to whom Árni had promised a catalogue of his manuscripts. On 26 May 1707 Reitzer replied that he had met the emissary before he left Copenhagen and assured him that the catalogue would be ready within a year. On 3 September Árni explained to Reitzer that he had not yet finished the catalogue and only had a preliminary version in Icelandic to hand, but if it was not completed during the winter he would take it with him to Copenhagen in

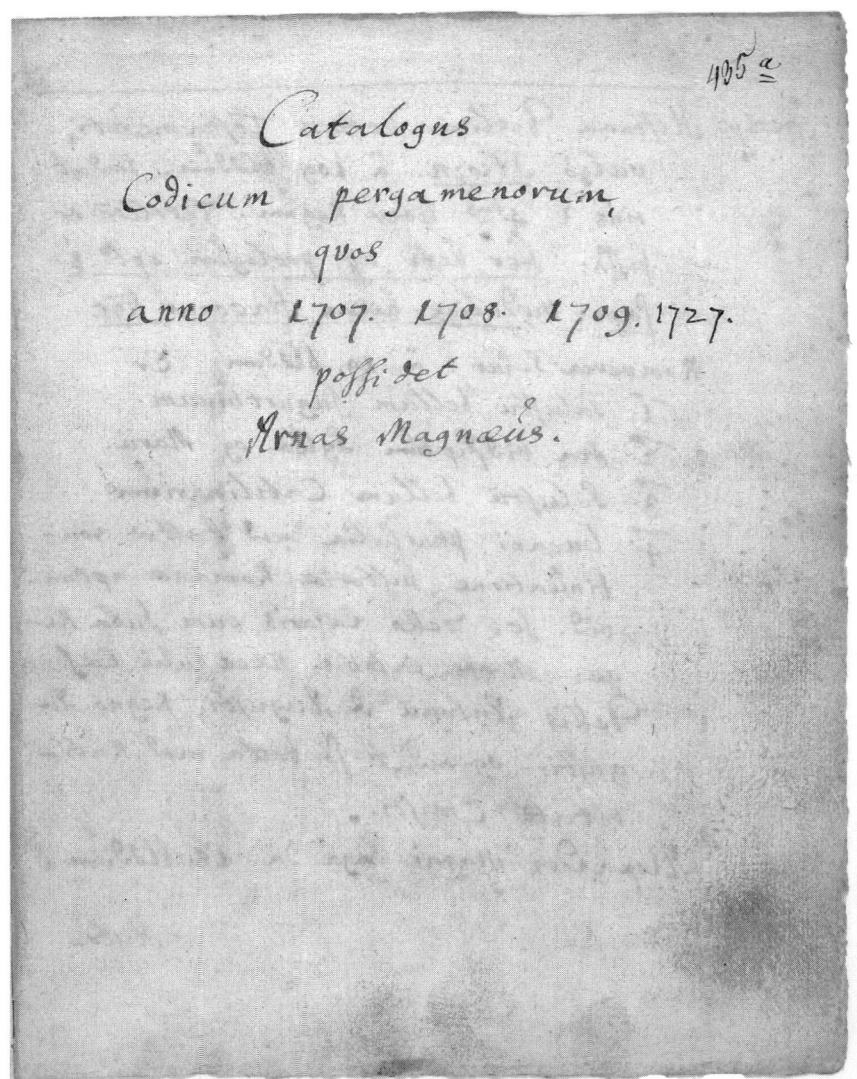

Figure 11. The front page of Árni's provisional catalogue of his vellum manuscripts (AM 435 a 4to: 1r).

whatever state of completion it was (*PB*: 371, 374, 378). Whether or not his excuses were truthful it is certain that in the winter of 1707–8 Árni started compiling a catalogue of his manuscripts in Icelandic (AM 435 a 4to), finishing it after he came back from Copenhagen in 1709. The first entry in this 'Catalogus Codicum pergamenorum', as Árni called it, is a vellum of *Stjórn* (AM 226 fol.), acquired in May 1708 from Brynjólfur Þórðarson at Hlíðarendi. For each manuscript, Árni made a list of its contents and in most cases provided information about how and where he had acquired it. This way of doing things was less detailed and less comprehensive than the standard followed by Árni's contemporaries, such as Humfrey Wanley, who in 1697 reported to the curators of the Bodleian Library in Oxford on his method in a prospective catalogue of Greek and Latin manuscripts. Titles would be given 'with two or three words of each tract, and shewing in what page it may be found'. He would say whether the manuscript was 'in paper or parchment, and how old it is, how many leaves it be on the whole'. He would tell whether the text had been printed and if that was the case 'whether it agree or disagree with the printed editions, and such like' (C.E. Wright 1960: 125–6).

In Árni's catalogue *Stjórn* is followed by vellums containing hagiography and theological treatises. Then follow kings' sagas, *Sturlunga saga*, *Íslendingasögur*, *biskupasögur*, *Snorra Edda* and annals. *Lygisögur* are in turn followed by *Landnámabók* and other texts of erudition, and then by *Karlamagnús saga*, *Þiðreks saga* and *Konungs skuggsjá*. Árni did not include his lawbooks in the catalogue and instead compiled a separate list in which he provided each vellum with identifying letters (Kålund 1909: 56; cf. Finnur Jónsson 1930a: 155–6). The catalogue does not include his fragments and Árni in fact never made a list of them; in the first version of the catalogue he explained that they were uncountable and had not been registered: 'Minora fragmenta eru otelianleg, og hefi eg þau eigi registrerad' (Kålund 1909: 25). He handled them with care, though, as can be seen in a note on two leaves of *Knýtlinga saga* which he took with him from Copenhagen to Iceland in 1706 and placed among his other fragments: 'nu 1706. eru þau komin saman vid önnur fragmenta' (AM 20 c fol.: 16r).

Apographa

Árni had a long-standing interest in medieval charters, not only because of his work on Bartholin's ecclesiastical history but also for his own research on Icelandic, Norwegian and Danish history. While in Copenhagen he had received a number of charters from Hólar as well as some fairly accurate copies. In a letter to Bishop Björn Þorleifsson on 14 May 1698 he asked that every transcription be furnished with information on whether its source was an original document, a good or bad copy, and that dates and names be exactly transcribed (*PB* 560). When it was decided that he would go to Iceland as representative of the king, he seems to have added to the description of his tasks that he should have unlimited access to documents (*Jarðabók* XIII: 10). It is also probable that it was his idea to ask landowners to provide an inventory of their property with supporting documentation (see p. 136). At that point, the concept of an all-encompassing archive of Icelandic historical documents may have been born, and while in Iceland Árni collected both original charters and old transcriptions. He also had copies made by his scribes, all on octavo-sized pages with a clearly defined method, albeit with some variations.

By the end of his life, Árni's collection contained around 2000 Icelandic charters and 6000 transcripts of charters and other documents from the twelfth century to the end of the seventeenth century, the so-called Icelandic *apographa*.[2] Árni rarely wrote comments on the charters but rather many on the transcripts, providing information on the originals and their owners. Most of these transcriptions are undated but one out of every ten ends with a verification (*vidisse*) of their exactitude signed by the scribe and other participants in Árni's project. At present

[2] The charters (indicated as AM Fasc) are divided between the National Archives of Iceland and the Árni Magnússon Institute in Reykjavík but have not been catalogued. The Icelandic *apographa* (AM Ap. Isl.) are kept at the Institute and there is no catalogue. My discussion is based on my own research and on work done by three students at the University of Iceland in 1997–8: Pétur Jónsson, María Ásdís Stefánsdóttir and Hallgrímur J. Ámundason. Árni Magnússon's 2000 Norwegian documents and 3000 transcripts, as well as his 1700 Danish documents and 1400 transcripts, are kept at the Arnamagnæan Institute in Copenhagen, and are also unregistered. They will only be mentioned sporadically in the present discussion.

the Icelandic *apographa* are kept in 76 bundles divided into six series, numbered in pencil by the librarian Kristian Kålund in the late nineteenth century, presumably in the order established by Árni. Series I contains documents ordered regionally from Þingeyjarsýsla to Árnessýsla (AM Ap. Isl. 1–1981). Series II covers the remaining districts but mostly relates to Skálholt, with items arranged to some extent in chronological order (1982–2855). Series III is dedicated to monasteries all over the country (2856–3048) but one of the bundles in Series I has transcripts of charters from the monastery at Þingeyrar (438–499). Series IV relates to Hólar cathedral, partly ordered chronologically from 1300 to 1600 (3049–3835). Series V is a jumble containing documents loosely ordered according to provenance at first (3836–4528) and subsequently in chronological order from 1551 to the end of the seventeenth century (4529–5509, 4720b–4819b). The remaining items are documents of diverse nature ordered by regions or years (5510–5909). Series VI deals with Vestmannaeyjar alone (5910–5942). At some point later Árni seems to have made an inventory of these transcripts in order to keep track of their ever-growing number, but no such document is preserved. There are however instances where he notes that documents have, or have not, been 'entered in' chronologically or according to the owners of the originals, for example that some documents dated 1561–70 had not been put in the list (4690–4776) and that documents borrowed in 1711 had been compared with the originals but not registered (4181–4292; cf. 114, 181–206).

The idea of gathering all these documents had probably been formed in Árni's mind in the autumn of 1702, when he asked Magistrate Lauritz Gottrup for access to all extant charters of the former monastery at Þingeyrar. Gottrup replied on 30 March 1703 and confirmed that he had given all the charters he had found written on parchment to Páll Vídalín (*PB*: 164). The first dated transcript in this 'new' project was made at Skálholt on 30 April 1703 and was certified by Benedikt Einarsson and Árni Gíslason (AM Ap. Isl. 5376). Árni Magnússon certainly had documents transcribed while at Bær on Rauðasandur in the summer of 1703 (AM Ap Isl. 1359). On 9 September 1703 he acknowledged that the *Amtmaður* Müller had lent him 121 parchment documents about the landed property of monasteries. Árni still had them in the spring of 1710 (*PB*: 56, 339). Hans Petersen Becker, who travelled to Iceland with Árni in 1702 and was fluent in Icelandic, transcribed two documents while at Skarð on Skarðsströnd in November 1703 and January 1704 (AM Ap. Isl. 5768, 5909). Two *apographa* were made in Skálholt in April 1704 (AM Ap. Isl. 1657, 2304) and a few more in Vestmannaeyjar while Árni was there in May and June (AM Ap. Isl. 14, 5192, 5917, 5928). Documents were thus copied *in situ* whenever possible, but it was of course more convenient for Árni to borrow them from the owners and make copies during the winter months in Skálholt. That was to become his policy, indicated as early as 28 January 1704 in a letter to the farmer Ásmundur Ketilsson who had asked for assistance in a dispute about landed property. In his reply, Árni asked for a good copy of a document from 1400 which Ásmundur had mentioned and explained his principles:

> I inquire for such old documents wherever I can, as well as for leaves from old Icelandic vellum books, and if you have some more of those or can procure them from others in your vicinity, please have them sent to me, at least on loan, if that is the only option.

> Eg spyrst og vidast epter þvilikum gömlum brefum, sem og einstaka blödum ur gömlum islendskum kalfskinns bókum, hvar af, ef þier nockud frekara hafed edur þar kringum ydur utvega kunned, þá bid eg ydur mier þess ad unna, i þad minsta til láns, ef ei ödruvis missast kann (*PB*: 271–2).

Árni wrote to people all over the country asking to borrow charters and documents. On 10 June 1704 Bessi Guðmundsson, sheriff of Múlasýsla, wrote that he had not found more documents written on parchment at Skriðuklaustur other than those he had already sent (*PB*: 171). Two days later, from the opposite side of the country, Magnús Magnússon at Eyri in Seyðisfjörður reported that he had already sent all the documents he had (*PB*: 311). On 5 June 1705 his daughter-in-law, Ingibjörg Pálsdóttir, explained to Árni that her brother, the Reverend Halldór Pálsson, had taken most of the documents written on parchment with him. She forwarded the remainder to Árni, who duly noted their receipt in the margin of her letter: 'medteked'. On 15 June Halldór sent the charters and other documents that he had taken from Eyri (*PB*: 350, 353).

THE DISTRIBUTION OF 346 TESTIFIED ICELANDIC *APOGRAPHA*	
Skálholt 2 November 1706–15 May 1707	13
Skálholt 5 December 1707–28 April 1708	44
Skálholt / Hvammur 7 September 1709–14 July 1710	49
Skálholt 2 October 1710–25 July 1711	78
Skálholt 9 September 1711–14 September 1712	162

Note: These transcripts may be representative of the whole collection but more secure results will only be reached after a study of all the scribes who worked for Árni.

Not many transcripts were made while Árni was in Copenhagen in 1705–6. When he returned to Iceland he took with him the charters of Stavanger in order to take notes on the ecclesiastical history of Norway (*PB*: 60–1). That indicates a growing interest in documents and after 1706–7 there was a sharp increase in the production of *apographa*, as can be seen in the box. More copies were made every year and documents poured in from everywhere. In December 1707 Árni had borrowed a number of charters from Grenjaðarstaður and promised to return them at the next *Alþingi*, while still hoping to obtain further documents from that church (*PB*: 601). On 30 June 1708 Eggert Snæbjörnsson confirmed that all the documents he had sent to Árni had been returned (*PB*: 469). On 14 January 1711 Ari Þorkelsson asked for charters which Árni had not sent back (*PB*: 533). On 4 July that year the Reverend Jón Þórarinsson thanked Árni for the return of the parchment charters belonging to the church in Hjarðarholt (*PB*: 513). In 1711 Þórður Þórðarson looked for documents in his trip to the Eastfjords (*PB*: 35, 126) and on 29 March 1712 Árni thanked the sheriff

Markús Bergsson of Ísafjarðarsýsla for old documents he had sent: 'þau medfylgiande gömlu bref' (*PB*: 46). Erlendur Jónsson wrote on 26 April that the documents which Árni had asked for were lost but that there were others available for consultation (*PB*: 230).

Árni transcribed hundreds of documents himself and his brother Jón even more, but others were paid to do the rest of the work and given instructions on how to proceed. Most of these scribes lived in Skálholt. Árni's two nephews, Snorri Jónsson and Ormur Daðason, were students, as were Gísli Bjarnason, Grímur Magnússon, Magnús Einarsson, Páll Hákonarson and Þorgils Sigurðsson. Others had positions at Skálholt, such as the cathedral priest Þorleifur Halldórsson, the steward Arngrímur Bjarnason, the schoolmaster Magnús Markússon and the printer Styr Þorvaldsson. While Árni was in Iceland his full-time assistants were the aforementioned Hans Becker and Þórður Þórðarson, both of whom transcribed hundreds of documents. Þórður, for instance, wrote from Skammbeinsstaðir on 6 January 1712 that he had not yet finished his transcription of the parchment charters he had with him: 'Ecke eru kalfskinna brefen buen, sem hiá mier eru' (*PB*: 523). A few scribes lived elsewhere and the documents were sent to them. The most important one was Eyjólfur Björnsson, who had previously worked with Árni (see p. 78); he made copies of most of the Stavanger charters (AM 222 8vo: 113r) and in January 1707 Árni sent him 89 old documents together with a supply of paper and tobacco (AM Ap. Isl.: between 348 and 349).

The *apographa* fall into two major categories, as Árni explained clearly in a note on copies made by Styr Þorvaldsson in Copenhagen on 7 June 1709. The oldest documents had been copied with great exactitude and the more recent ones only word by word: 'antiqvora her af eru accuratè skrifud, recentiora ordriett confererud' (AM Ap. Isl. 4443–4467). Exactitude meant that abbreviations and superscript signs were shown as they appeared in the originals. This applied, for example, to the transcripts of the sizable collection of charters from Þingeyrar. The orthography of the more recent documents was considered to be less important. They were thus copied with less detail, word by word: 'Ordriett epter originalnum' (AM Ap. Isl. 4862). This same distinction had governed Árni's earliest projects of transcribing medieval vellum manuscripts (see pp. 74, 78).

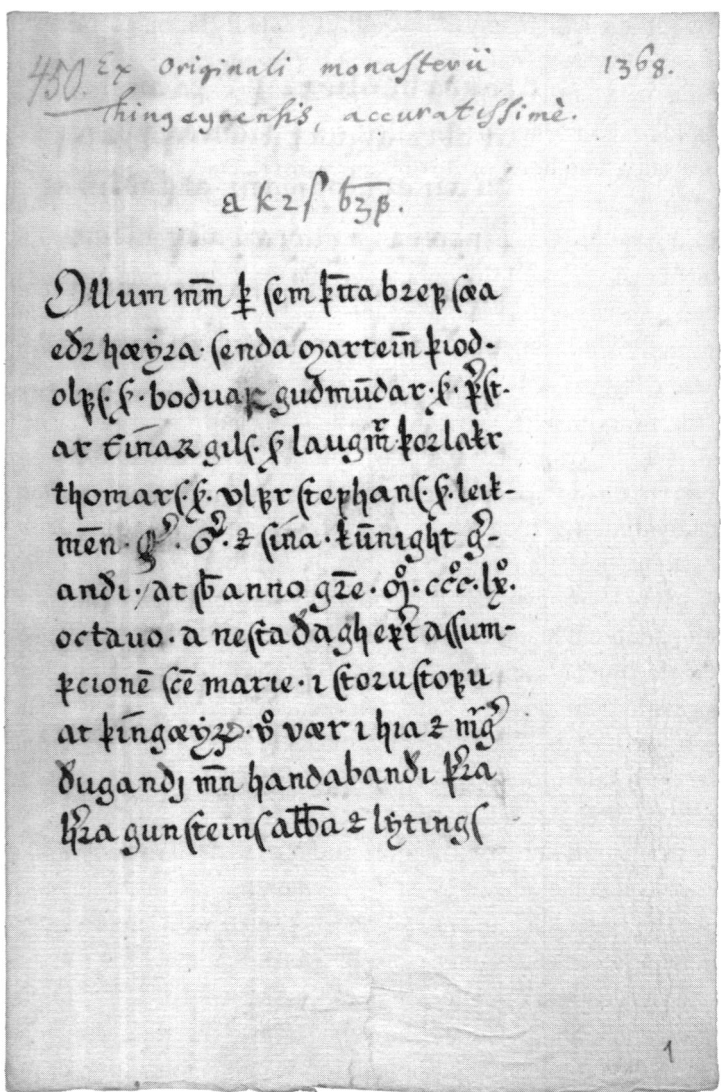

Figure 12. This document of 16 August 1368 was copied 'Ex originali monasterii Thingeyrensis, accuratissimè'. Árni Magnússon and Páll Hákonarson testify to the transcription in Skálholt on 10 August 1712. Árni describes two extant seals. Drawings of these seals are included as well as examples of letter-forms (AM Ap. Isl. 450: 1r).

Apographa

Árni supervised the project closely and seems to have compared the majority of his *apographa* with the originals. When necessary, he corrected the text between the lines or in the margins (cf. Stefán Karlsson 1963: lxvi). When the original text was difficult to decipher or damaged, the scribes left empty spaces, and sometimes Árni adopted an even more detailed method. In a comment to a document from 1476, to take only one example, he explained that underlined words were conjectures about text which was no longer visible due to damage, whereas dots referred to text which was barely legible (AM Ap. Isl. 2362). On another occasion Árni speculated on the possible readings of two unclear words, concluding that an error could arise when two similar letters were looked at rapidly (AM Ap. Isl. 51). The year in which the document itself was written, if known, was added above the beginning of the text, almost always by Árni himself, who often added the place where the original document came from and whether it was written on parchment or paper; for example 'Ex Origin. Vatzfiord. accuratissimè' (AM Ap. Isl. 892) and 'Ex originali chartaceo Einholtensi' (AM Ap. Isl. 2037). When he had completed these checks he could be content, as can be inferred from a note on copies of documents from Kirkjuból in Skutulsfjörður; they had been accurately copied and compared with the originals, and as the seals had also been sufficiently studied he had drawn all he could from the documents: 'in summa, usus sum til fullz' (AM 222 8vo: 68r).

On almost a third of these documents Árni describes how many seals were originally attached or how many were left and comments on their condition (e.g. Stefán Karlsson 1963: 28, 34, 51, 59, 64, 136–7). During his years in Iceland Árni also put together three special volumes about the seals of bishops, abbots, governors, sheriffs and farmers (AM 216–218 8vo) for 'historical', 'philological' and 'antiquarian' use as he stated on two of the three title pages (*Sigilla* II: 124, 223). Árni himself drew simple pictures, making primitive reproductions of the images or letters, and then copied the inscriptions separately (e.g. *Sigilla* II: 130, 134, 139, 225). More competently drawn reproductions were made by the Reverend Hjalti Þorsteinsson and Magnús Einarsson, some of them even based on several seals from the same person (e.g. *Sigilla* I: 88, 91, 184, 227, 316–26; *PB*: 636; AM 222 8vo: 139r, 141r). Árni sometimes checked whether a reproduction was accurate and once commented that he might have been wrong when he wrote that a particular seal was correctly drawn (*Sigilla* II: 44–5). As when comparing texts he speculated on details such as whether the letters of an inscription had faded, and he put dots under those that were not legible to the naked eye (*Sigilla* II: 120–1; cf. I: 41, 158–9). There were, thus, clear guidelines within a project that had the ambitious goal of securing in one place all available documents relating to the medieval history of Iceland.

Árni's notes are systematic in the sense that they provide the same kind of information for most of these texts, in particular on the original documents and the seals. On the other hand, they show the inconsistencies of Árni's somewhat erratic interest in particular items. When inspired by some detail he would write a note, but without noting comparable details in other documents or manuscripts. Given the magnitude of the task this seems understandable. Most of Árni's energy was devoted to keeping all threads together and his success can only be explained by his unwavering certainty that he was doing everything correctly. On one occasion he even wrote a comment on his capacity of not jumping to conclusions or being careless in his work: 'Þvi eg plaga ecki ad þviliku ad hrapa, eda ógiætiliga ad giöra' (*Sigilla* II: 192). Sometimes the task of keeping control over the material overwhelmed him, but he was confident that the problem would eventually be solved, as when he could not locate the copies of certain documents; they would indeed be found: 'Þær finnast þó vel sidan' (AM 222 8vo: 62r; cf. *Sigilla* I: 220, 252; II: 123, 184).

During his years in Iceland Árni also had copies made of manuscripts, mostly of vellums whose owners were reluctant to part with them for more than a short time. At Skarð on Skarðsströnd there was a collection of *postulasögur* (AM SÁM 1) whose owners would only lend it to Árni so that he could describe it and have it copied, but they refused to sell it or give it away (Eiríkur Magnússon 1892; cf. AM 85 8vo). Árni had accurate copies made by Eyjólfur Björnsson (AM 628 4to, AM 631 4to, AM 636 4to). Eyjólfur also made a copy of *Maríu saga* (AM 634–635 4to) from a now-lost vellum sent to him by Árni on 28 May 1712 (*PB*: 78). Eyjólfur copied *Guðmundar saga* (AM 397 4to) and *Nikulás saga* (AM 638 4to) from a vellum that Árni had borrowed from the University

Library in 1706 (see p. 146). When Árni asked Eyjólfur to transcribe *Guðmundar saga* he instructed him to write clearly with good margins and accurately according to the orthography of the original: 'accuratissime epter orthographia'. He wanted abbreviation marks to be copied as well as superscript strokes and majuscules, whether correct or not, and some particular letter forms were to be maintained, such as the long and round varieties of 's' and 'r.': 'Eins um lang s. og krók s. lang r. og krók r. et similia' (Guðvarður Már Gunnlaugsson 2001: 97, 102–3).

Eyjólfur's copy of *Ágústínus saga* (AM 648 4to) from a vellum in Árni's possession (AM 234 fol.) is not as accurate as those described above, nor are the copies he made from a collection of sagas (AM 152 fol.): *Göngu-Hrólfs saga* (AM 338 4to), *Gautreks saga ok Hrólfs* (AM 356 4to), *Grettis saga* (AM 476 4to) and *Mágus saga* (AM 535 4to). These copies may have been made for Árni's friends as gifts or as loans. Þórður Þórðarson, on the other hand, copied *Gyðinga saga* (AM 654 4to) and *Rómverja sögur* (AM 541 4to) with great exactitude from a vellum (AM 226 fol.) acquired by Árni in 1708. Þórður also transcribed *Hálfdanar saga brönufóstra* (AM 296 4to), *Sturlaugs saga starfsama* (AM 336 4to), *Egils saga einhenda* (AM 526 4to) and *Kirjalax saga* (AM 588 g 4to) from a vellum (AM 589 4to) provided by Bishop Björn Þorleifsson. Árni's brother Jón prepared an accurate copy (AM 467 4to) of *Njáls saga* (AM 468 4to); that vellum was sent to Árni in 1707 by his friend Niels Foss who had purchased it in Holland eleven years earlier (Kålund 1909: 31–2; *PB*: 153, 374, 379; Jón Helgason 1962: xv–xvi; Jón Þorkelsson 1879–89: 651).

Disgrace

In the autumn of 1706, at the instigation of Árni's political adversaries, Magnús Sigurðsson left for Copenhagen where he died in March 1707. The verdict in his case (see p. 141) had then been appealed to the Supreme Court (Már Jónsson 1998: 233–4). Árni and Páll met in Akranes in early June 1707, where Páll had already started working on the land register. They spent a week writing letters and Árni returned to

Skálholt while Páll continued with his task (*Annálar* I: 703; *Jarðabók* IV: 113–98; *Emb*: 224–5). They both attended the *Alþingi* and then travelled to Snæfellsnes. They finished their annual reports to Copenhagen on 17 September at Slitvindastaðir, where the Reverend Páll Ketilsson now lived (*Emb*: 240–94). Before arriving there, Páll Vídalín had been at Arnarstapi for the land register but was forced to leave as the region had become infested with smallpox; the disease had reached Iceland earlier in the summer in the clothing of a student who had died in Copenhagen and had thereafter spread rapidly. Three of Páll's men fell ill and one of them died. When Páll came to Slitvindastaðir Árni was in good health but his nephew Ormur Daðason was seriously ill. They left on 1 October and passed through Hvammur, where most people were sick. Páll was on his way to Víðidalstunga and Árni to Skálholt (Már Jónsson 1998: 256–7).

In the summer of 1707 a new man arrived on the Icelandic political scene. The young and wealthy Oddur Sigurðsson had spent the winter in Copenhagen and secured for himself the position of vice-magistrate to Lauritz Gottrup. Oddur was also to assist Árni and Páll with their work but instead criticised them harshly. On 4 September 1707 he wrote a stern letter to the *Stiftamtmaður* Ulrik Christian Gyldenløve, an illegitimate son of King Christian V, complaining that the commissioners had been at work on the land register for five years and only covered a quarter of the country. However, Árni still retained the support of King Frederik IV, who on 30 January 1708 asked Gyldenløve to order the *Amtmaður* Müller not to disturb Árni while he was in Iceland. In his reply to Gyldenløve, on 14 February, Müller asserted that Árni hated all honest Danes and wanted to get rid of them so that he could rule Iceland with his evil friends. This sufficed to persuade Gyldenløve to suggest to the king that Árni should be told to finish his business in Iceland and avoid all conflict in the meantime (Már Jónsson 1998: 253–6). Because of old age, Müller had been allowed to spend the whole year in Copenhagen. As his representative in Iceland he appointed Paul Beyer, whose nomination to the Royal Commission had been rejected by Árni six years earlier (see p. 134). Müller had in the past represented Gyldenløve, who despite being governor of Iceland had never set foot in the country. In the spring

Disgrace

of 1708, in what seems to have been a direct confrontation with Árni and Páll, Gyldenløve appointed Oddur Sigurðsson as his representative (Már Jónsson 1998: 258). King Frederik went along with his half-brother and on 21 May 1708 insisted that the commissioners should hasten their work. No results had been presented and he doubted whether the whole project would be of any use to the country (*Lovsamling* I: 657). Árni's enemies had now gained the upper hand in Denmark as well as in Iceland.

Among the tasks given to the commissioners in 1702 was to look into accusations concerning judicial malpractice in the last decades of the seventeenth century. This they did and immediately after the *Alþingi* of 1708 published their verdicts on four cases from the years 1678–99. The most important decision was that the recently retired Magistrate Sigurður Björnsson was found guilty of having made an agreement with the farmer Jón Hreggviðsson convicted for murder in 1684, promising to leave him alone if he did not insist on appealing the case to the Supreme Court in Copenhagen. These verdicts can be seen as a last resort in Árni and Páll's struggle against increasingly powerful detractors, whose friendship with Gyldenløve could sway the king's favour. On 3 September Sigurður asked the king to annul the verdict, arguing that after thirty years as a magistrate he had been stripped of his property and his reputation because of verdicts which had not been challenged before. Oddur, Müller and Gyldenløve supported Sigurður, who on 4 May 1709 was allowed to appeal the verdict to the Upper Court at the *Alþingi* (Már Jónsson 1998: 258–60; Finnur Jónsson 1930a: 88–93).

On 9 September 1708 Árni left Iceland in order to defend his case against the deceased Magnús Sigurðsson before the Supreme Court. On 27 October he asked the king for more time to translate the relevant documents and insisted that the case had been made up by his enemies in order to destroy him: 'til at ruinere mig' (*Emb*: 309). On 21 March 1709, eight out of nine judges decided that since Magnús was dead, all former verdicts should be annulled. His accusations towards Árni and Þórdís were invalid and Árni's reputation untainted, but his treatment of Magnús had been too aggressive. The ninth judge was convinced that Árni and Þórdís had actually had an affair, which again had caused Árni to persecute Magnús; Árni thus should repay Magnús's heirs the 300 rigsdaler that the

Alþingi had ordered Magnús to pay (*Emb*: 311, 593–600; Finnur Jónsson 1930a: 97–8; Már Jónsson 1998: 238–9). In his younger years Árni had been reluctant to consider marriage (see p. 123) and he was sincerely shaken by Magnús Sigurðsson's malignant accusations of adultery. He appears to have had no interest in women. It might then seem strange that two months after the verdict Árni married, but that can only be seen as a coincidence. The marriage took place on 16 May 1709 and the bride was Mette Jensdatter Fischer, widow of the royal saddle-maker Hans Hendrichsen Wichmand who had died two years earlier. The bride was quite well off and 64 years old at the time, nineteen years older than the groom. Three young Icelanders wrote poems to celebrate the event, which were printed. One of them, Magnús Arason, describes how Vulcanus, the god of fire, made the Icelandic volcano Hekla his home, where his wife Venus kept her bonfires of love. As Árni Magnússon heard of this he hastened to observe the spectacle and was hit by an arrow, which then burned in his chest. In order to put out the fire he went to Copenhagen where Venus showed pity and led him to a woman called Fiskera; he should now take his bride in his arms. Six weeks after the ceremony Árni and Mette obtained permission to make a common will (Westergård-Nielsen 1966: 5–11, 18–24; Már Jónsson 1998: 260–2; Finnur Jónsson 1930a: 67–8; *LS* I, 2: 115–19; *Lovsamling* I: 662–3; *Emb*: 333).

On 20 June 1709, just before he left for Iceland, Árni sought permission to return to Copenhagen in the autumn. The delay in finishing the land register, he claimed, was due to the fact that the commissioners had been forced to attend to other matters; therefore they needed two more years to complete their task. His plan was to return to Copenhagen in the autumn and travel from there to Múlasýsla or Ísafjarðarsýsla in the spring of 1710, and then return again. He would thus only stay in Iceland during the summer. The government rejected his proposal on 29 June on the grounds that the completion of the land register would be further delayed. Árni should stay in Iceland (*Emb*: 320–31, 334). He left Helsingør on 7 July and just after his arrival in Þorlákshöfn, on 3 August, he informed his wife that the trip had gone well (*PB*: 286). In another letter at the end of September he lamented that the Danes were now leaving for home while he was compelled to stay. He sent 50 rigsdaler as a New Year's gift and told her to buy something nice. She also received a long list of errands and books to be put in storage (*PB*: 286–94; Már Jónsson 1998: 264–5). Árni also missed the city in which, as he remarks in a letter to the Royal Exchequer on 13 September, he could pursue his scholarly activities undisturbed (*Emb*: 338).

In the summer of 1710 the verdicts pronounced in 1708 by Árni and Páll were tried before the Upper Court at the *Alþingi*. Páll defended their conclusions in excruciating detail. On 21 July the court decided that Magistrate Sigurður Björnsson should swear that he had not made an agreement with Jón Hreggviðsson. Other cases in which Árni and Páll gave verdicts in 1708 were adjourned (*Emb*: 375–415; Már Jónsson 1998: 270–1). Instead of going to Þingvellir Árni had departed on his announced trip to Ísafjarðarsýsla. The first meeting with local farmers took place at Kirkjuból in Langidalur on 1 July. Magnús Einarsson took care of the land register and went on to Grunnavík and Aðalvík, where he was between the 8 and 14 July. Árni probably waited in Vatnsfjörður where his friend the Reverend Hjalti Þorsteinsson lived, and was still there on 24 July (AM Ap. Isl. 920). Besides Magnús, Árni's retinue consisted of Þórður Þórðarson, Þorsteinn Sigurðsson, Þorsteinn Ketilsson and Hans Becker, who had all transcribed documents for him. On 7 August, at Eyri in Skutulsfjörður, Árni paid for liturgical fragments received three years earlier and arranged for the delivery of eider down to his wife (*PB*: 295; *Jarðabók* VII: 140–317). Páll Vídalín joined him at Hrafnseyri in Arnarfjörður and for the next three weeks they wrote letters to Copenhagen. Bishop Jón Vídalín arrived on 15 September on his way to inspect churches in the region and was accompanied by four young men who had made copies for Árni: Gísli Bjarnason, Grímur Magnússon, Þorgils Sigurðsson and Vigfús Jóhannsson (Már Jónsson 1998: 271–3). From this trip there survive six testified transcripts of documents (AM Ap. Isl. 2344, 2348, 2349, 4498, 5227, 5380) and it is likely that many more were made.

During this journey Árni acquired a number of recent transcriptions of sagas (AM 407 4to, AM 408 b 4to, AM 537 4to, AM 545 4to, AM 582 4to and AM 539 4to which at the time included AM 554 h α 4to,

AM 630 4to and AM 779 c II 4to). The only complete vellums he added to his collection were two copies of *Jónsbók*, one of which he described as good and old: 'gott gamalt exemplar' (AM 168 a–b 4to). The other one (AM 48 8vo) attracted no such comment. A few fragments appeared too. Jón Hannesson at Reykjarfjörður close to Vatnsfjörður came up with three leaves of *Knýtlinga saga* which he had removed from books (AM 20 b II fol.). Árni himself identified fragments of *heilagramannasögur* (AM 238 I fol.) as the cover of an inventory of church property from Holt in Önundarfjörður. He made inquiries about *Reykjarfjarðarbók* (AM 122 b fol.) of *Sturlunga saga* and gathered some information on its destiny, but only acquired half a leaf from a farmer in Arnarfjörður (Már Jónsson 2009a: 89).

On 12 June 1710 the Exchequer granted Árni and Páll one more year to finish their work in Iceland. They received the letter on 9 October, after they were back in Hvammur. In their reply, dated 20 October, they repeated once more that they were being persecuted, mostly by Oddur Sigurðsson. Oddur also wrote to Copenhagen to explain his side of the story and asked the *Stiftamtmaður* Gyldenløve not to believe anything that the commissioners wrote. In the spring of 1711 Árni and Páll were allowed to launch an appeal to the Supreme Court in Copenhagen against the verdict of the Upper Court in the case of Magistrate Sigurður Björnsson. Árni did not attend the *Alþingi* for a third consecutive year, leaving Páll Vídalín to ward off their enemies (Már Jónsson 1998: 275–6). Árni aimed to work on the land register in Múlasýsla but was forced to turn back because of bad weather while on his way across Sprengisandur (Gunnar F. Guðmundsson 1990b: 35–6, 40). Their position became even weaker when, on 10 June 1711, the Exchequer reprimanded them and decided to allow no further expenses. Árni received the letter on 13 August (*Emb*: 432–3) and six weeks later explained that their reports from the previous year had perished at sea. He expected to leave for Copenhagen in the autumn of 1712 but would not take any documents with him because of the war between Denmark and Sweden. He also argued that it would take too much time to produce a copy of the entire land register (*Emb*: 471–4). In a letter to Bishop Jens Bircherod, dated 27 September 1711, he explained that he would not risk the commission papers in such dangerous times, as they could fall into the hands of the Swedes, and the same was true of the Stavanger charters which the bishop wanted back (*PB* 64).

VELLUMS ACQUIRED BY ÁRNI MAGNÚSSON IN 1711

Heilagramannasögur, c. 1400, one leaf (AM 235 fol.)
Elucidarius, fifteenth century, four leaves (AM 238 XVIII fol.)
Óláfs saga Tryggvasonar, fourteenth century, one leaf
    (AM 325 VIII 2 d 4to)
Hákonar saga Hákonarsonar, c. 1400, one leaf
    (AM 325 X 4to)
Guðmundar saga góða, c. 1500, one leaf (AM 220 II fol.)
Álaflekks saga, *Hálfdanar saga brönufóstra*, *Þorsteins þáttr
    bæjarmagns* and *Grettis saga*, sixteenth century, 12 leaves
    (AM 571 4to)
Bærings saga, *Rémundar saga* and *Elís saga*, fifteenth century,
    17 leaves (AM 574 4to)
Sigurðar saga þögla, fourteenth century, ten leaves (AM 596 4to)
Jónsbók, fourteenth century, 98 leaves (AM 127 4to)
Jónsbók, written in 1578, 126 leaves (AM 38 8vo)

A letter sent to Árni from Jacob Mathesius in the spring of 1712 shows that the commission had few supporters in Copenhagen. After describing how he had argued in their support within the royal administration, Mathesius declared that he was alone against everyone: 'Jeg er solus contra omnes' (*PB*: 334). The government was dismayed at the costs and appalled by the incessant quarrels between the commissioners and other officials. On 22 July the Exchequer alleged that it had received no satisfactory answers for two years. Árni was ordered to come to Copenhagen in the autumn and explain the delays, costs and disagreements. He could leave the commission's papers behind but had to bring excerpts from the most important parts of their work. Árni did not see this letter until he received a copy in the following year (see p. 173). He was unaware that he had been summoned to Copenhagen but had already decided to leave, not least because he wanted to be present when the Supreme Court tried the case against Sigurður Björnsson (*Emb*: 495–7; Már Jónsson 1998: 278–80). His resolve may have been strengthened when he received a letter from his wife on 21 June. They had not seen each other for almost three years and she looked forward to see him (*PB*: 296–8).

Árni did not go to the *Alþingi* this summer either, again leaving Páll to cope with their political adversaries. In July, Páll borrowed some Swedish medieval lawbooks printed in the seventeenth century (*PB*: 94; cf. Schück 1932-44, I: 81). He also, perhaps as a parting gift, came up with a leaf from *Andreas saga postula* (AM 238 II fol.). Just before Árni left ('under þad eg fra Islandi for'), the Reverend Árni Þorleifsson gave him two leaves from a vellum of *Nikulás saga* (AM 642 b 4to). On 16 August 1712 Árni informed Magistrate Gottrup that he had asked Páll to return the documents from Þingeyrar which had been on loan for a while (see p. 154). As a remuneration Árni sent a charter concerning a farm owned by Gottrup (*PB*: 162–3). On 3 September he was in Skálholt; he went from there to Reykjavík and on 19 September left Iceland for good (Már Jónsson 1998: 280).

7
Copenhagen

> I would rather spend my
> time reading an old book.
>
> [. .] vil eg miklu helldur eyda
> tidenne med ad horfa i gamla bók.
>
> Árni Magnússon in the spring of 1728 (*PB*: 97)

This chapter describes Árni Magnússon's work in Copenhagen after he left Iceland. Because of the Great Northern War he was forced to leave his manuscripts and documents behind in September 1712 and only got them back more than eight years later. He was reluctant to deliver a final report on the work of the Royal Commission and spent most of his time on scholarly matters. He attended to his jobs as archivist and professor, looked after his collection and published little as before.

Back home

After reaching far into Russia, Swedish forces were repulsed after the battle of Poltava in Ukraine on 8 July 1709. King Charles XII escaped to friendly territory in the Ottoman empire. In November the Danish government decided to join the war again in the hope of re-conquering Scania, which had been lost to Sweden half a century earlier. Danish troops enjoyed success at first but were put to flight four months later. Subsequently they took part in battles in northern Germany, aiding Russia and Saxony against Sweden. At the end of 1711, however, Swedish forces entered Holstein, thereby threatening Jutland. Sailing in the North Sea and Kattegat had become dangerous (Olsen 1970: 428–48). When Árni left Iceland his manuscripts and documents were in storage in Skálholt. Páll Hákonarson was entrusted with the keys to the

32 chests. According to an extant list, original charters and documents, as well as Árni's transcripts (*apographa*), were placed in six of these chests; the papers of the Royal Commission were kept in another five. Two chests were filled with printed books and a red chest contained Árni's scholarly notes, 'Collectanea varia'. Although there is no mention of manuscripts in the list they must have been stored in the remaining chests. Árni did make an inventory of the manuscripts he put in storage but tore it up in 1723, after his belongings had been transported from Iceland back to Copenhagen (*LS* II: 226–9; AM 267 8vo: 28r–52v; AM 1057 IX 4to: 60r–v).

Some of the manuscripts had been lent to his friends and collaborators. Ormur Daðason borrowed *Alexanders saga* (AM 519 a 4to) and *Örvar-Odds saga* (AM 344 a 4to), together with two vellums of *Jónsbók* (AM 344 fol., AM 351 fol.), as well as a number of printed books. Ormur also kept some recent genealogical collections with the intention of comparing them with other such manuscripts (Jón Helgason 1966: xix; AM 209 8vo: 63r–73v). Árni's other close collaborators were assigned a variety of tasks. Þórður Þórðarson was asked to compare the *postulasögur* (AM SÁM 1) on loan from Skarð to copies which had already been made. Magnús Einarsson was given some documents to copy; he was also to make drawings of seals and transcribe *Maríu saga* (AM 633 4to) from a now-lost vellum. Páll Hákonarson was to copy documents and compare the text of various sagas (*PB*: 176–7). He did that meticulously, to say the least, and indicated variant readings with Greek letters and other elaborate proof-reading signs, as can be seen in two paper manuscripts containing *Jómsvíkinga saga* (AM 288 4to) and *Trójumanna saga* (AM 597 b 4to; cf. Jón Helgason 1960b: 12; Jón Helgason 1970b: 355–6; *LS* II: 157).

Because of the war, merchant ships sailing from Iceland to Copenhagen first went to Norway where they waited for naval escort (Olsen 1970: 491). Sigurður Sigurðsson, son of Magistrate Sigurður Björnsson, was with Árni on the ship that left Reykjavík on 19 September 1712, heading for Copenhagen. Sigurður wrote a journal which provides fascinating details on a hazardous trip that took almost five months to complete. Sigurður's task was to defend his father's case before the Supreme Court in the hope of overthrowing Árni and Páll's verdicts of

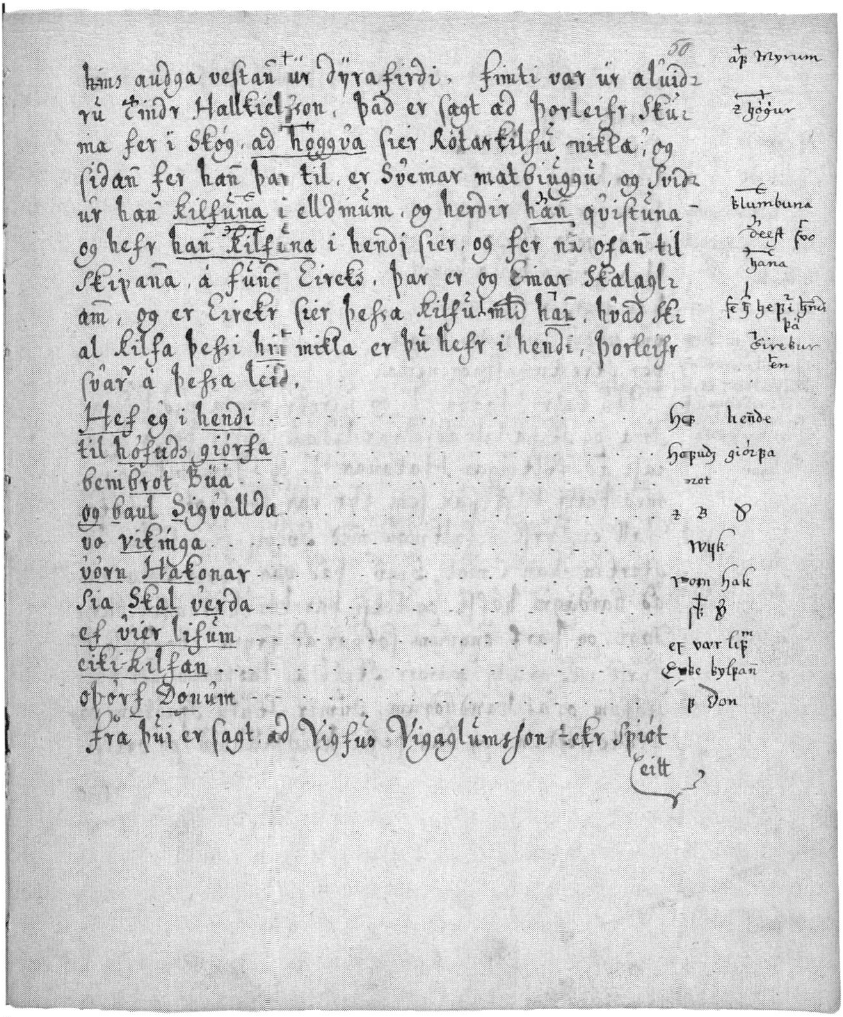

Figure 13. An impressive way of showing variants designed by Páll Hákonarson c. 1712 (AM 288 4to: 50r).

1708 (see p. 163). Despite their legal dispute the two men got on well. Due to bad weather it took the ship three weeks to reach Skudesnes, not far from Stavanger. On Wednesday 12 October Árni and Sigurður went on horseback to visit Þormóður Torfason at Stangeland and stayed for the night. On Sunday Árni went back to Stangeland and rejoined the ship a week later (Lbs 427 8vo: 40r–43r).[1] Þormóður was now 76 years old and had suffered a stroke six years earlier. Since they last met, in 1698, he had been productive. *Series dynastarum et regum Daniæ* (see pp. 127–8) had appeared a few months after Árni left for Iceland in 1702 (*BT*: 362; Finnur Jónsson 1930a: 47). It received immediate praise in learned journals, such as the French publication *Mémories de Trévoux*, where Þormóður is called a 'destroyer of lies' ('destructeur du mensonge') and a 'restorer of truth' ('restaurateur de la verité'). Árni had the French text copied and Otto Sperling translated it into Latin (AM 219 8vo: 136r–138r, 145r–146r). In 1705, Þormóður published *Historia Vinlandiæ antiqvæ*, about the discovery of America, and *Historia Hrolfi Kraki*, an annotated and paraphrased version of *Hrólfs saga kraka*. In 1706, he published *Gronlandia antiqva*, on medieval Greenland, and in 1707, *Trifolium historicum*, about three early kings of Denmark. The first two volumes of his *Historia rerum Norvegicarum* appeared in 1711 (Halldór Hermannsson 1954: 86–90; *BT*: xx–xxi; Þormóður Torfason 2008: 149–58; Dahl 1914).

While at Stangeland, Árni made an inventory of Þormóður's collection of 51 manuscripts, most of them written by Ásgeir Jónsson, who had left Þormóður's service in 1705 and died two years later. Árni had old inventories for comparison and noticed that many items had disappeared (Kålund 1909: 82–91). He also went through Þormóður's working papers and threw away drafts of translations made for King Frederik III half a century earlier. He assumed that the finished translations were in the Royal Library and reasoned that since the drafts were badly written and incorrect they would not be needed (Kålund 1909: 89). As payment for these efforts Árni received a manuscript of *Sturlunga saga* transcribed by Jón Erlendsson (AM 115 fol.), a collection of *rímur* (AM 732 a I 4to), an Icelandic book of prayers (AM 424 12mo), a description of Greenland

---

[1] I thank Gísli Baldur Róbertsson who showed me this text and provided a transcript.

in Danish (AM 777 a 4to) and a copy of *Völuspá* made by Guðmundur Andrésson (AM 165 8vo). He also borrowed recently-transcribed annals (AM 410 4to) and *rímur* on King Óláfr Tryggvason (AM 605 g 4to), and was promised that he would receive the whole collection when Þormóður died (Már Jónsson 1998: 288).

Árni and Sigurður left Skudesnes on 24 October. They travelled down the coast by boat and on horseback, arriving two weeks later at Flekkerøy, where eighteen merchant ships which had not reached Iceland during the summer were still waiting to be escorted. On this journey, Árni made notes on megaliths (*bautasteinar*) and churches. In the town of Stavern the two men secured passage on a ship that left on 6 December heading for Fladstrand in Jutland. The weather was extremely bad and while Árni was allowed to stay in the captain's cabin Sigurður had to sit with the other passengers, soaked and freezing (Lbs 427 8vo: 47v). After two weeks at sea the captain decided to return to Norway. Árni and Sigurður left Stavern for a second time on 19 December but that vessel also returned to port. Finally, on 5 February 1713, a military convoy left Stavern for Fladstrand with six thousand soldiers. The two Icelanders boarded the same ship on which they had left Iceland almost five months earlier. This time the crossing took just one day. On 20 February they left for Copenhagen by land, arriving on 2 March (Lbs 427 3vo: 54r–56r; Hødnebø 1988; Már Jónsson 1998: 288–9).

In the winter of 1711–12 the city of Copenhagen had been hit by a devastating plague, to which at least a third of its sixty thousand inhabitants succumbed. According to Árni's wife Mette, who wrote to him on 4 April 1712, seven thousand young women were among the dead, two of whom had been in her service (*PB*: 296). She herself was not affected and when Árni returned he took up residence in her house on Slotsholmen. One of his first tasks was to obtain a copy of the letter of 22 July 1712, in which the Exchequer had ordered his return to Copenhagen (see p. 168). The letter never reached Iceland and may have been on one of the ships waiting to go to Iceland which Árni saw at Flekkerøy. He received a copy on 26 March 1713 and decided not to reply until he had seen the original. That was the beginning of a protracted struggle with the government concerning the results, or rather the perceived lack of results, of his and Páll

Vídalín's work in Iceland. A lot of money had been spent and nothing seemed to have come out of it (Már Jónsson 1998: 308). To make things even worse the Supreme Court on 15 May 1713 overturned the commissioners' verdict against Magistrate Sigurður Björnsson, who was freed of all charges and awarded 300 rigsdaler in compensation for the unjust accusations against him, to be paid by Árni and Páll. In a note written on a copy of the Supreme Court's decision Árni expressed his fear that his enemies in Iceland would react by confiscating his belongings ('töi') in Iceland, which probably, in his mind, meant the manuscripts too (Már Jónsson 1998: 307).

On 21 November 1713 the Exchequer decided not to wait any longer and asked for a report on the Royal Commission. On 16 December Árni explained that little work remained to be done on the land register and added that he had only left Iceland to be present when Sigurður Björnsson's case came before the Supreme Court. He was still angry at the injustices that he and Páll Vídalín had suffered at the hands of Oddur Sigurðsson and Paul Beyer, but declared that he would not pursue the matter since the letter would be too long and nothing was to be gained by revealing too much of the truth. Árni also wished to be informed about the allegations made by the *Stiftamtmaður* Gyldenløve. They would have to be refuted, he wrote, if his reputation were to remain intact. The Exchequer, on 6 January 1714, refused to provide the details of the accusations and instead demanded a report on the land register, claiming that Árni would surely know enough about his work to produce one, even though the papers had been left in Iceland (*Emb*: 502–6; Már Jónsson 1998: 308–9). Árni did not reply and nothing happened until nine years later, as the Exchequer in a letter of 26 February 1723 asked him to hand over the complete land register (*Emb:* 555). He replied on 17 July and said that he had been almost forced to go to Iceland in 1702; adding that the land register was already at the Exchequer and had been since February 1721. He provided a detailed description of what had been written on each and every farm and offered to take all the individual registers, around 120–30, to his home, put them in the correct order and have them bound in 10 or 12 volumes at his own expense (*Emb:* 562–5). The Exchequer did not accept that and insisted repeatedly that he should come and take a look at the papers (*Emb:* 566–7, 571); adding on 5 July 1727 that the whole thing ought to be translated into Danish (*Emb:* 573). The Royal Archives were adjacent to the Exchequer and it would have been easy for Árni to comply, but by not reacting he demonstrated his discontent with how the commissioners had been treated. He finally succeeded in having the chests sent to his home, which happened on 23 July 1727; he promised to have each district (*sýsla*) bound in a separate volume and to write a report on what could be done with the land register as a whole (*Emb:* 578). In June 1728 and March 1729 the Exchequer politely asked how the translation was progressing. Árni never replied (*Emb:* 580–1, 588–9; Már Jónsson 1998: 311–12).

After the Reformation of 1536–7 Copenhagen University had taken over a number of large houses with sizeable gardens which had previously belonged to the cathedral. They came to be used as residences for professors who had a seat on the *Consistorium* (Már Jónsson 1998: 289–90). Árni had become a member in 1710, thus receiving the title of 'assessor', and on 13 March 1714 he chose a house on Store Kannikestræde where his colleague and friend Christian Reitzer had lived. Árni and Mette had already moved there by then, however, as an auction of books was held in his 'Canicke-strædet' house on 28 December 1713. Around 400 books were to be sold, among them Árni's 1695 Leipzig edition: 'Chronicon Danicum editum ab Arna Magnæo' (*Fortegneise paa en Deel Bøger*: 8vo nr. 66). On 15 January 1714 King Frederik IV bought Mette's house on Slotsholmen for 3000 rigsdaler with the intention of bringing it down to make space for buildings for his administration (*Emb*: 507–9; Már Jónsson 1998: 289–90; Westergård-Nielsen 1966: 25–6).

Not much is known of Árni's duties as secretary to the Royal Archives, which were kept in the cellar of Rosenborg castle. A few traces remain of his work there, most notably notes on the relocation of several medieval documents from one shelf to another. On 26 November 1715 he noted that Rostgaard had borrowed two volumes of a description of Finnmark. At Copenhagen University Árni was tutor (*præceptus*) to 175 students in the years 1713–29, fifteen of whom were Icelanders (Finnur Jónsson 1930a: 116; Már Jónsson 1998: 319). In 1713–22 he lectured on Saxo and Danish medieval historiography. At the end of 1720, when

Professor Hans Bircherod died, Árni became professor of history and geography. In the years 1725–7 he lectured on the geography and history of Europe. No lecture notes survive and there is no way of knowing how he performed (*Lectiones publicæ professorum*; cf. Már Jónsson 1998: 312; Ellen Jørgensen 1931: 150; Slottved 1978: 155). It may be, though, that some paragraphs on the discipline of history, assembled under the heading *De historiâ*, were teaching notes which he jotted down in the years immediately after his return. He starts with the dictum of the Greek historian Thucydides that history is a beautiful mirror of the human condition and, rather surprisingly given his personal preference for medieval manuscripts, argues for the need for teaching contemporary history. He also claims that the explanation of causes and context is the historian's most important task. Last but not least he tackles the question of how best to cite documents in books of history. Some scholars, he says, cite documents within the body of their text but others prefer to include them as appendices. Árni favoured the latter method, even while conceding that it would be advantageous for the reader to read the documents without having to refer to the end of the book (AM 228 8vo: 83r–93v; *LS* II: 123–6; Árni Magnússon 1998).

Árni should have served as Dean of the Faculty of Philosophy over the winter of 1714–15 but allowed Søren Lintrup, who was next in line, to assume those duties. In the academic year 1720–21, when it was again his turn, Árni asked Hans Gram to take his place, an arrangement which was repeated six years later. Árni may have thought that the position was too time-consuming. He did not turn his back on all administration, however, and was present at every other meeting of the *Consistorium* (Már Jónsson 1998: 314). He assumed other tasks too. The University Library had moved in 1657 to the top floor of Trinitatiskirken with an entry from the fourth floor of the newly completed Round Tower (Rundetårn). The walls and the furniture were painted in yellow, red and green, and the bookshelves decorated with designs meant to quicken the visitors' minds and encourage them to read. In 1723 the library was open on Wednesdays and Saturdays, from eight to ten in the morning and from one to four in the afternoon. Manuscripts could only be read in the presence of a librarian (Ilsøe 1980: 333–6; Villadsen 1980: 168–70). Árni became second librarian on 19 July 1721, after the death of Professor Caspar Bartholin. Árni attended to the books and oversaw the daily running of the library. The head librarian, Professor Hans Bartholin, supervised the accounts. Caspar and Hans were brothers of Thomas the younger, professor and royal antiquarian. Árni may have become head librarian in 1725, when Hans died, but as the acts of the *Consistorium* for that year have been lost this cannot be confirmed (RA. KU 12.03.16: 538, 828; Birket Smith 1882: 59). Nothing is known about Árni's activities as librarian, except that he ordered the binding of two or three vellum manuscripts of *Heimskringla* (Kålund 1900: xiv–xv; Finnur Jónsson 1930a: 117).

Another of Árni's duties as professor was to evaluate books that had been proposed for publication or were to be reissued. In 1720 his friend Joachim Wieland had big plans for publishing books. Wieland's first project a year earlier had been Árni's edition of the testament of King Magnús Hákonarson of 1277 (see p. 199) and he had just started a weekly journal on learned matters: *Nye Tidender om lærde Sager* (Søllinge and Thomsen 1988: 88–9). When asked for his opinion, Árni objected to the publication of a book on Luther's *Little Catechism* and found it risky to encourage excessive diversity in public opinion. He thought it was better, in matters of religion, that everyone thought alike. On the other hand, Árni was in favour of a new edition of Peder Syv's collection of folksongs (*viser*), noting that people liked legends. His tolerance, however, did not extend to adventure stories and comedies sold in the street which were read only for pleasure. He favoured a book in Latin on the Danish church on the grounds that it would strengthen Denmark's reputation abroad. He refused to comment on a book dealing with politics, concluding that state officials would have to decide on its suitability, as one never knew what such writings could lead to (*Emb*: 534–7; Már Jónsson 1998: 316).

Professors did not have a fixed salary but instead shared the substantial profits of the university's landed property and tithes in parishes around Copenhagen. As secretary to the Royal Archives Árni received 500 rigsdaler per year, the same as the director Frederik Rostgaard. The highest officials earned between 600 and 800 rigsdaler. Árni's overall income probably came close to this sum (Slottved and Thøgersen 1980:

1–2, 28–9, 39–40, 43–5; Már Jónsson 1998: 323). His social standing was thus quite high and this is indeed reflected in his expenses. In these years, for example, Árni and Mette had four servants and owned a carriage and two mares. In 1720 their residence was assessed at 690 rigsdaler and was among the largest houses in the neighbourhood. Árni was responsible for its maintenance, such as the decoration and installation of new window panes. The incessant repairs of the carriage were even more costly, as the wheels were constantly being damaged. For the upkeep of two horses Árni paid 20 rigsdaler per year. As all respectable men he wore a wig and thus needed the services of a barber twice a week, at an average annual cost of four rigsdaler. He employed a tailor to make and alter his clothes but his maid-servants undertook minor repairs, and in his private papers there are receipts for buttons for shirts and dresses and camel-hair for linings. In the years 1716–20 Árni had eleven pairs of shoes made for himself and eight for his servants. Coffee and tea were regularly purchased. In 1721 he had a coffee pot made for 42 rigsdaler and a much smaller teapot for only four rigsdaler. That same year, on 22 May, he bought five bottles of Mosel wine from the merchant Peter Abbesté. Other luxury items frequently appear in receipts which have been preserved among his papers: sugar and rice, raisins and prunes, nutmeg, cinnamon and cardamom (Már Jónsson 1998: 326–8; based on AM 452 fol.: 295–470).

After King Frederik IV bought Mette's house and other buildings on Slotsholmen they were demolished to make space for a building for the royal administration. A special three-storey house, adjacent to the Royal Library, was built for the Royal Archives. On 11 April 1720 the holdings were transported with military escort from Rosenborg castle. Árni had estimated the manpower requirements; for instance that four men were needed to carry big chests full of documents whereas two men could carry smaller chests. The next day Frederik Rostgaard handed the old keys over to the king and recited a poem he had composed on the importance of moving the documents from a damp cellar to safe custody in a wonderful new house. In December 1721 Rostgaard was made head of the Danish Chancery, keeping his post as director of the archives. Three years later it emerged that he had received bribes. A lock was put on the doors of the archive building to prevent his access and on 17 January 1725 he was relieved of all his positions. In early February Rostgaard handed over the archives to Árni in the presence of soldiers (Már Jónsson 1998: 319–21; Bruun 1870a: 219–20, 322–62, 382–3; Adolf D. Jørgensen 1884: 64–8, 270–1).

Manuscripts

Árni took most of his manuscripts to Iceland in 1706 (see p. 146), placing the remainder in the custody of the University Library (*Emb*: 200; *PB*: 197–8). Back in Copenhagen he took stock of them and in 1713 found two leaves of *Óláfs saga helga* (AM 325 XI 2 a 4to) in the spine of an inventory of the income of the Cathedral of Trondheim, made in 1618, which he had bought at an auction in 1702; he had not examined it carefully until then (Overgaard 1996: 267). That same year Árni made an exact copy of a list of bishops in Trondheim that he discovered on a mouldy vellum leaf which had been appended to a Norwegian lawbook (AM 93 4to) given to him by Þormóður in 1712. Árni reported on his use of dashes and dots (cf. p. 159):

> This leaf was damaged by mould, as can be seen in this copy, in which – short or long, under the letters, means that these underlined letters had completely disappeared from the vellum leaf. Dots . . . . under the letters mean that the letters with dots under them were unclear, even though they had not rotted completely, and could just about be read.

> Var þetta blad til skemmda fued, so sem merki má siá a þessare Copiu, hvarinne – stutt edur langt, under bokstöfunum merker, að þeir sömu understrikuðu bokstafer voru ölldunges burt trosnader ur pergaments bladenu. Punktar . . . . under stöfunum merkia ad þeir underpunktudu staferner voru óskirer, iafnvel þott þeir eige være ölldungis burtufuner, og yrde nockurn veginn lesner (AM 258 b II 8vo: 2r–v).

Árni carried on collecting manuscripts and documents, although on a smaller scale. Before leaving for Iceland in the spring of 1713 Sigurður Sigurðsson gave him seventeenth-century legal documents (AM 64 8vo). The following year Árni acquired a paper manuscript in Copenhagen which contained *Njáls saga* and *Ragnars saga loðbrókar* (AM 282 4to, AM 465 4to). At an auction he bought a Danish translation of *Hirðskrá* (AM 107 4to) and a copy of Þormóður Torfason's 1664 essay on Danish kings (AM 862 4to). Thomas Bartholin the youngest, son of Thomas the antiquarian, obtained for Árni a vellum containing Gualteri's poem *Alexandreide* (AM 824 4to); the new owner had seen it in Leipzig almost twenty years earlier (Jón Helgason 1967). When Páll Vídalín, who managed to finish the land register in the summer of 1714, came to Copenhagen a year later, he brought with him a leaf of *Óláfs saga Tryggvasonar* (AM 325 VIII 2 h 4to) and another from *Rómverja saga* (AM 598 III γ 4to). Þorsteinn Sigurðsson arrived from Iceland that same autumn with various fragments (AM 162 A δ fol., AM 238 I fol., AM 655 XVI 4to, AM 656 II 4to, AM 80 b 8vo). In the years 1715–17 Ormur Daðason sent remnants of the vellum *Pseudo-Vatnshyrna* (AM 445 b 4to), a leaf of *Óláfs saga helga* (AM 325 XI 2 b 4to) and two leaves from *Njáls saga* (AM 162 B ε fol.), together with transcriptions of documents (AM Ap. Isl. 1407–1416). In 1719 Jón Þorkelsson presented Árni with a leaf of *Óláfs saga helga* which had been used as cover for one of his printed books. Árni recognised it as belonging to a vellum that he had acquired earlier (AM 325 VII 4to) and so placed it where it belonged.

Árni also borrowed manuscripts and documents that belonged to Copenhagen University and on 17 January 1716 was asked to arrange its disordered collection of documents. He promised to do so when he had the time in the spring. On 5 December he borrowed 390 charters which had belonged to the monastery in Klarekloster and promised to return them undamaged (RA. KU 12.03.16: 111, 147; Már Jónsson 1998: 315). Over the years 1714–17 he and his scribes copied numerous legends of Danish saints from the Bartholinian volumes of 1686–90 (see p. 76) as well as various texts from manuscripts in the University Library (AM 300 4to, AM 1049 4to), besides the documents he still had on loan from Norway. Árni compared those copies favourably with the copies he and his friends had made for Thomas Bartholin: in the 1680s: 'Minar copiur er eg nu giöri (1714–15) eru miklu betri en Bartholini' (AM 222 8vo: 110r; cf. AM Ap. Norv. XII–XV). At the same time transcripts were made of Danish documents by Hans Becker and Magnús Einarsson. Becker worked for Árni until going into business for himself in 1716; he sold herring to Árni and Mette in 1717–19 and firewood in 1727–9. Magnús was in Copenhagen from at least the autumn of 1715 to the summer of 1718 and probably lived at Árni's house (Már Jónsson 1998: 291; cf. *LS* II: 200). Magnús wrote accurately as before, for instance a copy of the older church laws of Eiðsivaþing (AM 77 c 4to) and Gulaþing (AM 77 e 4to), besides the speech of King Sverrir against the bishops (AM 689 4to), aided by Árni. Magnús also made exquisite drawings of seals (e.g. AM Ap. Dan. V: 1283, VI: 1331, VIII: 1427, XII: 1097; cf. Már Jónsson 1998: 291–9; *ÍÆ* III: 415; Ólafur Halldórsson 1994: 53). Árni himself, in 1714, made an exact copy of a damaged fourteenth-century *jólaskrá* (AM 683 c 4to) which he had removed from a manuscript of the Norwegian national law of 1274 (*LS* II: 185–6). Together they produced a sizable collection of medieval religious poetry (AM 1032 4to).

On 11 December 1718 King Charles XII of Sweden fell in battle in Norway. Fighting continued for some months but a peace treaty between Denmark and Sweden was signed on 3 July 1720 (Olsen 1970: 498–509). The *Stifamtmaður* Gyldenløve died on 8 December 1719 and was succeeded by Admiral Peter Raben who on 6 March 1720 was ordered to go to Iceland and the Faeroe Islands. On 25 March King Frederik IV asked him to retrieve the papers of the Royal Commission. Two months later, in a letter to Árni, the Exchequer claimed that he had still not reported on that project and had used the war as an excuse for leaving the papers in Iceland. Árni was informed that Raben had been asked to bring them back. Árni should arrange for them to be transported to the frigate *Søeridderen*. This vessel was one of the biggest ships in the Danish navy, with a crew of 140 men and armed with 24 canons (*Emb*: 538; Már Jónsson 1998: 292).

While in Iceland Raben remained on board his frigate in Hafnarfjörður harbour. On 4 July 1720 he informed Bishop Jón Vídalín in Skálholt, where Árni had left his manuscripts and documents in storage eight years earlier (see pp. 169–70), that the king wanted all of it to be transported to Copenhagen. Raben repeated the request nine days later. Sheriff Brynjólfur Þórðarson provided 30 horses and on 20 July Bishop Jón informed Raben that Þórður Þórðarson would take care of the transport. Nine days later Jón and Þórður arrived in Hafnarfjörður with Árni's chests and cases. Raben could now leave and on 27 August, while off the Faeroe Islands, he informed his superiors that he had Árni's papers with him in 55 chests, besides a sealed package containing documents (Már Jónsson 1998: 293).

Back in Copenhagen again Raben did not mention his cargo in letters to the king until 28 October 1720, when he informed him that he had brought some unspecified 'antiqviteter'. Raben also forwarded a report from Bishop Jón Vídalín about a drinking-horn kept at Skálholt and the axe 'Remegie', which was thought to have belonged to Skarphéðinn Njálsson, one of the heroes of *Njáls saga*. On 1 November the king decided that Raben, Rostgaard and Árni should meet and agree on what to do with the chests from Skálholt. They never met and on 12 November Árni complained to the king that someone must have lied to him about the cargo. The chests were his property, he claimed, and explained that he had taken books and manuscripts to Iceland to work on them during the winter months; some of them were vellums but most were written on paper. He had also brought quite a few charters on loan from Norway to have them transcribed, and he added an explanation that the Icelandic language was similar to the old Norwegian language (Már Jónsson 1998: 294–5, 384). He then described his collecting activities:

> On my journeys in Iceland I encountered some old books and also a number of illegible documents, 200 to 300 years old and a few even older. All of these items I have acquired by payment when the owners did not mind, and the remainder which the owners could not or would not part with I have had copied solely to ensure that such materials should be saved from destruction, as most people in that country at present have little interest in such things.

> Paa mine reiser udi Iisland, forekom mig nogle gamle bøger, item een deel ulæslige breve 2 à 300 aar gamle og nogle faae ældre. Dette haver ieg, hvor eiermændene icke skiøtte derom, tilhandlet mig for betaling, og det øfrige som eiermændene icke kunde eller vilde miste, haver ieg ladet afcopiere alleene til den ende at slige sager kunde blive conserverede fra undergang, efterdi de fleeste i landet nu icke stort skiøtte om slige ting (Bruun 1870b: 117).

Árni went on to explain that because of the war he had not taken the papers of the Royal Commission with him when he left Iceland in 1712, but had put them in two purpose-made chests (*kister*). He had not risked his own property either and stored his manuscripts and documents in 53 small cases (*casser*). When Raben left Denmark to bring back the commission papers, Árni had asked him to bring his belongings back as well. He now regretted having asked this favour, as Raben on his return wanted to take everything which was given to him in Iceland to his own house. Árni had persuaded the Exchequer and the Customs to have all chests and cases placed in storage but Raben had decided that Árni should not be allowed to remove any items without royal permission. Árni asked the king that Raben be ordered to stop harassing him, as he was an honest man and a long-time servant of the king. The property confiscated by Raben had cost him a lot of money and many a sleepless night, and if he did not get his things back it would be impossible for him to report the results of the Royal Commission. Árni clearly had no wish to meet Raben in person and proposed that custom officials should go through his cases, whereas the two chests should be transported unopened to the Exchequer. Árni also suspected that Raben had told the king that some of the contents of his cases belonged to the Royal Archives and suggested that Rostgaard should inspect everything (Már Jónsson 1998: 295; Bruun 1870b: 116–20).

As the king did not reply, Árni wrote an almost identical letter on 7 January 1721. This time he emphasised that all the items he had collected over the last thirty years were meant to increase the reputation of the king and his lands. He also asked for royal protection against those who were unfairly working against him (*Emb*: 539–43; Bekker-Nielsen and Widding 1972: 31–2). Five weeks later, on 14 February, Rostgaard was told that Árni could have his cases back as soon as two officials had inspected them. Árni was to show his old documents to Rostgaard, who would decide whether some of them should be placed in the Royal Archives. The two chests of the commission were to be transported unopened to the Exchequer. Three days later Raben sent the Exchequer two sealed packages with Árni's name; one of them contained papers from Páll Vídalín, the other the keys to the two chests (Már Jónsson 1998: 296; Bruun 1870b: 122–3; *Emb*: 544–5).

Nothing is known about the moment of Árni's reunion with his beloved collection but after these events he spent most of his time attending to his manuscripts, documents and transcriptions. There was bookbinding and copying to be done, unnecessary items to be dispensed with and disparate leaves to be reunited whenever possible. He seems to have wanted to arrange his collection in such a way that it would be accessible to scholars after his death. He started by checking whether all the items from his cases had arrived safely after the inspection. In April 1723 he tore up a list of vellums that he had made in Iceland and had indeed found a few items missing (Kålund 1909: 55–6). Four years later he finished the inventory which he had started in 1707–8 (see p. 152), often writing identical notes on paper, which he attached to the manuscripts themselves. His collection continued to grow but new items consisted mostly of fragments and incomplete vellums, although some complete lawbooks arrived. In 1722, Árni's friend Johann Brøgger in Bergen sent a fourteenth-century vellum containing the Norwegian national law (AM 56 4to; *PB*: 85). Four years later Árni bought a number of manuscripts, mostly paper, at the auction of Frederik Rostgaard's library (Kålund 1909: 95–107; Bruun 1870a: 387–94; Larsen 1970: 111; Rasmussen 2007: 185–6).

As before, most of the manuscripts came from Iceland, where Árni's contacts did their best to help. In the autumn of 1721, his nephew the Reverend Snorri Jónsson sent a number of vellum leaves (see frame), as well as some transcripts of documents (AM 269 4to, AM Ap. Isl. 3567, 3581). That same year Páll Vídalin sent two vellums of *Jónsbók* and a year later asked someone to make a copy of *Karlamagnús saga* for Árni (*PB*: 677, 679). In 1721 Ormur Daðason, who had become sheriff of

> FRAGMENTS SENT TO ÁRNI BY SNORRI JÓNSSON IN 1721
>
> *Óláfs saga helga*, fourteenth century, four leaves (AM 75 c fol.)
> *Egils saga*, thirteenth century, two leaves (AM 162 A γ fcl.)
> *Guðmundar saga*, fifteenth century, two leaves (AM 220 IV fol.)
> *Stjórn*, fourteenth century, one leaf (AM 229 I fol.)
> *Stjórn*, c. 1400, one leaf (AM 229 III fol.)
> *Barlaams saga*, c. 1400, two leaves (AM 231 I fol.)
> *Barlaams saga*, fourteenth century, one leaf (AM 231 V fol.)
> *Gyðinga saga*, c. 1300, two leaves (AM 238 XVII fol.)
> *Hirðskrá*, c. 1500, one leaf (AM 173 d C 3 4to)
> *Orkneyinga saga*, c. 1300, two leaves (AM 325 III α 4to)
> *Óláfs saga Tryggvasonar*, c. 1400, one leaf (AM 325 VIII 2 e 4to)
> *Sverris saga* and *Hákonar saga Sverrissonar*, fourteenth century, one leaf (AM 325 VIII 4 a 4to)
> *Bevers saga*, fourteenth century, one leaf (AM 567 II 4to)
> *Adoníus saga*, fifteenth century, one leaf (AM 567 VI β 4to)
> *Göngu-Hrólfs saga*, fifteenth century, two leaves (AM 567 XI β 4to)
> *Nítíða saga*, sixteenth century, two leaves (AM 567 XVIII 4to)
> *Tveggja postula saga Jóns ok Jakobs*, fourteenth century, four leaves (AM 653 a 4to)
> *Tveggja postula saga Jóns ok Jakobs*, fourteenth century, two leaves (AM 653 b II 4to)
> *Michaels saga*, *Drauma-Jóns saga*, *Hákonar þáttr Háreks sonar* and *Clarus saga*, fourteenth century, several leaves (AM 657 a–b 4to)
> *Maríu saga*, fourteenth century, two leaves (AM 667 III 4to)

Barðastrandarsýsla, provided a leaf of *Mágus saga* (AM 567 XVII γ 4to). Three years later he sent some leaves from *Pseudo-Vatnshyrna* (AM 445 b 4to) and a leaf from what he thought to be *Þórðar saga hreðu*. Árni identified it as being from *Hrólfs saga Gautrekssonar* (AM 357 4to). In

1726 Ormur sent four leaves of *Veraldar saga* (AM 655 VII–VIII 4to) and a year later he discovered a twelfth-century Latin *lectionarium* in a pile of papers: 'i brefarusli' (AM 788 4to). In the summer of 1728 the Reverend Jón Halldórsson sent a fourteenth-century vellum containing *Margrétar saga* (AM 428 a 12mo); Árni received it on 10 July. On 30 August the Reverend Frans Ibsson, Árni's roommate at Regensen more than forty years earlier (see p. 53), sent him a leaf of *Barlaams saga* (AM 231 X fol.) with the student Erlendur Ólafsson, who arrived in Copenhagen on 27 October, a few days after the Great Fire (Jón Ólafsson 2005: 33).

Árni continued to ask for documents and have copies made. He made some of the transcriptions himself but also corrected those made by his assistants. Most of them were copied on octavo leaves, where each document is separate, but some copybooks were copied in their entirety, such as the books of bishops Ögmundur Pálsson (Lbs 62 8vo) and Gissur Einarsson (Lbs 63 8vo). Páll Hákonarson sent some transcriptions in 1721 (AM Ap. Isl. 2110–2130) and also Böðvar Pálsson, Árni's nephew, a year later (AM Ap. Isl. 5385, 5414). Copies arrived in 1723 from the Reverend Þorsteinn Ketilsson at Hrafnagil (AM Ap. Isl. 4535, 4891, 4936) and in 1726–9 from Grenjaðarstaður (AM Ap. Isl. 5–7, 79, 144, 599, 600, 4218, 4250). Original documents arrived in 1723 as gifts from Páll Vídalín's son, Jón the younger (AM Ap. Isl. 288, 418). On 22 May 1723 Árni wrote to Oddur Sigurðsson concerning some manuscripts that he wished to borrow but also requested whatever old documents Oddur could lay his hands on (*PB*: 438). Snæbjörn Pálsson at Mýrar in Dýrafjörður provided some charters in 1725 (*PB*: 356–7). Three years later, on a ship from Vatneyri, Ormur Daðason sent transcripts with drawings of seals made by Magnús Einarsson, as well as some original documents and vellum fragments. The ship perished close to Norway (*PB*: 108). Árni's brother Jón sent numerous copies of documents during these years (AM Ap. Isl. 3898–3955, 4103–4180). On 13 October 1729 he informed Árni that copies which he had sent the previous year had gone down with the ship from Hofsós but he would try to borrow the originals again (*PB*: 304). Bishop Steinn Jónsson at Hólar had sent some old documents on the same ship, and as he lamented the accident on 9 October

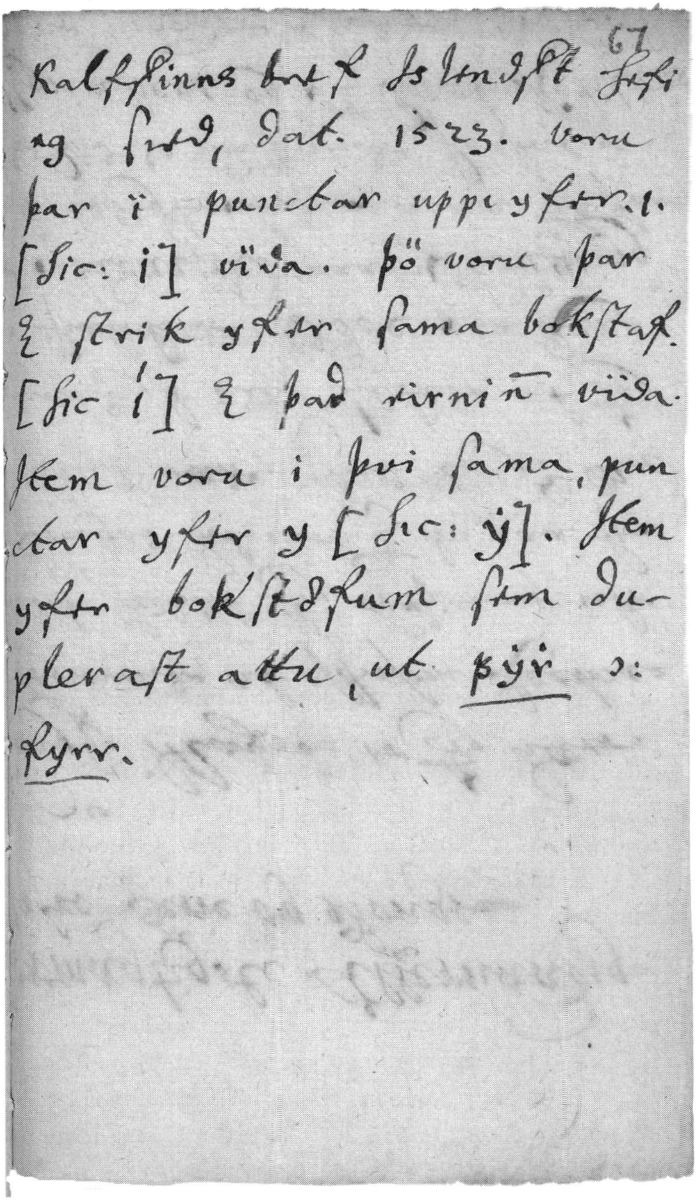
67
dat. 1523. voru
þar i punctar uppi yfer. i.
[sic: i] viða. þo voru þar
ʒ strik yfer sama bokstaf.
[sic í] ʒ það viða.
Item voru i þvi sama pun
ctar yfir y [sic: ẏ]. Item
yfir bokstöfum sem du-
plerast attu, ut þẏr ɔ:
þyrr.

Figure 14. Here Árni makes a perspicacious note on dots over the letter 'i' in a charter (AM 256 8vo: 67r).

1729 he consoled Árni by indicating that Jón Magnússon had already sent someone to Hólar for copybooks that he would now transcribe again in order to replace all that had been lost in the shipwreck (*PB*: 256–7). From at least February 1727 to May 1728 the students Einar Jónsson, Finnur Jónsson, Jón Ólafsson, Jón Sigurðsson and Sigurður Kárason produced *apographa* for Árni in Copenhagen (AM Ap. Isl. 241–248, 264, 274, 2300–2301). They made transcriptions of sagas too, but on a smaller scale. In 1727, Jón Sigurðsson thus copied *Eiríks saga víðförla* (AM 346 3 4to) from a damaged copy made by Ásgeir Jónsson, and earlier or later also *Yngvars saga víðförla* (AM 343 b 4to) from a vellum in Árni's collection (AM 343 a 4to); also *Bærings saga* (AM 525 4to) from another of his vellums (AM 180 a–b fol.). He made a copy (AM 745 4to) of *Snorra Edda* and eddic poems (AM 748 I a–b 4to), together with Jón Ólafsson (AM 746 4to), who also made a copy (AM 744 4to) of another vellum containing a grammatical treatise (AM 757 a 4to).

Work

Árni's commitment to his collection captured the imagination of his contemporaries, if one is to believe that Ludvig Holberg, professor and playwright, when asked about his colleague, answered that he most likely sat at home gnawing on his old vellums: 'Han sidder vel hjemme og gnaver paa sine gamle Skindpjalter'. This remark was recorded by Finnur Magnússon in 1813, whose source was his maternal uncle, Bishop Hannes Finnsson. He had heard the remark from his father Finnur Jónsson, who worked for Árni during his last years in Copenhagen (Finnur Magnússon 1813: 190). Such an image of Árni seems truthful in the sense that he was interested only in his manuscripts and documents; and indeed he appears to have handled every single item of his collection, some of them with great care. He thus made a special envelope for a leaf of *Hákonar saga Hákonarsonar* (AM 325 VIII 5 c 4to), given to him by his colleague Hans Gram, who had removed it from a printed book. Árni also put five tiny and unidentifiable bits of parchment within a folded piece of paper and wrote that they had been taken from the spine of a book: 'Islensker perments geirar, aptanaf kiöl á bok' (AM 921 VI 4to). He repaired some manuscripts himself, including a fourteenth-century vellum containing Þorláks saga (AM 382 4to). It was bound in ugly leather ('ohrysselegt liott ledur') which he removed, lamenting that three quires had been cut off by a barbarian: 'barbarâ manu' (Jón Sigurðsson et al. 1858–73, I: xlii–xliii). A note on a bifolium containing the sixteenth-century poems *Píslarminning* and *Hjónasinna* (AM 720 a X 4to) offers a rare glimpse into Árni's treatment of his vellums as he separated the two leaves in order to wash one of them in water, realising that the other would not survive the treatment: 'Eg skar þau hvert frá ödru, til ad þvo það fyrra, med því eg sá, ad það sídara ecki þolde vatned'.

Árni occasionally dismembered his vellums, for instance *Örvar-Odds saga* (AM 344 a 4to) and *Alexanders saga* (AM 519 a 4to), as he was certain that the two parts did not belong together. He frequently removed leaves that had been added to vellums and did not belong there, such as *Vilhjálms saga sjóðs* (AM 599 4to) discovered at the beginning of an older and more respectable vellum containing hagiography (Kålund 1909: 29). He investigated his vellums painstakingly and wrote in detail on many of them, such as a thirteenth-century *Konungs skuggsjá* (AM 243 b α fol.), on whose provenance he had written extensively while in Iceland (Holm-Olsen 1952: 191–7). He made lists of contents and noted whether the text was complete, such as in a fifteenth-century collection of fifteen sagas (AM 343 a 4to). He checked whether leaves were missing and made notes on the lower margins where relevant; for instance in two manuscripts containing the Swedish and Norwegian national laws (AM 53 4to: 15v, 111v, 112v, 113v; AM 74 4to: 4v, 12v, 29v, 31v, 35v).

Most collectors contemporary with Árni, such as John Bagford in London, were interested in fragments as 'specimens of ancient manuscripts' for their illuminations or the variety of scripts (McC. Gatch 1985: 97–8, 107, 112). For Árni the text mattered more than anything else and he did his best to ascertain whether his fragments belonged together or had been part of vellums he already had. As a first step he tried to identify the text. There were a few surprises, such as when he read a leaf taken from the cover of a book. Árni had never seen the text before. It concerned a certain Grega who lived in Britain and went to look for his brother, helping a lion on his way. Árni concluded that this was from a fable that he could as of yet not recognise: 'Ur fabula einne, sem eg ennnu ecki firer mig kem huer ad se' (AM 567 XXVI 4to; cf. Loth 1960c: 201). This finding was less spectacular than Humfrey Wanley's discovery of the manuscript of the poem *Beowulf* around 1700 (Ruth C. Wright 1939–40: 192), but must nonetheless have been gratifying. In most cases Árni was right in his identification of texts, although of course not always. What he for instance believed to be *Ísfirðinga saga* is actually *Hrafnkels saga* (AM 162 I fol.). The next step was to put the pieces together, if possible. In 1707 Guðrún Ögmundsdóttir in Flatey had given him a leaf of *Óláfs saga helga* and twenty years later Magnús Arason sent him another from the same codex. Árni rightly placed them together (AM 325 XI 2 m 4to). Another leaf of *Óláfs saga* (AM 325 IV β 4to) appeared at first sight to be part of a vellum already in Árni's possession but in 1722 he concluded otherwise; this was not the case, and he had no codex where this leaf fitted in: 'Þetta sie eg nu, ad eigi er so. Einga bok ä eg, sem þetta eige heima i' (Louis-Jensen 1970: 141).

Yet another leaf of *Óláfs saga* (AM 325 XI 2 d 4to) turned out to belong to one of the Resenian volumes in the University Library. At first Árni found the handwriting to be similar but then changed his mind, saying only that it appeared to be the same. The holes in the spine did fit: 'göten i kiölnum accordera nærre lage' (*LS* II: 159). On the basis of Roman numeration on two leaves containing hagiography (AM 238 VIII fol.) he decided that they could not have been part of a vellum of *Karlamagnús saga* (AM 180 a–b fol.), despite the similar handwriting. By 1721 he had put together forty leaves of *Óláfs saga helga* from around 1300 (AM 75 c fol.) but later doubted that some of them belonged to the vellum. Somewhat surprisingly he concluded that this did not matter much: 'Þar á rydr eigi mikit'.

Most of Árni's ruminations on vellums take the form of stray thoughts on specific items. In 1721 he received two leaves containing the last chapters of *Þórðar saga hreðu* (AM 564 a 4to: 3r–4v) from Ormur Daðason and immediately set about transcribing them (AM 475 4to). In both places he commented that this version of the saga was different from all others and that the fragment was priceless: 'egregium fragmentum'.

The same applies to his remarks on the age of manuscripts. In the first decades of the eighteenth century scholars such as Humfrey Wanley in London and Bernard Montfaucon in Paris ventured to ascribe codices to a certain century, basing their judgment primarily on the writing. In 1701, while in Bologna, Montfaucon quite correctly dated a certain manuscript to the sixth or seventh century and another to the eleventh. That same year Wanley composed a short treatise on how to judge the age of manuscripts and in his catalogue of Anglo-Saxon manuscripts, published five years later, he made an effort to provide approximate dates. Earlier scholars had been content with saying that manuscripts were 'ancient' or 'old' (Easterling 1977; Gain 2003: 260; C.E. Wright 1960: 108–9, 126–7). In the rare moments that Árni reflected on the age of his manuscripts he vacillated between these two ways. He thus characterised the writing in his two late twelfth-century leaves from *Grágás* as 'antiqvissima scriptura' (AM 315 d fol.) and in around 1720 he stated that a slightly younger fragment of an Icelandic homily (AM 686 c 4to) was what remained of a very old book: 'ex antiqvissimo libro' (AM 686 d 4to: 2r). In his notes on *Hungrvaka* he claimed to have an 'antiqvissimum fragmentum membraneum' containing the miracles of Bishop Þorlákur, and probably referred to the manuscript AM 645 4to from the early thirteenth century (*LS* II: 143). In around 1715, as he copied a *jólaskrá*, he noted that the writing was ancient ('forn'). He first suggested that it had been written around ('hier um') 1340, 1350 or 1360, and later put a line over 'eda 60' (AM 737 I 4to: 1r). Two other 'exemplaria' of this text were in his opinion written 'circa 1350' (6r). A fragment of a Latin life of Bishop Þorlákur, now lost, was not particularly old ('ikke meget gammel'), probably from around 1460. He later changed that to around 1440 (AM 670 e 4to: 24r). Two vellums of *Jónsbók*, one from the late fifteenth century (AM 160 4to) and the other from the sixteenth century (AM 153 4to), got the same verdict of not being particularly old: 'non admodum vetustus'. Again, Árni could be wrong, as he underestimated the age of an early fourteenth-century manuscript of *Snorra Edda* with eddic poems (AM 748 I a–b 4to), saying in a note that it was part of a recent parchment manuscript: 'Snorra Eddu fragment. recentior membrana'.

Paper manuscripts were far more numerous in Árni's collection and at times he evaluated their worth too, for instance explaining in a note that a recent copy of *Laxdæla saga* (AM 128 fol.) could be useful for comparison with the vellum *Möðruvallabók* (AM 132 fol.) where the latter was difficult to read. A recent copy of *Sögubrot* (AM 1 b fol.), on the other hand, was totally corrupt and worth nothing: 'nullius momenti'. The same could be said of paper copies of diverse *biskupasögur* (AM 384 4to), which were of no use to him whatsoever: 'mier ölldungis ónyt'.

Another preoccupation was how best to arrange manuscripts in his library if they contained many sagas or various texts, which many of the paper manuscripts actually did. Already while in Iceland Árni borrowed a paper manuscript from the Reverend Jón Torfason at Breiðabólstaður and took it apart to facilitate its use, as he explains in a note: 'ad faciliorem usum' (AM 226 a 8vo: 88r; *LS* II: 220). He left some of his recent saga collections untouched, such as one written by Jón Erlendsson (AM 160 fol.), a gift to Árni from the *Stiftamtmaður* Gyldenløve. A collection of sagas transcribed by Jón Gissursson ended up in five parts (Loth 1960b; Slay 1960a: 143–62). Another collection containing *Landnámabók* and some *Íslendingasögur*, purchased in 1711, was divided into eight parts (AM 110 fol., AM 125 fol., AM 163 a–d fol., AM 164 i fol., AM 202 g fol.). A manuscript given to Árni by Markús Bergsson in 1710 was partitioned into no fewer than nineteen items (Kålund 1909: 29–30). If the beginning or the end of a particular text was cut off during this process, Árni had an assistant copy whatever was lacking on a separate leaf, which was then glued approximately where it belonged; the text was thus complete. In most cases Árni left identical notes attached to each part of the manuscript.

This procedure of separating texts made for a sizeable investment in binding, and although Árni may have done some of the work himself it was mostly undertaken by professionals. Lists that he made in 1725–8 for the bookbinder Bertel Wolck refer to almost 600 manuscripts and printed books, including his old copy of *Járnsíða* (AM 119 4to) and vellums containing *Óláfs saga Tryggvasonar* (AM 310 4to) and *Sverris saga* (AM 327 4to). Wolck's last day of work for Árni was 13 October 1728, a week before the Great Fire (Springborg 1996: 18–20). Árni checked these lists by crossing out the books which had been bound and putting a mark against those ready to be bound. In many cases vellum leaves were used as covers and were in fact provided by Árni himself, who in that respect was no better than those Icelanders whom he had scolded for decades for their negligent treatment of manuscripts. Most of these leaves were taken from liturgical manuscripts which in his view were of limited value unless they contained text relevant to Icelandic history, such as a vellum from around 1200 (AM 98 I 8vo), acquired in Iceland in 1702, which turned out to contain material relating to St. Magnús and St. Óláfr (Gjerløw 1980, I: 29–30). He did keep some of these manuscripts, mainly the calendars, for example one which contained a Latin-Icelandic glossary (AM 249 1 fol.; Kålund 1909: 24; *AMKat*. I: 210–13, 226–32). On one occasion he kept the *calendarium* (AM 249 b fol.) of an English twelfth-century manuscript but used some of the psalter part for binding manuscripts (Gjerløw 1930, I: 191–2; Geert Andersen 2008: 97–8). He also retained samples, so to speak; for instance keeping two leaves of a liturgical manuscript from the church in Gufudalur (AM 266 4to) while using the remaining 34 or more leaves for bindings (Geert Andersen 2008: 10; cf. Sveinbjörn Rafnsson 1987: 314). It is therefore an exaggeration, as Jón Helgason has maintained, that Árni 'had no interest in Catholic liturgical books in Latin' and failed to see 'that they were proud monuments of the Icelandic book tradition' (Gjerløw 1980, I: 7). Árni did indeed write copious notes on liturgical manuscripts and transcribed texts that he found interesting (AM 241 b IX fol.; AM 209 8vo: 136r–224v, partly in *LS* II: 217–20; Gjerløw 1980, I: 49, 82, 118). He also kept a *breviarium* from around 1400 and studied it closely, indicating where leaves were missing (AM 415 12mo: 12v, 95v). He was indeed interested in these vellums, or at least intrigued by them, and decided for example to preserve four fragments of a Latin *obituarium* (AM 80 a 8vo) found in the spine of a book.

The fate of winding up as material for binding books was also met by a sixteenth-century manuscript of *Jónsbók* (AM Access 25), which was dismembered by Árni and the leaves used as covers for a number of paper manuscripts (Geert Andersen 2008: xii). Árni may have thought that he already had enough vellums of *Jónsbók*; and indeed his collection included at least fifty complete lawbooks and dozens of fragments. Another recent vellum manuscript of *Jónsbók* (AM 173 d A 30 4to) was already damaged when he got it, so he decided to keep a bifolium but destroy the rest: 'hveriu eg fargad hefi'. Not all vellums were thus indispensable and they could even be discarded if they were in bad shape or unremarkable. This is what happened to a vellum containing religious poetry, written around 1580–90 according to Árni, who decided to keep one leaf as a sample (*AMKat*. II: 148–9; Jón Sigurðsson et al. 1858–78, II; 509). After carefully comparing the first page of his grandfather's copy of *Bárðar saga* (AM 491 4to) with 'a recent vellum', which lacked the end, he had one of his scribes finish the task. Afterwards, Árni destroyed the vellum: 'Kalfskinns kvered sialft er eydilagt, epter þad þad hier vid samanlesed var' (*LS* II: 172).

Paper manuscripts were in danger too and if Árni concluded that they were redundant he did not hesitate to dispose of them. In 1719 he thus destroyed a Danish translation of *Orkneyinga saga* (AM 103 fol.) as its text would only confuse ignorant readers: 'icke uden til at forføre ukyndige' (*AMKat*. I: 70). Five years later he destroyed a transcription of an annal that had belonged to Þormóður Torfason (AM 410 4to) and had probably been written by Hjalti Þorsteinsson in Copenhagen thirty years earlier. Árni owned the original and did not want the transcript to mislead others. He also discarded an abridged version of an Icelandic annal transcribed by the Reverend Jón Egilsson in 1601 on the grounds that it contained nothing that he did not have elsewhere; besides that he owned the original (*LS* II: 163; Storm 1888: xvi–xvii, xlix). In 1725 Árni disposed of a compilation put together from four medieval annals copied by the Reverend Jón Erlendsson. Árni first compared its text with the originals (which he owned) and then wrote a scathing thirty-page report on Jón's unsatisfactory transcription method (AM 436 4to: 19r–34r; Storm 1888: lvii–lxvi). Árni also destroyed a copy of annals acquired in Iceland twenty years earlier written by Grímur Árnason, who had transcribed a copy made by the Reverend Jón Halldórsson in his youth (AM 411 4to). Árni was shocked by Grímur's inexactitudes and tore the manuscript to shreds so that nobody would be misled by it: 'reif eg þad í sundur og eydilagdi so engan villa skyldi' (Storm 1888: lxvii–lxviii; *LS* II: 163–4).

Árni did not spare his own work either. To his dismay he repeatedly discovered how uncritical he had been in his youth and actually threw away some copies he had made himself. In 1724 he checked his 1688–9 transcript of the thirteenth-century *Resensannáll*. It turned out to be inexact in a few places and, what was worse, he had skipped things that at the time he had regarded as unimportant. All entries until the discovery of Iceland were omitted and he had jumped over accounts of supernatural phenomena. He now considered such omissions to be quite unacceptable and, again, in order not to mislead future readers who could not know where this text was taken from ('hvadan þad tekid væri'), he destroyed it and made a better copy (AM 424 4to) of the vellum, which belonged to the University Library (*LS* II: 164–5).

As a scribe, Árni was more careful in his later years than he had been as a young man. His comments, analyses and methods also became more exact. His copy of a text from *Hauksbók* about rivers, lakes and ponds, Paradise and the sons of Noah (AM 765 4to: 1r–14r), written in around 1725, can serve as an example. The abbreviations are silently expanded but the transcript is otherwise made letter by letter. In a note he indicates that the first page of the manuscript, which was hard to decipher, had been carefully compared to the original: 'accuratissime confererud'. On the first four pages he underlined a few words or parts of words, or put dots under them, apparently to signal where the text was uncertain. Similarly, as he copied the annals of the fourteenth-century *Reynistaðarbók* (AM 764 4to), he put square brackets around uncertain words or letters, or placed dots underneath them (AM 765 4to: 17r–28v). Árni also transcribed the concordat of 1277 from AM 350 fol. quite exactly word by word (AM 116 4to), besides a number of medieval annals (AM 423 4to, AM 424 4to, AM 426 4to, AM 427 a 4to, AM 428 4to) and the preface to *Óláfs saga helga* (AM 78 b fol.) from a vellum which Peder Resen had given to the University Library, observing that it was copied accurately and that illegible letters were marked by dots underneath. He expanded the abbreviations but copied some of them in the margins, perhaps in order to remember how they looked.

Árni's understanding of textual variation, however, had not become any sharper. He was good at making copies but continued to compare various texts uncritically. Some of his projects are so incomprehensible that Jón Helgason, who knew Árni's work well, was moved to express his surprise at how much time he had invested in 'inadequate abridgments and mediocre transcripts' (Jón Helgason 1960b: 12). Árni's work on *Hungrvaka* is a case in point. In 1690–1700, Þorbergur Þorsteinsson made a transcript for Árni from a vellum manuscript (AM 379 4to) made for Bishop Þorlákur Skúlason in the mid-seventeenth century. Árni compared that copy with a manuscript written by Jón Gissursson (AM 205 fol.) and wrote variant readings in the margins of Þorbergur's transcript. After that he asked Jón Torfason to make a copy (AM 376 4to) of Þorbergur's copy and leave out the variants which Árni had written in the margins. In 1724 Árni went back to *Hungrvaka* and compared Jón Torfason's copy (AM 376 4to) carefully ('accuratissime') with Bishop Þorlákur's vellum (AM 379 4to), correcting what he termed Jón's erroneous orthography: 'þá raungu literaturam'. Árni went on to compare Jón's corrected copy with another manuscript made for Bishop Þorlákur (AM 380 4to) and wrote some variants in the margins of Jón's copy. After this thorough comparison Árni wrote, with apparent satisfaction, that Jón Torfason's copy contained an exact collation of Þorlákur's two manuscripts; he could therefore dispense with Þorbergur's copy as it was inaccurate and thus of no use to him or anyone else: 'hverki mier ne ödrum ad gagni' (*LS* II: 159; Már Jónsson 1998: 303–5). This seems to have been the only point of the whole exercise; he could get rid of a paper manuscript! Of course it was convenient to have variants from more than one manuscripts in one place, just as scholars wrote variants from manuscripts in the margins of printed editions if they planned a new edition (cf. Gasnault 2008: 153–4). It may also have simplified things for Árni to have fewer manuscripts of a single text, but what was he going to do next? It cannot be denied that this way of proceeding appears confusing. As in his youth he lost his way when he worked on more than one manuscript at a time (see p. 90).

Árni reassessed other old projects, most importantly his edition of *Íslendingabók*, but did not finish anything. On 19 March 1719, in a letter to Adolf Frederik Bassewitz, Prussian envoy to Sweden, who had visited him to see the collection, Árni explained that in his youth he had translated *Íslendingabók* into Latin and still hoped to finish his work (*PB*: 44;

cf. Finnur Jónsson 1930a: 120–1, 127). It appears that he had never given up that idea, abandoned in 1691 (see p. 93). During his years in Iceland he had gathered material that was intended to throw light on Ari fróði's text. Around 1720 he made an exact copy (AM 366 4to) of the better copy made by Jón Erlendsson (AM 113 b fol.). Árni had probably realised long before that his old transcript (AM 365 4to) was not good enough. Despite that he had continued to compare useless copies with great exactitude, for instance one he had borrowed in Iceland in 1703 with another one in his possession (AM 113 d fol.), concluding that they were exactly alike and had the same errors; and that his comparison had been exhaustive: 'i henne er eingu gleymt'.

Árni preserved most of his commentary but copied some of it and made small changes. He revised a number of items, however, for instance his conclusions relating to what learned authors had speculated on the thorny issue of how many years had passed from the creation of the world to the birth of Christ, a fiercely disputed subject at the time (AM 364 4to: 290v–292v; *LS* II: 36–7; cf. Grafton 1983, II: 262–3). Under the heading 'Loca veterum de Arone Multiscio' he gathered citations from medieval texts which mentioned Ari fróði or anything related to his writings. He also tracked words and place-names that appear in *Íslendingabók* (AM 364 4to: 64r–104v; AM 254 8vo: 152r–272r). In an effort to reconcile differences arising from various sources he prepared detailed chronological tables for the lives of Ari, Hallur from Haukadalur and the first bishops in Iceland, Ísleifur Gissurarson, Gissur Ísleifsson and Jón Ögmundsson (AM 364 4to: 2r–14r). Another of his concerns was the reliability of Ari's informants. After some reflection he concluded that one of them, Þuríður Snorradóttir, would have been forty-two years older than Ari. This meant that when she was sixty he would have been eighteen and thus could have learned many instructive things from her: 'kunne hann þá margt frodlegt af henni ad læra'. Árni thought that Þuríður's father, Snorri goði, died in 1033 when she was six years old and that she could have learned stories from those who had heard them from her father (AM 364 4to: 29r–v; cf. the truncated edition in *LS* II: 16–19). To Árni, this chain of events meant that Ari's information on Snorri goði could be trusted. At one point he assigned himself a few tasks:

Materials concerning Ari the wise to be read through.
Two leaves at the back of the Icelandic picture book, which I received from the Reverend Þórður Oddsson.
The miracles of St. Þorlákur and the apostles' sagas at the back.
Gregory the Great's homilies 4to longo.
Varia in an old booklet in 8vo.
Various old fragments from numerous books belonging to me.

Til literaturam i Ara froda ad lesa i gegnum.
2. blöd aptanvid þá Jslendsku billede bok, sem eg feck af Sr. Þordi Oddzsyne.
Miracula S. Thorlaci og Postula Sögurnar þar aptanvid.
Homilias Gregorii 4to longo.
Varia i gömlu qvere in 8vo.
atskilianleg gömul fragmenta ur ymsum bokum, fra mier (AM 254 8vo: 274r).

Árni's edition of *Íslendingabók* was never published, nor did he finish an edition of *Alexanders saga*, despite his claims over a period of thirty years (AM 519 b 4to). In his first edition of *Bibliotheca Latina* from 1712, the scholar Johann Albert Fabricius in Hamburg wrote that Árni intended to publish an Icelandic version of the saga. The claim also appears in the second edition of 1722 but in a third one of 1735 it is stated that Árni did not manage to complete the project before his death (Erik Petersen 1998: 421–2, 559, 580–1; Jón Helgason 1967: 208–9). In addition to his book *Incerti Auctoris Chronica Danorum* published in 1695 (see p. 113), Árni only produced one edition of another short text in Latin. This happened in 1719 with the appearance of King Magnús Hákonarson's political will of 1277, *Testamentum Magni Regis Norvegiæ, conscriptum Anno Christi M CC LXX VII*. On the title page Árni claims that this document was seeing the light of day for the first time (Árni Magnússon 1719; Finnur Jónsson 1930a: 119). In a short preface he explained that King Magnús deserved to be remembered for his legislation and that his will, written three years before his death in 1280, was preserved in a 400-year-old vellum in the Royal Library. Árni had transcribed the document without any intention of publishing it, but Joachim Wieland had encouraged him after learning that the text was not included in Þormóður Torfason's recent history of Norway. The text, Árni went on, contained valuable and otherwise unavailable information about the number of ships provided for war in each district of Norway. Árni explained the term 'skipreiða' as the district in which a certain number of ships would be held ready in times of war. He claimed to avoid further commentary so that the preface would not become longer than the text itself and concluded by expressing his hope that the reader would appreciate the book and encourage him to undertake further editions (Árni Magnússon 1719: 3–4).

Writings

In September 1713, soon after he returned to Copenhagen, Árni had composed a short biography of Þormóður Torfason in Danish (*LS* II: 127–135). At some point after Þormóður's death in 1719, Árni started to work on an edition of the correspondence between Þormóður and the Danish scholar Otto Sperling. Among Árni's papers there are proofs from one quire containing four letters which had already been printed, with Árni's minor corrections. He also prepared some notes for the introduction, in Latin, in which the two scholars are compared. Sperling's letters were in Árni's collection by then and his colleague Hans Gram owned some of Þormóður's letters; the remainder was preserved in Þormóður's copybooks. These letters were to be edited with the utmost care: 'accuratissime hic editis' (*LS* I: 234–5); but they never were. Towards the end of his life, then, Árni had published very little – and in fact had not written much. Nonetheless, a few perceptive essays among his papers (some only in draft form) might have been publishable in learned journals, although they were probably intended for private circulation among his Danish friends; for example short passages from *Knýtlinga saga* in Latin (AM 20 c fol.: 5r–10v) and a piece on the place-name Gandvík written around 1720, where he objected to the notion that it referred to the White

Sea. He also criticised scholars, especially those in Germany, who identified places and place-names on the basis of garbled forms mentioned in old sources; dismissing such explanations as pure nonsense: 'meras nugas' (AM 436 4to: 125r–135v; *LS* II: 288–90). In another short piece Árni argued against the belief of Swedish scholars, such as Olof Verelius, that medieval Icelandic sagas were written in the 'Old Gothic' language, the ancestor of modern Swedish. He observed that the language written in medieval Sweden was quite different from the Icelandic language that appeared in those texts. Árni stressed that his goal was to avoid confusion, just as one should avoid using incorrect names for familiar things (AM 436 4to: 1–2; *LS* II: 109–10). In the 1720's Árni wrote a short text on early medieval migrations in Northern Europe, perhaps intending it to be a late contribution to a dispute between Otto Sperling and Gottfried Wilhelm Leibniz, published in the journal *Nova Literaria Maris Baltici et Septentrionis* twenty years earlier. The text survives only in a rather chaotic draft (*LS* II: 111–13; AM 228 8vo: 96r–102r; AM 436 4to: 3r–5v; cf. Ekenvall 1953: 29–35; Davillé 1909: 152–3). A few very short essays are written in Icelandic, such as a study on the age and contents of *Langfeðgatal*, which concluded that the text was a list of kings rather than a genealogy (AM 1 f fol.: 29r–50v; *LS* II: 136–8). Árni wrote a somewhat more accomplished essay on the Poetic Edda, in which he compared its author's ideas about Óðinn and other deities to information provided by Snorri Sturluson (AM 739 α 4to: 2r–4v; *LS* II: 193–6). Árni's most refined piece of writing discusses skaldic verse, which in his opinion represented by far the oldest available historical sources: 'allra ellztu monumenta historica' (AM 266 8vo: 91r; cf. 11r–69r on individual poets in alphabetical order; also Sveinbjörn Rafnsson 1987: 300). Árni argued that such poems had at first been preserved by oral tradition, as they were transmitted from one individual to another. The poems were short, he added, and would have been of little value to those who were not familiar with the events described or alluded to in them, and would be of little benefit to posterity without an accompanying oral narrative: 'munnleg expositio'. Much learning was involved in knowing the poems by heart and in being able to explain the stories that lay behind these poems; this was evident from *Snorra Edda*, the compiler of which had been well versed in pagan poetry and had known how to interpret it. He had recast the poetry as prose and added a commentary; otherwise, the poems about the pagan gods would have been incomprehensible. However, Árni conjectured, when these explanations turned out to be either incorrect or too brief the meaning of the poems was lost. Later, as scholars began to write books about the events of former times, they offered their own understanding of the old poems, drawing also on such explanations as other learned men could offer. This methodology, he concluded, had dire consequences:

> That is how most of the old poems, which until then had been known by heart, were lost, because only the most important verses were considered to be worth citing. Accordingly, hardly any of these poems are preserved in their entirety. And we might not even possess half of what we do have, had not the elegance of the fragments that are cited tempted writers to include them in their books.

> Þar med leid under lok meste partur þeirra gömlu kvæda, sem menn þangad til utan bokar i minne haft höfdu: Med þvi eigi þotti vert ad citera ur kvædunum nema þad sem mest á reid. Og hier af kiemur þad, ad vær snart eingen þessarra kvæda nu heil höfum. Og hefdum vær, kannske, eigi halfpartinn af þvi sem vær höfum, ef eigi elegantia þeirra fragmentorum, sem citerast, hefde lockad scriptores til ad færa þau inn i sinar bækur (AM 266 8vo: 93r–v).

Árni's reluctance to write books may be related to his inability to finish anything larger than short notes and disquisitions on details concerning single manuscripts. On the other hand, there is some truth in the explanation he offered to Jón Ólafsson from Grunnavík, his assistant from the autumn of 1726 onwards. Árni allegedly said that there was no shortage of vain books in the world and there was no reason for him to add to the pile: 'kvad hann veröldina alt of fulla af hiegomabokum þo eigi bætti hann vid'. He confessed to Jón that he had never intended to write books and was convinced that a man could spend almost his whole life putting together a little booklet: 'lítinn bækling' (*LS* I, 2: 41–2). Árni's failure to become a more productive scholar (in a formal sense) may thus be attributed in part to his lack of interest in divulging the results of his research and his failure when he tried to compose longer works. On the other hand, he was anything but lazy and far from being unproductive. In the 1690s he often complained that he was too busy to do anything at all (see pp. 87, 99, 128) and he made such complaints until the last years of his life. In 1727, for example, Magistrate Benedikt Þorsteinsson requested the loan of some manuscripts and Árni promised to send them to Iceland when he had looked through them, only to explain, on 20 June 1728, that he had been too busy throughout the winter to do this: 'Eg hefe haft so margt ad sysla... ad eg hefe ecke feinged tom til ad siá þesse exemplaria i gegnum, so ad mier næge' (*PB*: 628). This was clearly a pattern in his working life; he promised to do things but could not deliver. He never had enough time. In a sense he led what now might be called a stressful life; there were too many manuscripts, too many documents, too many books, too many official chores at the archives and the university, not forgetting the incessant demands of the Exchequer concerning the results of the Royal Commission.

8
Last months

> We are now becoming old men.
> Vid tökum nu til ad giorast gamler menn.
>
> Árni Magnússon 2 June 1727 (*PB*: 639)

When Árni Magnússon wrote these words to his old friend the Reverend Hjalti Þorsteinsson at Vatnsfjörður he had spent more than six years organising his manuscripts and documents so that they would be of use to future scholars. A year later the collection came close to being destroyed by fire. This chapter describes that event and Árni's reactions, as he tried to understand what had happened and what could be done to restore what had been lost. The last months of his life were difficult and despite his successes Árni appears to have died a rather disappointed man.

Conflagration

On 3 July 1728 Árni had a set of bookshelves made for just over a rigsdaler. On 25 September the wheels of his carriage needed repairing, which was not unusual. Since December 1718 Jens Andersen had been to the house of 'Alle Magnusen' no less than 34 times to undertake various repairs to the carriage and had received a total of 50 rigsdaler for his work. An undated estimate suggests that a new carriage would have cost 145 rigsdaler (Már Jónsson 1998: 326, 329). Little did Árni know that he would soon need this carriage to prevent the destruction of the collection of manuscripts, documents and books which he had spent more than forty years assembling. Late in the afternoon on Wednesday 20 October a fire broke out in a house just within the city walls, a few metres from the westernmost gate of Vesterport and no more than five hundred metres from Árni's residence in Store Kannikestræde. Apparently, a boy of seven who was looking for his toy in a barn dropped his candle. Strong wind from the southwest caused the fire to spread with alarming speed. In the ensuing panic another fire broke out in Nørregade. The firefighting squads of the city and several army regiments proved to be inefficient and disorganised. In the evening, six Icelandic students came to Árni's house and offered to move his books and manuscripts to a safer place. One of them, Jón Ólafsson, later reported that Árni looked out of the windows on both sides of his house and concluded that there was no reason to worry; the fire would soon be under control. At ten o'clock the next morning, as Vorfruekirke caught fire, Árni finally decided to act. Two of the students, Jón Ólafsson and Finnur Jónsson, returned and were helped by Árni's servants. First, Mette and another professor's wife were brought to safety. One of the wheels of the carriage then came off and had to be fixed. Four or five loads of furniture, manuscripts and books were then moved to the house of Hans Becker, Árni's friend and former assistant, who lived at Hallandsås, now the corner of Gothersgade and Kongens Nytorv. After six hours, and with his house in flames, Árni was compelled to abandon it. He is said to have pointed to the book-lined shelves he was forced to leave behind and to have said that no such collection of books would ever be seen again until Doomsday: 'Þar eru þær bækur sem aldrei er að fá til dómadags' (Jón Ólafsson 2005: 102; cf. Þórhallur Vilmundarson 1979: 389, 403–4; Már Jónsson 1998: 329–31).

Árni's house burnt to the ground, as did all the other houses in the street apart from Borchs Collegium, which was made of brick. Its library, however, was destroyed. Hours after Árni left his house the fire ravished the Trinitatiskirke, where the University Library was kept. Neither Árni, as the library's custodian, nor any of the other professors did anything to save its books and manuscripts, all of them being busy trying to save their own libraries (Olrik 1889: 153–4; Birket Smith 1882: 59–60). On Saturday night the fire was brought under control. At least one third of the city had been destroyed, around three thousand houses. Sixteen thousand inhabitants had lost their homes. At mass in the Nikolaikirke on 14 November the Reverend Morten Reenberg compared the fire to the devastation of Jerusalem and Sodom, but rejoiced that five churches were still standing. Árni and Jón Ólafsson compared the city to an Icelandic desert landscape with its rocks and lava: 'eins og storgrytt hollt edur hraun' (Jón K. Margeirsson 1975: 161; Jón Ólafsson 2005: 96; Már Jónsson 1998: 330).

Thus, in six hours, with the help of a rickety old carriage, the medieval textual and codicological legacy of Iceland was saved from obliteration. Árni could have started to remove the manuscripts and books from his house the evening before. He could have taken the initiative in having students undertake similar work in the University Library. But like other professors and officials he was misled by his confidence that the fire would soon be under control. After abandoning his house he walked down Højbrostræde with Jón Ólafsson and went alone with his pouch of money to the wine-merchant Peter Abbesté (Jón Ólafsson 2005: 101–2). Already by 30 October King Frederik IV had given a thousand rigsdaler to the poor and almost as much to soldiers who had fought the fire, while officials who had lost their belongings received 6500 rigsdaler. The Reverend Reenberg and Professor Anckersen received 600 rigsdaler each and Christian Worm, professor of theology and bishop of Seeland, got 900. In November a further twenty thousand rigsdaler were distributed. Árni received 200 on 10 November as did his colleague Peter Horrebow. In a census made on 8–9 November, Mette Magnussen and three of her servants were registered as living at Hans Becker's house. They also appear, along with Árni, in the house of Peder Ørsleff, chaplain to Holmens kirke, at Størrestræde. On 21 December Árni paid out two and a half rigsdaler for bookshelves. Further purchases, early in the new year, included four beds, two bookshelves, two tables and a stand for his wig, together with other items needed for their new home (Már Jónsson 1998: 334–5).

The University Library was ravaged by the fire. Only manuscripts on loan to a few professors were saved. A vellum of *Guðmundar saga* (AM 399 4to) had been with Árni since 1706 and he also had some manuscripts relating to Danish medieval history (Birket Smith 1882: 64–71). All the vellums containing kings' sagas perished including *Fagurskinna* A and B, *Kringla*, *Jöfraskinna* and *Gullinskinna*; they had been returned from Stangeland a few years earlier, after the death of Þormóður

Torfason. Among the manuscripts given to the library by Peder Resen (see p. 59) were *Óláfs saga Tryggvasonar*, *Óláfs saga helga*, *Konungs skuggsjá*, medieval annals and *Vatnshyrna*, a collection of Icelandic sagas, as well as Norwegian lawbooks. Among the Danish manuscripts there were annals, lawbooks and copies of charters. Luckily, many of these Danish texts had been copied by Árni and other students while he worked for Thomas Bartholin. A fragment containing the text of Saxo's *Gesta Danorum* perished (Saxo 1979–80: 13) and also a vellum of Adam of Bremen's church history, which earlier had been consulted by Árni (Gram 1907: 192; Otto 1930: 21–3).

Soon after the fire the royal historiographer Andreas Højer wrote to an unidentified correspondent that Árni Magnússon's collection of manuscripts had been completely destroyed. Højer and other friends implored Árni to write a detailed account of his losses but in spite of promises to that end he did nothing (Birket Smith 1882: 64). For some months he appears to have been in a state of shock and he may never have known what he had lost and what had been preserved. In letters to friends in Iceland in the spring of 1729 he greatly exaggerated his loss. He wrote in detail to Ormur Daðason on 2 June 1729 and to the Reverend Jón Halldórsson on 22 June. Almost all his printed books had perished, he asserted, just like most of the books in the city. He pined for his collection, which had taken thirty years to assemble but only thirty minutes for the fire to devour; it would be a long time before he could put together an equally good library, the value of which he estimated at 5–6000 rigsdaler. To his relief most of his saga vellums had been saved, as he explained to the Reverend Jón: 'Eg feck ad sönnu biargad flestum minum Sögubókum' (Jón K. Margeirsson 1975: 149). In his letter to Ormur he had been less optimistic, saying that many of his manuscripts had burnt to ashes: 'Þar brann og til ösku hia mier miked og margt af minum skrifudu bókum' (*PB*: 98; cf. Finnur Jónsson 1930a: 171–3).

His friends were told that many copybooks and documents from the seventeenth century had perished, along with chronicles and diverse sources on contemporary Iceland, such as the pirate raids of 1627. These papers would never be replaced. Innumerable Norwegian, Danish and Swedish documents had also been lost, as well as some Icelandic ones.

Árni even thought that nearly all his transcripts of documents (*apographa*) older than 1550 had perished, except for copies of charters made at Skálholt and diverse churches, and others which Ormur had recently forwarded to Copenhagen; the rest had gone up in smoke. Gone too were his notes on learned Icelanders, poets and officials, all quite useful, even though many were imperfect. He had made lists of sagas and poems, with short comments intended for those scholars who would later write the literary history of Iceland; not a single page was left from all these labours (*PB*: 98–9; Jón K. Margeirsson 1975: 145–6). To the Reverend Ólafur Stefánsson Árni wrote that he would not gather more information about learned men, as everything he had written so far had been destroyed (Jón K. Margeirsson 1975: 132). Nothing could be done, however, and Árni thanked God that he at least had the means to live in reasonable comfort for the rest of his days. Most of what had made him happy did not exist anymore. Nothing remained for him but to prepare himself for a good end and to try to abandon all worldly vanities, of which, when properly considered, his books and manuscripts were a major part. The loss disturbed him greatly and a kind of dizziness invaded his mind. At times, though, he could also smile at himself and his vain thoughts: 'stundum brose eg ad mier siálfum og minum hiegomlegu þaunkum' (Jón K. Margeirsson 1975: 146).

Kristian Kålund (*AMKat*. II: xi–xiii) and Þórhallur Vilmundarson (1979: 407–11) have concluded that only some twenty vellums from Árni's collection perished in the fire, with an unknown number of fragments: *Maríu saga* (three or four manuscripts), *De Cruce Christi* and *Niðurstigningar saga*, *Maríu saga Magdalenæ* also containing *De Cruce Christi*, *Óláfs saga helga* and *Magnúss saga Eyjajarls*, *Norna-Gests þáttr* (fragment), *Víga-Glúms saga*, *Karlamagnús saga* (three manuscripts), *Þiðreks saga af Bern* (three manuscripts), *Konungs skuggsjá*, *Jónsbók* (at least four) and *Heiðarvíga saga* which had been on loan from Stockholm since 1725 (Jón Helgason 1925: 42–3; Sveinbjörn Rafnsson 1979: 85). Many more paper manuscripts were destroyed, such as the originals of seventeenth-century annals, protocols of the *Alþingi* and collections of poems. For instance, nothing remains of fifteen paper copies of the Poetic Edda which appear in a list that Árni made not long before

Last months

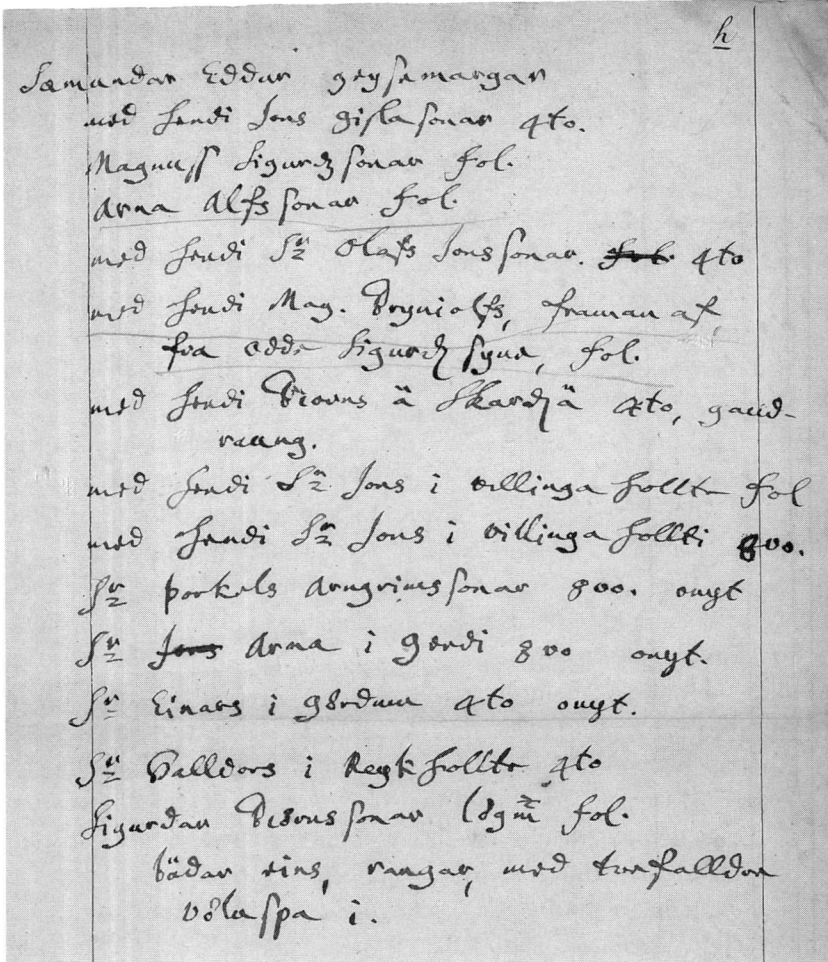

Figure 15. A list of recent and not so recent paper copies of the Poetic Edda in Árni's possession a few years before the Great Fire, in which they all perished (AM 739 a 4to: 9r).

the fire; indeed he wrote to the Reverend Jón Halldórsson that all of his 'Sæmundar Eddur' had perished: 'eru allar brunnar' (Jón K. Margeirsson 1975: 147).

In 1725–8 Oddur Sigurðsson had lent several manuscripts to Árni, most of them of recent vintage, such as travel descriptions written by Icelanders. These all perished with Árni's house (*PB*: 437–8, 445–50). The land register of the Royal Commission had been sent to Árni by the Exchequer in the summer of 1727 (see p. 175). The registers of Múlasýsla and Skaftafellssýsla are not extant, but the register of Barðastrandarsýsla (AM 469 fol.) was saved from the fire, whereas those from other districts were found in Árni's office at the Royal Archives after his death (*Jarðabók* 1: v). As for his working papers and notes, his assistant Finnur Jónsson later reminisced that a chest containing notes on learned men and other scholarly matters had to be left behind as there was no room in the carriage on its last trip (Jón Ólafsson 2005: 99). Árni himself subsequently wrote to the Reverend Eyjólfur Jónsson at Vellir in Svarfaðardalur that he felt as if he had no hands ('sem handlaus madur'), since his notes had been devoured by the fire (Jón K. Margeirsson 1975 154). Some of these notes seem to be preserved, however, such as an incomplete inventory ('opus inchoatum') of medieval authors (AM 434 4to), studies on medieval and later chronology (AM 250 fol., AM 729 4to, AM 732 a XII 4to), notes on the Icelandic language (AM 481 12mo, AM 226 b 8vo; cf. *LS* II: 252–4) and a complete set of nicely drawn genealogies from *Landnámabók* (AM 432 4to; cf. Loth 1977).

As concerns his transcripts of documents (*apographa*), Árni was certainly wrong when he wrote that they had all perished (see p. 154). In some of his letters in the spring of 1729, for instance to Hans Scheving, Árni noted that because of the small apartment many of his documents were still stored in chests: 'þad salverada er i kistum nidurpackad sokum hús þreyngsla'. He may simply not have examined all the surviving items and thus exaggerated his loss (Jón K. Margeirsson 1975: 156; cf. 144, 148). Similarly, not all of his printed books disappeared in the ruins of his house; a few hundred of them are indeed still extant (*AMKat.* II: 616–50; Geert Andersen 2008: xix).

Last months

Death

The months after the Great Fire were extremely cold. On 19 January 1729 Jón Ólafsson noted in his diary that he had walked on ice towards some small islands close to the city. At that time Árni lived in Størrestræde and despite the cold he kept his habit of walking to work on Slotsholmen (Jón Ólafsson 2005: 34; Már Jónsson 1998: 335–6). He had been in charge of the Royal Archives since Rostgaard's dismissal in January 1725 (see p. 179) and on 4 March 1729 Christian Ludvig Harboe was hired as his assistant there (*Emb*: 586; Adolf D. Jörgensen 1884: 68). In his letters to Iceland in the spring of 1729 Árni constantly complained about the cramped living conditions and used this as an excuse for not working on his manuscripts and documents (Jón K. Margeirsson 1975: 133, 149). He did not expect to live for long and said in one of his last letters that if he managed to survive for a year or two he would have time to arrange his scant belongings (Jón K. Margeirsson 1975: 150). In what remained of his life Árni made no transcriptions and had no manuscripts bound. He stopped writing notes on manuscripts and nothing became of his plans to make a complete inventory of his collection (*LS* I, 2: 54). After Árni's death Jón Ólafsson prepared a catalogue which seems to be based on the order of the manuscripts as they had been arranged after the Great Fire, perhaps partly by Árni or even more likely by Jón himself after his master's death (Ólöf Benediktsdóttir 2005). In Jón's catalogue the manuscripts are numbered by size (folio, 4to, 8vo, 12mo) and within those groups by genre and titles. The numbers, still in use with some modifications, were Jón's invention (AM 456 fol., AM 477 fol., Thott 1046 fol.).

Despite his depression, or perhaps in order to fight it, Árni decided to recover as many as possible of the documents which he believed to have perished, explaining to Bishop Steinn Jónsson that this was a way of passing the time: 'dægrastytting' (Jón K. Margeirsson 1975: 143). In his many letters in the spring of 1729 he asked for copies of documents and other texts that he thought were lost. He asked his brother Jón, as well as Magnús Einarsson, to work for him and he asked Magnús Pálsson, son of Páll Vídalín, to send, as a gift or on loan, whatever old letters he could find; and to do this for as long as Árni lived (Jón K. Margeirsson 1975: 136; cf. Finnur Jónsson 1930a: 176–8). Nothing much came of these requests, although on 13 October 1729 Jón Magnússon sent all the copies he had made, just under seventy in total, and promised to keep looking for documents (*PB*: 303–4). Magnús Einarsson could do nothing to help. Just before Easter that year his right hand had become so weak that he could not move it. The pain receded and he was able to write a letter on 5 September, albeit very slowly (*PB*: 108, 130). Magistrate Magnús Gíslason replied to Árni's request that he only had some documents from Reykhólar and insisted that not much remained in the country, as Árni had taken it all: 'þad lited þier effterskylldud' (*PB*: 161). Þorsteinn Sigurðsson and Markús Bergsson promised to do whatever they could (*PB*: 48, 468). Friends among bishops and priests lamented Árni's loss and consoled him with reference to the words and intentions of God (*PB*: 33, 257, 276–7, 641). In the autumn of 1729 Árni may have received only a single vellum leaf which had been removed from a schoolbook belonging to Bjarni Sigurðsson, who had just finished his first year at Skálholt school. Bjarni had no idea where the leaf came from (AM 226 a 8vo: 111r; *ÍÆ* I: 190–1).

During the summer of 1729 Árni purchased a black dresscoat and two pairs of trousers for himself, and some clothes for his servants. His household moved from Størrestræde to the nearby Laxegade and again in the autumn to a more spacious apartment in Admiralsgade. Before this final move Árni contracted influenza, which had claimed the lives of many people in the city. Finnur Jónsson had left for Iceland in the summer, having failed to repay Árni a debt of eight rigsdaler. His brother Vigfús arrived in Copenhagen that autumn and borrowed a further four rigsdaler from Árni, but settled the entire debt on 1 December. Árni was still alert as he noted, after weighing the coins, that one of them was French and too light. That same day Hans Becker sent him some firewood and a further consignment three weeks later. On Christmas Eve the weather grew colder. At eight o'clock in the evening Árni became ill and for three days he was unable to sleep or eat, and was quite constipated. The king's doctor, Hieronymus Laub, managed to deal with that, but then Árni became afflicted with diarrhoea and with so heavy a lethargy that he could hardly stay awake. According to Jón Ólafsson, who was present, Árni suffered from stomach ache, vomiting, chest congestion and flatulence. He could not eat and only drank a little. His head remained clear, though, except for the first night of his illness and again towards the end. He was able to walk from his bed to the table and sit there for a while, but could neither stand, sit nor lie still for any length of time. His friends came to visit, some of them twice every day. Árni always talked as if he were in good health and never complained (*LS* I, 2: 30–1; *BE*: 30–1; Már Jónsson 1997b; Már Jónsson 1998: 336–8).

Two days before his death Árni could no longer hold a pen and Hans Becker needed to help him sign his will. On the evening of 6 January Árni was unable to see his last guests to the door; he bade them farewell, saying that he was half-dead. After that his condition deteriorated and he was never able to stand up again. He did not sleep the whole night and spoke to no one, but recited prayers in Icelandic and French. In his two biographies Jón Ólafsson does not mention whether Árni's wife Mette was present, but as he seems to have disliked her intensely he may have deliberately chosen not to mention her. Árni's feet grew cold and little by little his whole body too. The pain grew worse and Árni could no longer drink. His last words were heard only by his housekeeper, as he three times repeated his wish that God would receive his soul. He died quietly as the clock showed quarter to six on Saturday morning 7 January 1730; and the clock allegedly stopped too. He was 66 years old (*LS* I, 2: 31–2, 37; *BE*: 31–2). Among those who had visited him the previous day was his colleague Hans Gram, who wrote to the Reverend Hjalti Þorsteinsson on 19 June 1730 that Árni's death was an irreparable loss; a light had been extinguished the like of which would never be seen again: 'med hannem er udslukt et Lius, som vore Tider neppelig, ja vel aldrig meere faaer at see igien optændt'. A year later Gram thanked Hjalti for his words on Árni, whose memory ought not to be allowed to fade: 'hvis hukommelse aldrig bør uddø' (AM 410 fol.: 1v, 3v; Gram 1907: 24, 27).

A few hours after Árni's death the university cashier arrived to seal his belongings and took with him a box containing money (*LS* I, 2: 37). The funeral took place at the Trinitatiskirke on Thursday 12 January. Twelve students carried the coffin and Árni was buried to the north in the choir of the Vorfruekirke, which had been badly damaged in the Great Fire. Ludvig Holberg succeeded him as professor of history and geography and Edvard Londemann, whose mother was Icelandic, replaced Holberg. Mette received her share of Árni's income from the Faculty of Philosophy in August, but she herself died on 15 September and was buried with Árni (Már Jónsson 1998: 339). Soon afterwards, it appears, someone spread a story that Árni's body had been dragged from the grave and thrown on the floor but Jón Ólafsson claims to have successfully silenced this infamous tale (*LS* I, 2: 32).

Árni was not well known in learned circles in Europe. Fabricius had informed the public of his plans to edit *Alexanders saga* (see p. 198), and when the German scholar Johann Mosheim spent some weeks in Copenhagen in 1722 he went to see his collection and got to transcribe some Latin texts (*LS* I, 2: 161–3). In Christian Gottlieb Jöcher's multi-volume lexicon on erudite men, published in the mid-eighteenth century, Árni figures as the Danish editor of a Danish annal in 1695: 'MAGNAEUS (Arnas), ein Däne, hat 1695 incerti Autoris chronica Danorum & præcipue Sialandiæ ab anno 1028 ad 1282 ediret' (Jöcher 1750–51, III: 39). Nothing more was known. In Iceland, on the other hand, Árni was famous, although not everyone had a high opinion of his legacy. In a letter to Hans Gram on 5 September 1730, Bishop Jón Árnason of Skálholt lamented that Árni had taken so many documents and manuscripts to Copenhagen, where, he understood, they had perished. Árni had spent his life collecting and reading these texts but never published anything of value for his countrymen. Bishop Jón noted that it should come as no surprise that someone, whose devotion to worldly things did nothing to promote the glory of God, had suffered such a cruel fate (*PB*: 33; Finnur Jónsson 1930a: 178). As it turned out, the bishop, whose deranged son Árni had helped in Copenhagen, was wrong in his account of the losses and he may have been misled by Árni's own exaggerations in letters written to Iceland in the previous year. Writing in the mid-eighteenth century Jón Marteinsson also lamented that Árni had taken documents that belonged in Iceland and never returned them. He suggested that this should be done immediately, either in the original or via copies (Thott 961 fol.: 15). Around 1780 the Reverend Þorsteinn

Last months

Pétursson at Staðarbakki observed that Árni had collected documents and vellums, conveyed them to Copenhagen and despite all promises had failed to return them. He concluded that Árni had done nothing for the benefit of the country (Páll Vídalín 1985: 160). Soon enough, however, other voices made themselves heard and Árni was placed on a pedestal as a scholarly hero, surrounded with symbols of learning and knowledge, echoing the words of his friend Magnús Arason that he was Iceland's honour: 'Arne er Islands Ære' (*BE*: 49). Árni was appreciated for having collected and produced sources for Icelandic history. Patriotism was identified as the common motivation behind all he did, as Jón Ólafsson remarked already in 1738: 'Han var alletider den største Islands Patriot' (*BE*: 29).

The Royal Commission failed in its mission because of endless disputes. The census of 1703 remained unknown for more than two centuries and nobody used the surviving land registers until late in the eighteenth century. Árni was not a politician or official by nature, but he did try to improve the conditions of the common people in relation to landowners, merchants and the state. In his mind, however, manuscripts were more important than contemporary issues and he thought of little else for almost half a century. There are few instances when he did not obtain the items that he wanted, perhaps only *Skarðsbók postulasagna* (AM SÁM 1), which he had on loan and Eyjólfur Björnsson copied (see p. 160). Without his labours, and despite the Great Fire, there would not be as many Icelandic manuscripts extant today. The destruction of vellums had indeed intensified just before Árni started collecting manuscripts in 1685 and, turning the tide, he saved innumerable items. The most remarkable manuscripts of *Njáls saga*, *Grettis saga* and *Guðmundar saga góða*, for example, are in his collection (Jón Þorkelsson 1879–89; Guðvarður Már Gunnlaugsson 1994: 293–8; Stefán Karlsson 1983: xi, xxx, liv, cvi). Even more remarkable was his persistence in collecting fragments, which he perhaps began to seek out as early as 1685 (see p. 67) and for which he was still on the lookout in 1729. In one of his last letters, written to the Reverend Þorsteinn Ketilsson, he explains that he would retain a few leaves (AM 237 a fol., AM 237 b fol.) which he had removed from a manuscript borrowed the previous year, as he preferred

Death

to hold on to such fragments himself (Jón K. Margeirsson 1975: 158). Many younger manuscripts would probably not have been preserved without his efforts either. After Árni and Mette died his manuscripts and books became the property of the University Library (*LS* I, 2: 117; Finnur Jónsson 1930a: 199; Halldór Hermannsson 1929: 67). Around half of the manuscripts were transferred to Iceland between 1972 and 1997, along with the original Icelandic charters and copies, and other Icelandic manuscripts from the Royal Library. The remaining manuscripts, charters and transcripts are still in Copenhagen (Sigrún Davíðsdóttir 1999: 368–70; websites of *Den Arnamagnæanske Samling* and *Stofnun Árna Magnússonar í íslenskum fræðum*).

We thus have good access to the results of Árni Magnússon's tireless efforts and we also know much about his systematic procedures – what he did, how and when. It is true that Árni arrived too late, in the sense that the destruction of medieval vellums was well under way by the time he started out as a collector and scholar. This was not his fault, of course, and it is my hope that in this book I have shown that, with the sole exception of liturgical manuscripts, he could not have done a better job at collecting and transcribing manuscripts and documents, preserving texts for posterity that would otherwise be lost. More research could and needs to be done on many aspects of his work – and it may even happen that we will come closer to an understanding of what exactly was behind Árni's urge to collect these objects from the past. What possessed him to do this? The readers of this book will be aware that I have not provided an explanation of the shadow around his eyes, which according to his assistant Jón Ólafsson hinted at hidden things in his heart (see p. 22). I won't even try. Let's keep this simple: Árni was a dedicated scholar who realised that historical and literary sources were vanishing. He decided, because others did not care, to do what he could to save them for posterity. He was lucky enough to have the means to do this and we are fortunate that instead of pursuing the highly valued goal of writing books, which would now be obsolete, he concentrated almost entirely on his collection. In a way, one could say that he did what he did for us, people he did not know. We should be grateful and do much more to ensure that the memory of this remarkable man does not fade.

List of figures

1	Barth. X: 1	51
2	Barth. XII: 9	57
3	AM 555 h 4to: 1r	73
4	AM 761 b 4to: 291v	88
5	AM 364 4to: 109r	91
6	AM 909 E 4to: 66r	109
7	AM 1 e β II fol.: 28v	112
8	AM 267 8vo: 3r	118
9	Royal administration in Iceland	134
10	Map of Iceland	139
11	AM 435 a 4to: 1r	151
12	AM Ap. Isl. 450: 1r	158
13	AM 288 4to: 50r	171
14	AM 256 8vo: 67r	187
15	AM 739 α 4to: 9r	208

Figures 1, 2 © Det Kongelige Bibliotek, Copenhagen – Fotografisk Atelier.

Figures 3, 4, 5, 12 © Stofnun Árna Magnússonar í íslenskum fræðum, Reykjavík – Photographer: Jóhanna Ólafsdóttir.

Figures 6, 7, 8, 11, 13, 14, 15 © Den Arnamagnæanske Samling, Copenhagen – Photographer: Suzanne Rietz.

References

Manuscripts

Arnamagnæan institutes, Copenhagen and Reykjavík

AM 1 b fol. *Sögubrot af fornkonungum* from the late seventeenth century.
AM 1 d α fol. *Sögubrot af fornkonungum* written by Árni Magnússon c. 1690.
AM 1 e ß I fol. *Sögubrot af fornkonungum* from c. 1300.
AM 1 e ß II fol. Árni Magnússon's notes on *Sögubrot af fornkorungum*.
AM 18 fol. *Knýtlinga saga* written by Árni Magnússon c. 1688.
AM 20 c fol. Árni Magnússon's notes on *Knýtlinga saga*.
AM 20 d fol. *Knýtlinga saga* written by Árni Magnússon c. 1690.
AM 20 h fol. *Knýtlinga saga* with a Latin translation partly written by Árni Magnússon c. 1684–5
AM 34 4 fol. *Hversu Noregur byggðist ok fannst* written by Ásgeir Jónsson in 1689.
AM 39 fol. *Heimskringla* from the fourteenth century.
AM 40 fol. *Heimskringla* written by Eyjólfur Björnsson c. 1688.
AM 41 fol. *Hulda* written by Ásgeir Jónsson c. 1697.
AM 45 fol. *Heimskringla* (*Fríssbók*) from the fourteenth century.
AM 47 fol. *Heimskringla* (*Eirspennill*) from the fourteenth century.
AM 51 fol. *Fagurskinna B* written by Eyjólfur Björnsson c. 1688.
AM 53 fol. *Óláfs saga Tryggvasonar* from the fourteenth century.
AM 58–60 fol. *Óláfs saga Tryggvasonar* written by Ásgeir Jónsson c. 1697.
AM 67 a fol. *Skáldasaga Haraldar hárfagra* written by Ásgeir Jónsson c. 1697.
AM 67 b fol. *Skáldasaga Haraldar hárfagra* written by Ásgeir Jónsson c. 1697.
AM 68 fol. *Óláfs saga helga* from the early fourteenth century.
AM 69 fol. *Óláfs saga helga* and *Orkneyinga þáttr* written by Ásgeir Jónsson in 1689.
AM 77 a fol. *Óláfs saga helga* written by Ásgeir Jónsson c. 1688.
AM 78 a fol. *Óláfs saga helga* written by Eyjólfur Björnsson c. 1688.

References

AM 78 b fol. Preface to *Óláfs saga helga* written by Árni Magnússon c. 1725.
AM 79 fol. *Sverris saga* written by Ásgeir Jónsson c. 1697.
AM 87 fol. *Sverris saga* and *Hákonar saga Sverrissonar* written by Eyjólfur Björnsson c. 1688.
AM 88 fol. *Hákonar saga Hákonarsonar* written by Eyjólfur Björnsson c. 1688.
AM 89 fol. *Hákonar saga Hákonarsonar* written by Ásgeir Jónsson and Eyjólfur Björnsson c. 1688.
AM 113 a fol. *Íslendingabók* written by Jón Erlendsson c. 1650.
AM 113 b fol. *Íslendingabók* written by Jón Erlendsson c. 1650.
AM 113 d fol. *Íslendingabók* from the late seventeenth century.
AM 113 g fol. *Íslendingabók* from the late seventeenth century.
AM 128 fol. *Íslendingasögur* from c. 1640.
AM 162 C fol. Fragments from a fifteenth-century collection of sagas.
AM 162 I fol. *Hrafnkels saga* from the fifteenth century.
AM 222 fol. *Jóns saga helga* in an autograph Latin translation by Árni Magnússon c. 1690.
AM 231 X fol. *Barlaams saga* from the fifteenth century.
AM 234 fol. *Heilagramannasögur* from the fourteenth century.
AM 238 VIII fol. *Heilagramannasögur* from the fifteenth century.
AM 241 b IX fol. Árni Magnússon's notes on liturgical manuscripts.
AM 243 b α fol. *Konungs skuggsjá* from the thirteenth century.
AM 243 n fol. *Konungs skuggsjá* partly written by Árni Magnússon c. 1685.
AM 249 l fol. *Calendarium latinum* from the twelfth century.
AM 250 fol. Árni Magnússon's notes on chronological issues.
AM 282 fol. Þormóður Torfason's copybook 1666–89.
AM 283 fol. Þormóður Torfason's copybook 1689–91.
AM 285 b fol. Þormóður Torfason's received letters 1681–1706.
AM 308 fol. *Gulaþingslög eldri* written by Árni Magnússon in 1688.
AM 310 fol. *Frostaþingslög eldri* written by Ásgeir Jónsson c. 1688.
AM 311 fol. *Frostaþingslög eldri* from c. 1690.
AM 312 fol. Fragment of *Frostaþingslög eldri* written by Árni Magnússon c. 1688.
AM 315 d fol. *Grágás* from the late twelfth century.
AM 327 fol. Church laws of Archbishop Jón rauðr and King Sverrir written by Jón Gíslason c. 1690.
AM 334 fol. *Grágás* and *Járnsíða* (*Staðarhólsbók*) from the late thirteenth century.

AM 339 fol. *Grágás* written by Hákon Ormsson c. 1650.
AM 344 fol. *Jónsbók* and *Kristinréttr Árna* (*Ljárskógabók*) from the fourteenth century.
AM 346 fol. *Jónsbók* and *Kristinréttr Árna* (*Staðarfellsbók*) from the fourteenth century.
AM 347 fol. *Jónsbók*, *Kristinréttr Árna* and *Kristinna laga þáttr* (*Belgsdalsbók*) from the fourteenth century.
AM 352 fol. *Kristinna laga þáttr* and Norwegian church laws with a Latin translation, written by Árni Magnússon c. 1690.
AM 355 a fol. Norwegian and Icelandic church statutes written by Árni Magnússon c. 1690.
AM 355 b fol. *Kristinréttr Árna* written by Jón Erlendsson c. 1650.
AM 410 fol. A collection of letters from the early eighteenth century.
AM 440 fol. The papers of the Royal Commission III.
AM 441 fol. The papers of the Royal Commission IV.
AM 444 fol. The papers of the Royal Commission VII.
AM 452 fol. Árni Magnússon's household papers after 1710.

AM 53 4to. The Swedish national law from the fourteenth century.
AM 65 4to. The Norwegian national law and the church law of Archbishop Jón from the fourteenth century.
AM 66 4to. *Gulaþingslög eldri* written by Ásgeir Jónsson c. 1688.
AM 67 4to. The Norwegian national law written by Árni Magnússon in 1686.
AM 68 4to. The Norwegian national law and the older church law of Eiðsivaþing from the fourteenth century.
AM 69 4to. The Norwegian national law from the fourteenth century.
AM 74 4to. The Norwegian national law from the fourteenth century.
AM 76 a 4to. The town law of Bergen written by Jón Gíslason c. 1688.
AM 77 c 4to. The older church law of Eiðsivaþing written by Magnús Einarsson c. 1715.
AM 77 d 4to. The older church law of Eiðsivaþing written by Árni Magnússon in 1686.
AM 77 e 4to. The older church law of Gulaþing written by Magnús Einarsson c. 1715.
AM 78 4to. Norwegian church laws from the fourteenth century.
AM 116 4to. The concordat of 1277 written by Árni Magnússon c. 1727.
AM 119 4to. *Járnsíða* written by Árni Magnússon in 1686.
AM 122 4to. *Grágás* written by Jón Magnússon, probably in 1636.
AM 153 4to. *Jónsbók* and *Kristinréttr Árna* from the sixteenth century.

References

AM 160 4to. *Jónsbók* and *Kristinréttr Árna* from the fifteenth century.
AM 169 4to. *Jónsbók* from the early fourteenth century.
AM 173 d A 30 4to. *Jónsbók* from the sixteenth century.
AM 179 4to. *Kristinréttr Árna* written by Ásgeir Jónsson c. 1697.
AM 180 4to. *Kristinna laga þáttr* written by Ásgeir Jónsson c. 1697.
AM 269 4to. *Sigurðarregistur* written by Snorri Jónsson c. 1721.
AM 288 4to. *Jómsvíkinga saga* from the late seventeenth century.
AM 300 4to. Danish annals written by Árni Magnússon c. 1690 and 1714–17.
AM 302 4to. *Fagurskinna B* written by Eyjólfur Björnsson c. 1688.
AM 310 4to. *Óláfs saga Tryggvasonar* by Oddr the monk from the thirteenth century.
AM 311 4to. *Óláfs saga Tryggvasonar* written by Ásgeir Jónsson c. 1688.
AM 312 4to. *Óláfs saga Tryggvasonar* written by Eyjólfur Björnsson c. 1688.
AM 325 VII 4to. *Óláfs saga helga* from the thirteenth century.
AM 325 VIII 5 c 4to. *Hákonar saga Hákonarsonar* from the fourteenth century.
AM 325 XI 2 d 4to. *Óláfs saga helga* from c. 1400.
AM 325 XI 2 m 4to. *Óláfs saga helga* from the fourteenth century.
AM 326 b 4to. *Hemings þáttr* written by Árni Magnússon and Ásgeir Jónsson in 1689.
AM 328 4to. *Hákonar saga Sverrissonar* written by Jón Vídalín c. 1688.
AM 329 1 4to. *Þáttr af Sigurði konungi slefu* written by Árni Magnússon in 1689.
AM 329 3 4to. *Helga þáttr ok Úlfs* written by Ásgeir Jónsson in 1689.
AM 343 a 4to. Saga collection from the fifteenth century.
AM 343 b 4to. *Yngvars saga víðförla* written by Jón Sigurðsson c. 1727.
AM 344 b 4to. *Örvar-Odds saga* and *Hálfdanar saga Eysteinssonar* written by Jón Torfason c. 1698.
AM 346 3 4to. *Eiríks saga víðförla* written by Jón Sigurðsson in 1727.
AM 348 4to. *Norna-Gests þáttr* written by Ásgeir Jónsson in 1689 (ff. 26–9).
AM 349 4to. *Þorsteins þáttr tjaldstæðings* and *Sneglu-Halla þáttr* written by Árni Magnússon in 1689.
AM 354 4to. *Hervarar saga ok Heiðreks* written by Ásgeir Jónsson c. 1697.
AM 364 4to. Árni Magnússon's commentary and notes on *Íslendingabók*.
AM 365 4to. *Íslendingabók* written by Árni Magnússon with his Latin translation written by Hjalti Þorsteinsson c. 1687–8.
AM 366 4to. *Íslendingabók* written by Árni Magnússon c. 1725.
AM 369 4to. Christian Worm's unfinished edition of *Íslendingabók* c. 1695–7.
AM 372 4to. *Hungrvaka* written by Frans Ibsson c. 1700.

Manuscripts

AM 376 4to. *Hungrvaka* written by Jón Torfason c. 1698.

AM 401 4to. *Guðmundar saga biskups* written by Ásgeir Jónsson and Eyjólfur Björnsson c. 1688.

AM 408 g 4to. *Biskupaannálar* of Jón Egilsson written by Frans Ibsson c. 1700.

AM 408 h 2 4to. *Biskupaannálar* of Halldór Þorbergsson written by the author in 1678.

AM 411 4to. Annals 70–1430 written by Jón Halldórsson c. 1685.

AM 412 4to. *Hólaannáll* 636–1394 from the early seventeenth century.

AM 423 4to. Annals 1328–1372 written by Árni Magnússon c. 1725.

AM 424 4to. *Resensannáll* written by Árni Magnússon c. 1725.

AM 425 4to. *Flateyjarannáll* written by Árni Magnússon in 1689.

AM 426 4to. A medieval annal written by Árni Magnússon c. 1725.

AM 427 a 4to. A medieval annal written by Árni Magnússon c. 1725.

AM 428 4to. *Skálholtsannáll forni* written by Árni Magnússon c. 1725.

AM 429 b 3 4to. Notes and passages on Icelandic church history written by Árni Magnússon c. 1690.

AM 432 4to. Genealogies from *Landnámbók* made by Árni Magnússon.

AM 434 4to. Árni Magnússon's notes on Icelandic medieval authors.

AM 435 a 4to. Árni Magnússon's catalogue of vellum manuscripts made in 1707–27.

AM 436 4to. Árni Magnússon's essays and notes.

AM 442 4to. *Eyrbyggja saga* written by Ketill Jörundsson c. 1640–70.

AM 447 4to. *Eyrbyggja saga* written by Þorsteinn Þórðarson c. 1670.

AM 448 4to. *Eyrbyggja saga* written by Ásgeir Jónsson and Árni Magnússon c. 1688.

AM 450 a 4to. *Eyrbyggja saga* written by Ásgeir Jónsson and Árni Magnússon c. 1697.

AM 453 4to. *Egils saga* written by Ketill Jörundsson c. 1640–70.

AM 460 4to. *Egils saga* written by Eyjólfur Björnsson c. 1688.

AM 461 4to. *Egils saga* written by Ásgeir Jónsson c. 1697.

AM 470 4to. *Njáls saga* written by Ketill Jörundsson c. 1640–70.

AM 475 4to. *Þórðar saga hreðu* written by Árni Magnússon c. 1725.

AM 481 4to. *Gísla saga* written by Ketill Jörundsson c. 1640–70.

AM 484 4to. *Svarfdæla saga* written by Jón Eggertsson c. 1687.

AM 491 4to. *Bárðar saga* written by Ketill Jörundsson c. 1640–70.

AM 495 4to. *Gull-Þóris saga* written by Ásgeir Jónsson c. 1697.

AM 497 4to. *Hallfreðar saga* written by Eyjólfur Björnsson c. 1688.

AM 499 4to. *Harðar saga* written by Ketill Jörundsson c. 1640–70.

References

AM 501 4to. *Hænsa-Þóris saga* written by Ásgeir Jónsson c. 1688.
AM 502 4to. *Hávarðar saga Ísfirðings* written by Ketill Jörundsson c. 1640–70.
AM 503 4to. *Kjalnesinga saga* written by Ásgeir Jónsson c. 1688.
AM 504 4to. *Kjalnesinga saga* written by Ketill Jörundsson c. 1640–70.
AM 505 4to. *Kormáks saga* written by Árni Magnússon and Ásgeir Jónsson c. 1688.
AM 506 4to. *Krókarefs saga* written by Jón Torfason c. 1698.
AM 508 4to. *Víga-Glúms saga* written by Árni Magnússon and Ásgeir Jónsson c. 1688.
AM 512 4to. *Víglundar saga* written by Jón Torfason c. 1698.
AM 516 4to. *Flóamanna saga* written by Ketill Jörundsson c. 1640–70.
AM 517 4to. *Flóamanna saga* written by Ásgeir Jónsson c. 1686.
AM 519 b 4to. Árni Magnússon's notes on Gualteri's *Alexandreide*.
AM 525 4to. *Bærings saga* written by Jón Sigurðsson c. 1727.
AM 534 4to. *Mágus saga* from the fifteenth century.
AM 554 a β 4to. *Bandamanna saga* written by Ketill Jörundsson c. 1640–70.
AM 554 a δ 4to. *Hænsa-Þóris saga* written by Ketill Jörundsson c. 1640–70.
AM 554 d 4to. *Laxdæla saga* written c. 1650.
AM 555 h 4to. *Stjörnu-Odda draumr* and *Bergbúa þáttr* written by Árni Magnússon in 1686.
AM 559 4to. *Vatnsdæla saga* written by Ásgeir Jónsson c. 1688.
AM 561 4to. *Íslendingasögur* from c. 1400.
AM 562 k 4to. *Þorsteins þáttr austfirska* written by Jón Torfason c. 1698.
AM 564 a 4to. *Pseudo-Vatnshyrna* from c. 1400.
AM 564 c 4to. *Bergbúa þáttr*, *Kumlbúa þáttr* and *Draumr Þorsteins Síðuhallssonar* written by Árni Magnússon in 1686.
AM 566 b 4to. *Fóstbræðra saga* written by Árni Magnússon and Ásgeir Jónsson c. 1688.
AM 567 XXVI 4to. *Grega saga* from the fourteenth century.
AM 576 a 4to. Summaries of sagas written by Einar Eyjólfsson c. 1690.
AM 576 c 4to. Árni Magnússon's notes and summaries of *lygisögur*.
AM 587 b 4to. *Hrómundar saga Gripssonar* written by Ásgeir Jónsson and Eyjólfur Björnsson c. 1688.
AM 599 4to. *Vilhjálms saga sjóðs* from c. 1600.
AM 649 b 4to. Árni Magnússon's list of words from *Jóns saga postula*, written c. 1690, with two transcriptions of the saga's *formáli*, one of them written by Árni c. 1725.
AM 663 c 4to. *Játvarðar saga helga* written by Ásgeir Jónsson in 1689.

AM 670 e 4to. Saints' lives in Latin written by Árni Magnússon's scribes c. 1725.
AM 683 c 4to. *Jólaskrá* from the fourteenth century and a copy made by Árni Magnússon in 1714.
AM 686 c 4to. Fragment of an Icelandic homily from c. 1200.
AM 686 d 4to. Fragment of an Icelandic homily written by Árni Magnússon c. 1686 and c. 1720.
AM 689 4to. *Ræða Sverris konungs* written by Magnús Einarsson c. 1715.
AM 715 d 4to. *Píslargrátur* written by Jón Torfason c. 1698.
AM 716 n 4to. *Heimsádeila* written by Jón Torfason c. 1698.
AM 716 o 4to. *Hugbót* written by Jón Torfason c. 1698.
AM 716 p 4to. *Hjónasinna* written by Jón Torfason c. 1698.
AM 729 4to. Árni Magnússon's notes on chronology.
AM 732 a XII 4to. Árni Magnússon's notes on chronology.
AM 737 I 4to. *Jólaskrá* written by Árni Magnússon c. 1725.
AM 739 4to. Árni Magnússon's notes on *Snorra Edda*.
AM 744 4to. *Snorra Edda* written by Jón Ólafsson c. 1727.
AM 745 4to. *Snorra Edda* written by Jón Sigurðsson c. 1727.
AM 746 4to. *Snorra Edda* written by Jón Ólafsson c. 1727.
AM 748 I a–b 4to. *Snorra Edda*, a grammatical treatise and eddic poems from the fourteenth century.
AM 761 a–b 4to. Árni Magnússon's collection of skaldic poetry.
AM 844 4to. Danish annals written by Árni Magnússon c. 1690.
AM 907 4to. Scania's church law written by Árni Magnússon c. 1690.
AM 909 A–E 4to. Árni Magnússon's notes from Leipzig in 1694–6.
AM 921 VI 4to. Five unidentifiable pieces from Icelandic vellums.
AM 922 4to. *Hrólfs saga kraka* written partly by Árni Magnússon and with his Latin translation c. 1634–5.
AM 950 4to. *Kristnisaga meistara Adams* written by Árni Magnússon in 1689.
AM 1005 4to. *Knýtlinga saga* from the first half of the seventeenth century.
AM 1008 I 4to. *Hversu Noregr byggðist ok fannst* written by Ásgeir Jónsson in 1689.
AM 1008 V 4to. *Grænlendinga þáttr* written by Ásgeir Jónsson in 1689.
AM 1008 VI 4to. *Ölkofra þáttr* written by Ásgeir Jónsson c. 1688.
AM 1009 4to. From *Óláfs saga helga* and poems by Einar Skúlason written by Árni Magnússon in 1689.
AM 1021 4to. *Járnsíða* written by Árni Magnússon in 1686.
AM 1027 4to. Jón Ólafsson's autograph Icelandic biography of Árni Magnússon written in 1738.

References

AM 1032 4to. Medieval religious poetry written by Árni Magnússon, Magnús Einarsson and others c. 1715.
AM 1037 4to. Jón Magnússon's autograph biography of Árni Magnússon written in 1730.
AM 1045 4to. Árni Magnússon's register of Don. var. 1 fol. Bartholiniana A–F., made c. 1725.
AM 1049 4to. Saints' lives written by Árni Magnússon and his assistants c. 1714–17.
AM 1057 4to. Árni Magnússon's letters and notes.

AM 85 8vo. Árni Magnússon's description of the *postulasögur* at Skarð (SÁM 1).
AM 116 II 8vo. *Hrafnkels saga* and *Gunnars þáttr keldugnúpsfífls* from the early seventeenth century.
AM 128 8vo. *Ármanns rímur* by Jón Guðmundsson the learned from the seventeenth century (three copies).
AM 129 8vo. *Andra rímur* from the latter part of the seventeenth century.
AM 222 8vo. Árni Magnússon's notes on documents.
AM 226 a 8vo. Árni Magnússon's notes on documents and sagas.
AM 226 b 8vo. Árni Magnússon's notes on the Icelandic language.
AM 228 8vo. Árni Magnússon's msicellaneous notes.
AM 231 a–f 8vo. Árni Magnússon's notes from Leipzig in 1694–6.
AM 254 8vo. Árni Magnússon's notes on *Íslendingabók*.
AM 256 8vo. Árni Magnússon's notes on charters.
AM 258 b 8vo. *Series Archiepiscoporum et Episcoporum Provinciæ Nidrosiensis* written by Árni Magnússon in 1713–25.
AM 267 8vo. Árni Magnússon's notes on manuscripts.

AM 415 12mo. *Breviarium Romanum* from c. 1400.
AM 428 a 12mo. *Margrétar saga* from the fourteenth century.
AM 434 d 12mo. Magical incantations from the seventeenth century.
AM 481 12mo. Árni Magnússon's notes on the Icelandic language.

Steph. 1 a. *Gulaþingslög eldri* written by Árni Magnússon c. 1688.

Apographa Danica.
Apographa Islandica.
Apographa Norvegica.

Manuscripts

National Library in Reykjavík
ÍB 225 4to. *Laxdæla saga* written by Ásgeir Jónsson c. 1686.
JS 98 fol. A collection of private letters from the eighteenth and nineteenth centuries.
JS 435 II 4to. *Droplaugarsona saga* written by Ásgeir Jónsson c. 1688.
Lbs 62 8vo. Bishop Ögmundur Pálsson's copybook written by Árni Magnússon and his scribes c. 1727.
Lbs 63 8vo. Bishop Gissur Einarsson's copybook written by Árni Magnússon and his scribes c. 1727.
Lbs 427 8vo: 24r–66r. Autobiographical notes of Sigurður Sigurðsson c. 1720.

Royal Library, Copenhagen
Don. var. 1 fol. Bartholiniana X–XIII. Antiqvitates Danicæ I–IV. Passages from manuscripts and books written by Thomas Bartholin and Árni Magnússon c. 1684–5.
Don var. 1 fol. Bartholiniana XIV–XXI. Annals of Danish ecclesiastical history by Thomas Bartholin c. 1687–90.
Don. var. 1 fol. Bartholiniana B–K. Transcriptions of documents and manuscripts for Thomas Bartholin's ecclesiastical history made by himself, Árni Magnússon and Icelandic students c. 1687–90.
Don. var. 153 4to. Inventory of books of theology owned by Thomas Bartholin c. 1675.
NKS 637 4to. Danish translation of parts of Thomas Bartholin's *Antiquitates* c. 1770.
Thott 961 fol. Jón Marteinsson, 'Islands nærværende Tilstand', c. 1750.

States Archives, Copenhagen (RA)
Københavns universitet
KU 12.03.14. Acta Consistorii 1693–1704.
KU 12.03.15. Acta Consistorii 1705–13.
KU 12.03.16. Acta Consistorii 1714–24.

Royal Library, Stockholm
Papp. 60 fol. Saga collection written by Jón Eggertsson in 1686–7.
Papp. 67 fol. Saga collection written by Jón Eggertsson in 1686–7.
Papp. 15 4to. Saga collection from the latter part of the seventeenth century.
Papp. 16 4to. Saga collection mostly written by Þórður Jónsson in 1654.

References

National Library, Oslo
NB Oslo 371 fol. *Fagurskinna B* written by Ásgeir Jónsson c. 1690.
NB Oslo 372 fol. *Hulda* written by Ásgeir Jónsson c. 1690.
UB Oslo. Ms. 4to, 73. Peder Deichmann's travel diary 1688–92.

British Library in London (BL)
Add. 11.1184: 67r–77r. Árni Magnússon's commentary of his *dróttkvæði* to Thomas Bartholin in *Antiquitates* (1689), written c. 1750.

Printed works

Acta Medica et Philosophica Hafniensia. 5 vols (1671–9).
Aðalgeir Kristjánsson. 1975. 'Upphaf handritasöfnunar Árna Magnússonar'. *Opuscula* 5: 377–82.
Akhøj Nielsen, Marita. 2004. *Anders Sørensen Vedels filologiske arbejder.* 2 vols. Copenhagen: C.A. Reitzels forlag.
Alþingisbækur Íslands 1570–1800. 17 vols. Reykjavík: Sögufélag, 1912–90.
Andersson, Theodore M. 1964. *The Problem of Icelandic Saga Origins. A Historical Survey.* New Haven: Yale University Press.
Annálar 1400–1800. 6 vols. Ed. Hannes Þorsteinsson, Jón Jóhannesson, Þórhallur Vilmundarson and Guðrún Ása Grímsdóttir. Reykjavík: Hið íslenska bókmenntafélag, 1922–87.
Antognazza, Maria Rosa. 2009. *Leibniz. An Intellectual Biography.* Cambridge: Cambridge University Press.
Arna Björk Stefánsdóttir. 2008. *Pappír sem ritfang. Yfirtaka pappírs á Íslandi á 16. og 17. öld.* BA-thesis in history at the University of Iceland.
Auger, Marie-Louise. 2003. 'Les mauristes et l'histoire des provinces de France'. In *Érudition et commerce épistolaire. Jean Mabillon et la tradition monastique,* ed. Daniel-Odon Hurel, 103–11. Paris: J. Vrin.
Árni Magnússon. 1695. *Incerti Auctoris Chronica Danorum & præcipuè Sialandiæ.* Leipzig.
—. 1955. *Chorographica Islandica.* Ed. Ólafur Lárusson. Safn til sögu Íslands. Annar flokkur I, 3. Reykjavík: Hið íslenska bókmenntafélag.
—. 1998. 'Um sögu – De historiâ'. Trans. Hanna Óladóttir. *Tímarit Máls og menningar* 59, 1: 66–72.
—. 2008. 'Ævi Sæmundar fróða (1690)'. Trans. Gottskálk Jensson. In *Í garði Sæmundar fróða,* ed. Gunnar Harðarson and Sverrir Tómasson, 143–70. Reykjavík: Hugvísindastofnun Háskóla Íslands.

Printed works

Bartholin, Thomas. 1676. *Dissertatio historico-philologica de Langobardis*. Copenhagen.

—. 1677. *De Holgero Danico, qui Caroli Magni tempore floruit, Dissertatio historica*. Copenhagen.

—. 1689. *Antiqvitatum Danicarum de causis contemptæ a Danis adhuc gentilibus mortis libri tres ex vetustis codicibus & monumentis hactenus ineditis congesti*. Copenhagen.

Baumgarten, Lisbeth. 1984. *Thomas Bartholins bog om danernes dødsforagt (1689) i samtid og eftertid*. Speciale til magisterkonferens i nordisk, Odense University.

Bekker-Nielsen, Hans and Ole Widding. 1963. *Arne Magnusson: den store håndskriftsamler*. Copenhagen: Gads forlag.

—. 1972. *Arne Magnusson. The manuscript collector*. Trans. Robert W. Mattila. Odense: Odense University Press.

Bergkamp, Joseph Urban. 1928. *Dom Jean Mabillon and the Benedictine historical school of Saint-Maur*. Washington: The Catholic University of America.

Birket Smith, Sophus, ed. 1890–1912. *Kjøbenhavns Universitets Matrikel*. 3 vols. Copenhagen: Gyldendal.

Bjarni Einarsson, ed. 1955. *Munnmælasögur 17. aldar*. Íslensk rit síðari alda 6. Reykjavík: Hið íslenska fræðafélag.

Bjarni Jónsson. 1949. *Íslenzkir Hafnarstúdentar*. Akureyri: Bókaútgáfan BS.

Bjerre Jensen, Birgit. 1987. *Udnævnelsesretten i enevældens magtpolitiske system 1660–1730*. Copenhagen: Rigsarkivet.

Björn Sigfússon. 1944. *Um Íslendingabók*. Reykjavík: Author.

Bogi Benediktsson. 1881–1932. *Sýslumannaæfir*. 5 vols. Ed. Jón Pétursson and Hannes Þorsteinsson. Reykjavík: Hið íslenska bókmenntafélag.

Boserup, Ivan. 1981. 'The Angers fragment and the archetype of Gesta Danorum'. In *Saxo Grammaticus. A Medieval Author between Norse and Latin Culture*, ed. Karsten Friis-Jensen, 9–26. Copenhagen: Museum Tusculanum Press.

Bruun, Christian. 1870a. *Frederik Rostgaards liv og levnet*. Copenhagen: Samfundet til den danske Literaturs Fremme.

—. 1870b. *Frederik Rostgaard og hans samtid. Anden del. Aktstykker og breve*. Copenhagen: Gyldendal.

Bæksted, Anders. 1959–60. *Besættelsen i Tisted*. 2 vols. Copenhagen: Ejnar Munksgaard.

Böðvar Kvaran. 1971. 'Útgáfa Íslendingabókar í Oxford'. *Árbók Landsbókasafns Íslands* 28: 157–68.

References

Catalogus Librorum In qvalibet Facultate & Lingva Rarissimorum b. m. Thomæ Bartholini. Copenhagen 1691.

Chesnutt, Michael. 2005a. 'Stockholm Perg. 4:o nr. 7, bl. 57r–58v'. *Opuscula* 12: 209–18.

—. 2005b. 'Tekstkritiske bemærkninger til C-redaktionen af Egils saga'. *Opuscula* 12: 228–62.

Chiffoleau, Jacques. 2008. 'Baluze, les papes et la France'. In *Étienne Baluze, 1630–1718. Érudition et pouvoirs dans l'Europe classique*, ed. Jean Boutier, 163–246. Limoges: Presses universitaires de Limoges.

Clunies Ross, Margaret. 1998. *Prolonged Echoes. Old Norse myths in medieval Northern society* II. The Viking Collection 10. Odense: Odense University Press.

Dahl, Svend. 1914. 'Forfattervilkaar i Holbergs tidsalder. Thormod Torfæus og hans bogtrykkere'. *Nordisk tidskrift för bok- och biblioteksväsen* 1: 335–52.

Davillé, Louis. 1909. *Leibniz historien. Essai sur l'activité et la méthode historiques de Leibniz*. Paris: F. Alcan.

Dibon, Paul. 1976. 'Les échanges épistolaires dans l'Europe savante du XVIIe siècle'. *Revue de synthèse* 97: 31–50.

Diplomatarium Islandicum – Íslenzkt fornbréfasafn. 16 vols. Copenhagen and Reykjavík: Hið íslenska bókmenntafélag, 1857–1972.

Dolmer, Jan. 1673. *Jus aulicum antiqvum Norvagicum... Hird-Skraa vocatum*. Ed. Peder Resen. Copenhagen.

Doni Garfagnini, Manuela. 1988. *Lettere e carte Magliabechi: inventario cronologico*. Roma: Istituto storico italiano.

Easterling, Patricia. 1977. 'Before Palaeography: Notes on Early Descriptions and Datings of Greek Manuscripts'. In *Studia Codicologica*, ed. Kurt Treu, 179–87. Berlin: Akademie-Verlag.

Eberhard, Johann August and Johann Georg von Eckhart. 1982. *Leibniz-Biographien*. Hildesheim and New York: Olms.

Ehrencron-Müller, H. 1924–35. *Forfatterlexikon omfattende Danmark, Norge og Island indtil 1814*. 12 vols. Copenhagen: H. Aschehoug & Co.

Einar Gunnar Pétursson. 1998. *Eddurit Jóns Guðmundssonar lærða. Þættir úr fræðasögu 17. aldar*. 2 vols. Reykjavík: Stofnun Árna Magnússonar.

Eiríkur Magnússon. 1892. 'Kodex Scardensis af postulasögur'. *Arkiv för nordisk filologi* 8: 238–41.

Eithun, Bjørn, Magnus Rindal and Tore Ulseth, ed. 1994. *Gulaþingslög eldri*. Oslo: Riksarkivet.

Eken, Thorsten. 1963. *Gammelnorske membranfragment i Riksarkivet* I. Oslo: Riksarkivet.

Ekenvall, Asta. 1941. 'Om de första lärda tidskrifterna'. *Lychnos. Lärdomshistoriska samfundets årsbok*: 161–90.

—. 1953. *Eric Benzelius d. y. och G. W. von Leibniz*. Linköping: Linköpings bibliotek.

Ekrem, Inger. 1994. 'Historiography in Norway (1536–1614)'. In *Acta Conventus Neo-Latini Hafniensis. Proceedings of the Eighth International Congress of Neo-Latin Studies*, ed. Rhoda Schnur, 401–7. Binghampton: Medieval & Renaissance texts & studies.

Erasmus, H.J. 1962. *The origins of Rome in historiography from Petrarch to Perizonius*. Assen: Van Gorcum & Comp.

Eriksson, Gunnar. 1984, 'Olof Rudbeck d. ä.' *Lychnos. Lärdomshistoriska samfundets årsbok*: 77–119.

Erler, Georg, ed. 1909. *Die iüngere Matrikel der Universität Leipzig 1559–1809* II. Leipzig: Giesecke & Devrient.

Faulkes, Anthony. 1964. 'The Sources of Specimen Lexici Runici'. *Íslenzk tunga* 5: 30–138.

—. ed. 1985. *Codex Trajectinus. The Utrecht manuscript of the Prose Edda*. Early Icelandic Manuscripts in Facsimile 15. Copenhagen: Rosenkilde and Bagger.

Fell, Christine E. 1996. 'The first publication of Old Norse literature in England and its relation to its soures'. In *The Waking of Angantyr. The Scandinavian past in European culture*, ed. Else Roesdahl and Preben Meulengracht Sørensen, 27–57. Aarhus: Aarhus University Press.

Feller, Joachim. 1686. *Catalogus Codicum Mssctorum Bibliothecae Paulinae in Academia Lipsiensi*. Leipzig.

Finnur Jónsson, ed. 1887. *Íslendingabóc*. Copenhagen: Hið íslenska bókmenntafélag.

—. 1930a. *Ævisaga Árna Magnússonar*. Safn Fræðafélagsins um Ísland og Íslendinga 8. Copenhagen: S.L. Möller.

—, ed. 1930b. *Árni Magnússons levned og skrifter*. 2 vols. Copenhagen: Gyldendal.

Finnur Magnússon. 1813. 'Om Holbergs haarde Dom over Nordens Oldsager og gamle Histories Studium'. *Athene. Et Maanedsskrift* 1: 187–98.

Foote, Peter, ed. 2003. *Jóns saga Hólabyskups ens helga*. Editiones Arnamagnæanæ A, 14. Copenhagen: C.A. Reitzels forlag.

Fortegnelse paa en Deel Bøger som først-kommende 28. Decembris, fra Klokken 2 om Eftermiddagen ved offentlig Auction, og for reede Penge, skulle selges udi Professor og Archiv-Secreterer Arnas Magnussens Huus beliggende i Canicke-strædet. Copenhagen 1713.

Frantzen, Allen J. 1990. *Desire for Origins. New Language, Old English, and Teaching the Tradition*. New Brunswick and London: Rutgers University Press.

Friedrichsen, Per and Chr. Gorm Tortzen, ed. 2001. *Ole Rømer. Korrespondance og afhandlinger samt et udvalg af dokumenter*. Copenhagen: C.A. Reitzels Forlag.

Friis-Jensen, Karsten. 1989. 'Humanism and Politics. The Paris Edition of Saxo Grammaticus's *Gesta Danorum* 1514'. *Analecta Romana Instituti Danici* 17–18: 149–62.

Fubini, Riccardo, ed. 1964–9. Poggius Bracciolini, *Opera omnia*. 4 vols. Torino: Bottega d'Erasmo.

Gain, Benoît. 2003. 'Les documents mauristes et leurs utilisation'. In *Érudition et commerce épistolaire. Jean Mabillon et la tradition monastique*, ed. Daniel-Odon Hurel, 255–68. Paris: J. Vrin.

Gasnault, Pierre. 2008. 'Baluze éditeur de textes anciens'. In *Étienne Baluze, 1630–1718. Érudition et pouvoirs dans l'Europe classique*, ed. Jean Boutier, 129–40. Limoges: Presses universitaires de Limoges.

Geert Andersen, Merete. 2008. *Katalog over AM Accessoria 7. De latinske fragmenter*. Bibliotheca Arnamagnæana 46. Copenhagen: C.A. Reitzels forlag.

Geertz, Martinus Clarentius, ed. 1917–22. *Scriptores Minores Historiæ Danicæ Medii Ævi*. 2 vols. Copenhagen: Selskabet for udgivelse af kilder til dansk historie.

Gísli Baldur Róbertsson. 2004. 'Áform um endurskoðun íslenskra laga'. In *Jónsbók. Lögbók Íslendinga*, ed. Már Jónsson, 35–54. Reykjavík: Háskólaútgáfan.

—. 2005. 'Snurðan á þræði Reykjarfjarðarbókar'. *Gripla* 16: 161–95.

—. 2010. 'Nýtt af Bjarna Jónssyni lögbókarskrifara á Snæfjallaströnd'. *Gripla* 21: 335–87.

Gjerløw, Lilli. 1980. *Liturgica Islandica*. 2 vols. Bibliotheca Arnamagnæana 35. Copenhagen: C.A. Reitzels forlag.

Gottskálk Jensson. 2008. '„Ævi Sæmundar fróða" á latínu eftir Árna Magnússon'. In *Í garði Sæmundar fróða*, ed. Gunnar Harðarson and Sverrir Tómasson, 135–42. Reykjavík: Hugvísindastofnun Háskóla Íslands.

Grafton, Anthony. 1983. *Joseph Scaliger. A Study in the History of Classical Scholarship*. 2 vols. Oxford: Clarendon Press.

—. 1985. 'The World of the Polyhistors: Humanism and Encyclopedism'. *Central European History* 18: 31–47.

—. 1991. *Defenders of the Text. The Traditions of Scholarship in an Age of Science, 1450–1800*. Cambridge and London: Harvard University Press.

—. 1999. 'Jean Hardouin: The Antiquary as Pariah'. *Journal of the Warburg and Courtauld Institutes* 62: 241–67.

Gram, Herman, ed. 1907. *Breve fra Hans Gram, etatsraad, geheimearchivar, professor, 1685–1748*. Copenhagen: V. Thaning & Appels forlag.

Grape, Anders. 1914. 'Om bröderna Salan och deras handskriftssamling'. *Nordisk tidsskrift för bok- och biblioteksväsen* 1: 207–38.

Guðrún Ása Grímsdóttir. 2007. 'Drög að skrá yfir handrit með hendi sr. Jóns Erlendssonar í Villingaholti'. *Árnesingur* 8: 165–70.

Guðvarður Már Gunnlaugsson. 1994. 'Lesbrigði í AM 455 fol Vitnisburður um týnd handrit?' In *Sagnaþing helgað Jónasi Kristjánssyni sjötugum*, ed. Gísli Sigurðsson, Guðrún Kvaran and Sigurgeir Steingrímsson, 289–305. Reykjavík: Hið íslenska bókmenntafélag.

—, ed. 2000. *Reykjaholtsmáldagi*. Reykholt: Snorrastofa.

—. 2001. 'Leiðbeiningar Árna Magnússonar'. *Gripla* 12: 95–124.

Gunnar F. Guðmundsson, ed. 1990a. *Jarðabréf frá 16. og 17. öld. Útdrættir*. Reykjavík: Hið íslenska fræðafélag.

—. 1990b. 'Pappírar Árna Magnússonar'. In *Brunnur lifandi vatns. Afmælisrit til heiðurs Pétri Mikkel Jónassyni prófessor sjötugum*, ed. Guðmundur Eggertsson et al., 35–43. Reykjavík: Háskólaútgáfan.

Gödel, Vilhelm. 1892. *Katalog öfver Upsala Universitets Biblioteks fornisländska och fornnorska handskrifter*. Uppsala: Almqvist & Wiksells boktryckeri.

—. 1897. *Fornnorsk-isländsk litteratur i Sverige I. Till Antikvitetskollegiets inrättande*. Stockholm: Ivar Hæggströms boktryckeri.

—, ed. 1897–1900. *Katalog öfver Kongl. Bibliotekets fornisländska och fornnorska handskrifter*. Stockholm: P.A. Norstedt & söner.

—, ed. 1912. 'Arne Magnusson till Johan Peringskiöld. Ett bref från 1699'. *Arkiv för nordisk filologi* 28: 269–71.

Hagland, Jan Ragnar and Jørn Sandnes, ed. and trans. 1997. *Bjarkøyretten. Nidaros eldste bylov*. Oslo: Det Norske Samlaget.

Hakluyt, Richard. 1598. *The Principal Navigations, Voiages, Traffiqves and Discoueries of the English Nation* I. London.

Halldór Hermannsson. 1922. *Icelandic Books of the Seventeenth Century*. Islandica 14. Ithaca and New York: Cornell University Library.

—. 1929. *Icelandic Manuscripts*. Islandica 19. Ithaca and New York: Cornell University Library.

—. 1954. 'Þormóður Torfason'. *Skírnir* 128: 65–94.

References

Halldór Laxness. 1993. *Íslandsklukkan*. Fifth edition. Reykjavík: Vaka-Helgafell.

—. 2003. *Iceland's bell*. Trans. Philip Roughton. New York: Vintage Books.

Harris, Richard Lynn, ed. 1992. *A Chorus of Grammars. The correspondence of George Hickes and his collaborators on the Thesaurus linguarum septentrionalium*. Toronto: Pontifical Institute of Mediaeval Studies.

Harth, Helene, ed. 1984–7. Poggio Bracciolini, *Lettere*. 3 vols. Florence: L.S. Olschki.

Hast, Sture, ed. 1960. *Harðar saga*. Editiones Arnamagnæanæ A, 6. Copenhagen: Ejnar Munksgaard.

Heer, Gall. 1938. *Johannes Mabillon und die Schweizer Benediktiner. Ein Beitrag zur Geschichte der historischen Quellenforschung im 17. und 18. Jahrhundert*. St. Gallen: Verlag Leobuchhandlung.

Helk, Vello. 1991. *Dansk-norske studierejser 1661–1813*. 2 vols. Odense: Odense Universitetsforlag.

Heussi, Karl. 1904. *Die Kirchengeschichtschreibung Johann Lorenz von Mosheims*. Gotha: Friedrich Andreas Perthus.

Hickes, George. 1689. *Institutiones grammaticæ Anglo-Saxonicæ et Moeso-Gothicæ*. Oxford.

Holm-Olsen, Ludvig. 1952. *Håndskriftene av Konungs skuggsjá. En undersøkelse av deres tekstkritiske verdi*. Bibliotheca Arnamagnæana 13. Copenhagen: Ejnar Munksgaard.

—. 1981. *Lys over norrøn kultur. Norrøne studier i Norge*. Oslo: Cappelen.

Hreinn Benediktsson, ed. 1965. *Early Icelandic Script*. Icelandic Manuscripts, series in folio, vol. 2. Reykjavík: The Manuscript Institute of Iceland.

—, ed. 1972. *The First Grammatical Treatise*. Reykjavík: Institute of Nordic Linguistics.

Huet, Pierre-Daniel. 1942. *Traité de l'origine des romans. Édition critique*. Ed. Arend Kok. Amsterdam: N.V. Swets & Zeitlinger.

Hødnebø, Finn. 1988. 'Árni Magnússon i Norge 1712–13'. In *Saga og kirkja. Afmælisrit Magnúsar Más Lárussonar*, ed. Gunnar Karlsson et al., 199–209. Reykjavík: Sögufélag.

Ilsøe, Harald. 1973. 'Historisk censur i Danmark indtil Holberg'. *Fund og forskning* 20: 45–70.

—. 1980. 'Universitetets biblioteker til 1728'. In *Københavns Universitet 1479–1979. Bind IV. Gods. Bygninger. Biblioteker*, ed. Svend Ellehøj and Leif Grane, 289–364. Copenhagen: Gads forlag

—. 1988. 'Lærde forbindelser mellem Danmark og Sverige ca. 1660–1720. Breve – bøger – besøg'. In *Bøger Biblioteker Mennesker. Et nordisk Fest-*

skrift tilegnet Torben Nielsen, ed. Erland Kolding Nielsen et al., 547–70. Copenhagen: Det kongelige Bibliotek.

Ilsøe, Harald and Kai Hørby. 1980. 'Historie'. In *Københavns Universitet 1479–1979. Bind X. Det filosofiske fakultet 3*, ed. Povl Johs. Jensen, 309–526. Copenhagen: Gads forlag.

Israel, Jonathan I. 2001. *Radical Enlightenment. Philosophy and the Making of Modernity 1650–1750*. Oxford: Oxford University Press.

Jacobowsky, C. Vilh. 1932. *J. G. Sparwenfeld. Bidrag till en biografi*. Stockholm: Kurt Lindberg.

Jakob Benediktsson, ed. 1944. *Veraldar saga*. STUAGNL 61. Copenhagen: Samfund til udgivelse af gammel nordisk litteratur.

—, ed. 1948. *Ole Worm's Correspondence with Icelanders*. Bibliotheca Arnamagnæana 7. Copenhagen: Ejnar Munksgaard.

—, ed. 1950–7. *Arngrimi Jonae Opera latine conscripta*. 4 vols. Bibliotheca Arnamagnæana 9–12. Copenhagen: Ejnar Munksgaard.

—. 1968. *Íslendingabók – Landnámabók*. 2 vols. Íslensk fornrit 1. Reykjavík: Hið íslenska fornritafélag.

Jarðabók Árna Magnússonar og Páls Vídalíns. 13 vols. Copenhagen and Reykjavík: Hið íslenska fræðafélag, 1913–90.

Johannesson, Kurt. 1991. *The Renaissance of the Goths in Sixteenth-Century Sweden. Johannes and Olaus Magnus as Politicians and Historians*. Los Angeles and Berkeley: University of California Press.

Johnsen, Oscar Albert. 1908. 'Norske geistlige og kirkelige institutioners bogsamlinger i den senere middelalder'. In *Sproglige og historiske afhandlinger viede Sophus Bugges minde*, 73–96. Christiania (Oslo): H. Aschehoug & Co.

Johnsen, Oscar Albert and Jón Helgason, ed. 1941. *Den store saga om Olav den hellige*. Oslo: Jacob Dybwad.

Jón Ma. Ásgeirsson og Þórður Ingi Guðjónsson. 2007. *Frá Sýrland til Íslands. Arfur Tómasar postula*. Reykjavík: Háskólaútgáfan.

Jón Eiríksson. 2009. *Thormod Torfesens Levnetsbeskrivelse*. Stavanger: Saga-Bok.

Jón Helgason. 1925. *Jón Ólafsson frá Grunnavík*. Copenhagen: S.L. Möller.

—, ed. 1942. *Úr bréfabókum Brynjólfs biskups Sveinssonar*. Safn Fræðafélagsins 12. Copenhagen: Hið íslenska fræðafélag.

—, ed. 1950. *Móðars rímur og Móðars þáttur*. Íslensk rit síðari alda 5. Copenhagen: Hið íslenska fræðafélag.

—, ed. 1955. *Kvæðabók úr Vigur. AM 148, 8vo. Inngangur*. Íslensk rit síðari alda 2, 1. Copenhagen: Hið íslenska fræðafélag.

References

—, ed. 1956. *The Saga Manuscript 9. 10. Aug. 4to in the Herzog August Library Wolfenbüttel*. Manuscripta Islandica 3. Copenhagen: Ejnar Munksgaard.

—. 1958. *Handritaspjall*. Reykjavík: Mál og menning.

—, ed. 1960a. *Hauksbók. The Arna-Magnæan Manuscripts 371, 4to, 544, 4to, and 675, 4to*. Manuscripta Islandica 5. Copenhagen: Ejnar Munksgaard.

—. 1960b. 'Til Hauksbóks historie i det 17. århundrede'. *Opuscula* 1: 1–48.

—, ed. 1962. *Njáls saga. The Arna-Magnæan manuscript 468, 4to*. Manuscripta Islandica 6. Copenhagen: Ejnar Munksgaard.

—, ed. 1963. *Íslenzk fornkvæði* 4. Editiones Arnamagnæanæ B, 13. Copenhagen: Ejnar Munksgaard.

—, ed. 1966. *Alexanders Saga. The Arna-Magnæan Manuscript 519A, 4to*. Manuscripta Islandica 7. Copenhagen: Ejnar Munksgaard.

—. 1967. 'Arne Magnussons erhvervelse af tre Alexandreis-håndskrifter'. *Opuscula* 3: 204–9.

—. 1970a. 'Om Perg. fol. nr. 8 og AM 304 4to'. *Opuscula* 4: 1–24.

—. 1970b. 'Et par notitser om Páll Hákonarson'. *Opuscula* 4: 353–6.

—. 1975a. 'Fra en seddelsamlings versosider'. *Opuscula* 5: 383–91.

—. 1975b. 'Biskop Þórður Þorláksson og Thomas Bartholin'. *Opuscula* 5: 406–8.

—. 1977. 'Athuganir Árna Magnússonar um fornsögur'. *Gripla* 4: 33–64.

—. 1985. 'Sylloge Sagarum. Resenii Bibliotheca. Vatnshyrna'. *Opuscula* 8: 10–53.

—. 2005. 'Observations on some manuscripts of Egils saga'. Trans. Michael Chesnutt. *Opuscula* 12: 3–47.

Jón Jóhannesson, ed. 1956. *Íslendingabók Ara fróða. AM. 113 a and 113 b, fol.* Icelandic Manuscripts 1. Reykjavík: University of Iceland.

Jón K. Margeirsson, ed. 1975. 'Bréf Árna Magnússonar til Íslands 1729 og fleiri skjöl hans í Ríkisskjalasafni Dana'. *Opuscula* 5: 123–80.

Jón Ólafsson. 1836. 'Biographiske Efterretninger om Arne Magnussen'. Ed. E.C. Werlauff. *Nordisk Tidsskrift for Oldkyndighed* 3: 1–166.

—. 2005. *Relatio af Kaupinhafnarbrunanum sem skeði í október 1728*. Ed. Sigurgeir Steingrímsson. Reykjavík: Góðvinir Grunnavíkur-Jóns.

Jón Sigurðsson, Guðbrandur Vigfússon, Þorvaldur Björnsson and Eiríkur Jónsson, ed. 1858–78. *Biskupa sögur*. 2 vols. Copenhagen: Hið íslenska bókmenntafélag.

Jón Þorkelsson. 1879–89. 'Om håndskrifterne af Njála'. In *Njála* II, ed. Konráð Gíslason and Eiríkur Jónsson, 647–787. Copenhagen: Det kongelige nordiske oldskrift-selskab.

Printed works

Jón Þorkelsson and Hannes Þorsteinsson, ed. 1903–15. *Biskupasögur Jóns prófasts Halldórssonar í Hítardal*. 2 vols. Reykjavík: Sögufélag.

Jónas Kristjánsson, ed. 1966. *Svarfdæla saga*. Reykjavík: Stofnun Árna Magnússonar.

Jucknies, Regina. 2009. *Der Horizont eines Schreibers. Jón Eggertsson (1643– 1689) und seine Handschriften*. Frankfurt am Main: Peter Lang.

Jöcher, Christian Gottlieb. 1750–51. *Allgemeines Gelehrten-Lexicon*. 4 vols. Leipzig: Johann Friedrich Gleditsch.

Jørgensen, Adolf D. 1884. *Udsigt over de danske Rigsarkivers historie*. Copenhagen: Bianco Luno.

Jørgensen, Ellen. 1915. 'Italienske humanisters manuskriptrejser til Danmark'. *Nordisk tidsskrift för bok- och biblioteksväsen* 2: 76–80.

—. 1917. 'Stephanus Johannis Stephanii manuskriptsamling'. *Nordisk tidsskrift för bok- och biblioteksväsen* 4: 19–28.

—. 1919. 'Biskop Christen Worms manuscriptsamling'. *Nordisk tidsskrift för bok- och biblioteksväsen* 6: 74–9.

—. 1931. *Historieforskning og historieskrivning i Danmark indtil aar 1800*. Copenhagen: Bianco Luno.

Jørgensen, Jon Gunnar. 1996. 'Et kort utdrag av Heimskringla'. *Opuscula* 10: 212–55.

—. 2007. *The lost vellum Kringla*. Bibliotheca Arnamagnæana 45. Copenhagen: C.A. Reitzels forlag.

Kirby, Anne-Mette. 1997. 'Kongelig Antiquarius Thomas Bartholin og den danske stoicisme'. *Magasin fra Det kongelige Bibliotek* 12, 1: 60–7.

Kjartan G. Ottósson. 2006. 'Árni Magnússons samling av skalcedikt i AM 761 a–b 4to. Ein førebels rapport'. In *The Fantastic in Old Norse/Icelandic literature. Sagas and the British Isles*, ed., John McKinnell, David Ashurst and Donata Kick, 749–58. Durham: The Centre for Medieval and Renaissance Studies.

Klemming, G.E. 1880–2. *Ur en antecknares samlingar*. Uppsala: E. Berling.

Konráð Gíslason, ed. 1858. 'Brudstykker af den islandske Elucidarius'. *Annaler for Nordisk Oldkyndighed og Historie*: 51–172.

Kålund, Kristian. 1888–94. *Katalog over den Arnamagnæanske håndskriftsamling*. 2 vols. Copenhagen: Gyldendal.

—, ed. 1889–91. *Laxdæla saga*. STUAGNL 19. Copenhagen: Samfund til udgivelse af gammel nordisk litteratur.

—. 1900. *Katalog over de oldnorsk-islandske håndskrifter i det store kongelige bibliotek og i universitetsbiblioteket*. Copenhagen: Gyldendal.

References

—, ed. 1909. *Arne Magnussons i AM. 435 A–B, 4to indeholdte håndskriftfortegnelser*. Copenhagen: Gyldendal.

—, ed. 1916a. *Árni Magnússon, Brevveksling med Torfæus (Þormóður Torfason)*. Copenhagen: Gyldendal.

—, ed. 1916b. *Árni Magnússon, Embedsskrivelser og andre offenlige aktstykker*. Copenhagen: Gyldendal.

—. ed. 1920. *Arne Magnussons private brevveksling*. Copenhagen: Gyldendal.

Larsen, Knud. 1970. *Frederik Rostgaard og bøgerne*. Copenhagen: Gads forlag.

Lectiones publicæ professorum in Universitate Hauniensi. Copenhagen 1713–27.

Leibniz, Gottfried Wilhelm. 1994. *Writings on China*. Trans. and ed. Daniel J. Cook and Henry Rosemont, Jr. Chicago and La Salle: Open Court.

Levine, Joseph M. 1987. *Humanism and History. Origins of Modern English Historiography*. Ithaca and London: Cornell University Press.

Lindberg, Kirsten. 1996. *Sirenernes stad København. By- og bygningshistorie før 1728*. 3 vols. Copenhagen: Sortedam.

Loth, Agnete, ed. 1960a. *Membrana Regia Deperdita*. Editiones Arnamagnæanæ A, 5. Copenhagen: Ejnar Munksgaard.

—. 1960b. 'Sønderdelte arnamagnæanske papirhåndskrifter'. *Opuscula* 1: 113–42.

—. 1960c. 'Fragment af en ellers ukendt Grega saga'. *Opuscula* 1: 201–6.

—. 1960d. 'Om nogle af Ásgeir Jónssons håndskrifter'. *Opuscula* 1: 207–12.

—, ed. 1964. *Thomasskinna. Gl. Kgl. Saml. 1008 fol. in the Royal Library, Copenhagen*. Early Icelandic manuscripts in facsimile 6. Copenhagen: Rosenkilde and Bagger.

—. 1977. 'Árni Magnússon og Sturlubók'. In *Sjötíu ritgerðir helgaðar Jakobi Benediktssyni*, ed. Einar G. Pétursson and Jónas Kristjánsson, 533–43. Reykjavík: Stofnun Árna Magnússonar.

Louis-Jensen, Jonna, ed. 1963. *Trójumanna saga*. Editiones Arnamagnæanæ A, 8. Copenhagen: Ejnar Munksgaard.

—, ed. 1968. *Hulda. Sagas of the Kings of Norway 1035–1117. Manuscript no. 66 fol. in the Arnamagnæan Collection*. Early Icelandic Manuscripts in Facsimile 8. Copenhagen: Rosenkilde and Bagger.

—. 1970. 'Et forlæg til Flateyjarbók? Fragmenterne AM 325 IV β og XI, 3 4to'. *Opuscula* 4: 141–58.

—. 1979. 'To håndskrifter fra det nordvestlige Island'. *Opuscula* 7: 219–53.

—. 1994. 'Árni Hákonarson fra Vatnshorn'. In *Sagnaþing helgað Jónasi Krist-

jánssyni sjötugum, ed. Gísli Sigurðsson, Guðrún Kvaran and Sigurgeir Steingrímsson, 515–25. Reykjavík: Hið íslenska bókmenntafélag.

Lovsamling for Island. 21 vols. Copenhagen 1853–89.

Mabillon, Jean. 1990. *Brèves réflexions sur quelques règles de l'histoire*. Ed. Blandine Barret-Kriegel. Paris: P.O.L.

—. 2007. *Oeuvres choisies*. Ed. Daniel-Odon Hurel. Paris: Robert Laffont.

Magnús Már Lárusson and Jónas Kristjánsson, ed. 1965–7. *Sigilla Islandica*. 2 vols. Icelandic Manuscripts, series in octavo 1–2. Reykjavík: The Manuscript Institute of Iceland.

Magnús Ólafsson. 2010. *Specimen Lexici Runici and Glossarium Priscæ Linguæ Danicæ*. Ed. Anthony Faulkes and Gunnlaugur Ingólfsson. Reykjavík and London: Stofnun Árna Magnússonar and Viking Society for Northern Research.

Malm, Mats. 1996. *Minervas äpple. Om diktsyn, tolkning och bildspråk inom nordisk göticism*. Stockholm: Symposion.

Már Jónsson. 1997a. 'Scribal inexactitude and scholarly misunderstanding: a contribution to the study of Vatnshyrna'. In *Frejas Psalter. En psalter i 40 afdelinger til brug for Jonna Louis-Jensen*, ed. Bergljót Kristjánsdóttir and Peter Springborg, 119–27. Copenhagen: Det Arnamagnæanske Institut.

—. 1997b. 'Síðustu misseri Árna Magnússonar'. *Ný saga* 9: 87–94.

—. 1998. *Árni Magnússon. Ævisaga*. Reykjavík: Mál og menning.

—. 1999. 'Arnas Magnæus Islandus. A visiting scholar in Leipzig, 1694–96'. *Lias* 26: 213–32.

—. 2001. 'Textatengsl nokkurra elstu handrita Jónsbókar'. In *Líndæla. Sigurður Líndal sjötugur*, ed. Garðar Gíslason et al., 373–87. Reykjavík: Hið íslenska bókmenntafélag.

—. 2003. 'Megindlegar handritarannsóknir'. In Ezio Ornato, *Lofræða um handritamergð. Hugleiðingar um bóksögu miðalda*, trans. Björg Birgisdóttir and Már Jónsson, 7–34. Reykjavík: Sagnfræðistofnun Háskóla Íslands.

—. 2006. 'Skýringar Árna Magnússonar við eigið dróttkvæði frá 1689'. In *Lesið í hljóði fyrir Kristján Árnason sextugan*, 163–5. Reykjavík: Mettusjóður.

—. 2009a. 'Sorgarsaga Reykjarfjarðarbókar'. In *Sturlaðar sögur sagðar Úlfari Bragasyni sextugum*, 87–9. Reykjavík: Mettusjóður.

—. 2009b. 'Skrifarinn Ásgeir Jónsson frá Gullberastöðum í Lundarreykjadal'. In *Heimtur. Ritgerðir til heiðurs Gunnari Karlssyni sjötugum*, ed. Guðmundur Jónsson, Helgi Skúli Kjartansson and Vésteinn Ólason, 282–97. Reykjavík: Forlagið.

—. 2010. 'Manuscript Hunting and the Challenge of Textual Variance in Late Seventeenth-Century Icelandic Studies'. In *The Making of the Humanities. Vol. I: The Humanities in Early Modern Europe*, ed. Rens Bod, Jaap Maat and Thijs Weststeijn, 309–22. Amsterdam: Amsterdam University Press.

McC. Gatch, Milton. 1985. 'John Bagford as a Collector and Disseminator of Manuscript Fragments'. *The Library.* Sixth Series 7: 95–114.

McKinnell, John. 1970. 'The Reconstruction of Pseudo-Vatnshyrna'. *Opuscula* 4: 304–37.

Mencke, Johann Burckhardt. 1714. *Catalogue des principaux historiens, avec des remarques critiques.* Leipzig.

Momigliano, Arnaldo. 1990. *The Classical Foundations of Modern Historiography.* Berkeley: University of California Press.

Montfaucon, Bernard de. 1725. *The Antiquities of Italy.* Second Edition. London.

Mortensen, Jens, ed. 1594. *Norske Kongers Krønicke oc bedrifft, indtil unge Kong Haagens tid, som døde: Anno Domini 1263. Udset aff gammel Norske paa Danske.* Copenhagen.

Murphy, Michael. 1967. 'Abraham Wheloc's Edition of Bede's *History* in Old English'. *Studia Neophilologica* 39: 46–59.

Müller, Kurt and Gisela Krönert. 1969. *Leben und Werk von Gottfried Wilhelm Leibniz. Eine Chronik.* Frankfurt: Vittorio Klostermann.

Neveu, Bruno. 1966. *Un historien à l'école de Port-Royal. Sébastien le Nain de Tillemont.* The Hague: Martinus Nijhoff.

Norges gamle love. 5 vols. Ed. Rudolph Keyser and Peter Andreas Munch. Christiania (Oslo) 1846–95.

Nouvelles de la république des lettres 1684.

Nyrop, Camillus. 1870. *Bidrag til den danske boghandels historie.* 2 vols. Copenhagen: Gyldendal.

Olrik, Hans. 1889. *Borchs kollegiums historie i de første 40 år, 1689–1728.* Copenhagen.

Olsen, Gunnar. 1970. *Den unge Enevælde 1660–1721.* Danmarks historie 8. Copenhagen: Politiken.

Ordbog over det norrøne prosasprog. Registre. Copenhagen 1989.

O'Sullivan, William. 1956. 'Ussher as a Collector of Manuscripts'. *Hermathena* 88: 34–58.

Otto, Alfred. 1930. 'Beiträge zur Textgeschichte des Adam von Bremen'. *Neues Archiv der Gesellschaft für ältere deutsche Geschichtskunde* 49: 9–55.

Overgaard, Mariane. 1996. 'Manuscripta Rosencrantziana'. *Opuscula* 10: 262–85.

Ólafía Einarsdóttir. 1964. *Studier i kronologisk metode i tidlig islandsk historieskrivning*. Stockholm: Natur och kultur.

Ólafur Halldórsson, ed. 1958–2000. *Óláfs saga Tryggvasonar en mesta*. 3 vols. Editiones Arnamagnæanæ A, 3. Copenhagen: C.A. Reitzels forlag.

—, ed. 1968. *Kollsbók. Codex Guelferbytanus 42. 7. Augusteus quarto*. Íslensk handrit, series in quarto 5. Reykjavík.

—, ed. 1969. *Jómsvíkinga saga*. Reykjavík: Prentsmiðja Jóns Helgasonar.

—, ed. 1982. *The great Sagas of Olaf Tryggvason and Olaf the Saint. AM 61 fol. Early Icelandic Manuscripts in Facsimile* 14. Copenhagen: Rosenkilde and Bagger.

—. 1990. *Grettisfærsla*. Reykjavík: Stofnun Árna Magnússonar.

—. 1992. 'Samskipti Þormóðar Torfasonar og Árna Magnússcnar'. *Skáldskaparmál* 2: 7–19.

—. 1994. 'Maríujarteinir frá Mjóabóli'. In *Strengleikar slegnir Robert Cook*, 50–5. Reykjavík: Mettusjóður.

—. 1999. Review of Már Jónsson 1998 in *Saga* 37: 244–51.

—. 2000. 'Athugasemdir við bók Más Jónssonar um Árna Magnússon'. *Gripla* 11: 326–8.

—. 2006. 'Danakonungatal in Copenhagen, Royal Library Barth. D III. Fol.: An Edition'. In *Beatus vir. Studies in early English and Norse manuscripts in memory of Phillip Pulsiano*, ed. A.N. Doane and Kirsten Wolf, 107–74. Tempe: Arizona Center for Medieval and Renaissance Studies.

Ólafur Lárusson, ed. 1936. *Staðarhólsbók. The Ancient Lawbooks Grágás and Járnsíða. Ms. No. 334 fol. in The Arna-Magnæan Collection in the University Library in Copenhagen*. Corpus Codicum Islandicorum Medii Aevi 9. Copenhagen: Ejnar Munksgaard.

Ólöf Benediktsdóttir. 2005. 'Bókarugl í Víngarðsstræti'. In *Glerharðar hugvekjur þénandi til þess að örva og upptendra Þórunni Sigurðardóttur fimmtuga*, ed. Margrét Eggertsdóttir, Guðvarður Már Gunnlaugsson and Svanhildur Óskarsdóttir, 55–59. Reykjavík: Mettusjóður

Palumbo, Margherita. 1993. *Leibniz e la Res Bibliothecaria. Bibliografie, historiae literariae e cataloghi nella biblioteca privata leibniziana*. Rome: Bulzoni.

Páll Eggert Ólason. 1948–52. *Íslenzkar æviskrár frá landnámstímum til ársloka 1940*. 5 vols. Reykjavík: Hið íslenska bókmenntafélag.

Páll Vídalín. 1985. *Recensus poetarum et scriptorum Islandorum hujus et superioris seculi*. Ed. Jón Samsonarson. Reykjavík: Stofnun Árna Magnússonar.

References

Pertz, Georg Heinrich, ed. 1847. *Leibnizens geschichtliche Aufsätze und Gedichte* 4. Hannover.

Petersen, Carl S., ed. 1920. *Ludvig Holbergs samlede skrifter* 5. Copenhagen: Gyldendal.

Petersen, Erik. 1998. *Intellectum liberare. Johann Albert Fabricius. En humanist i Europa.* 2 vols. Copenhagen: Tusculanum forlag.

Petersen, Julius. 1898. *Bartholinerne og kredsen om dem.* Copenhagen: Gads forlag.

Petersens, Carl af and Emil Olson, ed. 1919–25. *Sögur Danakonunga.* STU-AGNL 36. Copenhagen: Samfund til udgivelse af gammel nordisk litteratur.

Petitmengin, Pierre. 2008. 'Baluze éditeur des Pères de l'Église'. In *Étienne Baluze, 1630–1718. Érudition et pouvoirs dans l'Europe classique*, ed. Jean Boutier, 141–61. Limoges: Presses universitaires de Limoges.

Piggott, Stuart. 1956. 'Antiquarian Thought in the Sixteenth and Seventeenth Centuries'. In *English Historical Scholarship in the Sixteenth and Seventeenth Centuries*, ed. Levi Fox, 93–114. London: Oxford University Press.

Rafn, Carl Christian, ed. 1829–30. *Fornaldarsögur Nordrlanda.* 3 vols. Copenhagen.

Rasmussen, Stig. 2007. 'Frederik Rostgaards *Museum Orientale*'. In *Umisteligt! Festskrift til Erland Kolding Nielsen*, ed. John T. Lauridsen and Olaf Olsen, 183–92. Copenhagen: Det kongelige Bibliotek.

Rechenberg, Adam. 1691. *De Studiis Academicis.* Leipzig.

Reynolds, L.D., and N.G. Wilson. 1991. *Scribes and Scholars. A Guide to the Transmission of Greek and Latin Literature.* Third edition. Oxford: Clarendon Press.

Riis, Thomas. 2006. *Einführung in die Gesta Danorum des Saxo Grammaticus.* Odense: University Press of Southern Denmark.

Robinet, André. 1988, *G.W. Leibniz Iter Italicum (Mars 1689–Mars 1690). La dynamique de la République des Lettres. Nombreux textes inédits.* Florence: L.S. Olschki.

Rowe, Elizabeth Ashman. 2005. *The Development of Flateyjarbók. Iceland and the Norwegian dynastic crisis of 1389.* The Viking Collection 15. Odense: The University Press of Southern Denmark.

Ruinart, Thierry. 1933. *Mabillon.* Paris: Desclée de Brouwer.

Röhn, Hartmut. 1994. 'Zur Überlieferung des althochdeutschen Georgsliedes'. In *Studien zum Altgermanischen. Festschrift für Heinrich Beck*, ed. Heiko Uecker, 513–26. Berlin and New York: Walter de Gruyter.

Rørdam, Holger Fr. 1893–7. 'Aktstykker til Universitetets Historie i Tidsrummet 1661–1732'. *Danske Magazin. Femte Række* 3: 182–247.

——. 1896. *Historieskriveren Arild Hvitfeldt, Danmarks Riges Kansler og Raad, Skoleherre for Herlufsholm*. Copenhagen: Thaning & Appel.

Sabbadini, Remigio. 1905–15. *Le scoperte dei codici latini e greci ne' secoli XIV e XV*. 2 vols. Florence: Sansoni.

Sagan Landnama Vm fyrstu bygging Islands af Nordmönnum. Ed. Einar Eyjólfsson and Þórður Þorláksson. Skálholt 1688 (facsimile edition, Reykjavík 1969).

Sanders, Christopher. 2001. *Bevers saga*. Reykjavík: Stofnun Árna Magnússonar.

Saxo Grammaticus. 1979–80. *The History of the Danes. Books I–IX*. 2 vols. Ed. Hilda Ellis Davidson. Trans. Peter Fisher. Cambridge: D.S. Brewer.

Schedæ Ara Prests froda vm Jsland. Ed. Einar Eyjólfsson and Þórður Þorláksson. Skálholt 1688.

Scheele, Meta. 1930. *Wissen und Glauben in der Geschichtswissenschaft. Studien zum historischen Pyrrhonismus in Frankreich und Deutschland*. Heidelberg: Carl Winters.

Schepelern, Harald D., ed. 1965–8. *Breve fra og til Ole Worm*. 3 vols. Copenhagen: Ejnar Munksgaard.

Schnapp, Alain. 1993. *La conquête du passé. Aux origines de l'archéologie*. Paris: Éditions Carré.

——. 1997. *The Discovery of the Past*. Trans. Ian Kinnes and Gillian Varndell. New York: Harry N. Abrams.

Schoeck, Richard J. 1982 'The Humanistic Concept of the Text: Text, Context and Tradition'. *Proceedings of the Patristic, Mediaeval and Renaissance Conference* 7: 13–31

Scholderer, Victor. 1949. 'Printers and Readers in Italy in the Fifteenth Century'. *Proceedings of the British Academy*: 25–47.

Schück, Henrik. 1932–44. *Kgl. Vitterhets Historie och Antikvitets Akademien. Dess Förhistoria och Historia*. 8 vols. Stockholm.

Seaton, Ethel. 1935. *Literary Relations of England and Scandinavia in the Seventeenth Century*. Oxford: Clarendon Press.

Seelow, Hubert. 1977. 'Ásgeir Jónsson und seine 'membranartige' Frakturschrift'. In *Sjötíu ritgerðir helgaðar Jakobi Benediktssyni*, ed. Einar G. Pétursson and Jónas Kristjánsson, 658–64. Reykjavík: Stofnun Árna Magnússonar.

——. 1979. 'Páll Ketilssons Manuskript der Hálfs saga'. *Opuscula* 7: 254–9.

References

Shepherd, William. 1802. *The Life of Poggio Bracciolini*. Liverpool: J. M'Creery.
Sheringham, Robert. 1670. *De Anglorum Gentis Origine Disceptatio*. Cambridge.
Sigrún Davíðsdóttir. 1999. *Håndskriftsagens saga i politisk belysning*. Trans. Kim Lembek. Odense: Odense Universitetsforlag.
Sigurður Pétursson. 2007. 'Á slóð húmanista á Íslandi'. *Ritið* 7, 1: 143–58.
Sigurgeir Steingrímsson. 1982. 'Árni Magnússon och hans handskriftsamling'. *Scripta Islandica* 33: 45–59.
Sigurjón Páll Ísaksson. 1994. 'Magnús Björnsson og Möðruvallabók'. *Saga* 32: 103–51.
Skovgaard-Petersen, Karen. 1993. 'The Literary Feud between Denmark and Sweden in the Sixteenth and Seventeenth Centuries and the Development of Danish Historical Scholarship'. In *Renaissance Culture in Context. Theory and Practice*, ed. Jean R. Brink and William F. Gentrup, 114–20. Aldershot: Scolar Press.
—. 2002a. *Historiography at the Court of Christian IV (1588–1648). Studies in the Latin Histories of Denmark by Johannes Pontanus and Johannes Meursius*. Copenhagen: Museum Tusculanum Press.
—. 2002b. 'Et håndskriftfund i Lübeck ca. 1620. Om den spinkle overlevering af to norske nationalklenodier'. *Fund og forskning* 41: 107–27.
—. 2007. 'Biblioteksfaglig vejledning i 1670'erne – om Thomas Bartholins forelæsninger som universitetsbibliotekar'. In *Umisteligt! Festskrift til Erland Kolding Nielsen*, ed. John T. Lauridsen and Olaf Olsen, 137–52. Copenhagen: Det kongelige Bibliotek.
Slay, Desmond. 1960a. *The Manuscripts of Hrólfs saga kraka*. Bibliotheca Arnamagnæana 24. Copenhagen: Ejnar Munksgaard.
—. 1960b. 'On the Origin of Two Icelandic Manuscripts in the Royal Library in Copenhagen'. *Opuscula* 1: 144–50.
Slottved, Ejvind. 1978. *Lærestole og lærere ved Københavns Universitet 1537–1977*. Copenhagen: Samfundet for Dansk Genealogi og Personalhistorie.
Slottved, Ejvind and Mogens Thøgersen. 1980. 'Universitetets gods'. In *Københavns Universitet 1479–1979. Bind IV. Gods. Bygninger. Biblioteker*, ed. Svend Ellehøj and Leif Grane, 1–126. Copenhagen: Gads forlag.
Soll, Jacob. 2008. 'Entre bibliothécaire et agent d'information. Baluze au service de Jean-Baptiste Colbert'. In *Étienne Baluze, 1630–1718. Érudition et pouvoirs dans l'Europe classique*, ed. Jean Boutier, 79–91. Limoges: Presses universitaires de Limoges.

Speed Kjeldsen, Alex, ed. 2005. 'AM 162 A ð fol (Reykjavík)'. *Opuscula* 12: 71–153.

Springborg, Peter. 1969. 'Nyt og gammelt fra Snæfjallaströnd. Bidrag til beskrivelse af den litterære aktivitet på Vestfjordene i 1. halvdel af det 17. århundrede'. In *Afmælisrit Jóns Helgasonar*, ed. Jakob Benediktsson et al., 288–327. Reykjavík: Heimskringla.

—. 1977. 'Antiqvæ historiæ lepores – om renæssancen i den islandske håndskriftproduktion i 1600-tallet'. *Gardar* 8: 53–89.

—. 1996. 'The care taker by Árni Magnússon of the manuscripts in his collection. A study of the records'. In *Care and conservation of manuscripts 2. Proceedings of the second international seminar held at the University of Copenhagen 16th–17th October 1995*, ed. Gillian Fellows-Jensen and Peter Springborg, 7-20. Copenhagen: The Royal Library.

Steenbuch, Hans. 1684. ΑΛΕΚΤΟΡΟΦΩΝΙΑ. *Æliano conformata, Christi verbis fundata, Marc: XIII. comm. 35. Dissertatione Physico Historicâ...* Respondente ARNA MAGNÆO ISLANDO. Copenhagen.

Stefán Karlsson. 1960, 'Um handrit að Guðmundar sögu bróður Arngríms'. *Opuscula* 1: 179–89.

—, ed. 1963. *Islandske originaldiplomer. Tekst*. Editiones Arnamagnæanæ A, 7. Copenhagen: Ejnar Munksgaard.

—. 1970a. 'Resenshandrit'. *Opuscula* 4: 269–78.

—. 1970b. 'Um Vatnshyrnu'. *Opuscula* 4: 279–303. Reprinted in Stefán Karlsson 2000: 336–59.

—. 1977. 'Ættbogi Noregskonunga'. In *Sjötíu ritgerðir helgaðar Jakobi Benediktssyni*, ed. Einar G. Pétursson and Jónas Kristjánsson, 677–704. Reykjavík: Stofnun Árna Magnússonar.

—, ed. 1983. *Guðmundar sögur biskups 1*. Bibliotheca Arnamagnæana B, 6. Copenhagen: C.A. Reitzels forlag.

—. 2000. *Stafkrókar*, ed. Guðvarður Már Gunnlaugsson. Reykjavík: Stofnun Árna Magnússonar.

Stolpe, P.M. 1878–82. *Dagspressen i Danmark, dens Vilkaar og Personer indtil Midten af det 18. Aarhundrede*. 2 vols. Copenhagen: Samfundet til den Danske Literaturs Fremme.

Storm, Gustav. 1873. *Snorre Sturlassöns historieskrivning. En kritisk undersögelse*. Copenhagen: Bianco Luno.

—, ed. 1888. *Islandske annaler indtil 1578*. Christiania (Oslo): Det norske historiske Kildeskriftfond.

—, ed. 1899. *Laurents Hanssøns Sagaoversættelse*. Christiania (Oslo): Videnskabsselskabet.

References

Sveinbjörn Rafnsson. 1979. 'Heimild um Heiðarvíga sögu'. *Gripla* 3: 85–95.

—. 1987. 'Árni Magnússons historiska kritik. Till frågan om vetenskapssynen bakom Den Arnamagnaeanska samlingen'. In *Över gränser. Festskrift för Birgitte Odén*, ed. Ingemar Norlid et al., 293–316. Lund.

Søllinge, Jette D. and Niels Thomsen. 1988. *De danske aviser 1634–1989*, vol. 1. Odense: Odense Universitetsforlag.

Tamm, Ditlev. 1991. 'Københavns Universitet 1621–1732'. In *Københavns Universitet 1479–1979. Bind I. Almindelig historie 1479–1788*, ed. Svend Ellehøj et al., 199–314. Copenhagen: Gads forlag.

Timpanaro, Sebastiano. 1990. *La genesi del metodo del Lachmann*. Padova: Liviana Editrice.

Utermoehlen, Gerda. 1976, 'La correspondance de Leibniz et son édition'. *Revue de synthèse* 97: 95–106.

Valdimar Tr. Hafstein. 2003. 'Bodies of Knowledge. Ole Worm and Collecting in Late Renaissance Scandinavia'. *Journal of European Ethnology* 33: 5–20.

Vedel, Anders Sørensen. 1967. *Den danske krønicke. Saxo-oversættelse 1575*. Ed. Allan Karker. Copenhagen: Gads forlag.

Verelius, Olof, ed. 1664. *Gothrici & Rolfi Westrogothiæ regum historia*. Uppsala.

—, ed. 1666. *Herrauds och Bosa saga*. Uppsala.

—, ed. 1672. *Hervarar saga på gammal Götska*. Uppsala.

Villadsen, Villads. 1980. 'Universitetets bygninger'. In *Københavns Universitet 1479–1979. Bind IV. Gods. Bygninger. Biblioteker*, ed. Svend Ellehøj and Leif Grane, 127–288. Copenhagen: Gads forlag.

von Heinemann, Otto. 1894. *Die herzogliche Bibliothek zu Wolfenbüttel, 1550–1893*. Wolfenbüttel.

Völkel, Marcus. 1987. *Pyrrhonismus historicus und fides historica. Die Entwicklung der deutschen historischen Methodologie unter dem Gesichtspunkt der historischen Skepsis*. Frankfurt and New York: Peter Lang.

Wallette, Anna. 1999. 'Sammanskrefven på gammal svenska. Isländska sagor i stormaktstidens svenska fornforskning'. *Gardar* 30: 5–16.

Walser, Ernst. 1914. *Poggius Florentinus. Leben und Werke*. Leipzig and Berlin: B.G. Teubner.

Wattenbach-Levison. 1952–63. *Deutschlands Geschichtsquellen im Mittelalter*. Weimar: Hermann Böhlaus Nachfolger.

Weber, Jens Jacob, ed. 1775. 'Breve til Arnas Magnussen fra Frederik Rostgaard'. *Samlinger til den danske Historie, Lovkyndighed og andre Materier*: 113–27.

Werlauff, E.C. 1832. 'Ole Worms Fortienester af det nordiske Oldstudium'. *Nordisk Tidsskrift for Oldkyndighed* 1: 283–368.

Westergård-Nielsen, Christian. 1966. *Hvem var Arne Magnussons formand?* Århus: Universitetsforlaget.

—, ed. 1971. *Skálholtsbók eldri. Jónsbók etc. AM 351 fol.* Early Icelandic Manuscripts in Facsimile 9. Copenhagen: Rosenkilde and Bagger.

Whelan, Ruth. 1989. *The Anatomy of superstition: a study of the historical theory and practice of Pierre Bayle*. Oxford: The Voltaire Foundation.

Widding, Ole. 1963. 'Árni Magnússon and his Collection. An Appreciation on the Tercentenary of his Birth'. *Scandinavica* 2: 93–107.

Wieselgren, Harald. 1883. 'Leibniz' bref till Sparfvenfelt'. *Antiqvarisk tidskrift för Sverige* 7, 3: 1–64.

Worm, Christian. 1693–4. *De Corruptis Antiqvitatum Hebræarum apud Tacitum et Martialem Vestigiis.* 2 vols. Copenhagen.

Worm, Ole, ed. 1633. *Norske Kongers Chronica*. Copenhagen.

Wright, C.E. 1949–53. 'The Dispersal of the Monastic Libraries and the Beginnings of Anglo-Saxon Studies. Matthew Parker and his Circle: A preliminary Study'. *Transactions of the Cambridge Bibliographical Society* 1: 208–37.

—. 1960. 'Humfrey Wanley: Saxonist and Library Keeper'. *Proceedings of the British Academy* 46: 99–129.

Wright, Ruth C. 1939–40. 'Letters from Humfrey Wanley to Eric Benzelius and Peter the Great's Librarian'. *Durham University Journal* 32: 185–97.

Wäckerlin, Herbert. 2004. 'A manuscript collector's "commonplace books". Árni Magnússon (1663–1730) and the transmission of conscious fragmentation'. *Variants* 2–3: 221–44.

Þorkell Jóhannesson, ed 1950. *Merkir Íslendingar* 4. Reykjavík: Bókfellsútgáfan.

Þórhallur Vilmundarson. 1979. 'Bruninn mikli í Kaupmannahöfn 1728'. In *Söguslóðir. Afmælisrit helgað Ólafi Hanssyni sjötugum*, 389–415. Reykjavík: Sögufélag.

Internet Resources

British Library, Incunabula Short Title Catalogue: http://www.bl.uk/catalogues/istc

Den Arnamagnæanske Samling: http://nfi.ku.dk/om_instituttet/arnamagnaeansk

Stofnun Árna Magnússonar í íslenskum fræðum: http://arnastofnun.is

Index of manuscripts

Stofnun Árna Magnússonar í
íslenskum fræðum, Reykjavík,
and Den Arnamagnæanske
Samling, Copenhagen

AM 1 b fol. 192
AM 1 d α fol. 111
AM 1 e ß I fol. 111
AM 1 e ß II fol. 56, 111, 112
AM 1 f fol. 200
AM 18 fol. 79
AM 20 b I fol. 111
AM 20 b II fol. 37, 166
AM 20 c fol. 152, 199
AM 20 d fol. 79
AM 20 h fol. 59, 65
AM 34 4 fol. 86
AM 39 fol. 67
AM 40 fol. 79
AM 41 fol. 119
AM 45 fol. 79, 122
AM 47 fol. 31, 79, 122
AM 51 fol. 79
AM 53 fol. 55, 145
AM 54 fol. 143
AM 58–60 fol. 119
AM 61 fol. 33, 87, 88, 99, 119
AM 62 fol. 121
AM 66 fol. 55, 79, 87, 119
AM 67 a fol. 119

AM 67 b fol. 119
AM 68 fol. 33, 79, 145
AM 69 fol. 86
AM 75 c fol. 185, 190
AM 77 a fol. 79
AM 78 a fol. 79
AM 78 b fol. 195
AM 79 fol 119
AM 81 a fol. 65, 121
AM 87 fol 79
AM 88 fol. 79
AM 89 fol. 79
AM 103 fol. 122, 194
AM 110 fol. 192
AM 113 a fol. 72, 89, 90
AM 113 b fol. 72, 90, 197
AM 113 d fol. 197
AM 113 g fol. 89
AM 113 i fol. 144
AM 115 fol. 172
AM 122 a fol. 120, 149, 150
AM 122 b fol. 13, 39 43, 102, 120, 149, 166
AM 125 fol. 192
AM 128 fol. 122, 192
AM 132 fol. 33, 65, 78, 99, 117, 192
AM 133 fol. 55, 121, 150
AM 152 fol. 33, 161

Index of manuscripts

AM 160 fol. 192
AM 162 A α fol. 69, 147
AM 162 A γ fol. 185
AM 162 A δ fol. 37, 180
AM 162 A θ fol. 145
AM 162 B ε fol. 180
AM 162 C fol. 38
AM 162 F fol. 150
AM 162 I fol. 190
AM 163 a–d fol. 192
AM 164 i fol. 192
AM 179 fol. 69
AM 180 a–b fol. 33, 39, 120, 188, 190
AM 180 c fol. 145
AM 202 g fol. 192
AM 205 fol. 196
AM 219 fol. 37, 148
AM 220 II fol. 150, 167
AM 220 IV fol. 185
AM 222 fol. 77
AM 225 fol. 120
AM 226 fol. 33, 152, 161
AM 227 fol. 33, 121
AM 228 fol. 99
AM 229 I fol. 150, 185
AM 229 III fol. 185
AM 231 I fol. 145, 185
AM 231 V fol. 185
AM 231 X fol. 186
AM 232 fol. 33, 121
AM 233 a fol. 33, 145
AM 234 fol. 77, 121, 161
AM 235 fol. 121, 167
AM 237 a fol. 10, 214
AM 237 b fol. 214
AM 238 I fol. 166, 180
AM 238 II fol. 168
AM 238 VIII fol. 190

AM 238 XVII fol. 185
AM 238 XVIII fol. 167
AM 241 b IX fol. 193
AM 242 fol. 33, 61
AM 243 a fol. 121
AM 243 b α fol. 122, 189
AM 243 d fol. 121, 144
AM 243 e fol. 143
AM 243 k fol. 150
AM 243 n fol. 59
AM 243 q fol. 144
AM 249 b fol. 193
AM 249 d fol. 144
AM 249 l fol. 193
AM 249 o fol. 145
AM 249 q I–VIII fol. 145
AM 250 fol. 209
AM 282 fol. 87
AM 283 fol. 81, 96, 98
AM 285 b fol. 38, 43, 47, 59, 62-5, 69, 86, 95
AM 308 fol. 79
AM 310 fol. 80
AM 311 fol. 80
AM 312 fol. 80
AM 315 b fol. 144
AM 315 d fol. 191
AM 327 fol. 100
AM 334 fol. 70, 71, 84, 120
AM 339 fol. 69
AM 343 fol. 143
AM 344 fol. 66, 119, 170
AM 346 fol. 66, 77, 119
AM 347 fol. 66
AM 350 fol. 121, 195
AM 351 fol. 77, 121, 170
AM 352 fol. 77
AM 354 fol. 77, 121
AM 355 a fol. 77

Index of manuscripts

AM 355 b fol. 69
AM 410 fol. 212
AM 440 fol. 138
AM 441 fol. 146
AM 444 fol. 140
AM 452 fol. 178
AM 456 fol. 210
AM 469 fol. 209
AM 477 fol. 210

AM 53 4to 189
AM 56 4to 184
AM 65 4to 100
AM 66 4to 79
AM 67 4to 71
AM 68 4to 71, 145
AM 69 4to 121
AM 74 4to 189
AM 76 a 4to 100
AM 77 c 4to 181
AM 77 d 4to 71
AM 77 e 4to 131
AM 78 4to 100
AM 93 4to 179
AM 102 4to 33
AM 107 4to 180
AM 116 4to 195
AM 119 4to 70, 71, 192
AM 122 4to 70, 84
AM 123 a 4to 71
AM 126 4to 99
AM 127 4to 167
AM 128 4to 147
AM 132 4to 122
AM 133 4to 143
AM 134 4to 144
AM 151 4to 147
AM 153 4to 191
AM 155 a–b 4to 150

AM 160 4to 191
AM 168 a–b 4to 166
AM 169 4to 36
AM 173 d A 30 4to 194
AM 173 d B 1 4to 145
AM 173 d C 2 4to 145
AM 173 d C 3 4to 185
AM 174 I A 4to 144
AM 175 a, c 4to 77, 121
AM 179 4to 119
AM 180 4to 119
AM 182 a 4to 102
AM 191 4to 147
AM 266 4to 144, 193
AM 269 4to 136, 184
AM 282 4to 180
AM 288 4to 55, 170, 171
AM 296 4to 161
AM 300 4to 77, 180
AM 302 4to 79
AM 304 4to 144
AM 310 4to 33, 79, 146, 192
AM 311 4to 79
AM 312 4to 79
AM 325 III α 4to 185
AM 325 IV β 4to 190
AM 325 V 4to 147
AM 325 VII 4to 180
AM 325 VIII 1 4to 144, 145
AM 325 VIII 2 c, e–n 4to 12, 185
AM 325 VIII 2 d 4to 167
AM 325 VIII 2 f 4to 143
AM 325 VIII 2 h 4to 180
AM 325 VIII 4 a 4to 185
AM 325 VIII 5 c 4to 188
AM 325 IX 1 a 4to 143
AM 325 X 4to 147, 150, 167
AM 325 XI 2 a 4to 179
AM 325 XI 2 b 4to 180

Index of manuscripts

AM 325 XI 2 d 4to 190
AM 325 XI 2 m 4to 150, 190
AM 326 b 4to 86, 119
AM 327 4to 119, 192
AM 328 4to 79
AM 329 1 4to 86
AM 329 2 4to 150
AM 329 3 4to 86
AM 335 4to 121
AM 336 4to 161
AM 338 4to 161
AM 343 a 4to 188, 189
AM 343 b 4to 188
AM 344 a 4to 100, 170, 189
AM 344 b 4to 119
AM 346 3 4to 188
AM 348 4to 86
AM 349 4to 86
AM 354 4to 119
AM 356 4to 161
AM 357 4to 185
AM 364 4to 14, 43, 90, 91, 197
AM 365 4to 89, 90, 197
AM 366 4to 197
AM 369 4to 131
AM 371 4to 33, 119, 148
AM 372 4to 53
AM 376 4to 119, 196
AM 379 4to 37, 196
AM 380 4to 37, 196
AM 382 4to 143, 189
AM 383 I 4to 145
AM 383 IV 4to 37
AM 384 4to 192
AM 397 4to 160
AM 398 4to 37, 38
AM 399 4to 59, 79, 146, 205
AM 401 4to 79
AM 406 a I 4to 121

AM 407 4to 165
AM 408 b 4to 165
AM 408 g 4to 53
AM 408 h 2 4to 15
AM 410 4to 173, 194
AM 411 4to 55, 194
AM 412 4to 15, 92
AM 414 4to 33
AM 420 a 4to 121
AM 420 b 4to 121
AM 420 c 4to 121
AM 423 4to 195
AM 424 4to 195
AM 425 4to 86
AM 426 4to 195
AM 427 a 4to 195
AM 428 4to 195
AM 429 b 3 4to 77
AM 432 4to 209
AM 434 4to 209
AM 435 a 4to 151, 152
AM 436 4to 194, 200
AM 442 4to 147
AM 445 b 4to 180, 185
AM 445 c I 4to 145
AM 447 4to 67
AM 448 4to 74, 77
AM 450 a 4to 117, 119
AM 453 4to 67, 69
AM 458 4to 37
AM 460 4to 78
AM 461 4to 117
AM 465 4to 180
AM 466 4to 102
AM 467 4to 161
AM 468 4to 115, 161
AM 470 4to 55
AM 475 4to 190
AM 476 4to 161

Index of manuscripts

AM 481 4to 67
AM 482 4to 116
AM 484 4to 67, 75
AM 487 4to 116
AM 490 4to 33
AM 491 4to 194
AM 495 4to 119
AM 496 4to 150
AM 497 4to 78
AM 499 4to 67
AM 501 4to 74
AM 502 4to 75
AM 503 4to 74
AM 504 4to 67, 74
AM 505 4to 78
AM 506 4to 119
AM 508 4to 78
AM 510 4to 62
AM 512 4to 119
AM 516 4to 67, 74
AM 517 4to 74
AM 519 a 4to 100, 170, 189
AM 519 b 4to 198
AM 525 4to 188
AM 526 4to 161
AM 534 4to 54
AM 535 4to 161
AM 537 4to 165
AM 539 4to 165
AM 541 4to 161
AM 544 4to 119
AM 545 4to 165
AM 554 a b 4to 67
AM 554 a d 4to 67, 74
AM 554 d 4to 144
AM 554 h α 4to 165
AM 554 h β 4to 144
AM 554 i 4to 144
AM 555 h 4to 72, 73

AM 556 a–b 4to 150
AM 559 4to 74
AM 561 4to 119
AM 562 k 4to 119
AM 564 a 4to 12, 190
AM 564 c 4to 72
AM 566 a 4to 116
AM 566 b 4to 78
AM 567 II 4to 185
AM 567 VI β 4to 185
AM 567 XI β 4to 185
AM 567 XVII γ 4to 185
AM 567 XVIII 4to 185
AM 567 XXVI 4to 190
AM 570 a–b 4to 147
AM 571 4to 167
AM 573 4to 144
AM 574 4to 167
AM 576 a 4to 101
AM 576 c 4to 101
AM 580 4to 33, 61, 146
AM 582 4to 165
AM 587 b 4to 79
AM 588 a 4to 144
AM 588 g 4to 161
AM 589 4to 161
AM 593 a–b 4to 143
AM 596 4to 167
AM 597 b 4to 170
AM 598 II β 4to 143
AM 598 III γ 4to 180
AM 599 4to 189
AM 604 a–h 4to 150
AM 606 g 4to 173
AM 611 e 4to 144
AM 613 c 4to 144
AM 624 4to 122
AM 625 4to 147
AM 626 4to 150

Index of manuscripts

AM 628 4to 160
AM 630 4to 40, 166
AM 631 4to 160
AM 633 4to 170
AM 634–635 4to 160
AM 636 4to 160
AM 638 4to 160
AM 642 b 4to 168
AM 645 4to 191
AM 648 4to 161
AM 649 a 4to 77
AM 649 b 4to 77
AM 652 4to 40
AM 653 a 4to 185
AM 653 b II 4to 185
AM 654 4to 161
AM 655 I 4to 40
AM 655 VII–VIII 4to 12, 186
AM 655 XVI 4to 180
AM 656 II 4to 180
AM 657 a–b 4to 185
AM 658 III 4to 147
AM 661 4to 79
AM 663 c 4to 86
AM 667 III 4to 185
AM 670 e 4to 191
AM 671 4to 121
AM 673 a I 4to 147
AM 674 a 4to 122
AM 683 c 4to 181
AM 684 4to 147
AM 686 c 4to 67, 191
AM 686 d 4to 67, 191
AM 689 4to 181
AM 715 d 4to 119
AM 716 n 4to 119
AM 716 o 4to 119
AM 716 p 4to 119
AM 720 a X 4to 189

AM 729 4to 209
AM 732 a I 4to 172
AM 732 a VII 4to 10
AM 732 a XII 4to 209
AM 737 I 4to 191
AM 739 4to 125, 200, 208
AM 744 4to 188
AM 745 4to 188
AM 746 4to 188
AM 747 4to 144
AM 748 I a–b 4to 101, 188, 191
AM 748 II 4to 101
AM 757 a 4to 38, 188
AM 761 a–b 4to 87, 88
AM 762 4to 33
AM 764 4to 195
AM 765 4to 195
AM 777 a 4to 173
AM 779 c II 4to 166
AM 788 4to 186
AM 824 4to 180
AM 844 4to 77
AM 862 4to 180
AM 904 4to 119
AM 907 4to 77
AM 909 A–E 4to 106–10, 114, 115
AM 921 VI 4to 189
AM 922 4to 59, 65
AM 950 4to 86
AM 1005 4to 33, 59
AM 1008 I 4to 86
AM 1008 V 4to 86
AM 1008 VI 4to 78
AM 1009 4to 86
AM 1021 4to 70, 71
AM 1027 4to 18
AM 1029 4to 90
AM 1032 4to 181
AM 1037 4to 18

Index of manuscripts

AM 1045 4to 76, 87
AM 1049 4to 180
AM 1057 4to 170

AM 20 a 8vo 33
AM 38 8vo 167
AM 48 8vo 166
AM 64 8vo 180
AM 80 a 8vo 193
AM 80 b 8vo 180
AM 85 8vo 160
AM 98 I 8vo 143, 193
AM 111 8vo 37
AM 116 II 8vo 120
AM 128 8vo 15
AM 129 8vo 15
AM 160 I 8vo 33
AM 165 8vo 173
AM 166 a 8vo 143
AM 209 8vo 170, 193
AM 216–218 8vo 159
AM 219 8vo 172
AM 222 8vo 157, 159, 160, 181
AM 226 a 8vo 72, 192, 211
AM 226 b 8vo 209
AM 228 8vo 176, 200
AM 231 a–f 8vo 107
AM 254 8vo 14, 67, 89, 93, 106, 130, 197, 198
AM 256 8vo 187
AM 258 b 8vo 179
AM 266 8vo 200, 201
AM 267 8vo 118, 170

AM 415 12mo 193
AM 424 12mo 172
AM 428 a 12mo 186
AM 428 b 12mo 36
AM 434 d 12mo 120

AM 481 12mo 209

AM Access 25 193

SÁM 1 160, 170, 214

Steph. 1 a 79

Apographa Danica 14, 181
Apographa Islandica 13, 153–9, 165, 180, 184, 186, 188
Apographa Norvegica 14, 181

Landsbókasafn Íslands – Háskólabókasafn, Reykjavík
ÍB 225 4to 74
JS 98 fol. 54
JS 435 II 4to 78
JS 435 III 4to 116
Lbs 62 8vo 186
Lbs 63 8vo 186
Lbs 427 8vo 172, 173

Det Kongelige Bibliotek, Copenhagen

Don. var. 1 fol. Barth. X–XIII 50–3, 56–8, 61
Don. var. 1 fol. Barth. XIV–XXI 76, 99
Don. var. 1 fol. Barth. B–K 48, 76, 87
Don. var. 153 4to 47

GKS 1002–1003 fol. 102
GKS 1005 fol. 11, 34, 62, 84, 86, 117
GKS 1008 fol. 35, 87
GKS 1009 fol. 35

Index of manuscripts

GKS 1010 fol. 35
GKS 1157 fol. 34, 81
GKS 1812 4to 35
GKS 2087 4to 35
GKS 2365 4to 35, 69, 81, 84
GKS 2367 4to 35
GKS 2845 4to 35
GKS 2868 4to 35
GKS 2869 4to 35
GKS 2870 4to 35
GKS 3270 4to 35

NKS 637 4to 84
NKS 1824 b 4to 35

Thott 961 fol. 213
Thott 1046 fol. 210

Nasjonalbiblioteket, Oslo

NB Oslo 371 fol. 79
NB Oslo 372 fol. 79
UB Oslo. Ms. 4to, 73 93

Riksarkivet, Oslo

NRA 2 38
NRA 57 38
NRA 69 38
NRA 80 38

Kungliga biblioteket, Stockholm

Papp. 22 fol. 12
Papp. 58 fol. 69
Papp. 60 fol. 75
Papp. 67 fol. 75
Papp. 15 4to 52
Papp. 16 4to 52

Perg. 1 fol. 44
Perg. 5 fol. 41
Perg. 7 fol. 44
Perg. 4 4to 44
Perg. 6 4to 69
Perg. 8 4to 44
Perg. 15 4to 44
Perg. 16 4to 44
Perg. 18 4to 44
Perg. 24 4to 44
Perg. 1 8vo 44

Universitetsbiblioteket, Uppsala

DG 4–7 40
DG 8 40
DG 9 40
DG 10 40
DG 11 40, 125

British Library, London

Add. 11.1184 82, 83

Herzog August Bibliothek, Wolfenbüttel

Aug 9 10 4to 115–17
Aug 42 7 4to 115
Weiss 103 115

Index of names

Abbesté, Peter 178, 205
Adam of Bremen 29, 50, 86, 206
Admiralsgade 211
Adoníus saga 185
Aðalvík in Ísafjarðarsýsla 165
Aimonius of Fleury 26
Akranes in Borgarfjarðarsýsla 161
Aldus Manutius 36
Alexanders saga 33, 44, 84, 100,
 170, 180, 189, 198, 203
Alexandria 115
Alþingi 23, 34, 42, 44, 63, 64, 66,
 71, 133, 134, 136, 138, 140,
 141, 143, 144, 146, 147, 150,
 156, 162–6, 168, 207
amendments, see *réttarbætur*
Amlóða saga 62
Amsterdam 19, 44, 71, 113
Anckersen, Matthias 205
Andra saga 62, 65
Andreas saga postula 168
Angantýr 96
annals 14, 35, 49, 55, 59, 76, 77,
 86, 92, 113, 121, 129, 142, 152,
 173, 194, 195, 206, 207, 213
Antwerp 108
Ari fróði Þorgilsson 9, 10, 38, 72,
 89, 92, 97, 197
Ari Þorkelsson 102, 120, 156
Arnarfjörður 39, 165, 166

Arnarstapi in Snæfellsnessýsla 162
Arngrímur Bjarnason 157
Arngrímur Jónsson 25, 30–3, 61,
 62, 77, 95
Arngrímur Vídalín 75
Asconius 26

Á
Ágústínus saga 161
Álaflekks saga 167
Áns saga bogsveigis 65
Árnessýsla 65, 154
Árni Álfsson 67
Árni Gíslason 154
Árni Guðmundsson 59, 149
Árni Hannesson 147
Árni Hákonarson 65, 72, 76, 79
Árni Þorleifsson 143, 168
Árni Þorvarðsson 66
Ásgeir Jónsson 74, 77–80, 82, 86,
 116, 117, 119, 123, 129, 172,
 188
Ásmundar saga berserkjabana 124
Ásmundur Ketilsson 155

B
Badius, Jodocus 26, 27, 110
Bagford, John 189
Baluze, Étienne 71
Bandamanna saga 60, 67, 75, 78

257

Index of names

Barðastrandarsýsla 39, 102, 120, 138, 185, 209
Barlaams saga ok Jósafats 121, 145, 185, 186
Baronius, Caesar 76
Bartholin, Caspar 177
Bartholin, Hans 177
Bartholin, Margrethe 47
Bartholin, Thomas, the elder 47, 48
Bartholin, Thomas, the younger 20, 25, 47–53, 56, 58, 59, 61–6, 69, 71, 75–8, 80–7, 89, 93–6, 98, 99, 106, 108, 113, 114, 119, 125, 126, 131, 153, 180, 181, 206
Bartholin, Thomas, the youngest 18, 180
Basel 28, 68
Bassewitz, Adolf Frederik 196
Bayle, Pierre 18, 94
Bárðar saga Snæfellsáss 52, 53, 194
Beatus Rhenanus 36
Becker, Hans Petersen 155, 157, 165, 181, 204, 205, 211, 212
Bede 26, 58
Belgsdalsbók 66
Belgsdalur in Dalasýsla 66
Benedikt Einarsson 154
Benedikt Magnússon 122
Benedikt Þorsteinsson 202
Beowulf 190
Bergen 27, 28, 39, 86, 87, 100, 119, 126, 184
Bergsbók 44
Berlin 107, 108, 113
Bessastaðir in Gullbringu- og Kjósarsýsla 136, 138, 141, 147

Bessi Guðmundsson 155
Bevers saga 69, 185
Beyer, Paul 135, 162, 174
Bible 10, 64, 68, 108, 116
Biondo, Flavio 108, 110
Bircherod, Hans 176
Bircherod, Jens 166
Bircherod, Johan 76
biskupasögur 10, 32, 37, 41, 108, 129, 148, 152, 192
Bjarkeyjarréttur 71
Bjarnar saga Hítdælakappa 101, 150
Bjarni Bjarnason 144
Bjarni Indriðason 149
Bjarni Pétursson 70
Bjarni Sigurðsson 211
Björn Jónsson, Skarðsá 39, 129, 144
Björn Jónsson, Staðarfell 66
Björn Magnússon 65
Björn Þorleifsson 17, 43, 75, 101, 102, 123, 126, 127, 136, 138, 142, 144, 150, 153, 161
Bockenhoffer, Johan Philip 82
Bodleian Library, Oxford 152
Bologna 191
Book of Icelanders, see *Íslendingabók*
Borch, Ole 82, 98
Borchs Collegium 99, 105, 204
Bósa saga 41, 60, 95, 96
Bósi 95
Bracelli, Jacopo 110
Brandenburg 107
Braunschweig 106
Bretasögur 144
Brinck, Iver 123, 124
Brodd-Helga saga 59, 60

Index of names

Brokey in Snæfellsnessýsla 144
Brynhildr Buðladóttir 97
Brynjólfur Sveinsson 34–6, 38, 40,
    41, 45, 68, 69, 72, 89, 90, 100
Brynjólfur Þórðarson 147, 152,
    182
Bræðratunga in Árnessýsla 140,
    141
Brøgger, Johann 184
Bureus, Johannes 40
Bustarfell in Múlasýsla 148
Bærings saga 146, 167, 188
Böðvar Pálsson 54, 186
Böðvars þáttr bjarka 75
Böglunga sögur 121

C
Casaubon, Isaac 71
Celsius, Olof 107, 108
Celtis, Konrad 26, 110
Charles, emperor 27
charters 11, 13, 14, 49, 77, 86, 87,
    126, 127, 138, 153–7, 167, 168,
    170, 180, 182, 186, 187, 206,
    207, 215
China 105, 106
chivalric sagas, see riddarasögur
Christ 64, 197, 207
Christiania 87, 126
church law 71, 77, 100, 147, 181
Cicero 26
Clarus saga 185
classical texts 25, 26, 29, 42, 64,
    67, 85, 94, 95, 113, 152, 176
Claussøn, Peder 33
Codex Trajectinus 72
Codex Wormianus 61
Conring, Hermann 94, 110
Consistorium 105, 146, 175–7

Constantinople 95
Copenhagen 9, 10, 12, 16, 20, 23,
    27, 29–35, 38, 41–5, 48, 49,
    52–5, 58, 59, 64, 65, 67, 72, 75,
    76, 78, 80–2, 84–7, 97, 100–2,
    105, 107, 110, 111, 113, 114,
    116, 117, 119, 120, 122–7, 129,
    130, 133, 135–8, 140, 143–6,
    148, 150, 152, 153, 156, 157,
    161–70, 173, 177, 179–82, 186,
    188, 194, 199, 207, 213–15
Copenhagen University 20, 28, 31,
    42, 45, 47, 48, 53, 54, 56, 58,
    63, 64, 74, 76, 78, 79, 82, 99,
    101, 105, 106, 110, 113, 114,
    123, 127, 130, 131, 135, 146,
    161, 175–7, 179, 180, 190, 195,
    202, 204, 205, 212, 213, 215

D
Daði Steindórsson 144
Dalasýsla 53, 54, 66, 70–2, 107
Danakonungatal 76
Danish Chancery 82, 114, 125,
    134, 178
Danske lov 137
Dámusta saga 101
De Cruce Christi 207
Deichmann, Peder 93
Denmark 25–32, 34, 38, 42, 44,
    48, 49, 63, 64, 75–7, 80, 83, 92,
    93, 97–9, 106, 110, 127, 128,
    163, 166, 172, 177, 181, 183,
    206
Diaconus, Paulus 110
Dolmer, Jan 42
Dom Lotineau 76
Donation of Constantine 71
Drangar in Snæfellsnessýsla 137

Index of names

Drauma-Jóns saga 52, 185
Droplaugarsona saga 59, 60, 62, 78
Dublin 115

E
Eastfjords 156
Eckhardt, Johann Georg von 18
Edvardsen, Edvard 100
Eggert Eggertsson 60
Eggert Snæbjörnsson 156
Egils saga 37, 52, 55, 58, 60, 65, 67, 69, 78, 115–17, 145, 147, 185
Egils saga einhenda 63, 96, 124, 125, 161
Einar Eyjólfsson 65, 71, 89, 101, 122
Einar Jónsson 188
Einar Magnússon 33
Einar Þorsteinsson 102
Einholt in Skaftafellssýsla 159
Einvaldsóður 103
Eiríks saga rauða 58, 60
Eiríks saga víðförla 86, 188
Eirspennill 31, 79, 122
Elisabeth, King Christian III's wife 27
Elín Björnsdóttir 54
Elín Þorláksdóttir 150
Elís saga 146, 167
Elucidarius 66, 122, 167
England 36, 48, 84, 97, 114, 123
Enoch di Ascoli 25
Erasmus of Rotterdam 68, 71
Erasmus Pálsson 54
Erlendur Jónsson 157
Erlendur Ólafsson 186
Espergærde 130

Europe 10, 11, 16, 17, 20, 26–8, 30, 35, 36, 80, 85, 93, 106, 113, 115, 122, 130, 176, 200, 213
Eyjafjörður 33, 38, 41, 148
Eyjólfur Björnsson 75, 78, 79, 157, 160, 161, 214
Eyjólfur Jónsson 209
Eyrarbakki in Árnessýsla 146
Eyrbyggja saga 28, 67, 72, 74, 77, 115–17, 147
Eyri in Seyðisfjörður, Ísafjarðasýsla 155, 156
Eyri in Skutulsfjörður, Ísafjarðasýsla 121, 165

F
Fabricius, Johann Albert 16, 18, 198, 213
Faeroe Islands 87, 181, 182
Fagurskinna 31, 79, 205
Feller, Joachim 107
Finnboga saga ramma 52, 59, 78
Finnmark 175
Finnur Jónsson, Kálfalækur 150
Finnur Jónsson, student 188, 204, 209, 211
Finnur Magnússon 188
First Grammatical Treatise 9, 10
Fladstrand 173
Flatey in Breiðafjörður 143, 190
Flateyjarannáll 86
Flateyjarbók 11, 34, 62, 84, 86, 117
Flekkerøy 173
Florence 14, 16, 25, 67
Flóamanna saga 67, 72, 74, 75
Flóvents saga 146
fornaldarsögur 10, 84, 142
Foss, Niels 107, 161
Fóstbrœðra saga 60, 78, 84, 116

260

Index of names

France 26, 48, 84, 94, 150, 172, 172
Frans Ibsson 53, 56, 186, 223
Friðþjófs saga 96, 122
Friis, Christian, of Kragerup 32
Fríssbók 79, 122
Frostaþingslög 80

G

Gandvík 199
Gardie, Magnus de la 40, 52
Garpsdalur in Barðastrandarsýsla 147
Gaulverjabær in Árnessýsla 38, 43, 90, 101, 119
Gautreks saga ok Hrólfs 41, 50, 95, 96, 161
Geir Markússon 75, 76
Gelenius 36
genealogies 9, 128, 142, 209
Geoffrey of Monmouth 26
Germany 14, 25, 93, 106, 108, 110, 169, 200
Gesta Danorum 27–9, 31, 36, 38, 113, 206
Giessen 106
Gissur Einarsson 186
Gissur Ísleifsson 197
Gísla saga 60, 67, 116, 145
Gísli Bjarnason 157, 165
Gísli Einarsson 75, 76
Gísli Jónsson 39, 40
Gísli Magnússon 53
Gísli Oddsson 54
Gísli Þorláksson 35
God / gods 29, 50, 83, 133, 164, 201, 207, 211–13
Goðdalir in Skagafjarðarsýsla 138
Goldast, Melchior 113

Golius, Jacob 115
Gothenburg 41
Gothersgade 204
Gottorp 130
Gottrup, Lauritz 66, 133, 135–7, 154, 162, 168
Gram, Hans 18, 176, 188, 199, 212, 213
Grágás 34, 65, 66, 69, 70, 81, 84, 119, 120, 144, 191
Greenland 106, 172
Grega saga 189
Gregory of Tours 26, 110
Gregory the Great 198
Grenjaðarstaður in Þingeyjarsýsla 144, 156, 186
Grettis saga 40, 52, 58, 60, 161, 167, 214
Grindavík in Gullbringu- og Kjósarsýsla 138
Gríms saga loðinkinna 60
Grímsey in Eyjafjarðarsýsla 150
Grímur Árnason 194
Grímur Einarsson 122
Grímur Magnússon, owner of manuscript 38
Grímur Magnússon, student 157, 165
Gronovius, Johann Friedrich 48
Grunnavík in Ísafjarðarsýsla 18, 148, 165, 201
Grænlendingaþáttr 86
Gualteri 180
Guarino Veronensis 26
Guðbrandur Þorláksson 30, 126
Guðlaug Erasmusdóttir 54
Guðmundar saga biskups 37, 59, 77, 79, 146, 150, 160, 161, 167, 185, 205, 214

Index of names

Guðmundur Andrésson 173
Guðmundur Guðmundsson 75, 76, 116
Guðmundur Ólafsson 116, 148
Guðmundur Þorleifsson 43, 144
Guðný Jónsdóttir 40
Guðrún Gísladóttir 143
Guðrún Ketilsdóttir 53
Guðrún Ögmundsdóttir 143, 150, 190
Gufudalur in Barðastrandarsýsla 144, 193
Gulaþingslög 79, 129
Gullinskinna 31, 205
Gull-Þóris saga 119
Gunnars saga þiðrandabana 62
Gunnars þáttur Keldugnúpsfífls 60
Gunnlaugs saga Ormstungu 63
Gunnlaugur Ormsson 37
Gyðinga saga 33, 161, 185
Gyldenløve, Ulrik Christian 162, 163, 166, 174, 181, 192
Göngu-Hrólfs saga 60, 161, 185

H
Hadorph, Johan 44, 52
Hafnarfjörður in Gullbringu- og Kjósarsýsla 181, 182
Hagi in Barðastrandarsýsla 39
hagiography, see *heilagramannasögur*
Hallandsås 204
Halldór Laxness 142
Halldór Pálsson 155, 156
Halldór Torfason 90, 101
Halldór Þorbergsson 120, 144
Halle 114
Hallfreðar saga 60, 78
Hallur from Haukadalur 197

Hamburg 16, 29, 198
Hannes Finnsson 188
Hannes Þorleifsson 42–4, 47–9, 56, 99, 120, 144, 147
Hanover 16, 116
Hans Scheving 209
Hanssøn, Laurents 28
Haraldar saga hilditannar 62
Harboe, Christian Ludvig 210
Harðar saga 60, 67
Haukadalur in Árnessýsla 197
Hauksbók 33, 100, 119, 148, 195
Hákon Hannesson 75
Hákon Ormsson 69
Hákonar saga Hákonarsonar 79, 121, 122, 167, 188
Hákonar saga Sverrissonar 79, 185
Hákonar þáttr Hárekssonar 60, 185
Hálfdanar saga brönufóstra 161, 167
Hálfdanar saga Eysteinssonar 60, 63, 119
Hálfdanar saga svarta 35, 86
Hálfsrekka saga 129
Hávamál 42
Hávarðar saga Ísfirðings 75, 190
Hearne, Thomas 71
Heidemann, Christopher 63, 65
Heiðarvíga saga 44, 101, 207
Heiðreks saga 41, 119
heilagramannasögur 10, 33, 36, 77, 108, 121, 142, 145, 152, 166, 167, 180, 189, 190, 193
Heimsádeila 119
Heimskringla 28, 30, 33, 40, 67, 79, 92, 95, 117, 124, 125, 144, 145, 177

Index of names

Hekla 164
Helga saga Droplaugarsonar 62
Helga þáttr ok Úlfs 86
Helgi Grímsson 12
Helgi Ólafsson 75, 76, 80
Helmstedt 114
Helsingør 164
Hemings þáttr 86, 119
Herodotus 95
Herrauðr 95, 96
Herrauðs ok Bósa saga 41, 60, 95
Hertel, Lorenz 116
Hervarar saga 41, 42, 50, 119
Hickes, George 123, 124
Hirðskrá 30, 42, 180, 185
Historia Norwegica 114
Hítardalur in Mýrasýsla 12, 67, 136, 150
Hjarðarholt in Dalasýsla 156
Hjalti Þorsteinsson 122, 159, 165, 194, 203, 212
Hjónasinna 119, 189
Hlíðarendi in Rangárvallasýsla 143, 152
Hofsós in Skagafjarðarsýsla 135, 186
Holberg, Ludvig 128, 183, 213
Holger the Dane 48
Holland 14, 44, 111, 114, 115, 161
Holmens kirke 205
Holstein 169
Holt in Önundarfjörður, Ísafjarðarsýsla 166
homilies 44, 67, 191, 193
Horrebow, Peter 205
Hólar in Hjaltadalur, Skagafjarðarsýsla 12, 30, 32, 34–8, 101, 120, 126, 127, 136, 138, 153, 154, 186, 188

Hrafnagil in Eyjafjarðarsýsla 186
Hrafnkels saga 120, 190
Hrafns saga 116
Hrafnseyri in Ísafjarðarsýsla 165
Hrokkinskinna 35
Hrotsvitha of Gandersheim 26, 110
Hrólfs saga Gautrekssonar 41, 50, 95, 96, 161, 185
Hrólfs saga kraka 59, 65, 84, 97, 102, 103, 172
Hrómundar saga Gripssonar 62, 79
Hugbót 119
Huet, Pierre-Daniel 84
Huitfeldt, Arild 30, 31
Hulda 55, 78, 119
Humlebæk 130
Hungrvaka 30, 77, 119, 141, 191, 196
Hvammur in Hvammsfjörður, Dalasýsla 53–5, 64, 70, 74, 136, 138, 156, 162, 166
Hversu Noregr byggðist 86
Hænsa-Þóris saga 67, 72, 74
Højbrostræde 205
Højer, Andreas 206
Høyer, Henrik 31

I

Illuga saga gríðarfóstra 63
Ingibjörg Jónsdóttir 66
Ingibjörg Pálsdóttir 143, 155
Italy 14, 26, 47, 106, 108

Í

Ísafjarðarsýsla 157, 164, 165
Ísleifur Einarsson 103
Ísleifur Gissurarson 197
Ísleifur Þorleifsson 121

263

Index of names

Íslendinga saga 62
Íslendingabók 9, 14, 38, 71, 72, 81, 89–94, 101, 106, 130, 144, 196–8
Íslendingasögur 10, 33, 35, 65, 80, 101, 122, 124, 142, 150, 152, 189, 192,
Ívens saga Artúskappa 144

J

Jacobsen, Holgeir 82
Japhet 28
Járnsíða 70, 71, 120, 192
Játvarðar saga helga 86
Jerusalem 204
Jordanes 50
Jóhanna Jónsdóttir 144
jólaskrá 181, 191
Jómsvíkinga saga 28, 30, 55, 61, 62, 83, 122, 170
Jón Árnason 146, 213
Jón Eggertsson 43–5, 52, 53, 58, 59, 63, 65, 67, 75, 80, 100
Jón Egilsson 194
Jón Einarsson, servant 144
Jón Einarsson, student 99
Jón Erlendsson 38, 69, 72, 89, 90, 101, 102, 172, 192, 194, 197
Jón Gissursson 192, 196
Jón Gíslason 75, 99
Jón Guðmundsson the learned 125
Jón Halldórsson 55, 75, 136, 150, 186, 194, 206, 209
Jón Hannesson 166
Jón Hákonarson 120, 143
Jón Hreggviðsson 163, 165
Jón Jónsson, Garpsdalur 147
Jón Jónsson Rúgmann 41
Jón Loftsson 66

Jón Magnússon, Árni's brother 18, 70, 137, 157, 188, 211
Jón Magnússon, Hagi 39
Jón Marteinsson 213
Jón Ormsson 53, 56
Jón Ólafsson of Grunnavík 18, 22, 55, 56, 114, 188, 201, 204, 205, 210, 212–15
Jón Ólafsson, Lambavatn 102
Jón Pálsson, Hólar 37, 150
Jón Pálsson Vídalín 186
Jón rauðr, archbishop 100
Jón Sigmundsson 103
Jón Sigurðsson, bishop 66
Jón Sigurðsson, student 188
Jón Torfason, Breiðabólstaður in Fljótshlíð 192
Jón Torfason, Copenhagen 117, 119, 196
Jón Torfason, Gaulverjabær 43
Jón Torfason, Staður in Súgandafjörður 148, 149
Jón Vídalín 75, 79, 120, 121, 135, 136, 140, 141, 143, 147, 165, 181, 182
Jón Þórarinsson 156
Jón Ögmundsson 197
Jóns saga biskups 30, 38, 60, 61, 77, 108
Jóns saga postula 77, 185
Jónsbók 11, 35, 36, 40, 41, 66, 70, 71, 77, 99, 115, 121, 122, 137, 143, 144, 147, 150, 166, 167, 170, 184, 191, 193, 194, 207
Jutland 87, 125, 169, 173
Jöcher, Christian Gottlieb 213
Jöfraskinna 31, 205
Jökuls þáttr Búasonar 52, 59

Index of names

K

Karlamagnús saga 33, 39, 43, 121, 145, 152, 184, 190, 207
Kattegat 169
Kálfalækjarbók 55, 121, 150
Kálfalækur in Mýrasýsla 150
Keflavík in Gullbringu- og Kjósarsýsla 145
Ketill Jörundsson 53, 54, 56, 67, 69, 74, 75, 144, 194
Ketill Pálsson 54
Ketils saga hængs 60
Kiel 107
King Charles XII 130, 169, 181
King Christian I 29
King Christian II 27
King Christian III 28
King Christian IV 30, 32, 34, 49, 137
King Christian V 25, 49, 61, 63, 99, 102, 129, 131, 137, 162,
King Dan 29, 128
King Frederik III 34, 41, 127, 172
King Frederik IV 20, 22, 129–31, 133, 135, 145, 162, 163, 175, 178, 181–3, 205
King Gautrekr 41
King Goðmundr 50
King Gormr 92
King Gustav Vasa 28
King Haraldr hárfagri 90, 92
King Hrólfr 41
King Magnús Hákonarson 177, 198
King Ólafr helgi 131
King Ólafr Tryggvason 173
King Skjöldur 128
King Sverrir 59, 100, 181
kings' sagas, see *konungasögur*
Kirchmann, Bernhard Caspar 114

Kirchmann, Johann 114
Kirjalax saga 43, 161
Kirkjuból in Langidalur, Ísafjarðarsýsla 165
Kirkjuból in Skutulsfjörður, Ísafjarðarsýsla 159
kirkjuskipanir 66, 87, 145
Kjalarnes in Gullbringu- og Kjósarsýsla 143, 145
Kjalnesinga saga 60, 67, 72, 74
Kjós in Gullbringu- og Kjósarsýsla 145
Klarekloster 180
Klerkarímur 103
Knudsen, Bertel 32
Knýtlinga saga 31, 33, 37, 59, 65, 79, 111, 146, 152, 166, 199
Kongens Nytorv 204
konungasögur 10, 27–9, 31, 34, 41, 55, 51, 78, 80, 87, 92, 111, 122–5, 142, 150, 152, 205
Konungs skuggsjá 28, 30, 59, 121, 122, 143, 144, 150, 152, 189, 206, 207
Kormáks saga 60, 65, 78, 150
Krag, Niels 30, 31
Kringla 31, 43, 53, 205
Kristinna laga þáttr 66, 119, 145
Kristinréttr Árna biskups 66, 69, 102, 119, 121, 147, 150
Kristín Jónsdóttir Vídalín 137
Kristni saga 61, 148
Kristnisaga meistara Adams 86
Króka-Refs saga 60, 72, 78, 119
Króksfjarðarbók 120, 149, 150
Kvennabrekka in Dalasýsla 9, 53

265

Index of names

L

Lambavatn in Barðastrandarsýsla 102
land register 136–8, 140, 141, 143, 145, 146, 161, 162, 164–6, 174, 175, 180, 209, 214
Landnámabók 30, 33, 58, 60, 61, 65, 71, 77, 83, 89, 148, 152, 192, 209
Langanes in Þingeyjarsýsla 135
Lange, Wilhelm 35, 38
Langebek, Jakob 17
Langfeðgatal 54, 200
Languedoc 76
Laub, Hieronymus 211
Laufás in Þingeyjarsýsla 32
Laurentius saga biskups 120, 121
Laxdæla saga 55, 60, 72, 74, 78, 85, 144, 147, 192
Laxegade 211
Leibniz, Gottfried Wilhelm 16, 18, 105, 106, 115, 116, 200
Leiden 19, 48, 106, 107
Leipzig 14, 19, 48, 71, 105–15, 123, 131, 175, 180
Leirá in Borgarfjarðarsýsla 39, 140
Liguria 110
Lindenbrog, Erpold 113
Lintrup, Søren 176
liturgical manuscripts 10–12, 36, 121, 122, 142–5, 144, 165, 193, 215
Liutprand of Cremona 26
Livy 25
Ljárskógabók 66, 119
Ljárskógar in Dalasýsla 66
Ljósvetninga saga 60
Londemann, Edvard 213
London 28, 48, 123, 189, 191

Lorentsen, Johan 127
Lorenzo di Medici 67
Lorenzo Valla 71
Lund 27, 87
Luther, Martin 12, 32, 177
Lübeck 114, 131
lygisögur 10, 44, 61, 62, 102, 121, 142, 143, 147, 152, 165

M

Mabillon, Jean 18, 71, 85, 94, 106, 113
Magliabechi, Antonio 16
Magnus, Johannes 28, 95
Magnussen, Mette 164, 173, 175, 178, 181, 204, 205, 212, 213, 215
Magnús Arason 143, 147, 164, 190, 214
Magnús Björnsson 33, 36, 39
Magnús Einarsson 157, 159, 165, 170, 181, 186, 210, 211
Magnús Gíslason 211
Magnús Gunnlaugsson 37
Magnús Jónsson, Árni's father 53, 56, 64
Magnús Jónsson, Leirá 39, 121
Magnús Jónsson, Vigur 17, 39, 43, 101, 120
Magnús Magnússon, Árni's brother 136
Magnús Magnússon, Eyri in Seyðisfjörður 155
Magnús Markússon 144, 157
Magnús Ólafsson 32, 33, 37, 100
Magnús Pálsson Vídalín 21, 210
Magnús Sigurðsson 140, 161, 163, 164
Magnúss saga Eyjajarls 193, 207

Magnúss saga Hákonarsonar 86
Magnúss saga lagabætis 147
Margrétar saga 36, 186
Maríu saga 44, 160, 170, 185, 207
Maríu saga Magdalenæ 207
Markús Bergsson 157, 192, 211
Mathesius, Jacob 167
Mazarin, cardinal 115
Mágus saga 62, 146, 161, 185
Meibom, Marcus 113
Meier, Reinhold 115, 123, 125, 129
Mencke, Johann Burckhardt 85
Mette Jensdatter Fischer, see Magnussen, Mette
Meursius, Johannes 34
Michaels saga 185
Milan 26, 106
Miltzow, Geertz 100
Montfaucon, Bernard de 14, 191
Morkinskinna 35
Mortensen, Jens 30
Mosheim, Johann 213
Moth, Matthias 82, 98, 99, 106, 110, 111, 113, 114, 125, 126, 129
Múlasýsla 155, 164, 166, 209
Múli in Reykjadalur, Þingeyjarsýsla 101
Müller, Andreas 105, 106, 116
Müller, Christian 47, 119, 130, 135, 136, 141, 147, 148, 154, 162, 163
Münster, Hans 28
Mýrar in Dýrafjörður, Ísafjarðarsýsla 186
Mýrdalur in Skaftafellssýsla 145
Möðruvallabók 33, 65, 78, 85, 99, 117, 192

N
Naples 106
Niðurstigningar saga 207
Nikolaikirke 204
Nikulás Einarsson 148
Nikulás saga 38, 44, 146, 160, 168
Nítíða saga 101, 185
Njáls saga 30, 35, 43, 55, 56, 59, 60, 78, 102, 115, 150, 161, 180, 182, 214
Noah 195
Noregskonungatal 117
Norna-Gests þáttr 52, 86, 207
Norske lov 99, 137
North Sea 169
Norway 13, 14, 25, 27, 28, 30–5, 38, 42, 44, 49, 58, 61, 71, 76–8, 87, 90, 92, 93, 95, 97–9, 106, 107, 114, 116, 122, 126, 128, 135, 136, 146, 153, 156, 170, 172, 173, 180–2, 186, 199, 206
Norwegian national law 27, 38, 71, 76, 78, 100, 121, 129, 145, 179, 181, 184, 189, 206
Norwegian town law 100
Nürnberg 26, 110
Nørregade 204

O
Oddi in Rangárvallasýsla 101
Oddur Sigurðsson 162, 163, 166, 174, 186, 209
Old Testament 95
Ordericus Vitalis 50
Orkney Islands 87, 96, 111, 116, 127, 129
Orkneyinga saga 28, 37, 52, 86, 96, 122, 185, 194
Ormarsrímur 103

Index of names

Orms þáttr Stórólfssonar 60
Ormur Daðason 12, 157, 162, 170, 180, 184, 186, 190, 206
Oslo, see Christiania
Ottoman empire 169
Ovid 95
Oxford 19, 48, 64, 106, 107, 125, 130, 152
Óðinn 200
Óláfs saga helga 33, 35, 40, 44, 55, 59, 60, 79, 86, 87, 99, 119, 122, 146, 147, 150, 179, 180, 185, 190, 195, 206, 207
Óláfs saga Tryggvasonar 12, 28, 33, 40, 41, 44, 56, 59, 60, 62, 79, 99, 119, 121, 141, 143, 145, 146, 167, 180, 185, 192, 206
Ólafur Einarsson 103
Ólafur Hallsson 38
Ólafur Hjaltason 36
Ólafur Jónsson 148
Ólafur Stefánsson 207

P

Papebroch, Daniel 108
Paris 19, 26, 27, 36, 48, 71, 106, 108, 110, 115, 191
Parker, Matthew 36
Parsberg, Holger 76
Páll, archbishop 66
Páll Hákonarson 157, 158, 169–71, 186
Páll Jónsson 37
Páll Ketilsson 17, 54, 56, 67, 120, 129, 137, 144, 150, 162
Páll Pálsson 54
Páll Torfason 143
Páll Vídalín 20, 21, 75, 121, 135–8, 145, 146, 154, 162, 165, 166, 174, 180, 184, 186, 210
Páll Þórðarson 149
Páls saga postula 38
Pedersen, Christiern 27, 29
Peringskiöld, Johann 116, 122, 124, 125
Peutinger, Konrad 110
Pétur Björnsson 148
Péturs saga postula 147
Pfautz, Christoph 107
Physiologus 147
Pistorius, Johannes 113
Píslargrátur 119
Píslarminning 189
Plessen, Siegfried von 128
Pliny 36
Plutarch 95
Poetic Edda 10, 35, 52, 65, 67, 69, 81, 84, 90, 101, 113, 116, 188, 191, 200, 207, 209
Poggio Bracciolini 25, 26
Poland 93
Poliziano, Angelo 67, 68, 71
Polonus, Martinus 110
Poltava 169
Pommern 93, 105
Pontanus, Johannes 34, 113
Pontusrímur 103
Pope Nicholas V 25
postulasögur 38, 40, 77, 147, 160, 168, 170, 185, 198, 214
Profectio Danorum Hierosolymam 114
Prussia 196
Pseudo-Vatnshyrna 180, 185

Q

Quintilian 26

R

Raben, Peter 181–4
Rafn, Carl Christian 111
Ragnar loðbrók 127
Ragnars saga loðbrókar 35, 65, 97, 180
Rangárvallasýsla 141
Rantzau, Otto 76, 79
Rasch, Jacob 135
Rechenberg, Adam 113
Reenberg, Morten 204, 205
Reimarus, Hermann Samuel 18
Reitzer, Christian 150, 175
Resen, Peder 42, 58, 59, 61, 67, 72, 79, 80, 190, 195, 206
Resensannáll 195
Reykdæla saga 102
Reykholt in Borgarfjarðarsýsla 10, 150
Reykhólar in Barðastrandarsýsla 211
Reykjarfjarðarbók 13, 39, 40, 43, 102, 120, 149, 166
Reykjarfjörður in Barðastrandarsýsla 39
Reykjarfjörður in Ísafjarðarsýsla 166
Reykjavík in Gullbringu- og Kjósarsýsla 12, 13, 23, 153, 168, 170
Reynistaðarbók 195
Rémundar saga 167
réttarbætur 66, 99, 129, 137, 144
Ribe 87
riddarasögur 10
Rif in Snæfellsnessýsla 64
rímfræði 35
rímur 103, 115, 142, 144, 150, 172, 173
romances, see *lygisögur*
Rome 25, 27, 28, 95, 106, 108
Rosenborg castle 49, 175, 178
Rosencrantz, Jens 76, 79, 122
Rostgaard, Frederik 17, 93, 98, 106, 130, 175, 177–9, 182–4, 210
Rostock 106
Round Tower 176
Royal Archives 20, 49, 76, 105, 114, 123, 127, 130, 135, 175, 177, 178, 183, 184, 209, 210
Royal Commission 16, 20, 133, 135–41, 145, 162–4, 166, 167, 169, 170, 174, 175, 181, 183, 184, 202, 209, 214
Royal Exchequer 38, 115, 134, 136, 165–7, 173–5, 181, 183, 184, 202, 209
Royal Library, Copenhagen 34, 35, 38, 42, 49, 58, 123, 146, 172, 178, 199, 215
Royal Library, Stockholm 41
Royal Museum 42
Rómverja sögur 33, 161, 180
Rudbeck, Olof 95
Ruinart, Thierry 18
Runólfur Jónsson 124
Russia 169
Rúgstaðir in Eyjafjarðarsýsla 41
Rømer, Ole 106, 135

S

Salan, Jonas 125
Salan, Peter 124, 125
Sauðafell in Dalasýsla 54, 64
Saurbær on Rauðasandur, Barðastrandarsýsla 154
Saurbær on Kjalarnes, Gullbringu- og Kjósarsýsla 143

Saxo Grammaticus 27–31, 36, 50,
  95–7, 113, 128, 175, 206
Saxony 169
Scaliger, Joseph 71
Scania 29, 30, 77, 169
Scoppe, Caspar 48
Seefeldt, Jørgen 41
Seeland 41, 130, 205, 213
Seerup, Jørgen 131
Selvogur in Árnessýsla 146
Seneca 68
Sextus Empiricus 94
Sheringham, Robert 84
Siegebert of Gembloux 26
Sighvatr Þórðarson 83, 88
Sigríður Jónsdóttir, Skálholt 120,
  140
Sigríður Jónsdóttir Vídalín 136
Sigurðar saga þögla 62, 84, 101,
  167
Sigurðar þáttr slefu 86
Sigurður Björnsson 71, 137, 143,
  150, 163, 165, 166, 168, 170,
  174
Sigurðr Fáfnisbani 97
Sigurður Kárason 188
Sigurður Sigurðsson 150, 170,
  172, 173, 180
Sigurgarðs saga 62
Skaftafellssýsla 141, 209
Skagafjörður 37, 43, 120, 138
Skagaströnd in Húnavatnssýsla
  42, 43
skaldic poetry 10, 82–4, 87, 128,
  200, 201
Skammbeinsstaðir in Rangárvalla-
  sýsla 157
Skarð on Skarðsströnd in Dalasýsla
  40, 55, 67, 74, 155, 160, 170

Skarðsá in Skagafjarðarsýsla 39,
  129, 144
Skálavík in Ísafjarðarsýsla 149
Skálda 32
Skálda saga Haraldar hárfagra
  119
Skálholt in Árnessýsla 20, 34, 38,
  53–5, 71, 89, 97, 100, 101, 111,
  120, 121, 126, 136, 138, 140,
  146, 154–8, 162, 168, 169,
  181, 207, 211, 213
Skjöldunga saga 30
Skriðuklaustur in Múlasýsla 155
Skudesnes 172, 173
Skúli Ólafsson 16, 39, 120
Skúli Þorláksson 144
Slitvindastaðir in Snæfellsnessýsla
  162
Slotsholmen 173, 175, 178, 210
Sneglu-Halla þáttr 60, 86
Snorra Edda 35, 37, 40, 42, 52,
  61, 72, 101, 113, 125, 143, 144,
  152, 188, 191, 200
Snorri Jónsson 157, 184, 185
Snorri Sturluson 81, 97, 128, 200
Snorri Þorgrímsson goði 197
Snæbjörn Pálsson 143, 186
Sodom 204
Sorø 25, 29
Spain 14, 48, 122
Sparwenfeld, Johan Gabriel 43,
  116
Sperling, Otto 172, 199, 200
Sprengisandur 166
St. Gallen 26
Staðarfell in Dalasýsla 66
Staðarfellsbók 66, 77, 119
Staðarhóll in Dalasýsla 70
Staðarhólsbók 70, 71, 84, 120

Staðarstaður in Snæfellsnessýsla 137
Staður in Grunnavík, Ísafjarðarsýsla 148
Staður in Steingrímsfjörður, Strandasýsla 146
Staður in Súgandafjörður, Ísafjarðarsýsla 148
Stangeland 35, 62, 63, 81, 82, 85–8, 92, 100, 117, 129, 146, 172, 205
statutes, see *kirkjuskipanir*
Stavanger 35, 126, 156, 157, 167, 172
Stavern 173
Steenbuch, Hans 64
Steindór Ormsson 40
Steinn Jónsson 75, 76, 186
Stephanius, Stephan 31, 40
Stephanus saga 79
Stettin 29, 105–7
Stjórn 33, 99, 120, 121, 150, 152, 185
Stjörnu-Odda draumr 72, 75, 84
Stockholm 41, 44, 58, 69, 75, 116, 124, 207
Store Kannikestræde 98, 175, 204
Strasbourg 26
Sturlaugs saga starfsama 60, 96, 103, 161
Sturlunga saga 10, 13, 17, 39, 55, 62, 102, 120, 124, 129, 149, 152, 166, 172
Stúfs þáttr Kattarsonar 60
Styr Þorvaldsson 157
Størrestræde 205, 210, 211
Størssøn, Matthis 30
Supreme Court 98, 125, 140, 161, 163, 166, 168, 170, 174

Svaning, Hans 28, 29
Svarfdæla saga 67, 75
Sverris saga 65, 79, 100, 119, 121, 122, 147, 185, 192
Sweden 14, 25, 28, 40–4, 50, 52, 63, 69, 75, 80, 84, 37, 93, 95, 97, 98, 101, 106, 107, 113, 116, 117, 123–5, 127, 130, 166–9, 181, 196, 200, 206
Swedish Institute of Antiquities 41, 44, 52, 63, 75, 80, 107, 116
Swedish national law 14, 168, 189
Switzerland 26, 106
Syv, Peder 177
Sæmundur fróði Sigfússon 81, 90, 142, 209
Sögubrot af fornkonungum 111–13, 192
Sörla saga sterka 63, 96

T
Tacitus 110
Temple, William 85
Theodoricus 114
theological texts 9, 10, 40, 108, 121, 122, 147, 150, 152
Thucydides 176
Tisdorph, Anne 98
Tisted in Jutland 125
Tithe law 66
Torfi Hallsson 40
Torfi Jónsson 38, 43 59, 62, 63, 65, 69, 100, 101
Torfæus, see Þormóður Torfason
Tómas saga erkibiskups 35, 87
Tómasskinna 87
Trinitatiskirke 176, 204, 212
Trondheim 86, 179

Trójumanna saga 66, 69, 143, 144, 170
Tveggja postula saga 185
Twysden, Roger 113

U
Ulfeldt, Korfitz 41
University Library, Copenhagen 31, 58, 61, 63, 76, 79, 105, 113, 123, 131, 146, 161, 176, 179, 180, 190, 195, 204, 205, 215
University Library, Leipzig 107
University Library, Uppsala 40, 58
Uppsala 40, 41, 58, 95, 116, 125
Ussher, James 36

Ú
Úlfljótslög 43

V
Valerius Flaccus 26
Valla, Lorenzo 71
Vallna-Ljóts saga 63
Vatican 106
Vatneyri in Barðastrandarsýsla 186
Vatnsdæla saga 55, 58, 60, 65, 72, 74
Vatnsfjörður in Ísafjarðarsýsla 122, 159, 165, 166, 203
Vatnshorn in Dalasýsla 71, 72
Vatnshyrna 72–5, 77, 84, 117, 180, 185, 206
Vatnsleysa in Árnessýsla 141
Vedel, Anders Sørensen 29–31, 42, 95
Vellir in Svarfaðardalur, Eyjafjarðarsýsla 209
Venice 36, 108
Venus 164
Veraldar saga 12, 147, 186

Verelius, Olof 41, 42, 50, 95, 96, 200
Verona 108
Vesterport 203
Vestmannaeyjar 141, 154
Vémundar saga 62
Viðey in Gullbringu- og Kjósarsýsla 138
Vigfús Jóhannsson 165
Vigfús Jónsson, Leirulækur 67
Vigfús Jónsson, student 211
Vigur in Ísafjarðarsýsla 17, 39, 43, 101, 120
Vilhjálms saga sjóðs 189
Vilmundar saga 62
Vinding, Rasmus 48
Vínland 172
Virgil 25, 95
Virgils saga víðfræga 101
Víðidalstunga in Húnavatnssýsla 136, 146
Víga-Glúms saga 60, 63, 78, 207
Víga-Skúta saga 65, 101
Víga-Styrs saga 101
Víglundar saga 52, 59, 119
Vítus saga 120
Vorfruekirke 204, 213
Vulcanus 164
Völsunga saga 35
Völuspá 42, 83, 173

W
Walter, Frederik 138, 140
Wanley, Humfrey 71, 124, 152, 190, 191
Werlauff, E.C. 19
Westfjords 149
White Sea 199
Wichmand, Hans Hendrichsen 164

Wieland, Joachim 177, 199
William of Malmesbury 50
Wittenberg 114
Wolck, Bertel 192
Wolfenbüttel 115–19
Worm, Christian 130, 131, 146, 205
Worm, Ole 31–4, 42, 52, 59, 61, 80, 93, 95, 96, 100, 115
Worm, Willum 49, 61, 78, 81, 98, 130

Y
Ynglingatal 117
Yngvars saga víðförla 188
Ytri-Hólmur in Borgarfjarðarsýsla 147

Þ
Þernuvík in Ísafjarðarsýsla 37
Þiðreks saga af Bern 84, 142, 152, 207
Þingeyjarsýsla 154
Þingeyrar in Húnavatnssýsla 154, 157, 168
Þingvellir in Árnessýsla 65, 136, 140, 143, 165
Þorbergur Þorsteinsson 196
Þorgils Sigurðsson 157, 165
Þorkell Arngrímsson 115
Þorláks saga helga 37, 143, 145, 189, 191, 198
Þorlákshöfn in Árnessýsla 146, 164
Þorlákur Grímsson 75, 76, 148
Þorlákur Skúlason 32, 34, 35, 37, 59, 150, 196
Þorleifs þáttr jarlaskálds 60
Þorleifur Halldórsson 157

Þorleifur Jónsson 144
Þormóðar saga Kolbrúnarskálds 60, 84
Þormóður Torfason 17, 35, 38, 43, 49, 56, 58, 59, 61–5, 68, 69, 79–82, 84–7, 89, 90, 92–100, 106, 107, 110, 111, 113, 115–17, 123–9, 133, 135, 141, 142, 146, 172, 173, 179, 180, 194, 199, 205
Þorsteinn Björnsson 59
Þorsteinn Ketilsson 165, 186, 214
Þorsteinn Ólafsson 144
Þorsteinn Pétursson 214
Þorsteinn Sigurðsson 165, 180, 211
Þorsteinn Þorleifsson 43
Þorsteinn Þórðarson 40, 44, 67, 74
Þorsteins saga Víkingssonar 94, 96
Þorsteins þáttr austfirska 119
Þorsteins þáttr bæjarmagns 58, 60, 167
Þorsteins þáttr Síðuhallssonar 116
Þorsteins þáttr tjaldstæðings 86
Þorsteins þáttr uxafóts 60
Þorvaldur Stefánsson 150
Þórarinn Eiríksson 35
Þórdís Jónsdóttir 140, 141, 163
Þórðar saga hreðu 44, 60, 185, 190
Þórður Jónsson, Hítardalur 67
Þórður Jónsson, Staðarstaður 90, 120, 121, 144
Þórður Oddsson 198
Þórður Steindórsson 150
Þórður Þorkelsson Vídalín 53, 122
Þórður Þorláksson 16, 53, 59, 65, 71, 77, 89, 100, 111, 143

Þórður Þórðarson 156, 157, 161, 165, 170, 182
Þóris saga háleggs 62
Þrúður Þorsteinsdóttir 142
Þuríður Snorradóttir 197
Þykkvabæjarklaustur in Skaftafellssýsla 103

Æ
Ævi Noregskonunga 84
ævintýri 121

Ö
Ögmundar saga akraspillis 62
Ögmundur Pálsson 60, 186
Ölfus in Árnessýsla 146
Ölkofra þáttr 60, 78
Ørsleff, Peder 205
Örvar-Oddr 96
Örvar-Odds saga 60, 96, 100, 119, 170, 189